$15.00

NMENT

Law and the Environment

Edited by Malcolm Baldwin and
James K. Page, Jr.

A Conservation Foundation Publication

The conservation movement has become
the environmental revolution and lawyers
are playing an increasingly vital role in it.

Yet environmental law itself is at a relatively primitive stage. Doctrine is unclear, strategies are uncertain and largely
untried, training is unspecific, and remun-
eration for the lawyer is often meager.
Even matters of professional ethics are, in
some instances, confused.

Therefore it is especially timely and
important that the most distinguished
practitioners and teachers of environmental law should have pooled their ideas, resources, and experiences in this volume.
And it is essential to the vitality and success of the conservation movement that
its supporters be familiar with the questions, the techniques, and the potential of
environmental law.

Does the citizen have a constitutional
right to a pollution-free environment?
Who has standing to sue? How can the
trial lawyer make the best use of scientific
witnesses in a field where the basic science itself is often uncertain? Who has
the burden of proof in environmental litigation? How should the law schools respond to the growing need for lawyers sophisticated in environmental matters, the
urgent and appealing cry for relevance,
and the constant requirement that lawyers
be trained primarily as lawyers, not conservationists?

g the basic questions
lmark volume, the re-
ouse Conference held
), and sponsored by
Foundation and the
esearch Foundation.
ven papers presented
developments in the
to meet these needs,
e transcription of the
n and an extensive
ant reports and arti-
ental law field, pre-
his publication.

is Senior Legal As-
rvation Foundation,
Environmental Law
Page, Jr., formerly
ral History Press, is
lker and Company.

LAW AND THE ENVIRONMENT

EDITED BY Malcolm F. Baldwin

and James K. Page, Jr.

A CONSERVATION FOUNDATION PUBLICATION

NEW YORK  WALKER AND COMPANY

First published in the United States of America in 1970
by the Walker Publishing Company, Inc.

Published simultaneously in Canada by The Ryerson Press, Toronto.

ISBN: 0-8027-0315-1

Library of Congress Catalog Card Number: 71-120406

Printed in the United States of America

Designed by Paula Wiener

CONTENTS

LAW AND THE ENVIRONMENT

A Conservation Foundation Publication

Edited by
Malcolm Baldwin
and James K. Page, Jr.

Foreword

In September, 1969, some fifty lawyers, law professors and conservation leaders, along with twenty-five observers, participated in a two-day conference on law and the environment. The group assessed evolving legal techniques for protecting and enhancing the quality of the environment and discussed the prospects for greater application of the law to conservation efforts.

The conference came about through a pleasant and productive collaboration of two organizations. The Conservation and Research Foundation met direct conference costs, and The Conservation Foundation staff handled preparations and physical arrangements.

In planning the conference, the two foundations were fortunate to enlist a distinguished steering committee consisting of Russell E. Train, then President of the Conservation Foundation and now Chairman of the federal Council on Environmental Quality; Wallace D. Bowman, Environmental Policy Division, Library of Congress; Professor George Lefcoe, Yale Law School; Professor Sheldon J. Plager, University of Illinois College of Law; Professor Joseph L. Sax, University of Michigan Law School; and William Van Ness, Jr., Special Counsel, U.S. Senate Committee on Interior and Insular Affairs. Malcolm F. Baldwin, Senior Legal Associate at the Conservation Foundation, served as conference secretary and guided the project from the initial planning stages to its completion.

Specially commissioned papers distributed to participants in advance of the conference and lively discussion during and between sessions gave abundant evidence that the law has matured and sharpened its focus within the environmental field in recent years. The conference itself had a significant impact on the legal profession by initiating fertile exchange among many lawyers who are breaking new ground. We are heartened by a growing public awareness of the need for new principles of environmental law and for a legal profession trained in their use. A step toward this development, and a direct outgrowth of the conference itself, has been the establishment of the Environmental Law Institute, which plans to publish an *Environmental Law Reporter.*

We hope that the thoughtful papers and discussion set forth in this volume will continue to advance the evolution of the law as a dynamic, positive force for environmental quality.

RICHARD H. GOODWIN
President
The Conservation and Research
   Foundation
SYDNEY HOWE
President
The Conservation Foundation

Introduction

It has been said that law is the profession of the uncommitted. Yet the eagerness with which lawyers are now embracing environmental law belies that adage. Indeed, the magnetism of the environmental revolution has given many lawyers a soul.

On September 10, 1969, as the conference participants made their way to Airlie House, they might have heard news broadcasts playing an appropriate overture to the discussions about to take place in Warrenton. The secretaries of Interior and Transportation and the Governor of Florida had held a meeting to assure the nation that in the controversy over a jetport planned for Dade County the ecological values of the Everglades would be preeminent. Far to the north, a record price was reported in the state of Alaska's auction of vast North Slope areas to the oil industry. And in Colorado, a citizens' group pressed court action in the matter of Project Rulison, claiming that the A.E.C. had not taken adequate precautions against the hazards of an underground atomic blast to the people and the ecology of the region.

Meanwhile, oil continued to seep to the surface of the Santa Barbara Channel while the Corps of Engineers was receiving oil company requests for permits to conduct new exploratory drilling and to add a new platform in the channel. Appropriately, therefore, on the morning of September 11, the conference took up the Santa Barbara issue as a test "case," to explore the strategies and potential remedies available to the environmental lawyer. From this beginning it was apparent that, in spite of the experience rapidly being accumulated by lawyers, a great deal about environmental law remained unclear.

In the discussions at Airlie House, and in the papers, there was a striking absence of any attempt to define environmental law. A decade before, a definition might have been attempted, but the lawyers present, recognizing that environmental decay was a hideous fact, focused on ways for the law to respond; the response would, in turn, define the field.

It was generally accepted that by opening up and democratizing the legal process, at every level, environmental abuse could be curtailed. Nevertheless, there was pervasive conflict, and conference debate was not always along predictable lines. Did an environmental crisis warrant radical legal reform and innovation or was there time for evolutionary approaches? Several professors and practitioners endorsed the broad, swift remedy of a constitutional attack, a Supreme Court appeal, and greater use of the courts' equitable powers in order to develop some new environmental doctrine in the law. Others preferred the philosophically more opaque strategy of mixing legislative and judicial remedies by taking what one participant called the "subliminal" approach to court intervention. Then there were those who, though believing environmental deterioration was indeed rapid, still questioned whether radical changes in the roles of courts, legislatures and law schools were feasible or desirable; they were concerned that in our haste to reform we would destroy the sustaining forms.

Several unresolved anxieties permeated the discussion. One of the most serious—and obvious—was financial. Can any public-interest lawyer, let alone an environmental lawyer, support himself by fees from clients who are likely to be just a cut above the indigent? In addition, the public-interest lawyer is haunted by professional standards, laid down years ago by the states, that forbid the fund-raising, client-gathering, and public information programs frequently necessary to combat powerful adversaries. Lastly, of course, because environmental law is in such a primitive stage, even the most imaginative and industrious environmental lawyer may feel a general professional frustration at the doctrinal and procedural obstacles he must face.

Not surprisingly, the environmental lawyer eyes law schools as a rich source of badly needed help. Although he may have emerged from his own law school with the altered mind expected of him, he could seldom credit his training with any environmental exposure. That was gained after law school, and with no thanks to bar associations. Now, however, a new generation of law students receive environmental training that was unheard of even five years ago. Conservation law student groups are prolific. The practicing environmental lawyer favors active law school programs of student research, services, and professorial help to boot. But how are law schools to mix relevance with the educative purpose? While environmental law can provide skills, it may not be the law school's proper function to develop conservation zealots.

It is evident from the discussions that to accomplish our environmental objectives, we will need legal reform based on far-reaching changes in social, economic and political thought. A world made livable for future generations can only result from a translation into legal forms of new, internationally conceived public policies that recognize man's common biological limitations and diverse spiritual and cultural needs. In this regard, then, the conference may have ended at the beginning, and have shown how limited the traditional scope of a lawyer's inquiry may be.

Few questions were settled at Airlie House, but one lawyer suggested that there be follow-up conferences in the future, because the pooling of experience and ideas of so many people had, for him at least, been valuable. It is in this same spirit that this volume is offered to the legal profession in particular and to environmentalists in general.

It should be noted that since the conference, Congress passed the highly significant National Environmental Policy Act, signed by the President on January 1, 1970. The act incorporated many of the ideas discussed at the conference by establishing a three-man Council on Environmental Quality and by requiring environmental factors to be taken into consideration by all federal agencies. Several provisions of this act have had an immediate and intriguing impact on judicial response to citizen environmental litigation, and lawyers will be watching and evaluating these results carefully in the years to come.

The participants at the conference are listed and identified in the pages that follow. There are, however, many other contributors to the creation of this book who were not present at the conference and the editors would like their contributions made known.

We are especially grateful to Wallace Bowman, a friend of the Conservation Foundation since its New York days, for the initial impetus that he gave to the conference idea and for his vital support thereafter. In organizing and managing a mass of details before and during the conference, Jacqueline Burke of the Conservation Foundation deserves special credit. Fortunately, she was ably succeeded by Rosannah Farley, who jumped into the midst of the conference follow-up with the requisite enthusiasm.

Special thanks are due to Richard Pardo for his research assistance and to Lynda Baldwin, for her invaluable contributions to the editorial style and organization of the conference transcript.

MALCOLM F. BALDWIN
JAMES K. PAGE, JR.

Biographies of Conference Authors

MALCOLM F. BALDWIN:
Senior Legal Associate, The Conservation Foundation, Washington, D.C.; BA, Haverford College, 1962; JD, University of Chicago Law School, 1965; Management Intern, Office of the Secretary of Defense, 1965-1966; Associate, The Conservation Foundation, since 1966; member, International Union for Conservation of Nature and Natural Resources—Commission on Legislation, and member of the Bar: District of Columbia.

EDWARD BERLIN:
Partner, Berlin, Roisman & Kessler, Washington, D.C.; BBA, College of the City of New York, 1958; LLB, Columbia University, 1961; LLM, Georgetown University, 1964; formerly an Assistant General Counsel, Federal Power Commission, and with the Appellate Section, Civil Division, United States Department of Justice; Member of the Bar: the State of New York, the District of Columbia, and the Supreme Court.

JAMES N. CORBRIDGE, JR.:
Vice President for Student Affairs, University of Colorado; AB, Brown University, 1955; LLB, Yale, 1963; Admitted to the Bar: New York, 1964; Associate, Lord, Day and Lord, New York City, 1963-65; Assistant Professor, University of Colorado, 1965-68, Associate Professor, University of Colorado School of Law, 1968-70; U.S.N.R., 1957-60, Lt. (j.g.).

CHARLES H. W. FOSTER:
Research Fellow, Harvard University, and Chairman, Advisory Board, New England Natural Resources Center; BA, Harvard College, 1951; BSF, University of Michigan, 1953; MS, University of Michigan, 1956; PhD, Johns Hopkins University, 1969; Executive Secretary, Wildlife Conservation, Inc., 1953-55; Natural Resources Consultant, Massachusetts Water Resources Commission, 1956-59; Commissioner, Massachusetts Department of Natural Resources, 1959-66; President, The Nature Conservancy, 1966-67; Consultant, The Conservation Foundation, 1967-69.

HAROLD P. GREEN:

Professor, George Washington University Law School; AB, 1942; JD, University of Chicago, 1948; Admitted to the Bar: Illinois, 1949, District of Columbia, 1954, Maryland, 1959; Private practice, Chicago, Illinois, 1949-50; Attorney, Atomic Energy Commission, Washington, D.C., 1950-54; Acting Counsel, Subcommittee on Reorganization, Senate Committee on Government Operations, 1955; Private practice, Washington, D.C., 1955-64; U.S. Army, 1944-46.

LOUIS L. JAFFE:

Professor, Harvard University Law School; AB, Johns Hopkins University; LLB, 1928; SJD, Harvard, 1932; Admitted to the Bar: California, 1928, New York, 1937; Graduate Fellow, Harvard Professor, Harvard, since 1950; Dean, University of Buffalo, 1948-50; Professor, 1936-48.

GLADYS KESSLER:

Partner, Berlin, Roisman & Kessler, Washington, D.C.; AB, Cornell University; LLB, Harvard Law School; formerly with NLRB, Executive Assistant to Senator Harrison A. Williams, Jr., Legislative Assistant to Representative Jonathan B. Bingham; Member of the Bar: the State of New York, the District of Columbia, and the Supreme Court.

JAMES E. KRIER:

Acting Professor, School of Law, University of California, Los Angeles; BS, 1961; JD, University of Wisconsin, 1966; Admitted to the Bar: Wisconsin, 1966; Law Clerk, Chief Justice Roger J. Traynor, Supreme Court of California, 1966-67; Associate, Arnold & Porter, Washington, D.C., 1967-69.

JAMES WATT MOORMAN:

Staff Attorney, The Center for Law and Social Policy, Washington, D.C.; AB, Duke University, 1959; LLB, Duke University School of Law, 1962; formerly with Davis, Polk, Wardwell, Sunderland & Kiendl, and the Lands and Natural Resources Division (General Litigation Section), Department of Justice. Member of the Bar: the State of New York and the District of Columbia.

ERNEST F. ROBERTS, JR.:

Professor of Law, Cornell Law School; BA, Northeastern University, 1952; LLB, Boston College, 1954; Private practice, Northampton, Massachusetts, 1956-57; Professor of Law, Villanova University, 1957-64; Visiting Professor, University of Nottingham (England), 1962-63; U.S. Army, 1954-56.

ANTHONY Z. ROISMAN:

Partner, Berlin, Roisman & Kessler, Washington, D.C.; AB, Dart-

mouth College, 1960; LLB, Harvard Law School, 1963; formerly
with the Tax Division, Department of Justice, Washington, D.C.;
Member of the Bar: the State of New York, the District of Columbia, and the Supreme Court.

DAVID SIVE:

Partner, Winer, Neuburger & Sive, New York, New York; AB,
Brooklyn College, 1943; LLB, Columbia University School of Law,
1948; formerly with Seligson, Morris & Neuberger (predecessor of
present firm); Executive Director, Committee on Natural Resources, New York State Constitutional Convention, 1967; Member of the American Bar Association, New York State Bar
Association, and Associate of the Bar, City of New York; Adjunct
Associate Professor, Graduate Division, New York University
Law School.

A. DAN TARLOCK:

Assistant Professor, Indiana University School of Law, Bloomington; AB, 1963; LLB, Stanford, 1965; Admitted to the Bar: California, 1966; Instructor, U.C.L.A., 1965-66; Assistant Professor,
University of Kentucky, 1966-68.

Participants

THOMAS ALDER
President
Public Law Education Institute
1346 Connecticut Ave., N.W., Rm. 620
Washington, D.C. 20036

MALCOLM F. BALDWIN
Senior Legal Associate
The Conservation Foundation
1250 Connecticut Ave., N.W.
Washington, D.C. 20036

WILLIAM M. BENNETT
Attorney-at-Law
35 Evergreen Dr.
Kentfield, Calif. 94904

EDWARD BERLIN
Berlin, Roisman & Kessler
1910 N Street, N.W.
Washington, D.C. 20036

PHILLIP BERRY
President
Sierra Club
1050 Mills Tower
San Francisco, Calif. 94104

WALLACE D. BOWMAN
Assistant Chief
Environmental Policy Division
Library of Congress
Washington, D.C. 20540

RUSSELL L. BRENNEMAN
Copp, Brenneman & Tighe
302 State Street
New London, Conn. 06320

DONALD M. CARMICHAEL
Assistant Professor
University of Colorado
School of Law
Boulder, Colo. 80302

DAVID F. CAVERS
President
Council on Law-Related Studies
1563 Massachusetts Avenue
Cambridge, Mass. 02138

BERNARD COHEN
Cohen, Hirschkop & Hall
110 N. Royal Street
Alexandria, Va. 22313

JAMES N. CORBRIDGE, JR.
Associate Professor
University of Colorado
School of Law
Boulder, Colo. 80302

DAVID P. CURRIE
Professor of Law
University of Chicago Law School
1111 E. 60 Street
Chicago, Ill. 60637

WILLIAM J. DUDDLESON
Director of Policy Studies
The Conservation Foundation
1250 Connecticut Ave., N.W.
Washington, D.C. 20036

MARVIN B. DURNING
Cary, Durning, Prince & Smith
1411 Fourth Avenue
Seattle, Wash. 98101

BROCK EVANS
Federation of Western Outdoor Clubs
4534½ University Way N.E.
Seattle, Wash. 98105

CHARLES H. W. FOSTER
Research Fellow, Harvard University
484 Charles River Street
Needham, Mass. 02192

RICHARD H. GOODWIN
President
The Conservation and Research
  Foundation
Department of Botany
Connecticut College
New London, Conn. 06320

HAROLD P. GREEN
Professor of Law
The National Law Center
George Washington University
Washington, D.C. 20006

RAYMOND A. HAIK
President
Izaak Walton League of America
900 Farmers & Mechanics Bank
  Building
Minneapolis, Minn. 55402

ROGER P. HANSEN
Director
Rocky Mountain Center on
  Environment
5850 East Jewell Avenue
Denver, Colo. 80222

N. WILLIAM HINES
Professor of Law
University of Iowa Law School
Iowa City, Iowa 52240

PHILIP H. HOFF
(Former Governor, State of Vermont)
Attorney-at-Law
109 S. Winooski Avenue
Burlington, Vt. 05401

SYDNEY HOWE
President
The Conservation Foundation
1250 Connecticut Avenue., N.W.
Washington, D.C. 20036

LOUIS L. JAFFE
Professor of Law
Harvard University Law School
Cambridge, Mass. 02138

ROBERT W. JASPERSON
General Counsel
Conservation Law Society
220 Bush Street
San Francisco, Calif. 94104

JAMES JEANS
Professor of Law
University of Missouri at Kansas City
  School of Law
Kansas City, Mo. 64110

THOMAS C. JORLING
Minority Counsel
Committee on Public Works
U.S. Senate
Washington, D.C. 20510

GLADYS KESSLER
Berlin, Roisman & Kessler
1910 N Street, N.W.
Washington, D.C. 20036

JAMES E. KRIER
Acting Professor
University of California School of Law
Los Angeles, Calif. 90024

GEORGE LEFCOE
Associate Professor
Yale Law School
New Haven, Conn. 06320

MICHAEL E. LEVINE
Assistant Professor
University of Southern California
  Law Center
Los Angeles, Calif. 90007

JAMES B. MACDONALD
Professor of Law
University of Wisconsin
  School of Law
Madison, Wis. 53706

J. MICHAEL MCCLOSKEY
Executive Director
Sierra Club
1050 Mills Tower Building
San Francisco, Calif. 94104

REP. PAUL N. MCCLOSKEY, JR.
U.S. House of Representatives
Washington, D.C. 20515

JAMES W. MOORMAN
The Center for Law and Social Policy
2008 Hillyer Place, N.W.
Washington, D.C. 20009

FRANK H. MORISON
Holland & Hart
Equitable Building
Denver, Colo. 80202

RALPH NADER
The Center for the Study of
  Responsive Law
1908 Q Street, N.W.
Washington, D.C. 20009

BENJAMIN W. NASON
Executive Secretary
Conservation Law Foundation
44 School Street
Boston, Mass. 02108

SHELDON J. PLAGER
Professor of Law
University of Illinois
  College of Law
Champaign, Ill. 61820

E. F. ROBERTS, JR.
Professor of Law
Cornell Law School
Ithaca, N. Y. 18450

NICHOLAS ROBINSON
Columbia University
  School of Law
435 W. 116 Street
New York City, N. Y. 10027

ANTHONY Z. ROISMAN
Berlin, Roisman & Kessler
1910 N Street, N.W.
Washington, D.C. 20036

NORMAN K. SANDERS
Assistant Professor
Department of Geography
University of California
Santa Barbara, Calif. 93106

JOSEPH SAX
Associate Professor
University of Michigan
  School of Law
Ann Arbor, Mich. 48104

DAVID SIVE
Winer, Neuburger & Sive
445 Park Avenue
New York City, N. Y. 10022

JAN STEVENS
Deputy Attorney General
State of California
Room 500, Wells Fargo Bank Bldg.
5th and Capitol Mall
Sacramento, Calif. 95814

ANN LOUISE STRONG
Director, Institute for Environmental
  Studies
University of Pennsylvania
3400 Walnut Street
Philadelphia, Pa. 19104

A. DAN TARLOCK
Assistant Professor
Indiana University
  School of Law
Bloomington, Ind. 47401

ROGER TIPPY
Counsel
New England River Basins
    Commission
Room 205
55 Court Street
Boston, Mass. 02108

PETER F. TUFO
Assistant to the Mayor of New York
    City
1730 K Street, N.W.
Washington, D.C. 20006

WILLIAM J. VAN NESS, JR.
Special Counsel
Committee on Interior and Insular
    Affairs
U.S. Senate
Washington, D.C. 20510

VICTOR J. YANNACONE, JR.
Attorney-at-Law
39 Baker Street
Patchogue, N. Y. 11772

PROBLEMS OF LITIGATION

The Santa Barbara Oil Spill

Malcolm F. Baldwin

The Santa Barbara oil spill of 1969, like the wrecks of the *Torrey Canyon* and the *Ocean Eagle*, and the spills from a host of other oil tankers, was an accident. So it differs a little from those daily environmental dislocations associated with industrial societies—pollution from automobiles, inadequate sewer plants, urban sprawl. But the environmental effects of these accidents are no less serious, and they are increasingly common. The way we decide to take all these environmental risks is both primitive and irrational.

This account of the events and conflicts before and after the spill has all the elements of a nightmare. In retrospect, we are unsure even now how it might have been averted, given the premises on which leasing decisions were based. We can see that before the spill even civic prophets did not see *how* pollution might occur, but the sticky mess (found underfoot in so many nightmares) did, in fact, end up on Santa Barbara's shores.

Since nightmares recur, the lessons of the Santa Barbara spill should be remembered. Hopefully, what follows may be helpful to lawyers and citizen groups as they consider their own potential impact on future government policies affecting oil development in Alaska, the development and deployment of the supersonic transport, and a variety of less glamorous matters involving highways, estuaries, strip mines, dams and open space.

BEFORE AND AFTER THE SPILL—A BRIEF CHRONOLOGY

The Interior Department began oil and gas leasing procedures in the Santa Barbara Channel in 1965, after the Supreme Court settled Channel jurisdiction disputes with California. State leasing of oil tracts just within the three-mile limit accelerated this federal process, and late in 1966 Secretary Udall authorized the leasing of one federal tract (1,995 acres) to forestall subsurface oil drainage from adjacent state wells. Phillips Petroleum bid $21,000,000 and was awarded this initial drainage tract in December, 1966. A week later the Bureau of Land Management asked oil and gas companies to nominate the channel tracts that they wanted the Interior Department to offer in a general leasing sale.

Santa Barbara residents noted these developments with some alarm. Early in 1967 Santa Barbara County officials and various municipal leaders began discussions with Interior's Assistant Secretary for Mineral Resources. They voiced concern that federal drilling would stimulate state oil drilling in the sixteen-mile-long, three-mile-wide state marine sanctuary along the Santa Barbara coast. County spokesmen urged a larger federal sanctuary to protect the ocean view and a one-year federal leasing moratorium. While these negotiations with Interior proceeded, oil companies conducted their own exploratory oil surveys of the channel's federal lands.

That fall Interior announced that it would prohibit any leasing in a two-mile buffer zone adjacent to the state sanctuary. The county requested a six-month leasing delay, a larger zone (that would include the area of Platform A, of future infamy), a general reduction in leasing acreage, and fewer platforms. The Department would not agree, and in December, 1967, announced a competitive lease sale of 500,000 acres of Channel lands. Nevertheless, its bidding notice required that platforms should be large enough for twenty or more wells, and be camouflaged and designed to help protect aesthetic values.

Just prior to this Interior action, the Corps of Engineers held public hearings on the application of Phillips for approval of its drainage tract platform. Testimony of the November, 1967, hearing covered aesthetic, geophysical, pollution, and fish and wildlife aspects of the proposed platform, in addition to navigational matters. The following January the Corps granted the permit on terms conforming to the Phillips lease from the Bureau of Land Management, and platform construction began.

In February, 1968, Interior finally held its general lease sale on Channel lands, accepting $603,000,000 for leases on seventy-one tracts (363,000 acres). A combination of Union Oil, Texaco, Gulf, and Mobile offered a record bid of $61,400,000 for Tract 402 in what is called the Dos Cuadras field, and Union was named operator of the lease. By March, Union had discovered oil, and in May it too requested Corps permits for platform construction. The permits were obtained several months later without a Corps hearing. (The City of Santa Barbara had asked for a hearing and then withdrew the request.) In discussions between Union and the U.S. Geological Survey, it was agreed that Union's Platform A should be designed for 56 separate wells.

As of January, 1969, the United States Geological Survey had approved five development wells; three had been sunk and sealed by then. The fourth and fifth wells were drilled that month. On January 28 the fourth well (A-21) was drilled to its total depth of 3,479 feet from the platform, crossing two large faults and other smaller faults and reaching the major oil deposits beneath the 3,000-foot level. As the drill was being withdrawn, gas and then oil gushed up the hole. The well was out of control.[1]

The next day the Coast Guard took charge of cleanup under the National Multi-Agency Oil and Hazardous Materials Pollution Contingency Plan, and Union Oil assumed full financial responsibility for the cleanup. Oil first hit the beaches on February 1 and continued to arrive as efforts to control the well failed. On February 7 Interior Secretary Walter Hickel, after some hesitation, ordered all production and drilling stopped in federal waters of the Channel. That same day well A-21 was finally closed, but seepage continued from several places on the ocean floor. (For this reason, the spill was not technically a blowout, where a well *itself* is out of control.)

While cleanup efforts accelerated, Presidential Science Advisor, Dr. Lee A. DuBridge, named a panel of fourteen experts to conduct a study of the spill in Santa Barbara, and on the panel's recommendation Secretary Hickel gave Union permission to perforate other Platform A wells and conduct temporary pressure-relief pumping.

In late February Secretary Hickel announced new regulations for existing and future lessees requiring absolute liability for cleanup costs from offshore platform pollution. In early March the Secretary asked Union Oil and other companies to supply geological, geophysical, and structural information that Interior lacked and did not normally require. Union provided the "proprietary" data based on Hickel's guarantee of no public inspection. Several weeks later the Secretary issued new detailed regulations for federal offshore oil drilling and production and established a 21,000-acre Ecological Preserve and 34,000-acre buffer zone in the Channel (*see map*).

In April the Secretary authorized resumption of drilling and production on five channel leases[2] under new regulations. That same month

---

[1]To put the spill in statistical perspective, of the 10,000 well completions in the Outer Continental Shelf, there have been 25 blowouts reported to USGS. Six were controlled in less than an hour, another six in less than a day, another four in less than two days, another four in less than two weeks (including Santa Barbara), and another five in more than two weeks. (The longest was three months.) Seventeen of these were gas only, four were oil only, and four were gas and oil. *Hearings on S.1219 Before the Subcommittee on Minerals, Materials and Fuels of the Senate Interior Committee,* 91st Cong., 1st Sess., at 68 (1969).
[2]One of these fortunate lessees, Humble Oil Company, reported in July that it had made

President Nixon asked Dr. DuBridge to assemble a second panel of experts to recommend future measures regarding the Union lease. Then in June, while the shutdown order continued for 67 leases as well as for Union's Platform A, that panel recommended resumption of drilling as the best cure for continued seepage.

Reserving immediate action on the panel report, Secretary Hickel announced in early August that limited shallow drilling and cement injection processes had indeed accounted for a reduced seepage around the Union platforms. Then in mid-August the Secretary endorsed the theory of the panel's report and announced that Sun Oil Company could resume drilling (and the construction of new platforms) on its lease, from which about one-third of the seepage was occurring. Finally, late in the same month, the Secretary announced final procedures on lease operations, information requirements, and intra-departmental procedures for deciding to lease.

Following the Secretary's review of federal Channel leases after the spill, the Corps of Engineers received requests for permits authorizing new exploratory drilling (in water as deep as 1,000 feet, as opposed to the 200 feet at Platform A) and, in the case of Sun Oil, a new Channel platform. In August Santa Barbara County objected to the permits and requested public hearings, none having been held by the federal government. In September, however, the Corps issued several exploratory permits without such hearings, and the County asked the U.S. District Court for temporary injunctions against issuance of more permits. When the Court held against the County, the Corps issued the remaining permits. [County appeals to the Court of Appeals and the U.S. Supreme Court in November, 1969, were unsuccessful. By the end of the year the Sun Oil platform was placed just east of Union's Platform A—the first new platform installed in the Channel since the spill.]

THE SPILL

Magnitude.

The spill magnitude has been estimated by one expert to have amounted to 3,250,000 gallons by the middle of May,[3] compared with 30,000,000 gallons from the *Torrey Canyon* that grounded off the coast of Cornwall, England.[4] This estimate, by Allan A. Allen of General Research Corpo-

a major oil discovery in the Channel in an area previously considered disappointing. *The Wall Street Journal*, July 10, 1969, at 7, col. 1.
[3] *Hearings on S.1219, supra* note 1, at 152.
[4] For details on the *Torrey Canyon* disaster *see*, *The Torrey Canyon: Report of the Great Britain Committee of Scientists on the Scientific and Technological Aspects*. (H.M.S.O. 1967)

ration, differs from those of Geological Survey (USGS) and Union Oil Company. Union recorded 500 barrels[5] of oil per day for the first 10½ days, while Allen believes the more accurate figure is 5,000 barrels per day. As of March 20 the total oil seepage was noted by USGS at between 3,000 to 6,000 barrels[6] whereas Allen's estimate was over 60,000 barrels. [By October, 1969, the spill had been substantially reduced. USGS and General Research Corporation studies agreed that the seepage from around Platform A was about 10 barrels a day.[7]]

Effects.

Immediate damage assessment by the Federal Water Pollution Control Administration (FWPCA) indicated no fish kills, "reasonably healthy" kelp beds, and general "abundance and variety" of planktonic and intertidal plants.[8] The review of the California Department of Fish and Game was similar.[9]

Early damage assessments were misleading, however. State testimony at the end of February noted that oil had "not reached San Miguel Island which has an extremely large population of marine mammals, including the rare fur seal and elephant seal, and it appears virtually impossible for the oil to reach this area." Three months later *Life* magazine pictured an oil-soaked shoreline of this island.[10] The Interior Department later confirmed the pollution, but disputed the reported damage to seals.[11]

Similarly, FWPCA assessment of bird damage on February 18, 1969, noted that of the reported 1,000 or more oil-damaged birds approximately half had died. By the end of February a 25 per cent survival rate was expected, but by mid May figures showed that of the 1,500 birds brought to rescue centers, about 90 per cent died. It could have been worse. Testimony of the Bureau of Sport Fisheries and Wildlife noted that bird losses were held down by fortunate weather conditions and migration schedules.[12]

It is possible that the long-term damage from oil pollution will be more

---

[5] One barrel equals 42 gallons.
[6] *Hearings on S.7 and S.544 Before the Subcommittee on Air and Water Pollution of the Senate Public Works Committee*, 91st Cong., 1st Sess., Ser. 2, Pt. 3, at 813 (1969)
[7] See, USGS Professional Paper 679, *Geology, Petroleum Development, and Seismicity of the Santa Barbara Channel*, at 45 (1969) and General Research Corporation Technical memorandum 1230, *Estimates of Surface Pollution Resulting from Submarine Oil Seeps at Platform A and Coal Oil Point*, Prepared for Santa Barbara County, at 19 (November, 1969).
[8] *Hearings on S.7 and S.544*, *supra* note 6, at 808.
[9] *Id.*, at 865.
[10] *Life*, June 13, 1969.
[11] Report, San Miguel Island, news release, Department of the Interior, June 29, 1969.
[12] *Hearings on S.7 and S.544*, *supra* note 6, at 847.

serious. Max Blumer of Woods Hole Oceanographic Institution outlined some of these problems.[13] Pointing out the complexity and individual characteristics of crude oil, Blumer noted the general lack of research into the "more serious long term and low level effects of crude petroleum" when "oil influx to the ocean is at least 1,000,000 metric tons a year (shipping losses only) and is likely to be 10 to 100 times higher." This ignorance is especially serious at a time when the risk of accidents increased as oil production shifted to continental shelf lands and deep water reserves.

Blumer's paper emphasizes that dangers from oil pollution may result from the fact that hydrocarbons in petroleum are highly stable in marine organisms—passing through the food chain without alteration.

> In the marine food chain hydrocarbons may not only be retained but they can actually be concentrated. This is a situation akin to that of the chlorinated pesticides which are as refractory as the hydrocarbons. These pesticides are concentrated in the marine food chain to the point where toxic levels may be reached.

The danger exists of eventual "accumulation in human food of long term poisons derived from crude oil, for instance, of carcinogenic compounds," since oil and residues contain hydrocarbons resembling those in tobacco tar. Without proper regard for ocean biological resources "we may do irreversible damage to many marine organisms, to the marine food chain, and we may eventually destroy the yield and the value of the food which we hope to recover from the sea."[14]

Cleanup.

While little is known about the lasting ecological effects of oil pollution, less was known at the time of the spill about how to clean it up. From experience with the *Torrey Canyon* spill it was determined that chemical dispersants, particularly detergents, not only had adverse long-term biological effects, but also were expensive and of doubtful effectiveness.[15] Therefore, at Santa Barbara, chemical dispersants were reportedly little used along the shore while some 300 barrels were used with FWPCA approval around the platform to protect the crew from fire danger.[16] Union Oil experimented with booms, brooms, straw, powdered cement, aluminum material and other trapping techniques to clean up or contain the oil. As late as May, 1969, Union was maintaining a force of 300 men

---

[13]*Id.*, at 1485.
[14]*Id.*, at 1488.
[15]See J.F. Smith, *Torrey Canyon—Pollution and Marine Life*, Cambridge (1968).
[16]*Hearings on S.7 and S.544, supra* note 6, at 803.

to clean up the beaches each day. Reviewing these practices at a symposium on oil pollution held that same month, experts agreed that cleanup treatment technology was still very primitive.[17]

THE SANTA BARBARA SETTING

The Santa Barbara coastline is one of the most beautiful areas of the country. It has been described by the County Planning Director as,

> a narrow plain hugging the shore, merging into rolling hills and rising to a mountain backdrop. The beaches are, for the most part, ideal for recreation and the water and climate is warm enough for year-round swimming. The ocean dominates the scene and building sites are oriented to the ocean with views of the shoreline and the Channel Islands 25 miles offshore. This unique setting, protected for 40 years by zoning, prohibitions against smoke and fumes, architectural controls and opposition to eyesores and ugliness, has given the Santa Barbara area its world-wide reputation for beauty and pleasant living.[18]

Santa Barbara County's 57 miles of east-west shoreline (from Point Conception to the Ventura County line) are protected in the south by the islands of Anacapa, Santa Cruz, Santa Rosa, and the U.S. Navy's San Miguel. The communities of Montecito, Carpenteria, Santa Barbara and Goleta border the shoreline and account for most of the county's 150,000 people.

The varied and conflicting interests within the county are revealed by a lengthy study prepared at its request while the federal offshore leasing program was being considered. It reported that revenues to the county in 1965 were $98,000,000 from oil and gas (of which 2 per cent was from offshore production); $78,000,000 from agriculture; $64,000,000 from manufacturing; $412,000 from commercial fishing; $28,000,000 from other mineral operations including on land; and $41,000,000 from tourism.[19] More recent estimates place tourism at some $53,000,000 annually.

Partly because of this tourist trade, one of the county's great concerns over the last 15 to 20 years has been to protect its environment from the adverse effects of the oil industry. Tideland oil was discovered and refined in the mid 1890's just east of the city of Santa Barbara, the first

---

[17]Oil on the Sea—A Symposium on the Scientific and Engineering Aspects of Oil Pollution at Sea, M.I.T., May 16, 1969. Charles O'Brien, Chief Deputy Attorney General of California, noted that after the spill "one man, one rake, one 10-foot punt, and one bale of hay" seemed to be the safest and most effective way to handle the spill. *Hearings on S.1219, supra* note 1, at 32.

[18]Statement by Richard Whitehead to Assistant Secretary of Interior Cordell Moore, Feb. 28, 1967.

[19]*Hearings on S.7 and S.544, supra* note 6, at 654.

place in the country where oil was drilled from ocean piers.[20] By the late 1920's oil was being produced from piers from the Ellwood field to the west of Santa Barbara. Then in 1938 the California State Lands Act legalized oil leasing in state tide lands out to the three-mile limit, and by the early 1950's oil companies had obtained state permits to conduct seismographic studies of the ocean floor.

At this time Santa Barbara residents and other conservationists lobbied for a sanctuary to preserve the shoreline view, and the state responded by creating a sanctuary out to the three-mile limit for 16 miles along Santa Barbara's coast.[21] Oil leasing in this sanctuary can be permitted only if the State Lands Commission finds that the sanctuary's oil is being drained from oil development outside the three-mile limit and that leasing would be in the "best interest of the state."[22] Thereafter, with this safeguard, the city and county of Santa Barbara enacted zoning controls for onshore protection.

In the decade following, the development of state tideland oil accelerated. The state permitted offshore drilling from platforms in 1957, and a year later the first platform in the Pacific was constructed two miles out from Summerland, serving what proved to be a rich oil and gas deposit. Not long after the U.S. Supreme Court decided *U.S. v. California*[23] (which rejected California claims to continental shelf lands in the Santa Barbara Channel beyond the three-mile limit), the state had leased all state shelf lands outside the sanctuary between the Ventura County line and Point Conception.[24] As a result of this state leasing and state-supervised core drillings in disputed channel lands, a great deal was learned by oil companies and the state about oil in the highly faulted, earthquake-prone ocean floor. The state information was not conveyed to the federal government.[25]

PRESSURES FOR AND AGAINST LEASING

The public record shows that there were strong pressures from the

---

[20]Evidence of natural-oil leakages had been noticed on the shore by Spanish missionaries in the 18th century. *Id.*, at 270. One account of oil pollution in 1793 is cited in *Science*, September 3, 1969, at 967.

[21]Cunningham-Shell Tideland Act, §6871.2 Calif. Public Resources Code (1955).

[22]Section 6872 Calif. Public Resources Code (1955).

[23]381 U.S. 139 (1965).

[24]At the time of the spill there were 159 oil and 12 gas wells producing on state lands, with eight platforms, four underwater completions, 12 onshore processing plants and five marine terminals. Total state revenue from these and other offshore leasing has come to $800,-000,000 at about $50,000,000 per year. *See Hearings on S.7 and S.544, supra* note 6, at 481.

[25]*Id.*, at 477-479. See also, *Hearings on S. 1219, supra* note 1, at 70, 71.

Bureau of the Budget and the oil industry favoring early federal leasing of offshore channel oil fields. The record also indicates opposition to proposals for an offshore sanctuary from the Assistant Secretary for Fish, Wildlife and Parks. The FWPCA was apparently not involved in the leasing decisions at all. Private opposition was essentially local and on aesthetic grounds.

The Budget Bureau.

Bonus revenues to the U.S. government from the 1,300 oil and gas leases on the Outer Continental Shelf (OCS) have totaled approximately $3 billion.[26] The 4,000 oil and gas wells presently producing there yield a steady source of annual royalties to the federal government. One of the beneficiaries of this revenue is the Land and Water Conservation Fund. Under the Land and Water Conservation Fund Act of 1968, OCS mineral revenues are available "in an amount sufficient to bring the income of the fund to a total of $200,000,000 for the fiscal years 1969, 1970, and 1971, and to a total of $300,000,000 for each of the remaining two years of fiscal 1972 and 1973."[27] At the time of the Act's passage this revenue guarantee was gratefully anticipated by conservationists in and out of government.

In July, 1967, while Interior was "negotiating" with Santa Barbara representatives over the nature of the leasing program in the channel, the Deputy Director of the Bureau of the Budget, Phillip Hughes, wrote to the Under Secretary of Interior Charles Luce asking about leasing administration and the financial implications of various alternative regulatory policies being considered by Interior.

> As you know, we are particularly interested in the Presidential decision to generate additional revenues from the leasing of the Nation's mineral resources. We are convinced that improved efficiency of Federal OCS policy, procedures, and regulations would lead to lower capital and operation costs for lessees. These lower costs would, we believe, be reflected in increased bonuses from OCS lease sales. Recent indications from oil economists, oil companies, and in oil trade journals are that the economic benefits through improved, more efficient practice would be exceedingly large.[28]

Under Secretary Luce noted in his reply the Department's concern over assertion by states of jurisdiction over Outer Continental Shelf resources, particularly Louisiana. The Secretary's jurisdictional assertion

---

[26] *Id.*, at 660.
[27] Senate Report (Interior and Insular Affairs Committee) No. 1071, *U.S. Cong. & Adm. News*, 1968, at 2618, 1968.
[28] Letter from Phillip Hughes to Charles Luce, July 11, 1967.

of December 30, 1966, had, he said, been delayed by disagreements with Louisiana and Texas, and within the federal government. There were various federal regulatory alternatives open to Interior, the most lucrative course being for the federal government to publish detailed oil regulations for Interior administration "to achieve maximum production at minimum cost consistent with good conservation principles, and without any necessary regard to the conservation regulations promulgated by the States." Luce went on to link this revenue potential to appropriate oil import or production quotas.

> It should be emphasized that increased production on OCS would proportionately increase our revenues only if it did not result in lower domestic oil prices. Thus to realize proportionately increased revenues it would be necessary to restrict oil imports in approximately the same amount as the increased production; or alternatively, the states would have to reduce their allowable production in that amount.[29]

(So far as the author has been able to determine, no changes were made in federal import policies or state production before or after leasing in order to bring in this additional revenue.) However, in the face of rising demand for oil, a static oil import policy would encourage offshore production.

The Under Secretary concluded by raising the Santa Barbara question, noting that "if we should decide not to offer any federal lands for leasing off Santa Barbara the decision would be very expensive in terms of immediate revenue to the United States." By offering a buffer zone along the state sanctuary "the cost would be less but still quite substantial." (A memorandum of April 10, 1967, by Eugene W. Standley, Staff Engineer for the Interior Department, on a meeting with the Under Secretary, placed the cost of a sanctuary buffer zone at roughly $40,000,000 to $100,000,000 in terms of lost bonus revenue.)

The Budget Bureau's interest in offshore leasing continued when several months later a memorandum to Secretary Udall from the Director of the Budget Bureau, Charles Schultz, reminded him of President Johnson's feelings on the subject.

> As you know, the President has on several recent occasions instructed us to make every attempt to produce additional revenues from Federal resources. Last fall after a successful sale off the Gulf Coast, he specifically asked me what might be done to increase revenues from offshore leasing.[30]

---

[29]Letter from Charles Luce to Phillip Hughes, July 14, 1967. For discussion of these policy relationships, see Allan T. Demaree, "Our Crazy, Costly Life With Oil Quotas," *Fortune*, June, 1969.

[30]Memorandum from Charles Schultz to Stewart Udall, November 20, 1967.

Schultz expressed special interest in the kind of regulations Interior would adopt on offshore leasing.

The Oil Companies.

Throughout 1967 the position of the oil companies interested in Santa Barbara offshore oil was unfavorable to leasing delays and extensive buffer zones near the sanctuary. Their financial investment had already been sizeable, and exploration by major oil companies since World War II had indicated that there were rich oil fields beneath the channel. These fields were believed to be structurally related to the on shore fields in Ventura, southwest of Santa Barbara, which had been producing since the late 1920's.

The Western Oil and Gas Association stated its position in a letter to Udall on December 2, 1967, prompted by the extensive reports and recommendations of the Santa Barbara County Board of Supervisors presented to Secretary Udall in November. The county requested more limited Channel leasing than Interior contemplated (or ultimately adopted).

> While the oil industry believes the danger to the sanctuary is exaggerated, the establishment of the proposed two-mile "buffer zone" is more than adequate to protect the Santa Barbara Sanctuary. Any further compromise would seriously neglect the need to (1) prevent drainage of oil from federal water-bottoms, (2) provide the federal government with an important new source of income in the form of bonuses and royalties from the leased lands, and (3) develop the known geologic structures so as to increase the petroleum reserves of federal lands.

The letter voiced the hope,

> ... that the bulk and length of the report will not serve to delay implementation of the proposals of the Department of the Interior dated September 20, 1967. ... *In good faith, the petroleum industry has spent over $100,000,000 gathering geological and geophysical information in order to be prepared to bid intelligently at the proposed sale.* This expenditure included numerous "twin" core-holes under a program authorized and encouraged by the Department of the Interior. Nominations were called for on December 29, 1966, and accepted until March 1, 1967. The lands proposed to be leased represented a consensus of the nominations received. A considerable amount of drilling equipment and personnel has been assembled on the West Coast in anticipation of this sale and is now idle because of the unexpected delay.[31]

----

[31]Letter from P.F. Sollars, Chairman, Exploration Committee, Western Oil and Gas Association, December 2, 1967. (Emphasis added.)

Public Opposition.

The opposition to these budgetary and oil interests was primarily local and grounded on aesthetics. That aesthetics were the primary concern of the Santa Barbara residents is partly due to the difficulty they had in obtaining information on the pollution problems that might result from offshore leasing, or information on problems potentially resulting from the geological structure of the Channel floor.

Discussing the pollution problem at Senate hearings, Santa Barbara Supervisor George Clyde remarked that

> ... you may well ask why we at the local level didn't stress spillage controls. The answer is simple. It was discussed many times, but always Interior Department and oil industry officials led us to believe we had nothing to fear. They said they had perfected shutoff devices that were foolproof even in such disasters as a ship running into the platform, or an earthquake.[32]

The minutes of the meeting between Interior officials and Santa Barbara County representatives on May 12, 1967, provide other examples of Mr. Clyde's observations, as does the record of the one-day hearing of the Corps of Engineers on the Phillips platform, November 20, 1967. Citizens there did discuss the potential hazards resulting from earthquakes, faults, and other unique features of the Channel floor,[33] but safety assurances were offered by platform contractors and oil and marine supply companies.[34] No other public hearing on these matters was held.

Santa Barbara citizens faced several problems in getting information on the geological and technical aspects of offshore drilling. First, certain data is protected by the USGS as proprietary.

> In order to protect the interest of the lessee, geological and geophysical interpretations required by this section shall, upon request of the lessee, be classified as not available for public inspection until such time as the supervisor determines the release of such information is required and necessary for the proper development of the field or area.[35]

This regulation is consistent with one of the exceptions to public disclosure allowed by the Public Information Act.[36] The act exempts from public inspection "matters that are ... geological and geophysical information and data, including maps, concerning wells."[37]

[32] Hearings on S.7 and S.544, supra note 6, at 281.
[33] Corps of Engineers Public Hearings on Permit Application by Phillips Petroleum Company on Proposed Drilling Platform Hogan at Carpenteria, California, November 20, 1967.
[34] Id., at 71, 78.
[35] 33 C.F.R. §250.34(c).
[36] P.L. 89-487, codified by P.L. 90-23 in 5 U.S.C. §552.
[37] 5 U.S.C. §552(b) (9). For discussion and evidence of USGS reluctance to release to the public the data it developed see, Hearings on S.7 and S.544, supra note 6, at 585 and 674-676.

Second, the information received by the USGS was limited. USGS regulations did not require that seismic and geophysical information acquired by oil companies in exploratory operations be made available to the government.[38]

Third, citizens faced difficulty in obtaining expert scientists free from industry ties and willing to assist in interpreting and investigating data related to offshore oil and gas exploration and production.[39]

The argument that offshore platforms were ugly was the simplest and most basic complaint of the Santa Barbara residents. The aesthetic arguments did win the two-mile wide buffer zone. But once it was determined by Interior that such a zone outside the state sanctuary would be sufficient to forestall state leasing in the sanctuary, no further aesthetic appeals were successful. Thus, in response to the November, 1967, report and requests of Santa Barbara County for a larger buffer zone, reduced leasing and fewer platforms, Assistant Secretary Moore stated:

> Further action of this sort would be beyond our original intention to prevent drainage of the state sanctuary. The two affected tracts cover the remainder of the Rincon trend and is the last of the prime acreage of our proposed sale. This would be "deferring" additional bonus money above that that could be received if we leased the two-mile buffer zone acreage. I cannot see how these people can expect us to absorb any additional revenue losses merely because of their further obsession to protect their view.
>
> ... At a time when the President has asked that we collect all revenues possible and when we can easily make additional multi-million dollar collections, I don't see how this additional "deferment" can be justified to either the White House or the Budget Bureau, and especially in view of the reason that the additional platforms are merely additional restrictions to the view. I especially hope that the Secretary is not placed in the position of explaining such additional action should the Budget Bureau chance to look into this matter, in conjunction with their recent letter on OCS leasing revenues. I do think that we can defend the sanctuary's protective measure but not any additional revenue deferrals.[40]

The Department thereafter adopted Assistant Secretary Moore's position and held the general Channel lease sale two months later.

Would litigation at this stage have changed the decision? One private group concluded that even this recourse was blocked. Early in 1968 an organization of citizens and lawyers considered an action to prohibit construction of offshore drilling facilities and the leasing of oil and gas

---

[38]New regulations would require somewhat more information. See discussion in a following section of this paper.

[39]For some discussion of this problem in litigation after the spill, see Science, April 25, 1969, at 411, and commenting letter Science, June 27, 1969, at 1466.

[40]Memorandum to the Under Secretary, Department of the Interior, December 1, 1967.

tracts in the Santa Barbara Channel. After extensive analysis of the problems and chances of success, the idea of litigation was dropped.

The difficulties and conclusions of the lawyers involved are instructive. They determined, first, that a successful challenge to the Secretary of Interior's leasing decision was unlikely to succeed given the language and background of the Outer Continental Shelf Lands Act. They decided not to argue against the constitutionality of that act. A second option, an action against the Corps of Engineers based on its permit role, looked unpromising in view of the Corps' uncertain authority even to refuse permits on non-navigational grounds. The third alternative, a suit against the oil company (Phillips) to prevent irreparable harm to the complainants, was judged to be prohibitively expensive. It was anticipated that the entire oil industry would oppose such a suit, and that the extensive scientific, engineering and other testimony needed to support the claim was not only difficult to find but impossible to finance. Finally, the subject itself did not appear to promise sufficient legal precedential value to warrant the expense of scarce legal and financial resources that were available; the combination of scenic values with oil-rich offshore areas was believed to be unique to the Santa Barbara Channel, and hardly a general feature of outer shelf lands.

FEDERAL STATUTES, PROCEDURES AND AGENCIES INVOLVED IN OFFSHORE LEASING DECISIONS. WHO PROTECTS THE PUBLIC?

Outer Continental Shelf Lands Act and the Department of the Interior.

Oil and other mineral development of the continental shelf of the United States is governed by the Outer Continental Shelf Lands Act.[41] The Act declares U.S. jurisdiction over submerged lands on the continental shelf that are seaward of lands confirmed to the states by the Submerged Lands Act.[42] Thus the outer shelf excludes state lands extending generally to three miles on the Atlantic and Pacific Coasts and to nine miles on the Gulf Coasts. Outer shelf limits extend, by terms of the 1958 Continental Shelf Convention (ratified by the United States March 24, 1961) to the 200-meter mark or "to where the depth of super adjacent waters" admits natural resources exploitation.[43]

---

[41]67 Stat. 462 (1953) 43 U.S.C. §1331, et. seq.
[42]67 Stat. 29 (1953) 43 U.S.C. §1301, et. seq.
[43]Geneva Convention on the Continental Shelf, April 29, 1958-June 10, 1964, 15 U.S.T. 471 (T.I.A.S. 5578).

Under Section 5 of the Act, the Secretary of Interior may "prescribe and amend such rules and regulations as he determines to be necessary and proper in order to provide for the prevention of waste and conservation of natural resources of the Outer Continental Shelf . . ."[44] His authority to grant oil and gas leases is explicit in Section 8.[45] The Act requires no public hearing before making such rules or regulations, but the Administrative Procedure Act states the *general* requirement that rules be published in the *Federal Register* 30 days before their effective date[46] and that "each agency shall give an interested person the right to petition for the issuance, amendment, or repeal of a rule."[47]

The Secretary is given the authority to cancel leases, subject to the right of judicial review, only if they are *non-producing*. Producing leases may be canceled only after an "appropriate proceeding" in the U.S. District Court, and only when the owner fails to comply with the statute, the lease, or regulations "in force and effect on the date of the issuance of the lease . . ."[48]

The Secretary has divided his authority between the Bureau of Land Management, to administer the leasing,[49] and the U.S. Geological Survey, to supervise and regulate actual operations on outer shelf lands.[50]

Leasing procedures followed by BLM and USGS before the Santa Barbara spill did not provide for public hearings or any evaluation by the Interior Department of other non-mineral uses of marine resources. BLM or USGS was required to publish in the *Federal Register* such procedural steps as the notice of map availability (whereby the public might see what areas were proposed for leasing), the call for nominations from oil companies for areas on which they wished to bid, and the notice of lease sale.[51] The material published and the terms used

---

[44]43 U.S.C. §133.
[45]43 U.S.C. §1337.
[46]5 U.S.C. §553(d).
[47]5 U.S.C. §553(e).
[48]43 U.S.C. §1334(b).
[49]43 C.F.R. §3380, *et seq.*
[50]30 C.F.R. §250, *et seq.*
[51]The principal steps in the oil and gas leasing procedures that were followed before the spill are summarized as follows: (a) The first (exploratory) phase began when oil companies obtained a letter from the USGS permitting them to gather data on oil and gas deposits by seismic surveys and drill core sampling. (West and Gulf Coast Region permits differed somewhat, but both required data submission to the USGS and other general operational requirements.) (b) The companies next indicated their interest in particular areas of shelf lands by requesting that the Secretary offer them for public lease. (c) USGS and the Bureau of Land Management analyzed these requests and jointly might recommend a lease sale. If the Secretary agreed, BLM prepared leasing maps of areas to be leased and excluded from nomination. Notice of map availability would be published in the *Federal Register*. (d) BLM

in the Register was, and remains, highly technical.

Apparently the Department of the Interior sought more than the usual amount of geological and geophysical information on Channel lands before deciding to lease. Secretary Udall announced soon afterward that

this particular portion of the continental shelf has been under intensive geologic investigation for several years. Undoubtedly more was known about it and in greater detail than any other area of comparable size along our entire coastline.[52]

However, after the spill, the Director of the U. S. Geological Survey reported that "without any question of doubt we did not have as much information on the detailed reservoir conditions as existed in the oil company files."[53]

The Regional Supervisor has broad discretion over the operations of the lessee and his approval is required before each operational stage.[54] Employing his operational discretion, the Regional Supervisor in the Pacific Region authorized a variance in the usual casing requirements for Union's A-21. Casing is necessary to enable drilling mud to circulate through the drill stem and, carrying away the drill cuttings, up the hole to the platform for recirculation.[55] Union Oil was permitted to set one string of conductor casing (20″ in diameter) 15 feet beneath the channel floor. Then it was permitted to drill 238 feet below the ocean floor (20 feet above the oil sands) and put in 13 3/8″ surface casing, which was cemented in place. Union was *not* required to put this surface casing to any greater depth.

But according to USGS regulations (OSC Order No. 2, March 31, 1965)

issued a call for nomination of units that companies might wish to have offered for lease sale. Publication in *Federal Register.* (For the Santa Barbara lease, 31 Fed. Reg. 16629, December 29, 1966.) (e) Oil and gas companies nominated areas by notifying USGS Regional Supervisor. (f) BLM published notice of lease sale in *Federal Register.* (For Santa Barbara, 32 Fed. Reg. 20884, December 28, 1967.) (g) At sale (for Santa Barbara, February 6, 1968) oil companies made sealed bids for tracts offered, each one required by statute to be no longer than 5,760 acres. The cash bonus offered by the oil companies, reflected the company's belief in the chances of oil and gas discovery. A royalty of not less than 12½% of the production value must be established by the Secretary. (16 2/3% for Santa Barbara.) (h) BLM, as executor of the lease, awarded it to the "highest responsible qualified bidder," the lease being for five years and as long thereafter as oil or gas is produced. (i) A drill plan of the oil company would be forwarded to the USGS Regional Oil and Gas Supervisor for approval along with various information from the exploratory drilling operations. After discovery, a development plan was to be submitted, and approved by USGS.
[52]Department of the Interior press release, February 7, 1968.
[53]*Hearings on S.1219, supra* note 1, at 69.
[54]30 C.F.R. §250.34. *See also* §250.10, *et seq.*
[55]For diagrams and explanations of this process, *see Hearings on S.7 and S.544, supra* note 6, at 557-565.

conductor casing must be set to not less than 300 feet below the ocean floor, and surface casing for such a well to at least 25% of the total depth, or 869 feet below the ocean floor.

One reason why a casing variance was granted was because the first competent bed to which such surface casing could be anchored was about 1400 feet below sea level— a greater depth than is usual for such casing. (Permission to set casing to only 238 feet from the ocean bottom was also granted for the four other wells on Platform A.) But according to the Vice President of Union Oil more casing might have contained the spill. "Had we had such a string of casing, it is probable that we would not have had the well come up through the ocean floor."[56]

In early 1965 the USGS Regional Supervisors of the Pacific and Gulf Coast Regions issued OCS order No. 7, which outlined in detail the pollution regulations for offshore oil, gas, and sulphur operations. The Supervisor for the Pacific Region subsequently required that the order be posted on all platforms.[57]

At the time of the Santa Barbara disaster the Regional Supervisor for the Pacific Region had four petroleum engineers available to carry out the necessary on-scene supervision and inspection, two of whom were based at Santa Barbara. Nevertheless, the Regional Supervisor testified that more inspections would not have avoided the spill, since Union Oil had complied with all USGS requirements.[58]

Fish and Wildlife Acts.

The Fish and Wildlife Service of the Department of the Interior is charged with making biological and economic investigations and reports on fish and wildlife resources. The Bureau of Commercial Fisheries and the Bureau of Sport Fisheries and Wildlife generally divide the authorities and duties provided for by the acts.[59]

Under the Fish and Wildlife Act of 1956 the Secretary of Interior "shall consider and determine the policies and procedures that are necessary and desirable in carrying out efficiently and in the public interest the laws relating to fish and wildlife," including such matters as steps "for the development, advancement, management, conservation, and protection of the fisheries resources."[60]

---

[56] *Id.*, at 572. See also discussion at 645, 646, and 683-691.
[57] *See Senate Hearings on S.7 and S.544, supra* note 6, at 786, for a compilation of Order No. 7 and other orders.
[58] *Id.*, at 673.
[59] 70 Stat. 119, 16 U.S.C. §742 (a), *et seq.*
[60] 16 U.S.C. §742(f).

The Fish and Wildlife Coordination Act of 1958[61] directs

that wildlife conservation shall receive equal consideration and be coordinated with other features of water-resource development programs through the effectual and harmonious planning, development, maintenance and coordination of wildlife conservation and rehabilitation . . .[62]

The Secretary of Interior is authorized ". . . to make surveys and investigations of the wildlife of the public domain, including lands and waters or interests therein acquired or controlled by any agency of the U.S."[63] The Act further states that

whenever the waters of any stream *or other body of water* are proposed or authorized to be impounded, diverted, the channel deepened, or the stream or other body of water otherwise *controlled or modified for any purpose whatever,* including navigation, and drainage, by any department or agency of the United States, or *by any public* or *private agency under Federal permit or license,* such department or agency first *shall consult with the United States Fish and Wildlife Service,* Department of the Interior . . . *with a view to the conservation of wildlife resources by preventing loss of and damage to such resources* as well as providing for the development and improvement thereof in connection with such water-resource development.[64]

Pursuant to the Fish and Wildlife Coordination Act,[65] the 1899 Rivers and Harbors Act,[66] and the Federal Water Pollution Control Act,[67] the Secretaries of Interior and the Army entered into a Memorandum of Understanding on July 13, 1967. Procedures were agreed upon to insure that the Corps of Engineers considered pollution, fish and wildlife, and recreation interests in granting Corps permits for dredging, filling or excavation in navigable waters.

The Role of Fish and Wildlife Service in the Santa Barbara leasing. Involvement of the Assistant Secretary for Fish and Wildlife and Parks in Santa Barbara leasing decisions was apparently discussed within the Interior Department by April, 1967. At that time the Assistant Secretary, Stanley Cain, wrote the Assistant Secretary for Mineral Resources, Cordell Moore, that he

was encouraged when informed that the Fish and Wildlife Service will have an opportunity to review the leases to be issued for this area before they are

---

[61] 72 Stat. 563 (1958), 16 U.S.C. §661, *et seq.*
[62] 16 U.S.C. §661.
[63] *Id.*
[64] 16 U.S.C. §662(a). (Emphasis added.)
[65] 16 U.S.C. §661, *et seq.*
[66] 33 U.S.C. §401, *et seq.*
[67] 33 U.S.C. §466, *et seq.*

actually granted. We certainly appreciate this cooperation and are looking forward to seeing the leases when they are being prepared.[68]

The Assistant Secretaries had apparently made the judgment that the Fish and Wildlife Coordination Act quoted above did not require consultation for offshore leasing by BLM.

In a memorandum to Secretary Udall some six months before leasing, Assistant Secretary Cain came out in favor of creating the first national marine sanctuary in the Santa Barbara Channel that would bar federal leasing within its boundaries.

> The expected difficulty in establishing marine sanctuaries is that we often do not know what values may be foregone, such as mineral potential, but in most National Parks and Monuments the country has foregone these values in favor of preservation of habitat and landscape.
>
> In the Santa Barbara case, the oil is not really speculative, so we have to face squarely the question of preservation.

He went on to say that the Secretary might

> . . . seek to establish a national reserve[69] outside the sanctuary for whatever distance is feasible. I would favor this. I believe the time is ripe to take such actions. For one thing, they do not require land purchase.[70]

Several days later, after conversations with Assistant Secretary Moore, Cain's position changed. In writing again to Secretary Udall, Cain called attention to Moore's willingness to accept a two-mile buffer zone along the State sanctuary, and Moore's objection to Santa Barbara County's request for a one-year moratorium on leasing and drilling. Moore told Cain that if the Secretary were willing to

> accept the criticism such moratorium would draw from the oil companies and the budget people he [Moore] would go along. However, there is already enough known about the oil potentialities off the sanctuary and other related matters that a period of further study is scarcely needed.

Cain mentioned the deep water between the Channel Islands and the shore and his belief that

> the continental shelf that you might set aside as a sanctuary would not be able to prevent oil development in any case. On the basis of this information, and

---

[68]Letter from Stanley Cain to Cordell Moore, April 27, 1967.

[69]Section 12(a) of the Outer Continental Shelf Lands Act authorizes the President to "withdraw from disposition any of the unleased lands of the Outer Continental Shelf." The Key Largo Coral Reef Preserve was created in 1960 by the President under this provision [Pres. Proc. No. 3339 (1960)] and is now administered by the Secretary of Interior for Conservation and recreation purposes. 43 C.F.R. §15.1, *et. seq.*

[70]Memorandum from Stanley Cain to Stewart Udall, August 7, 1967.

especially because of the very high value of the resources and the public revenues therefrom, this would be a poor place to attempt to initiate the first marine sanctuary.[71]

The extent of Fish and Wildlife involvement in the Santa Barbara Channel leasing decisions is perhaps indicated when three months *after* the federal leasing sale Assistant Secretary Cain recommended against a Santa Barbara marine sanctuary study bill.

While the Federal Government has not leased much acreage in the Santa Barbara Channel, *a general sale is under active consideration.* Strong efforts are being made to develop adequate restrictions which will minimize the operational impact on the values of the Channel area and to prevent any possibility that the lands covered in the state sanctuary will be drained from adjacent OCS lands.[72]

Several months later a move was made within the Department to remedy the communication problem with Fish and Wildlife. In October, 1968, Secretary Udall created the Office of Marine Resources under a newly named Assistant Secretary for Fish and Wildlife, Parks, and Marine Resources. The action was announced

to strengthen the advancement and coordination of Interior's significant marine resources programs, including those related to marine geology, determination of mineral potential, mineral development, oil and gas exploration and leasing, marine hydrology and pollution . . . marine biology, commercial uses of the living resources of the sea, sport fisheries and recreation.[73]

The Assistant Secretary was charged with coordinating marine resources policies assisted by a nongovernmental Marine Resources Advisory Committee. Under his supervision, the Office of Marine Resources was directed to analyze, coordinate, review, report on and recommend policies on marine resource programs of Interior, "serving as the focal point for the Department's broad multi-bureau relationships in the field of marine resources . . . with other government agencies . . . private industries . . . and the public . . ."[74]

Federal Water Pollution Control Act.

The basic policy of the Federal Water Pollution Control Act, as amended,[75] is "to enhance the quality and value of our water resources

---

[71]Memorandum from Stanley Cain to Stewart Udall, August 11, 1967.

[72]Letter from Stanley Cain to Edward Garmatz, Chairman House Merchant Marine and Fisheries Committee, April 8, 1968. (Emphasis added.)

[73]33 Fed. Reg. 15916 (October 29, 1968).

[74]*Id.*

[75]33 U.S.C. §466, *et seq.*

and to establish a national policy for the prevention, control, and abatement of water pollution."[76] The Act directs the Secretary of Interior to cooperate with other federal, state and local agencies and to "prepare or develop comprehensive programs for eliminating or reducing the pollution of interstate waters and tributaries thereof and improving the sanitary condition of surface and underground waters."[77] The Federal Water Pollution Control Administration, created in 1965 under the Water Quality Act, was transferred to the Department of the Interior and functions under the Assistant Secretary for Water Quality and Research.[78]

Pursuant to the policies of the Federal Water Pollution Control Act, President Johnson issued Executive Order 11288, on Prevention, Control and Abatement of Water Pollution by Federal Activities. Of particular relevance to offshore leasing are the following provisions directed toward Secretarial and agency heads:

Section 1. *Policy.* The heads of the departments, agencies, and establishments of the Executive Branch of the Government shall provide leadership in the nationwide effort to improve water quality through prevention, control, and abatement of water pollution from Federal Government activities in the United States. In order to achieve these objectives . . .

(3) Pollution caused by all other operations of the Federal Government, such as water resources projects and operations under Federal loans, grants, or contracts, shall be reduced to the lowest level practicable;

(4) Review and surveillance of all such activities shall be maintained to assure that pollution control standards are met on a continuing basis; . . .

(7) Water pollution control needs shall be considered in the initial stages of planning for each new installation or project, and the head of each department, agency, and establishment shall establish appropriate procedures for securing advice and for consulting with the Secretary of the Interior at the earliest feasible stage. . . .

Section 7. *Review of facilities or operations supported by Federal loans, grants, or contracts.* (a) The head of each department, agency, and establishment shall conduct a review of the loan, grant, and contract practices of his organization to determine the extent to which water pollution control standards similar to those set forth in this order for direct Federal operations should be adhered to by borrowers, grantees, or contractors with respect to their operations in the United States. The head of each department, agency, and establishment shall review all such activities for which there is a significant potential for reduction of water pollution and develop appropriate recommendations for accomplishing such reduction. In conducting this review, necessary

[76]Water Quality Act, 79 Stat. 903 (1965); 33 U.S.C. §466.
[77]33 U.S.C. §466(a).
[78]Reorganization Plan No. 2 of 1966, 31 Fed. Reg. 6857, 80 Stat. 1608. The agency name has since been changed to the Federal Water Quality Administration, Water Quality Improvement Act, Pub. L. 91-224, §110 (April 3, 1970).

technical assistance should be sought from the Secretary of the Interior and the heads of other appropriate Federal agencies. A report on the results of this review shall be submitted to the Director of the Bureau of the Budget by July 1, 1966.

(b) The heads of departments, agencies, and establishments are encouraged to prescribe regulations covering loan, grant, or contract practices designed to reduce water pollution.[79]

[It should be noted here that until passage of the Water Quality Act in April 3, 1970 legislation on oil pollution specifically dealt with vessels and oil pollution in navigable waters, without mention (or application by the Interior Department) to offshore oil rigs.[80]]

The role of the Federal Water Pollution Control Administration in the Santa Barbara leasing. When the Corps held public hearings on the Phillips lease a representative of the FWPCA presented brief testimony. He cited the FWPCA requirements that adjacent water be free from pollution, and offered surveillance and enforcement assistance under Executive Order 11288 and other acts.[81] Other than this testimony there is scant evidence of FWPCA participation in the Santa Barbara offshore leasing processes.

In the same month the leasing took place, the Secretary of Interior, who, with the Secretary of Transportation, had just issued a joint report to the President on *Oil Pollution*, sent a memorandum to the Director of the Geological Survey on this very subject.

> Because of the local concern for scenic values and objections to leasing . . . it is essential that the Geological Survey, whose responsibility it is, take every precaution possible in its supervisory functions. Pollution from oil spills in drilling and production is an additional hazard which we must take every possible means to avoid.

The letter noted that the new operations and techniques required for deep water production required USGS to

> keep abreast of these so that our regulatory work does not impede this new effort by the industry, and is at the same time effective in carrying out our responsibilities.
>
> . . . I urge the Geological Survey to make available adequate manpower and funds to carry out this task on which I place a high priority. The assistance of other bureaus and offices of the Department, particularly the Federal Water Pollution Control Administration, should be enlisted as necessary.[82]

[79]E.O. 11288, 31 Fed. Reg. 9261, July 2, 1966.
[80]*See* Oil Pollution Act, 1924, as amended by Clean Water Restoration Act of 1966, November 3, 1966, P.L. 89-753, 80 Stat. 1252; 33 U.S.C. §431, *et seq.*
[81]Testimony of John C. Merrell, Jr., Southern California Field Station, FWPCA. Corps *hearing, supra* note 33, at 39.
[82]Letter from Stewart Udall to William Pecora, February 17, 1968.

The letter is further evidence of Interior's position that primary jurisdiction over pollution prevention controls on federal offshore oil operations belonged to USGS.

The apparent nonparticipation of the FWPCA in the leasing decision was subject to inquiry at Senate hearings. Former Secretary Udall agreed with Senator Muskie, Chairman of the Air and Water Pollution Subcommittee of the Senate Public Works Committee, that documents and minutes did not indicate an FWPCA role in the leasing discussions. Secretary Udall noted that "of course we have already brought out the fact that the oil spill was not the major policy issue that was developed here and this is really where we failed. . . ."[83] Udall pointed out that ". . . had anyone, including FWPCA, raised the question of oil spills as one of the major considerations to be analyzed in making that final judgment . . . we would have had a different process . . ."[84]

Jurisdiction of the Corps of Engineers.

The authority of the Secretary of the Army over offshore oil rigs was specified in the Outer Continental Shelf Lands Act. Section 4(f) of the Act states:

> The authority of the Secretary of the Army to prevent obstruction to navigation in the navigable waters of the United States is extended to artificial islands and fixed structures located on the Outer Continental Shelf.[85]

The Army's navigational authority mentioned above is based on provisions of the 1899 Rivers and Harbors Act. Section 9 of that act states:

> *It shall not be lawful to construct or commence the construction* of any bridge, dam, dike, or causeway over or in any port, roadstead, haven, harbor, canal, navigable river, or other navigable water of the United States until the consent of Congress to the building of such structures shall have been obtained and *until the plans for the same shall have been submitted to and approved by the Chief of Engineers and by the Secretary of the Army.*[86]

Section 10 states:

> *The creation of any obstruction not affirmatively authorized by Congress, to the navigable capacity of any of the waters of the United States is prohibited;* and *it shall not be lawful to build* or commence the building of any wharf, pier, dolphin, boom, weir, breakwater, bulkhead, jetty or other structures in any port, roadstead, haven, harbor, canal, navigable river, or other water of the United States, outside established harbor lines, or where no harbor lines have

---

[83] *Senate Hearings on S.7 and S.544, supra* note 6, at 1286.
[84] *Id.,* at 1288.
[85] 43 U.S.C. §1333(f).
[86] 30 Stat. 1151 (1899); 33 U.S.C. §401. (Emphasis added.)

been established, *except on plans recommended by the Chief of Engineers and authorized by the Secretary of the Army.*[87]

Regulations for the granting of Corps of Engineers construction permits under these sections were once based primarily on navigational effects of a proposed project. But in December, 1967, the grounds for denying a permit were broadened.

The decision as to whether a permit will be issued will be predicated upon the effects of permitted activities on the public interest including effects upon water quality, recreation, fish and wildlife, pollution, our natural resources, as well as the effects on navigation . . .[88]

One other statute affecting the Corps navigational authority should be noted. Broad pollution control authority is granted to the Corps under Section 13 of the 1899 Rivers and Harbors Act. The section declares it unlawful

to deposit, or cause, suffer, or procure to be deposited material of any kind in any place on the bank of any navigable water, or on the bank of any tributary of any navigable water, where the same shall be liable to be washed into such navigable water, either by ordinary or high tides, or by storms or floods or otherwise, whereby navigation shall or may be impeded or obstructed . . .[89]

The Secretary of the Army may, however, permit such deposits when "anchorage and navigation will not be injured."[90]

The Role of the Corps of Engineers in the Santa Barbara Leasing.

The Corps authorizes offshore oil operations in its Los Angeles District in three stages, none of which requires a public hearing. (1) It authorizes geophysical explorations for a six-month term by letter with no public notice or hearing. (2) Drill core exploration *outside* the Santa Barbara Channel is authorized by letter for a similar term with no public notice, while those explorations *within* the channel are advertised by public notice for 15 days and a three-year permit is issued for each tract. Public hearings are held at the Corps' discretion. Permit renewal is granted under the same procedures. (3) Applications to construct permanent

[87] 33 U.S.C. §403. (Emphasis added.)

[88] 33 C.F.R. §209.330(a). The authority of the Secretary of the Army to deny a *dredge* and *fill* permit on non-navigational grounds was recently denied by a U.S. District Court and is being appealed by the Justice Department. *Zabel and Russell v. Tabb* Civil No. 67-200 (M.D. Fla. Feb. 17, 1969), 37 U.S. L. W. 2502 (March 11, 1969), Appeal No. 27555.

[89] 33 U.S.C. §407. Oil discharges have been considered within the prohibitions of this Act. See *U.S. v. Ballard Oil Co.* 195 F.2d 369 (1st Cir. 1952).

[90] 33 U.S.C. §407. Violation of this section is a misdemeanor under 33 U.S.C. §411.

offshore platforms are publicly advertised for 30 days and a public hearing is held at the Corps' discretion. The permit requires construction within three years and may be revoked.[91]

The Corps, which authorized four platforms in the Los Angeles District plus a fifth platform not yet built, decided to hold public hearings in November, 1967, on the proposed drainage lease platform of the Phillips Company. At that time there was evident public interest in the potential effects of the proposed platform on coastal communities.

While the District Engineer stated that only the platform, not the offshore lease, was to be considered at the hearing, this distinction was not always maintained by witnesses—indicating the inherent ambiguity of the Corps offshore permit role. Ultimate permit approval was hardly in doubt.

The reasons were, first, that the Corps permit authority granted by Section 4(f) of the Outer Continental Shelf Lands Act relates to obstructions to navigation, while its authority under the 1899 Rivers and Harbors Act may be much broader. But disregarding this possible distinction at its Phillips Petroleum hearing in Santa Barbara, the District Engineer noted that he would hear testimony on "any matter pertinent to the structure which might bear on the public interest."[92] Thus, the Corps heard statements on pollution, recreation, aesthetics, and fish and wildlife, as well as navigation aspects of the proposed Phillips platform.

Second, under Section 1(c) of its lease[93] Phillips was given the right to construct an offshore platform, and platform approval had already been granted by the USGS, which requested rapid permit approval by the Corps at the hearing.[94]

Third, according to testimony by the drilling contractor at the hearing, from $1,750,000 to $2,000,000 had already been invested in the lease. The platform itself was nearing completion in a Gulf Coast shipyard and was expected to be delivered through the Panama Canal by the following month.

After the hearing, in January, 1968, the Corps recommended certain pollution control guarantees objectionable to the Phillips Company requiring:

> ... (m) That positive controls are provided for control of pollution from routine operations, and particularly in the event of damage to the installation by tsunamis or earthquakes.

---

[91] *Hearings on S.7 and S.544, supra* note 6, at 539-40.

[92] Corps *hearing, supra* note 33, at 4.

[93] The Phillips lease and Union Oil lease are similar, *see Hearings on S.7 and S.544, supra* note 6, at 322.

[94] Corps *hearing, supra* note 33, at 19.

(n) That the permittee will remove the structure upon proof that:

1. The work is causing pollution of navigable waters to the extent that adjacent beaches or marine life in the area are detrimentally affected.

2. There is a shut-down in production due to lack of oil or because further development of the area is no longer desirable, unless local interests desire at that time to take possession of the structure for utilization as an offshore marina development for small boat refuge.

(o) That the conditions of this permit shall be enforced by the District Engineer or such other agencies as he may designate.[95]

A detailed letter from the Phillips Company to the Corps District Engineer at Los Angeles objected to these provisions as being contrary to its lease, unnecessary in view of the USGS pollution requirements, and not within the area of the Corps' responsibility. It suggested a new provision (m) to incorporate these concerns, requiring that:

(m) The permittee, in the installation and maintenance of such structure at the authorized site, will take reasonable precautions for control of pollution to the navigable waters, particularly in the event of damage to the installation by tsunamis or earthquakes, and will observe and comply fully with these controls for pollution prescribed by the Code of Federal Regulations for OCS mineral and development operations.[96]

Several meetings were held between Corps and Interior officials to resolve these conflicts. Reporting after one such meeting, Eugene W. Standley, Staff Engineer for Interior, noted that Interior handled its

public relations business in Santa Barbara through city, county and state people and had chosen not to go the public hearing route. That we [Interior] had tried to warn L.A. District Engineer of Corps of what he faced and we preferred not to stir the natives up any more than possible. . . . All decided that more coordination and a better method of Corps permit handling could solve our problems. [The representative of the Corps will] . . . see about combining our approvals for platform installations to give companies a better service.[97]

The Corps adopted the substitute language suggested by Phillips. (The same provision was inserted in the permit granted to Union Oil for Platform A.)

Subsequent discussions by Interior and the Corps did not resolve the inherent ambiguity of the Corps permit role or determine how non-navigational considerations should be coordinated with Interior. The

---

[95] Letter of C. Rex Boyd, Division Chief Attorney, to Col. Norman E. Pherson, July 24, 1968.

[96] Id.

[97] Memorandum for the files, Department of the Interior, from Eugene Standley, February 15, 1968.

situation remained unclear when Union Oil requested a permit for Platform A but no hearing was held.[98] However, after the spill the Corps and Interior did reach an agreement regarding their respective roles in offshore exploration and platform construction. Under new Corps regulations only navigational and national defense matters will be considered by the Corps in granting permits for activities conducted outside territorial waters.[99] Notice of this limited jurisdiction was given to Santa Barbara residents when the Corps solicited comments on exploratory oil drilling proposals and Sun Oil's request for a platform construction permit.[100]

EXECUTIVE BRANCH RESPONSE AFTER THE SPILL

New standards.

In mid-February, 1969, USGS began a scientific study of the Santa Barbara Channel in cooperation with the State of California to investigate the nature of the channel floor and the need for new drilling procedures.[101] Partly as a result of this study, in March, 1969, Interior specified new drilling methods, covering such matters as safety and pollution control, equipment, casings, and testing procedures. In addition the order announced the creation of an ecological sanctuary and an adjacent buffer zone in the Channel.[102]

On February 17, Interior announced new regulations on outer shelf

---

[98]On June 12, 1968, the City of Santa Barbara requested a Corps public hearing (not otherwise required) on Union's application, protesting that (1) it posed a potential danger to water and air navigation, (2) it would be ugly to residents of the city, and (3) underwater facilities were possible. For reasons still unclear, on July 11, 1968, the city *withdrew* its hearing request while reasserting its objections. *See Senate Hearings S.7 and S.544, supra* note 6, at 546-548. The County of Santa Barbara did not respond to the Corps notice of permit application. *Id.*, at 540.

[99]"The decision as to whether a permit will be issued must rest on an evaluation of all relevant factors, including the effect of the proposed work on navigation, fish and wildlife, conservation, pollution, aesthetics, ecology, and the general public interest *except that* in the case of permits for fixed structures or artificial islands on *Outer Continental Shelf lands* under mineral lease from the Department of the Interior, the decision will be based on the effect of the work on *navigation* and *national security.*" 6.a. Corps of Engineers Reg. No. 1145-2-303, Change 4, December 3, 1969. (Emphasis added.)

[100]Letter from Norman E. Pherson, Colonel, Corps of Engineers, to the Board of County Supervisors, County of Santa Barbara, September 25, 1969. The Corps did not hold hearings on the oil company requests for exploratory drilling and platform permit requests and the County filed suit alleging that hearings were required. *County of Santa Barbara, et al. v. Robert J. Malley, et al. cert. denied,* November 25, 1969. Remanded to 9th Cir., Civil No. 25049.

[101]*Hearings on S.1219, supra* note 1, at 45.

[102]O.C.S. Order No. 10, March 21, 1969.

operations that provided for absolute liability of present lessees for oil pollution. A few days later the Federal Register stated

> It is the policy of the Department whenever practicable, to afford the public an opportunity to participate in the rulemaking process. This procedure is deemed unnecessary in this case because the amendment involves public property. Furthermore, it is contrary to the public interest to delay the effective date of this amendment. Accordingly, the amendment shall become effective on publication in the *Federal Register.*[103]

Subsequently in early May 1969, the Department proposed and published in the *Federal Register*, new provisions on pollution. On August 22, 1969, it announced the new §250.43 to read:

> §250.43 *Pollution and waste disposal.*
> (a) The lessee shall not pollute land or water or damage the aquatic life of the sea or allow extraneous matter to enter and damage any mineral-or water-bearing formation. The lessee shall dispose of all liquid and nonliquid waste materials as prescribed by the supervisor. All spills or leakage of oil or waste materials shall be recorded by the lessee and, upon request of the supervisor, shall be reported to him. All spills or leakage of a substantial size or quantity, as defined by the supervisor, and those of any size or quantity which cannot be immediately controlled also shall be reported by the lessee without delay to the supervisor and to the Coast Guard and the Regional Director of the Federal Water Pollution Control Administration. All spills or leakage of oil or waste materials of a size or quantity specified by the designee under the pollution contingency plan shall also be reported by the lessee without delay to such designee.
> (b) *If the waters of the sea are polluted by the drilling or production operations* conducted by or on behalf of the lessee, *and* such pollution damages or *threatens to damage aquatic life, wildlife, or public or private property, the control and total removal of the pollutant, wheresoever found, proximately resulting therefrom shall be at the expense of the lessee.* Upon failure of the lessee to control and remove the pollutant the supervisor, in cooperation with other appropriate agencies of the Federal, State and local governments, or in cooperation with the lessee, or both, shall have the right to accomplish the control and removal of the pollutant in accordance with any established contingency plan for combating oil spills or by other means at the cost of the lessee. Such action shall not relieve the lessee of any responsibility as provided herein.
> (c) The lessee's liability to third parties, other than for cleaning up the pollutant in accordance with paragraph (b) of this section shall be governed by applicable law.[104]

---

[103]34 Fed. Reg. 2503, February 21, 1969.
[104]34 Fed. Reg. 13547, August 22, 1969. (Emphasis added.) It is interesting to note that the proposed regulations of May called for "reparation of any damage to whomsoever occurring . . ." 34 Fed. Reg. 7481, May 7, 1969.

The oil industry indicated its opposition to the new policy on liability. Comments to USGS by the American Petroleum Institute noted that:

> The effect of a provision which would subject a lessee to unlimited liability for actions beyond his control would be to burden any lease evaluation with a large, undetermined risk. Since this risk is uninsurable, many prudent operators, and those without a substantial financial position, would find it difficult or impossible to bid on federal acreage. This would result in reduced competition for leases and in lower revenue to the government by reducing the value of the leases.[105]

Procedural Reform.

When Secretary Hickel ordered all wells closed and drilling halted on federal channel leases, he noted Interior's lack of knowledge about the channel floor. He therefore asked Union Oil and other companies to submit to USGS all engineering, geological, geophysical and other information normally regarded by the companies as proprietary and withheld from the U.S. The Secretary's request to Union Oil thus concluded with the assurance "that proprietary information will be safeguarded and not released for public inspection."[106]

In early May the Department proposed new regulations on information policies[107] to require submission of oil companies of certain structural interpretations as well as raw data (before exploratory programs as well as before development). The Department proposed that geological and geophysical interpretations be available to the public even against the lessee's wishes if it was "administratively determined" to be "in the public interest." Oil companies objected to these provisions as neither sufficiently protective nor "within the spirit of the competitive bidding intent of the O.C.S. Act . . ."[108] In late August new regulations were finally announced and the information retrieval and disclosure proposals of May were substantially modified.[109] Data such as drilling logs and charts, analysis of cores, and raw paleontological reports (specifically *not* paleontological *interpretations*)[110] must be made available to USGS "upon request of the supervisor.[111] Like the regulations supplanted, geophysical and geological data and interpretations would be made available

---

[105]Letter from Frank Ikard to William Pecora, June 4, 1969. *See also Hearings on S.1219, supra* note 1, at 111-113.

[106]Telegram from Walter Hickel to Fred Hartley, March 3, 1969.

[107]34 Fed. Reg. 7381, May 7, 1969.

[108]Letter from Frank Ikard to William Pecora, June 4, 1969. The companies did not refer to the Public Information Act exemption.

[109]34 Fed. Reg. 13544, August 22, 1969.

[110]30 C.F.R. §250.38 (34 Fed. Reg. at 13546).

[111]*Id.*

to the public against the lessee's wishes only when the *supervisor* determined that "such information is required and necessary for the proper development of the field or area."[112] The proposed reference to the public interest was dropped, and the public disclosure requirements remain substantially as they were before the spill.[113]

In June, 1969, the Interior Department proposed new pre-leasing procedures and after receipt of public comments issued substantially similar regulations in August, 1969.[114] When an area is initially considered for mineral leasing, BLM must request USGS to prepare reports on the mineral resources of the area and "other interested" Federal agencies to report on other resources and the effects of mining on the total environment.[115] After a leasing program is decided upon in a particular area, but prior to final selection of leasing tracts, the Director of the Bureau of Land Management must

> evaluate fully the potential effect of the leasing program on the total environment, aquatic resources, aesthetics, recreation, and other resources in the entire area during exploration, development and operational phases.[116]

Views of other agencies, none of them named, must at this stage be requested and considered, and the Director "*may* hold public hearings and *may* consult with State agencies, organizations and individuals to aid him in his evaluations and determinations."[117] Thereupon the Director alone is charged with developing special leasing stipulations to protect the environment, to be published in the *Federal Register* 30 days before the lease sale. The regulations contain no requirement for coordination with the FWPCA, Fish and Wildlife Service, or Office of Marine Resources which is theoretically charged with the coordination of marine resource policy.

In April, 1969, President Nixon asked his Science Advisor, Dr. DuBridge, to appoint a special panel of technical experts to recommend ways to stop the leak on Union Oil's lease. The eleven-man panel included several members from the President's fourteen-man panel on oil spills that was appointed the previous February, and was likewise staffed by the Office of Science and Technology.

The new panel met four times in formal sessions, along with various

---

[112]30 C.F.R. §250.97.
[113]For further discussion of this proprietary information problem, *see Hearings on S.1219, supra* note 1, at III-115.
[114]43 C.F.R. §3380, *et seq.* 34 Fed. Reg. 13548, August 22, 1969.
[115]43 C.F.R. §3381.2.
[116]43 C.F.R. §3381.4.
[117]*Id.*

conferences with scientists of the state of California, the federal government, several universities and the oil companies. At the end of their deliberations in June, they issued a two-page report recommending six steps in order of their priority. In effect the panel reported that the best way to stop the leak was to resume drilling.

> The Panel believes that it is less hazardous to proceed with development of the lease than to attempt to seal the structure with its oil content intact. In fact, the Panel is of the opinion that withdrawal of the oil from the Repetto zone is a necessary part of any plan to stop the oil seep and to insure against recurrence of oil seeps on the crest of the structure. The Panel concludes that it would be hazardous to withdraw from this lease at the present time.[118]

The report was immediately criticized as cursory and unduly secretive by residents of Santa Barbara and various Congressmen. A joint statement by Senators Muskie and Cranston noted that there was no discussion of alternative solutions, and no reference to panel procedures or sources of information used. They urged a new study by independent scientists.[119] The Director of USGS, Dr. William Pecora, responded to this criticism by emphasizing the limited mission of the Panel and the basic policy assumptions on which its recommendations were based.

> The Secretary particularly wanted a group of specialists on the Panel rather than an across-the-board intellectual group, to examine not only the geological characteristics, the sea floor characteristics, but also the reservoir characteristics.[120]

As for the charge that the Panel examined only industry information, its Executive Secretary noted that the members "were to examine the scientific data and evidence related to the technical questions they were asked. ... They believed that they have examined *all* the data available relating to these issues." Furthermore, "the Panel would like nothing better than to see the data which they examined made public. They are prevented by law as is Dr. DuBridge and the Department of the Interior from making this information public."[121]

Criticism of the Panel's "pump the reservoir dry" theory was presented before the Senate Interior Committee by Dr. Robert Curry, who noted that:

---

[118]Panel report, Office of Science and Technology press release, June 2, 1969.

[119]*Los Angeles Times*, June 6, 1969, part 1, at 22, col. 1 *See also* 115 Cong. Rec. 56119 (daily ed. June 9, 1969).

[120]*Hearings on S.1219, supra* note 1, at 62.

[121]Letter from John S. Steinhart, Technical Assistant, Office of Science and Technology, to Mrs. Ralph E. Allen, July 2, 1969.

We do not know how fast oil can refill the existing shallow reservoirs of unknown size, and to try to pump these dry and fail is asking for certain trouble, since the permeability of the whole field will then have been increased and existing capping sediments may be woefully inadequate.[122]

Dr. Curry's expertise on this subject was subsequently disputed by oil companies and USGS.[123]

LEGISLATIVE BRANCH RESPONSE AFTER THE SPILL

In the 90th Congress, several bills were introduced calling for Interior Department studies of potential marine sanctuaries. Two bills, H.R. 11460 and H.R. 11868, provided for a moratorium on oil and gas and other mineral or industrial development during the study period. These proposals were not endorsed by the Interior Department as noted above and were not passed by the House.

In the 90th Congress the House and Senate each passed new water pollution bills (separate versions of S. 3206), but in the hurry to adjourn failed to reach agreement and no act was passed. One of the points of disagreement involved liability treatment for oil pollution from offshore oil facilities.

Several bills were introduced in the 91st Congress dealing with oil pollution from offshore facilities. The Senate approved S.7, introduced by Senator Muskie as the Water Quality Improvement Act of 1969. Before the spill, S.7 was designed to subject owners or operators of offshore rigs to liability for oil cleanup costs of the U.S. government up to $15,000,000 for any negligent or willful oil discharge in navigable waters of the United States or on adjoining shorelines. After the spill, however, at hearings of the Muskie subcommittee, S.7 was criticized by Secretary Hickel for being limited to willful and negligent pollution and restricted to navigable waters and shorelines only. He recommended that the committee

adopt no language which would limit the existing law and regulations which require absolute liability, without limit, on those who operate on the Outer Continental Shelf.[124]

As finally approved by Congress, the Water Quality Improvement Act of 1970 affects offshore facilities by requiring generally that

Any applicant for a Federal license or permit to conduct any activity. . . which may result in any discharge into the navigable waters of the United States shall

---

[122] *Hearings on S.1219, supra* note 1, at 134.
[123] *Id.*, at 145, 146 and 115, 116.
[124] *Hearings on S.7 and S.544, supra* note 6, at 946.

provide. . . certification from the State in which the discharge originates or will originate, or, if appropriate, from the interstate water pollution control agency having jurisdiction. . . that there is reasonable assurance. . . that such activity will be conducted in a manner which will not violate applicable water quality standards.[125]

The act makes the owner or operator of any offshore facility absolutely liable up to $8,000,000 (barring act of God, war, negligence of the U. S. or act of a third party) for costs incurred by the United States in cleaning up oil discharge on U. S. navigable waters or adjoining shorelines. The act sets no limitation for discharge resulting from negligence,[126] but provides that cleanup costs can be recovered from the U. S. if the owner or operator can show, in an action before the U. S. Court of Claims, that he was not responsible for the spill and that he is not liable under the OCS act.[127]

The Water Quality Improvement Act of 1970, therefore, does not affect oil drilling liability beyond the three-mile limit. But it does add the requirement that persons in charge of onshore or offshore facilities, no matter where located, must notify the appropriate U.S. government agency of illegal oil discharges "immediately," or else be fined $10,000 or suffer a year's imprisonment or both. A civil penalty of $10,000 would be levied against offshore owners or operators for each separate illegal discharge of oil into navigable waters, adjoining shorelines and the contiguous zone.[128]

The new act includes a separate section on the control of hazardous substances besides oil. Section 12 provides for regulations affecting the introduction of such substances as are dangerous to public health, fish or wildlife, or shorelines into or upon U.S. navigable waters, adjoining shorelines and the contiguous zone. Thus, detergents and other chemicals, used so heavily after the *Torrey Canyon* spill, would be regulated by the President or his delegate.

After the spill various bills were introduced specifically to protect the Channel from oil pollution.

Senator Cranston introduced S.1219 to terminate all offshore drilling in the Channel and to suspend drilling in other California outer shelf areas until completion of an Interior Department study. The bill would direct the Secretary to investigate oil drilling, production, and transport meth-

[125] Water Quality Improvement Act, Pub. L. 91-224. §21(b)(1)(April 3, 1970).
[126] Pub. L. 91-224, §11(f)(3).
[127] Pub. L. 91-224, §11(i).
[128] Pub. L. 91-224, §11(b).

ods on the outer shelf, and to study ways of phasing out production from Channel leases. The Subcommittee on Minerals and Fuels of the Senate Interior Committee held two days of hearings on S.1219 at which time Senator Cranston presented petitions from 100,000 citizens urging a halt to Channel drilling. California's Office of the Attorney General endorsed[129] and Interior testified against the bill.[130]

On June 30, 1969, Representative Teague and Senator Murphy introduced a novel proposal designed to trade off another oil field for Channel leased tracts. Both H.R. 12541 and S. 2516 would terminate all federal lease contracts in the Channel, designate the area a Naval Petroleum Reserve, transfer Naval Petroleum Reserve #1 (Elk Hills, Kera County, California) to Interior as public domain land, and give oil companies operating in the Channel a credit toward competitive bids for Elk Hills leases.[131]

Legal Actions and Suits Pending.

There are more than a half dozen legal cases now pending in state or federal courts as a result of the Santa Barbara spill. The principal actions are summarized below.

Absolute Liability.

Petition of *Pauley Petroleum, Inc., et. al. v. United States, Civil No. 197-69 (Ct. Cl., Filed April 9, 1969)*. The plaintiffs in this action, federal lessees in the Santa Barbara Channel, claimed that the new Interior regulations on absolute liability were confiscatory and a breach of contract. On these and other grounds, they asked for recision of their offshore leases, and compensation for past investment and future profits.

Pauley Petroleum and several other oil companies had been awarded two federal oil tracts in the Santa Barbara Channel lease sale of February, 1968. They made a bonus payment of $74,000,000 for the two tracts, and their lease called for annual rental payments of $17,000 for each tract, plus royalties. In this action they alleged spending some $2,100,000 on preleasing exploratory activities and an additional $4,700,000 from March, 1968, to January, 1969, when oil was discovered.

The complaint alleged several facts potentially damaging to Union Oil Company in other suits arising out of the spill. Stated Pauley:

13. The United States also knew or should have known at this time, as plaintiffs did, that the Santa Barbara Channel area was characterized by deeper water,

---

[129] *Hearings on S.1219, supra* note 1, at 30-39.
[130] *Id.*, at 44-71.
[131] H.R. 12541 and S.2516, 91st Congress, 1st Session (1969).

greater tectonic activity, a greater density of subsurface faults and fault zones, and more frequent and more intense earthquake and other seismic activity than most, if not all, other areas in which offshore exploration for and production of oil and gas had theretofore been attempted and that each of these conditions increased the likelihood of well blow-outs, pipeline breakage, and other causes of inadvertent spillage or seepage of oil.[132]

14. The United States likewise knew or should have known at this time, as plaintiffs did, that it was generally understood in the petroleum industry that the possibility of well blow-outs is, roughly, inversely proportional to the available knowledge with respect to subsurface geologic conditions and that the geologic knowledge of the subsurface outer continental shelf areas under the waters of the Santa Barbara Channel was even more sketchy and uncertain than the geologic knowledge available with respect to on-shore oil-producing areas and most other submarine off-shore oil-producing areas in the United States.

15. Thus, when the United States solicited bids and substantial cash bonuses for oil and gas leases under the waters of the Santa Barbara Channel, it knew or should have known, as plaintiffs did, that no operator could guarantee that, even with the greatest degree of care, its exploration and production in the area would be free of well blow-outs or of other events which would give rise to the unintended discharge of oil into the surrounding waters.

Pauley further stated that the leases

are in deep water and in a known area of faulting which is subjected, from time to time, to earthquakes and tidal waves. Drilling in the leased areas requires operations which reach to the presently known limits of the relevant technology. Moreover, the leased areas are in a channel heavily travelled by ships and are only a short distance from a heavily populated portion of the coast of California in and about Santa Barbara.

As a result of the new regulations, being companies of "modest size and resources," plaintiffs alleged that it became "economically and practically impossible" for them to continue drilling and production. The burden of being an insurer was too great. Furthermore, the new liability rules were such a material change of circumstances that they frustrated plaintiffs' expectations. Had the regulations been in existence when the tracts were offered, plaintiffs claimed that they would not have bid. In fact, by "interdicting plaintiffs' efforts to exploit their rights as

---

[132] The oil companies apparently do not agree on this matter of the unique geologic dangers posed by Santa Barbara Channel drilling. Mr. Harry Pistole, of Humble Oil and Refining Company, testified that: "I have been responsible for my company's operations in many parts of the United States, including the Gulf of Mexico, for their drilling operations, and I have to tell you frankly that my experience tells me the Santa Barbara Channel, in terms of drilling without blowouts, is a much easier problem than in the Gulf of Mexico. *Hearings on S.1219, supra* note 1, at 101.

lessees . . . the Government had been unjustly enriched" to the tune of a $74,000,000 bonus and $69,000 in annual rentals.

On these grounds and other grounds plaintiffs asked for recision and a total of up to $231,000,000 for confiscating property contrary to the 5th Amendment and for breach of contract.

For their constitutional claims, the plaintiffs received support from the American Civil Liberties Union. On July 10, 1969, the ACLU filed an *amicus* brief in support of Pauley Petroleum on the grounds that (1) the government's absolute liability requirements were imposed without notice or opportunity for hearing, depriving Pauley of rights under the 5th Amendment, and (2) that the government action was unconstitutional by impairing the obligation of contracts.

Future Drilling.

(1)Complaint for Mandatory Injunction. County of Santa Barbara et al. v. Walter J. Hickel Secretary of Interior et al., Civil No. 69-636-AAH (D.C. Cal. filed April 4, 1969). In this suit against Secretary Hickel, the USGS Regional Supervisor, nine oil companies and two well-drilling contractors, and the county and city of Santa Barbara asked (1) for an injunction against all offshore drilling operations "adjacent to the shore of the State of California," and (2) for a declaration that the Outer Continental Shelf Act is unconstitutional.

Their first cause of action was based on alleged damage to property, fish and wildlife, natural beauty and other resources, injury to public health, and loss of public revenues due to the negligent oil drilling operations of the defendants and their failure to take reasonable precautions by not obtaining complete oceanographic information before drilling. The complaint stated that Secretary Hickel and USGS Regional Supervisor Solanas exceeded their authority by permitting an activity that was likely to cause pollution and damage and irreparable injury to plaintiffs, and that was ultrahazardous by California law.[133]

The second cause of action was based on the claim that the Outer Continental Shelf Lands Act was an unconstitutional delegation of legislative power to the executive branch, that the Secretary of Interior's powers were vague, and that proper leasing and regulatory standards were not established. Contrary to the due process clause of the 5th Amendment, plaintiffs claimed that neither the Act nor the actions of the Secretary provided for hearing procedures or the right to redress or compensation by persons adversely affected by the Act.

(2)Complaint for Injunction. Weigand et al. v. Hickel et al., Civil No.

---

[133] *See Green v. General Petroleum Corp.* 205 Cal. 328. 270 P. 952 (1928).

69-1317-EC (D.C. Cal., Filed July 10, 1969). This suit by the ACLU sought to enjoin Interior from carrying out recommendations of the President's panel on the Union oil lease. It was brought against government administrators and Union, Gulf, Mobil, and Texaco oil companies. Plaintiffs were Santa Barbara County property owners and/or personal users of Santa Barbara beaches, waters or environmental amenities of the county, whose enjoyment of the area was claimed to be diminished by the spill.

The complaint alleged that the personal or property rights of all but one plaintiff were abridged by the spill, that irreparable damage would be done by the drilling proposed by the panel. Plaintiffs argued that their personal and property rights under the 5th Amendment would be abridged by new drilling.

> The personal right is the right to live in, and enjoy, an environment free from improvident destruction or pollution; the property right is the right to the ownership, use and enjoyment of property, free from improvident invasion or impairment.

The complaint noted that the two-page Presidential panel report recommended drilling and producing from 50 or more wells, requiring from 10 to 20 years to complete the process. The validity of the report was questioned on the basis that the panel relied primarily on data from Union Oil and other oil companies—data apparently provided under the guarantee of Interior's proprietary safeguards.

The complaint alleged that the Secretary's refusal to give notice and hold public hearings on the panel recommendations and his reliance on the report without making public the data on which it was based violated the due process clause of the 5th Amendment. Plaintiffs therefore asked that Secretary Hickel be enjoined from implementing the panel report or from

> relying on any secret information without first according plaintiffs, members of the public and all interested parties, a full and fair hearing, after adequate notice, and without, prior thereto, according the plaintiffs and the public access to the data upon which said panel report and recommendations were based.

(3) Complaint for Injunction. Union Oil Company v. Minier, No. 69-712-S (D.C. Cal. Filed April, 1969). On April 10, 1969, the District Attorney for the county of Santa Barbara served the USGS Regional Oil and Gas Supervisor and three oil companies with a notice that Interior and the oil companies drilling and producing in the Santa Barbara Channel were maintaining a public nuisance that was a misdemeanor under the state penal code. The notice advised that oil operations cease "immediately

and permanently," that each day of operation would be a separate criminal offense. Oil companies requested and obtained a preliminary injunction in the U.S. District Court prohibiting the District Attorney from making any charges, arguing that the District Attorney's actions were outside his jurisdiction.

Damages.

(*1*) *Complaint of State of California et al. v. Union Oil et al., Civil No. 84594 (Super. Ct., County of Santa Barbara, Calif., Filed February, 1969).* This was an action for damages to property, fish and wildlife, submerged lands, waters, etc., by the state, the county of Santa Barbara and the cities of Santa Barbara and Carpenteria. Liability of four oil companies and one drilling company was alleged on the basis of (a) strict liability for pollution from oil drilling by the defendants, which under the California law is an ultrahazardous activity, (b) negligence in drilling, (c) negligence after the initial spill, (d) negligent destruction of fish and wildlife prohibited by State law, (e) liability for a state pollution penalty and for cleanup costs. For claims (a), (b), and (c) the state asked $500,000,000, for (d) $50,000,000, and for (e) a $6,000 fine, plus cleanup costs of $10,000,000.

The action raised preliminary problems involving state court jurisdiction over an action beyond the three-mile limit, and the state, federal, or international law applicable to the case.

(*2*) *Claim for damages by the State of California, County of Santa Barbara, and Cities of Santa Barbara and Carpenteria on Standard Form 95 filed with the Interior Department, February 18, 1969.* This claim for $500,000,000 was filed on the same form as one would use if he slipped and fell on the steps of a federal court house. The allegations are that the Interior Department was negligent in allowing Union to drill and in inspecting the operations. The damage claim is based on the 5th Amendment—the deprivation of property without due process of law.

QUESTIONS RAISED

The Santa Barbara oil spill is a classic illustration of how the environment is mismanaged by public agency and private business decisions. More practically, it provides us with a means to test the adequacy of various new management mechanisms favored by Congress and the President.

One idea long recommended was accepted by President Nixon in the late spring of 1969—an Environmental Quality Council, made up of the Secretaries of Health, Education and Welfare, Housing and Urban Development, Interior, and Agriculture. The Council was designed to assess environmental trends and programs and was staffed by a handful of men in the Office of Science and Technology.[134]

It is questionable whether the decision to lease in the Santa Barbara Channel would have been any different in 1968 if an executive branch council had existed, even if it *had* recommended to the President against leasing. The interests of the Bureau of the Budget, so manifest in this case, might just as easily have outweighed the aesthetic interests of Santa Barbara, or any national aesthetic values, even if the Council had been there to articulate those interests. Any doubts about adequate oil pollution control might just as easily have been outweighed in the President's eyes by the announced confidence and expertise of Geological Survey, the Bureau of Land Management, and the oil companies. Very probably any negative report of an Environmental Council would have been overruled by the Department of the Interior and the Bureau of the Budget.

These speculative conclusions are reinforced by two even more recent national issues, each of which is capable of affecting the environment in more serious ways than the spill—the trans-Alaska pipeline and the supersonic transport (SST).

In June, 1969, a consortium of oil companies asked permission of the Interior Department to build an 800-mile, 48-inch pipeline across Alaskan federal lands. The companies had discovered some five to 10 billion barrels of oil under state-owned lands of the North Slope, and had in September bid $900,000,000 for oil leases. Lacking a way to get the oil out, they proposed shipment of heated oil by pipeline across the tundra, and asked Interior for suspension of the land freeze that had been ordered by Secretary Udall pending federal settlement of extensive native land claims to public land.

Secretary Hickel, having promised the Senate and House Interior Committees that he would submit to them any decision to lift the freeze before claim settlement,[135] immediately appointed a task force to study the pipeline's environmental hazards. These included erosion, melting permafrost, wildlife barriers, and potential pipe-breaking earthquakes.

Three days before issuance of the task force report, the Assistant

---

[134]E.O. 11472, May 27, 1969. The function of the Council (renamed the Cabinet Committee on the Environment) was altered when the Congress passed and the President signed the National Environmental Policy Act of 1969 (P.L. 91-190, 83 Stat. 852, January 1, 1970). The act created a permanent three-man Council on Environmental Quality to advise the President and to assess the environmental programs of executive agencies.

[135]Secretary Hickel's commitment to submit any decision to lift the Alaska land freeze to Congressional committees is by no means clear (or clearly constitutional). It arose out of his dialogue with Senators Jackson and McGovern at hearings on his nomination. *See Hearings on Interior Nomination Before the Committee on Interior and Insular Affairs*, 91st Congress, 1st Session at 121-128 (1969).

Secretary of the Interior for Mineral Resources, Hollis M. Dole, announced to the American Association of Oilwell Drilling Contractors that "the first load of 48-inch pipe for the proposed trans-Alaskan pipeline—8½ miles of it—was landed at Valdez last week."[136] Then, on September 29, Secretary Hickel endorsed the pipeline concept; the task force had recommended his approval of a 48-inch pipeline as long as its construction could meet the Department's unusually detailed stipulations designed to protect the environment.[137]

Continued government subsidy of the SST was evaluated within the Executive Branch early in 1969, and in the spring it appeared likely that the subsidy would not be continued. Then in the fall President Nixon re-endorsed the concept. He asked Congress for $96,000,000 in fiscal year 1970 to develop an SST prototype, and the remaining $556,000,000 was to be requested before 1974, making a total subsidy of $1.3 billion for the entire project.[138] The President justified his action for reasons of balance of payments and national prestige.

Soon after his announcement it was revealed that an interdepartmental committee had studied the SST for the Department of Transportation and had concluded that the project should be suspended.[139] The administration made an attempt to keep the report secret,[140] but it was finally released and reprinted in the *Congressional Record*.[141] The reader of this report is struck by the conclusions that on the basis of economic need, technological and defense value, balance of payments, national prestige, and environmental effects, the SST program is, at this time, senseless.

From these two examples, one questions whether the lesson of Santa Barbara has been learned. It does not even appear, for example, that the President's Environmental Quality Council was involved in evaluating the pipeline or the SST. Furthermore, the federal pipeline task force did not have the authority to consider overall national oil policy or appropriate Alaskan land use. (Meanwhile, these were matters being examined by the President's Oil Import Task Force.) For the federal department that manages 90 per cent of Alaska, the pressures for pipeline approval have unquestionably been prodigious, but they were not primarily finan-

---

[136]Remarks of Hon. Hollis M. Dole, Assistant Secretary, Mineral Resources, before the American Association of Oilwell Drilling Contractors, September 26, 1969.

[137]Department of the Interior, Stipulations for the Trans-Alaska Pipeline System, September, 1969.

[138]*The New York Times*, September 24, 1969. The President requested $290,000,000 for SST prototype construction in FY 1971.

[139]Letter from Rep. Harry S. Reuss to Rep. John Moss, Chairman, House Subcommittee on Government Information, October 11, 1969.

[140]*Id.*

[141]115 Cong. Rec. H.10432 (daily ed. October 31, 1969).

cial, as with Santa Barbara; the federal government has not realized any revenue from oil-lease sales on the North Slope, and federal supervision of pipeline construction promises to be expensive.

As for the SST, however, its basic assumptions and problems *were* evaluated within the executive branch (although not by the Environmental Quality Council). But the evaluations had little effect since they were overruled.

Any discussion of Santa Barbara, the pipeline or the SST raises a basic question: what mechanisms should exist to evaluate new technology and to determine when or whether to employ it when its operation or malfunction could seriously affect the environment?

One useful tool for assessment is the public hearing, which might be required and given some administrative teeth whenever serious environmental conflicts arise. The new offshore leasing regulations of the Bureau of Land Management authorizing public hearings are at least a step in that direction. Clearly, however, the effectiveness of the hearing depends on adequate information, without which any new hearing procedures, such as the right to cross-examine government witnesses, have only limited utility.

Citizens protesting federal oil operations in the Santa Barbara Channel before and after the spill faced an especially difficult proprietary information restraint because of the specific exemption found in the Freedom of Information Act. But public policies guarding the competitive position of private industry are also manifest in such environmentally significant fields as oil shale development and pesticide use. These policies, not to speak of national security constraints, are serious deterrents to effective use of public hearings or other public assessment of new technology.

Certainly the government agency possessing *all* the information, charged as it is with the duty to protect the public welfare, should decide in favor of new development with some understanding of the government's ability to assess and legally respond to any potential environmental damage. (In the case of the Santa Barbara spill, the Interior Department had not expected the resulting damage. Furthermore it is hardly clear how it can settle conflicting damage claims against it without costly litigation.) It is well to ask to what extent these damage assessment determinations have been made respecting the pipeline or the SST.

Public agencies have not only had scant propensity to assess the damage from a new development's long-term ecological affect, but they have given little, if any, attention to aesthetic costs before or after a damaging event. Such public disregard for aesthetics is a primary flaw in the way we now manage environmental affairs. While we can presumably measure environmental decay in ecological or other technical terms, it is popularly and more obviously evident when things turn ugly; the aesthetic argument is nearly always the most basic cry against development, whether in terms of sight, sound, smell or taste. Santa Barbara citizens railed against offshore platforms because they were ugly, and against pollution because it too was ugly. A government concerned about the welfare of its citizens would be prudent not to deny or disparage this sixth sense whereby men can assess the present or future condition of their environment. When aesthetics are ignored, we seem to have environmental decay and civic discontent, and those who put their faith in the legal process must somehow account for both in their planning and decision-making.

The human need for a sane environment—balanced and diverse—has been forcefully expressed by a Santa Barbara corporate executive. His words summarize the lesson of the Santa Barbara spill and serve to forewarn:

> "We are so goddamned frustrated. The whole democratic process seems to be falling apart. Nobody responds to us, and we end up doing things progressively less reasonable. This town is going to blow up if there isn't some reasonable attitude expressed by the Federal Government—nothing seems to happen except that we lose."[142]

---

[142] *The Wall Street Journal*, August 27, 1969.

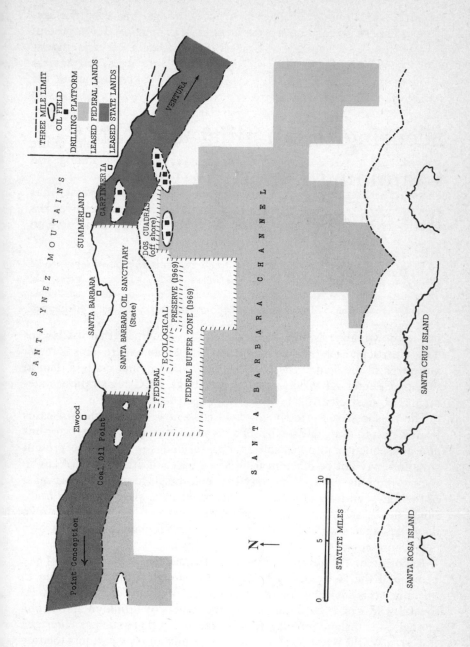

THREE MILE LIMIT

OIL FIELD

■ DRILLING PLATFORM

LEASED FEDERAL LANDS

LEASED STATE LANDS

SANTA YNEZ MOUTAINS

Point Conception

Elwood

Coal Oil Point

SANTA BARBARA

SUMMERLAND

CARPINTERIA

VENTURA

SANTA BARBARA OIL SANCTUARY
(State)

DOS CUADRAS
(off shore)

FEDERAL
ECOLOGICAL
PRESERVE (1969)

FEDERAL BUFFER ZONE (1969)

SANTA BARBARA CHANNEL

SANTA CRUZ ISLAND

SANTA ROSA ISLAND

N

0   5   10

STATUTE MILES

Securing, Examining and Cross-Examining Expert Witnesses in Environmental Cases

David Sive

It is a known lawyer's joke, kept carefully from laymen, that if a lawyer does a particular job once he may deem himself an expert. This is much more true in the field of the litigation of environmental matters than in that of Chapter XI arrangement proceedings, SEC registration statements, or most other fields of acknowledged legal expertise.

The reason is self-evident: the field is so new. The number of cases from which to draw one's experience is small, and the variety of forums and consequently of applicable procedural codes is large. The present situation may not be different from those cases of other fields of law in their evolutionary stages, midway between the stage of borrowing most of their substantive and procedural doctrines from all of the other traditional fields, and recognition as separate bodies of law, with their own doctrines, their own chapters in Corpus Juris Secundum, and their own law school courses.

Recognizing the newness of the field, the paucity of experience of any of us, and the fact that my being expert enough to be called upon to introduce this subject is the result much less of talent than of a fondness for the wild woods born long ago in the streets of Brooklyn and strong enough to withstand infantry duty in places and times such as Huertgen Forest in World War II—a fondness that family and law partners tolerate with amazing forbearance—I have accepted the invitation to lead into the assigned subject.

SCOPE OF THE PROBLEM AND DEFINITIONS

What are we talking about when we speak of the litigation of conservation matters, which I will call "environmental litigation"?

The litigation is, of course, before both judicial and administrative tribunals. The judicial proceedings include plenary actions and all types of special proceedings, before both federal and state courts. The administrative proceedings include licensing proceedings before federal agencies such as the Federal Power Commission and Atomic Energy Commission. Whether such proceedings are deemed quasi-judicial or not, they are within our subject matter if they are adversary and involve testimony under oath with examination and cross-examination of witnesses, a formal record of testimonial and documentary evidence, and findings and conclusions based only on that record.

Many legislative bodies and committees, as well as administrative agencies, conduct non-adversary "hearings" with formal records. They often involve the testimony and statements of large numbers of renowned experts, and a strong case can be made for urging that they are better instruments for ascertaining truth and wisdom than adversary proceedings. Unless they are adversary in nature, however, and involve the aspects of the proceedings described above, they are not within the scope of our discussion.

How do we delineate for ourselves the "environmental" nature of litigation? First, we are concerned with proceedings which determine the disposition or use of a major natural resource or aspect of our natural environment. Secondly, we are concerned only with the problems of, and look at the subject matter only through the eyes of, the conservationist protecting the resource of environment from one special disposition, use, or claim.

This limitation to the problems of the "good guys" is perhaps contrary to tradition, and may disqualify even the more polished and more fully annotated form of this paper from the prestigious law reviews. It is absolutely necessary, however, because the problems of the two sides are as vastly different as was the refining of the pebbles in David's sling from the buildup of the might of Goliath's brawn.

This limitation to the problems of the "protectors" delineates the party position of the client. In a plenary action, characteristically a declaratory judgment and injunction action, it is generally that of the plaintiff. In any administrative proceeding it is usually that of an opposing intervenor, that is, one opposing or seeking to condition the grant of a license or permit to use a resource.

Having defined our particular area of litigation and indicated generally our forums, forms of action and party status, let us list the specific aspects of the problem. Acknowledging that classification is by its nature in part arbitrary and subjective, I suggest the following: (1) selecting, securing, and compensating the expert witness; (2) the availability and conduct of discovery proceedings; (3) preparing the witness' direct testimony; (4) preparing the witness for cross-examination; (5) conduct of the examination and cross-examination on the hearing or trial.

SELECTING, SECURING, AND COMPENSATING THE EXPERT

The primary problem in selecting and securing the services of an expert is, of course, money. Protectors of resources and their lawyers, with very rare exceptions none of which lie in the experience of this writer, simply cannot go out into the market and pay the arms' length fees of experts entitled to $300 to $750 per day plus expenses. Something must be substituted for the money. The readiest substitute is dedication. That dedication exists to an inspiring degree among surprisingly large numbers of expert physical and social scientists and others who are officers, employees or merely members of the major conservation organizations or citizens' groups which assume the resources protection function.

A tremendous aid is the known fact—the explanation of which is as fascinating as it is beyond the scope of our subject matter—that conservation groups are always concentrated very heavily among college and university faculties. There the experts may be found. Cataloging the aptitudes of conservation organization members, secured by questionnaires sent to members as they join, or some similar technique, is of great help. The work is only a few clerical man hours per week.

Another helpful factor in securing expert witnesses whom the conservation organizations cannot afford to pay fairly, and frequently not pay at all, is the very public importance of the litigation and the public attention it receives. Expert testimony in an important environmental litigation is a mark of prestige in almost anyone's curriculum vitae, although many persons who have rendered great service in such cases hardly need any such additional credentials. And it is no derogation of the nobility and selflessness of those who have given many whole days and weeks, with no or ridiculously small compensation, to point out that such recognition may be helpful in securing the witnesses.

Balancing the advantages of dedication and evangelism against those of money I would say that where the expert testimony is concerned with the resources or planning issue itself we are fully as able to secure expert witnesses and testimony as our opposition. Where the testimony is more technical in nature, our zeal cannot match the opposition's dollars.

In my experience in seeking and finding expert witnesses I have been required to consider a number of seemingly unrelated questions. There follow several miscellaneous observations and comments which may make the task of a hopefully growing number of environmental litigators somewhat simpler.

A question often asked is that of whether the value of the services may be deducted against income, as a charitable deduction. The answer is clearly, "No". The explanation is simple: If the compensation were received it would be income and if the amount were donated back to the organization the net tax effect would be zero. (A more basic problem of deductibility exists, of course, with respect to this author's favorite donee of services, what a *New York Times Magazine* article has called the "litigious" Sierra Club. That problem is for the tax law journals.)

Statutory witness fees and mileage are taxable costs in the federal courts,[1] but the amount of compensation of expert witnesses is generally not taxable.[2]

Most expert witnesses testifying on behalf of the conservationists in environmental cases are not professional witnesses, and for many it is their very first experience in an adversary litigation, although they may have frequently been "witnesses" at legislative hearings. A special effort must be made to explain to them the difference between the two types of hearings. Some other problems of preparation for cross examination, peculiar to the experts with whom we are concerned, are discussed below.

THE AVAILABILITY AND CONDUCT
OF DISCOVERY PROCEEDINGS

The profound change brought about in the conduct of most litigation by the growth of discovery proceedings and practice, commencing with the adoption of the Federal Rules of Civil Procedure in 1938, is a whole chapter of legal history which need not be discussed herein except to cite as background 4 J. Moore *Federal Practice*.[3]

The conduct of an environmental litigation is governed perhaps even more by the availability of discovery proceedings—depositions on oral examination, inspection of documents and physical things, and written interrogatories—than most other litigations. This is primarily because of the tremendous inequality of knowledge, as between the conservation

---

[1] *H.C. Baxter & Bro. v. Great Atlantic & Pacific Tea Co.*, 44 F.R.D. 49 (1968).
[2] *Firtag v. Gendleman*, 152 F. Supp. 226 (D.D.C., 1957).
[3] §26.01-26.03, 1011-1061 (2d ed. 1968).

organization and the government agency or other resource user or developer, concerning the project under examination. The mountains of studies, plans and relevant files are all with the opposition. The hard evidentiary facts generally are buried deep in the platitudinous gobbledygook in which bureaucrats in general specialize, and in which resources agency personnel seem to reach closest to perfection.

Obtaining the hard evidence before trial is of special concern in connection with conservationists' expert testimony because only with those facts can their affirmative testimony be prepared. If the litigation is a plenary action the conservationist group is typically the plaintiff. Its case must go in first. Without discovery proceedings the very persons who would be examined on pre-trial depositions may have to be called as plaintiffs' witnesses, and although under most present day procedural codes one is not bound by his own witness if the witness is hostile,[4] learning the facts by day and preparing the testimony of one's own expert by night is not an efficient method of trial preparation.

At the very earliest point in preparing the case, and even before the proceeding is brought and as an important factor in determining *whether* the proceeding should be brought, the availability of discovery proceedings should, therefore, be ascertained. If there is a choice between some type of special proceeding and a plenary action, the general availability of discovery in the plenary action is almost controlling, in and of itself, in choosing a plenary action.

The rules of most federal resource regulation agencies do not permit discovery as a matter of right, but do authorize applications for discovery proceedings.[5]

Often discovery can be had, however, on an informal basis, encouraged by a hearing examiner who realizes the great savings in time. In the Storm King proceedings a vast amount of data has been disclosed by the applicant, on a voluntary basis or under gentle prodding by the hearing examiner.

The time factor may limit appreciably in many cases the use and value of discovery proceedings for preparation of the testimony of expert witnesses, or for other purposes. Whatever the disposition of the preliminary injunction motion that is usually made (because we typically commence our injunction actions in the very shadow of the bulldozer blades) the trial is generally expedited and the time for discovery and all other trial preparation severely abbreviated.

In the Hudson River Expressway cases, the sequence of preliminary injunction motions, appeals from their denial, court of appeals affirmance

---

[4] *See e.g.* Fed. R. Civ. P. 43(b).
[5] *See e.g.* Federal Power Commission Rules of Practice and Procedure, §1.24.

with direction that a trial begin in four weeks, depositions on almost a day-to-day basis, pretrial hearings and motions, and trial, severely limited the use upon the trial of testimony elicited in the discovery proceedings. The presentation of plaintiff's case was in many ways a continuation of the discovery process, plaintiff's main witnesses being officials of the government agency defendants.

The relationship of discovery proceedings to expert witnesses has two aspects, one of which has been noted: the use of the information discovered in the preparation of the experts' testimony. The second aspect is the examination before trial of the experts themselves. Such examination is very much limited, the usual rule in the federal courts requiring a showing of good cause and special circumstances.[6] The recent trend is toward liberalization, however, and what was said in a federal condemnation case concerning the necessity of examining expert witnesses should, in this writer's opinion, apply to environmental litigations where the experts are government officials or other witnesses who may testify as experts:

> I am inclined to think that such necessity or justification is implicit in every eminent domain case. There is nothing sacred about the rights of the government in eminent domain proceedings. The government ought to be as frank, fair and honest with its citizens as it requires its citizens to be with it.[7]

A distinction may be drawn between the factual portions of the testimony or report of an adverse party's expert and the opinions or conclusions per se.[8] And the opinions or conclusions of the government agency expert may be embodied in the reports or brochures issued in promotion of the project.

In general, it can safely be said that the ordinary limitations on pretrial discovery from an adverse party's experts are much weaker in environmental litigation than in most commercial or tort actions.

If discovery is available the drastic shortening of the procedure eases one problem of plaintiffs generally, the priority accorded defendants under most codes of civil procedure.[9]

Depositions will generally be scheduled on the basis of availability of witnesses and the convenience of counsel rather than according to priority gained by the first service of a notice.

It might be well, however, to point out two useful techniques for

---

[6] *Lewis v. United Airlines Transport Corp.*, 32 F. Supp. 21 (W.D. Pa. 1940).
[7] *United States v. 364.82 Acres of Land*, More or Less, in the County of Mariposa, State of California, 38 F.R.D. 411 (1965).
[8] *U.S. v. 284,392 Square Feet of Floor Space*, 203 F. Supp. 75 (E.D. N.Y. 1965).
[9] *See e.g.* Fed. R. Civ. P. 26; R. 3106 New York State Civil Practice Law and Rules.

plaintiffs' counsel in launching discovery almost simultaneously with the commencement of the action, again referring to the Federal Rules of Civil Procedure as illustrative: (1) the securing, *ex parte*, of an order permitting the taking of depositions before the 20th day after commencement of the action;[10] and (2) the availability of discovery by interrogatories to parties from and after the 11th day after commencement of an action.[11]

PREPARING THE WITNESS' DIRECT TESTIMONY

To the extent that there are special problems and considerations in the preparation of the direct testimony of experts in environmental litigation, as distinguished from other areas of litigation, they relate more to the substance than the procedure. The requirement that the attorney be as or more expert than the expert, the necessity of collection and ready availability of the materials upon which the testimony is based, the existence or non-existence of a rule rendering it unnecessary to elicit opinions by the traditional hypothetical question[12] and most of the other advice found in trial practice guides, apply to environmental litigations as to other actions. The special problems stem primarily from the subject matters of the expert testimony, which are often in the realm of aesthetics.

The Storm King litigation is perhaps the best example. The reversal by the Court of Appeals for the second circuit[13] of the grant of license by the Federal Power Commission was coupled with the remand of the proceeding to the Commission in the now classical language of the opinion of Circuit Judge Paul R. Hays:

> The Commission's renewed proceedings must include as a basic concern the preservation of natural beauty and of national historic shrines, keeping in mind that, in our affluent society, the cost of a project is only one of several factors to be considered.[14]

The Court's direction as to the nature of the renewed proceedings required an appraisal and analysis of the scenic beauty and of the place in history of Storm King Mountain and the surrounding area, for only by such an appraisal and analysis could the "basic concern" of "the

---

[10] *See e.g. Noer & Motor Freight, Inc. v. Eastern Railroad Presidents Conference*, 14 F.R.D. 189.

[11] Fed. R. Civ. P. 33.

[12] *See e.g.* New York State CPLR §4515.

[13] *Scenic Hudson Preservation Conference v. Federal Power Commission*, 354, F. 2d 608 (2d Cir. 1965) *cert. denied* 384 U.S. 941 (1966).

[14] 354 F. 2d at 624 (1965).

preservation of natural beauty and of national historic shrines" be properly considered alongside the "cost of [the] project".[15]

The scenic beauty could not, of course, be measured quantitatively. It could not, however, be claimed to be a purely subjective matter, for there would then be no standard by which the Commission or a court could hold Storm King Mountain to be more worthy of preservation than any other acreage which any other persons held particularly dear. In this connection it can be pointed out that prior to Thoreau's sojourn there Walden Pond was hardly known for any unique scenic beauty.

The task fell to the two active opposing intervenors—Scenic Hudson Preservation Conference and the Sierra Club—to prove, under the ordinary rules of evidence, the degree of natural beauty of Storm King. This was done primarily by the expert testimony of four leaders in the conservation movement, one leading planner and professor of planning, one professor of art history and one renowned cartographer. The conservation leaders were: Charles Callison, David Brower, Richard Pough and Anthony Wayne Smith, of the National Audubon Society, Sierra Club, Open Space Action Committee and National Parks Association, respectively. The planner was Professor Charles W. Eliot, 2d, of Harvard University; the professor of art history was Vincent J. Scully of Yale University; the cartographer was Richard Edes Harrison.

The testimony of the seven experts is a mixture of dry analysis and eloquence. I quote below only the most striking of the eloquence, Professor Scully's description of Storm King Mountain in his direct testimony:

It rises like a brown bear out of the river, a dome of living granite, swelling with animal power. It is not picturesque in the softer sense of the word but awesome, a primitive bodiment of the energies of the earth. It makes the character of wild nature physically visible in monumental form. As such it strongly reminds me of some of the natural formations which mark sacred sites in Greece and signal the presence of the Gods; it recalls Lerna in Argolis, for example, where Herakles fought the Hydra, and various sites of Artemis and Aphrodite where the mother of the beasts rises savagely out of the water. While Breaknect Ridge across the river resembles the winged hill of tilted strata that looms into the Gulf of Corinth near Calydon.

Hence, Storm King and Breaknect Ridge form an ideal portal for the grand stretch of the Hudson below them. The dome of one is balanced by the horns of the other; but they are both crude shapes, and appropriately so, since the urbanistic point of the Hudson in that area lies in the fact that it preserves and embodies the most savage and untrammeled characteristics of the wild at the very threshold of New York. It can still make the city dweller emotionally

[15]354 F. 2d at 620 (1965).

aware of what he most needs to know: that nature still exists, with its own laws, rhythms, and powers, separate from human desires.

The clearest and most direct opinion was rendered by Mr. Callison:

The Hudson River from its origin to the sea is a river of great beauty. Where it flows through the Highlands, from the breathtaking gateway at Storm King Mountain to Dunderberg downstream, the scenery from the river, or from either shore, is supreme. In my opinion this is the most beautiful stretch of river scenery in the United States.

The supremacy of the scenic beauty of the Hudson at Storm King is directly related, said Mr. Callison, "to the dominant geological feature of eastern United States, the Appalachian Mountains." The Hudson Gorge "is one of very few places where the main chain of the Appalachians is broken by a river." He compared the Hudson to the other rivers cutting through the Appalachian Mountains:

Moreover none of the other rivers has the history, the drama of the Hudson. None has been as much the very waterway of history, the gateway to the north and west, the "northwest passage" to an empire, if not to the Orient as Henry Hudson thought it might be. In short, the Highlands and Storm King Mountain are unique topographical and scenic features, not only in the East, but in the entire country. In the far West there are rivers that run through deeper gorges, the Colorado, the Snake, the Yellowstone, the Salmon, and the Columbia, to name a few. But none of them, except perhaps the Columbia, is so great a river of history, of commerce, and of empire, connecting great mountains and wilderness with a great city and seaport at its mouth.

The measurement of natural beauty and the balancing of it against purely economic considerations has been and will be involved in perhaps most environmental litigations. The litigation of that issue and of other issues to which expert testimony may be addressed in environmental litigations poses some special problems under the traditional rules governing most expert testimony.

One traditional rule is that expert testimony on the matter directly in issue is inadmissible, particularly if the issue be a mixed one of fact and of law.[16] The degree of scenic beauty of Storm King Mountain is, of course, a matter placed directly in issue by the Court of Appeals. The testimony of the experts named above was, however, received over objections based upon this traditional rule.

An even more basic and ultimate issue of fact and of law in the Storm King case is that of whether the project "will be best adapted to a

---

[16] *U.S. v. Roberts,* 192 F. 2d 893 (5th Cir. 1951).

comprehensive plan for improving or developing . . ." the waterway, the Hudson River and Valley.[17]

Expert testimony of both the applicants and opposing intervenors' witnesses was, however, received in the form of answers to almost the very question of whether the project "will be best adopted to [such] a comprehensive plan."

A second traditional rule is that expert testimony is not admissible if it deals with matters of common knowledge.[18] The beauty of a mountain or a river, or of a highway, it has been argued in environmental cases, including the Storm King and Hudson River Expressway cases, is a matter of common knowledge; and, the argument proceeds, any truck driver, as well as Charles Callison, is entitled to his opinion. Countering such arguments without appearance of condescension or conceit is a problem. And the problem is not solved simply because the testimony is received. Theories must be advanced under which the testimony will be granted due weight by the hearing examiner or trial judge.

One such theory advanced by one of the experts for the opposing intervenors in the Storm King case may not at the present time be said to be accepted, for the Hearing Examiner has recommended grant of the application (subject now to questions of safety of New York City's aqueducts, raised by New York City after the Hearing Examiner's report, but before any ruling by the full Commission). The theory is that beauty created by nature is equal in value to, and to be accorded reverence equal to that of, the beauty of music, art or poetry of man, and experts are available to testify as to degrees of natural beauty just as they are able to testify to the quality of mortals' art. From this it follows that the traditional rule concerning expert evidence as to matters of common knowledge should no more exclude, or preclude attaching substantial weight to, the testimony of Professor Scully concerning Storm King than it should do so to the testimony of Leonard Bernstein on the value of a work of music being litigated perhaps in an estate tax proceeding.

A third traditional rule governing expert testimony can hardly apply in environmental litigation—the rule that the facts upon which an opinion is based must be established by evidence.[19] This rule, of course, has several qualifications in ordinary non-environmental litigations. Some of the facts may be facts of which the court itself may take judicial cognizance. An expert may also rely on reports not in evidence if such reliance is in accord with the practice of his profession.[20]

---

[17] §10(a) Federal Power Act, 16 U.S.C. §803(a).
[18] *Noah v. Bowery Savings Bank*, 225 N.Y. 284, 122 N.E. 235 (1919).
[19] *Mozer v. Aetna Life Ins. Co.*, 126 F. 2d 141 (3rd Cir. 1942).
[20] *Jenkins v. U.S.*, 307 F. 2nd 637 (D.C. Cir. 1962).

None of the qualifications generally available, however, really supports the admissibility or weight of expert testimony such as that of Richard Pough in the Storm King case on an issue which at first blush may seem much too esoteric, but which attorneys for both of the active opposing intervenors believe may well determine the long controversy in its Second Court of Appeals stage or in the Supreme Court. The issue arose out of literally hundreds of pages of expert testimony, adduced by both sides, concerning the precise degree of visibility of the project works from many different angles and locations, in all seasons, all times of day and night, and all weather conditions.

Mr. Pough testified that any such mathematical computations were not important. The issue is the "integrity of the Mountain" itself, the meaning of the Mountain to those who observe it. Is it to be interpreted as a demonstration of the scientific, judicial and political prowess of the Consolidated Edison Company or as a uniquely beautiful creation of nature?

This issue was summarized as follows in the brief submitted by this writer on behalf of the Sierra Club:

> It is this character and "integrity of the Mountain" and the surrounding areas that must be borne in mind in determining the extent to which the Project, and all that goes with it, will mar the natural beauty of Storm King and its environs. If its meaning is changed, in the eyes of those who behold it, its supreme value as a preserver and embodiment of the spirit of the New World . . . to a whole nation, particularly the vast millions in its greatest metropolitan area, is forever lost. In that event, no combination of orders of this Commission, funds of the applicant, and skill of its eminent landscape architects, can be any more successful in putting the earth, rocks and trees of Storm King back together again, than were all the king's horses and all the king's men in the case of Humpty Dumpty. Painting concrete green[21] cannot deceive its beholders into believing that it is the handkerchief of the Lord, or, if it can, this Commission should not, in the absence of some overwhelming economic necessity, direct such deception.

The preparation of experts' direct testimony is a cooperative process between expert and lawyer. There is no problem of adversity of interest, although sometimes there are clashes of temperaments and techniques. The adverse party's expert cannot generally be called for direct testimony, for an expert may not be compelled, against his will, to render expert testimony.[22]

In the Hudson River Expressway cases, a situation unique in this writer's trial experience arose, which perhaps will arise frequently in future environmental litigations.

---

[21]Applicant's experts testified that the works would hardly be seen for, among other things, the concrete could be painted green.

[22]*Cold Metal Process Co. v. U.S Engineering & Foundry Co.*, 83 F. Supp. 914 (W.D. Pa. 1938).

At issue, although not determined, because of the resolution of the cases on other issues, was the impact of the project upon the fish in and around the area of the Hudson River to be filled in. Defendants' position was that the impact would be small. Plaintiffs alleged that it would be substantial and adverse. Plaintiffs had neither the finances nor the other resources necessary to prove it, but claimed that the government agencies concerned, both state and federal, had never adequately ascertained the impact because, among other failures, they had not measured the abundance of fish in the area.

Plaintiffs subpoenaed John Clark, employed by the Department of the Interior and head of the Sandy Hook (New Jersey) Marine Laboratory, an agency of the Department's Bureau of Sport Fisheries and Wildlife. Secretary Hickel was a defendant in the actions.

Mr. Clark was asked to testify as to the kind of study necessary, in his opinion, to determine adequately the impact of the project upon the fish, plaintiffs' position being that no such study had never been made.

The beginning of Mr. Clark's answer and the colloquy of the Court and plaintiffs' attorney follow:

A: The information that would be necessary to plan a research program to evaluate the effect of this project would require assembling all background information available from previous studies of the river and would require planning, suitable inventory and collection of additional specific information to come up with a scientific opinion as to the effect of this, and in addition there would have to be more information put at the disposal of the people doing the research and planning.

There would have to be more than these two paragraphs of information available.

Q: Well, can you please just describe—

THE COURT: I am just wondering about the fairness of this. Have you talked with the witness before, and did you tell him that you were going to ask him his expert opinion on the matters?

MR. SIVE: I have not talked to the witness, your Honor, beyond just telling him that I would subpoena him here.

THE COURT: I know, but don't you think it is a little unfair to call a man who is expert in the field and not tell him what he is going to be asked, whether it is necessary for him to do more work in order to form an opinion? I would think it must take men much longer to determine the nature and scope of a project than just the two minutes on the stand. Doesn't it, Doctor?

Don't you have to do a little thinking about it?

THE WITNESS: You certainly would have to spend considerable time. I only know what the general requirements for research plans are. I couldn't on this short notice give specifics.

MR. SIVE: Your Honor, I might state that I deliberately forebore conferring with the witness because he is an employee of the Department of Interior which is an adverse party.

THE COURT: All I am saying is you are asking him for his opinion as an expert without warning him what he was going to be asked, and my experience is that you have to give these men time.

The rule under which expert testimony cannot be compelled under subpoena was not invoked, because Mr. Clark was willing to give his opinion, despite the fact that it might be used in support of the positions taken by his employer, the Department of the Interior. Are there not, and will there not be, however, in many environmental litigations, experts who are employees of the very government agencies being sued and whose expert opinions, wrong or right, are at variance with the positions taken by the agency heads? In the ordinary commercial or tort litigation in which expert testimony is needed, each side secures its own expert who is well able to study the subject matter. If he must inspect documents or physical things or lands, the discovery process[23] is available.

In the environmental litigation in which the legality of a large public works project is at issue, financial, time and physical factors prevent the plaintiffs from getting the materials or data for their experts to study. Should they not, therefore, be permitted to examine experts employed by the adverse party, the government agency, both on deposition before trial and on trial, on direct examination and under subpoena? If their opinions are as much the property of the plaintiffs, whom we may grace with the good name "taxpayers," as the defendants, it would seem that the traditional rule of discovery and evidence should be modified.

PREPARING EXPERT WITNESSES FOR CROSS-EXAMINATION

The expert witness, who may have testified many times before legislative bodies on matters closely related to the matters involved in an environmental litigation, may not understand the nature of an adversary proceeding. This has been pointed out. It is also unnecessary to dwell at any length here on the instructions given to witnesses generally: to answer simply and truthfully, not to argue, not to regard cross examination as a game of wits, not to attempt to figure out whether an answer will be helpful or harmful, and to leave strategy and tactics to the lawyers.

What, then, are the special problems of the environmental expert witness? One is the degree to which opposing counsel will attempt to portray the witness as a composite of several objects of derision, among which are: the feminized male, the unworldly sentimentalist, the profes-

---

[23] See e.g. Fed. R. Civ. P. 35.

sor who has never met a payroll, the enemy of the poor who need more kilowatts and hard goods, and the intellectual snob.

An example is the cross examination of Richard Edes Harrison, who testified for the plaintiffs in the Hudson River Expressway cases as an expert cartographer. The issues to which his testimony was directed were those upon which the cases were decided: whether the proposed Expressway involved the construction of dikes, bridges and causeways within the meanings of those terms as used in 33 U.S.C §401.

On direct examination, based upon his examination of the plans and specifications set forth in the contract for the first stage of the project, he stated that the project did involve such structures.

On cross examination by the U.S. Attorney, Mr. Harrison was asked: (1) whether he had any feelings about the Expressway before the litigation began, to which he stated that he thought the project was unnecessary; (2) whether he had submitted at a departmental hearing a statement, on behalf of the New York City Parks Association, opposing the road, which he admitted doing; (3) what he had done on behalf of the "Save Central Park Committee," to which he answered that he worked to protect the park; (4) what was his "feeling and opinion on 'happenings,'" which precipitated the Alice-in-Wonderland colloquy and testimony set forth below; (5) whether he objected to "ball fields and tennis courts in Central Park," to which he answered that he thought they had been overdone; (6) whether he was a member of the Citizens Committee for the Hudson Valley (one of the three plaintiffs) as well as of the Sierra Club to which he referred on his direct testimony; to that question he answered no; (7) whether he was ever retained by the Sierra Club in any other matter, to which he answered that he was, in the Storm King case; (8) whether he was paid for his testimony, to which he answered no; (9) whether he was ever commissioned by the Sierra Club to write any books, to which he answered no.

The colloquy and testimony with respect to "happenings" follow:

> MR. SIVE: Objection, your Honor.
> THE COURT: Aren't we getting far afield now?
> MR. DE FELIPPI: I would like to proceed with a few more questions in this area with a motion to strike if irrelevant. I think it is germane in this action.
> MR. SIVE: If this is offered for comic relief I think we need it, but I object if it is being offered for any other purpose.
> THE COURT: I do not see any possible connection.
> MR. DE FELIPPI: I would ask the Court's indulgence for approximately three or four more questions, as I say, subject to a motion to strike if it is deemed by the Court to be irrelevant.
> MR. SIVE: Your Honor, I may make one other observation.

Certainly, everybody who comes in here and who testifies must answer anything that is relevant to the case, but obviously what has been done with this witness, as with others, is to search everything which the United States Attorney and the Attorney General can find about each of the witnesses and then throw it back here on some theory that it may be embarrassing or weaken the case. It seems to me it is a little bit unseemly as well as irrelevant.

MR. WALSH: If your Honor please, may I be heard?

On this both the United States Attorney and I have taken objections to the competency of the witness and the credibility of this witness as an expert, and I think that anything that bears on that is admissible at this point.

THE COURT: I think so too.

What I am disturbed about is whether one likes or dislikes "happenings"— whatever that means, I don't know—but I don't see how it is going to help me.

MR. DE FELIPPI: I will withdraw that question.

Q: What are your feelings and opinions on recreation centers in Central Park?

MR. SIVE: Objection, your Honor.

THE COURT: I do not see any harm in that. I will allow it.

Do you have any feelings on that, Mr. Harrison?

A: What do you mean by "recreational center"?

Q: You can define it.

A: Structure or a place?

Q: Any way you care to interpret it.

A: There is one recreation center which we successfully opposed about 10 years ago, which was a building in the ramble designed for the recreation of older people, 55-year-old respectable people, and it involved putting a 10-foot —an 8-foot chain link fence around the whole core of the ramble and providing a structure which would have the usual facilities, snack bar, restaurants, plus a radio room, television room, and a record-playing room. We deemed that this was not proper use for a park because a park was for outdoor recreation and not indoor recreation.

We oppose all forms of indoor recreation.

THE COURT: In Central Park.

THE WITNESS: Anywhere.

THE COURT: Anywhere!

Plaintiff's counsel found it necessary, on Mr. Harrison's redirect examination, to have him explain that his opposition to "indoor recreation" was to "anywhere" in Central Park, and not to such recreation anywhere at all:

MR. SIVE: Your Honor, I forgot one question. Please forgive me.

Q(By Mr. Sive): Mr. Harrison, on your direct testimony or on your cross examination you said, I think, that you opposed indoor recreation. What did you mean by that?

A: The question I thought was whether—

THE COURT: Your lawyer saw me sit back when you said that.

A: What I intended was indoor recreation in parks, because parks are for outdoor recreation.

Q: Were you speaking about indoor recreational structures within parks like Central Park?

A: That's right.

Q: You are not opposed to all indoor recreation, are you?

A: Of course not.

THE COURT: Anything else, gentlemen? All right. Tomorrow at 10:30.

The probing into the background, experience and opinions of conservationists' experts testifying in environmental litigations, on their cross-examinations, is not always more amusing than troublesome. Some experts are far more sensitive than Mr. Harrison. The extent to which they may have to be cross examined as to their opinions, backgrounds and associations can be a definite deterrent, particularly because the appeal to testify is made generally with the equivalent of merit badges rather than hard dollars. Moreover, on several occasions when it seemed to this writer that the hearing or trial was akin to some conducted by the deceased and now less famous of the two midwestern Senators McCarthy, the calmness or only calculated wrath which trial lawyers are supposed to maintain under all pressures gave way.

Not too troublesome, but worthy of note is the fact that in the Storm King litigation, Charles Callison was asked questions and gave answers which amounted to an admission that he was a professional conservationist. He was also referred to as a public relations man on the basis of his answers to questions concerning his past. David Brower could not be classified at all by the cross examiners.

The probing into the opinions and past activities and associations of conservationists' experts is largely justified, under ordinary rules of evidence. The expert's expertise may be impeached. The bases of his opinion are a fair field for questioning. Nothing said here is meant to be critical of the cross examiners of Messrs. Clark, Callison, Brower and others. If the subject matter of an expert opinion is the balancing of natural beauty against superhighways, rather than the permanency of a knee injury, the cross examiner has far greater latitude. The fact that this poses tactical problems for the conservationist's counsel, and even perhaps civil liberties problems, is just one more of a whole new set of problems to be worked out from case to case.

Another special problem which almost all conservationists' experts must meet on cross examination is what may be called the "wilderness problem." The defense of a Storm King Mountain, Mineral King or Central Park against charges that we would turn Times Square itself into a rain forest, or that we are hypocrites for riding automobiles or airplanes, is a chore everyone in the conservation movement, not only the lawyers and their expert witnesses, must handle. On cross examination by very fine trial lawyers it is difficult.

In the Hudson River Expressway cases, plaintiffs' expert on the beauty of the Tappan Zee area of the Hudson was an eminent artist who is also the chairman of the Rockland County (New York) Natural Beauty Commission. It was difficult, under cross-examination which featured references to the admitted existing blight of the waterfront in some of the areas of the proposed road, to defend halting construction of a roadway which would be much cleaner than some of the blighted areas. The answers involved subtle theories, psychological and artistic, on just when a scene may evoke feelings of nature's rather than man's skill and intelligence.

Much the same happened upon the cross examination of Professor Scully in the Storm King proceedings. Attorneys for Scenic Hudson and the Sierra Club were very much aided by the fact that Professor Scully had been a Marine Corps officer in World War II and presumably knew a good deal about the nuts and bolts part of the world, as well as of Artemis and Aphrodite.

There is no special solution in environmental cases to this problem of derision of an expert witness. The witnesses must simply have ready, in simple terms, basic theories of why and how man must remain a part of nature and nature a part of the life of man. The fact there have been and will be very few, if any, major environmental cases tried before a jury— the remedy sought in plenary actions generally including an injunction —can be of some reassurance to the witness. Particularly important is the instruction to a witness not to be concerned if the cross examining attorney indicates the deepest sadness or puzzlement or the sharpest pain —almost as though the witness and the attorney were Benedict Arnold and George Washington, respectively—at a statement, the basic meaning of which is really that man does not live by bread alone.

CONDUCT OF THE EXAMINATION AND CROSS EXAMINATION

The direct testimony of the conservationists' expert witness may be pre-filed in written form, if the proceeding is before the Federal Power Commission or an agency with similar procedural rules. In such case the first oral testimony of the witness will be on cross examination. If it is not pre-filed and is given orally it is best to have the questions written out beforehand, particularly the hypothetical questions if the rules prevailing, in by now a very small minority of jurisdictions, require such form of questions to elicit expert opinions.

The direct testimony should be as brief as possible if the witness is one who knows his subject matter thoroughly and is not given to ad libbing. Far more can often be accomplished on the cross-examination than on the direct, just as in other types of litigation. More often than not the attorney for the adverse party will not follow the instruction that most senior trial lawyers give to a young associate on his first case: In cross examination ask questions only when you know what the answers will be!

As more environmental cases are tried, attorneys defending the re-source-using agencies or companies will cross examine less. Charles Callison was cross examined at length at the Storm King hearings at which he gave the testimony quoted above. This writer correctly predicted that on the second occasion when he testified, at the hearings brought on by New York City's claim of danger to city aqueducts, he would not be cross examined at all. His testimony on the second occasion was addressed to the proposal to move the project site south of Storm King Mountain to Palisades Interstate Park lands.

Cross examination of the expert witness of the resource-using agency or company can be fruitful. Such experts, particularly those engaged in planning or construction, still, by and large, do not understand the con-cept that some parts of the world cannot be improved, or that public policy is not necessarily to have more of everything that we can build.[24]

This pursuit of bigness may not be as dramatically expressed as it was in the words of one of the company's planning experts on cross examina-tion in the Storm King proceedings—"Any large lake is handsomer than a small lake"—in comparing the proposed immense storage reservoir to the small pond now at its proposed site. Nor may the philosophy of improvement of everything by engineering be stated as clearly as in the following question and answer on cross-examination of a planner of the Storm King project:

> Q: Have you ever in your experience found an area which you decided was so beautiful that you didn't think that you could improve it?
>
> A: Personally I think practically anything can be improved. In my past experience I have not had any area which wasn't improved or something like that.

The philosophy will, in most cases, be manifested in some way which poses dramatically the issue of what the affluent society should seek.

Many of the experts cross examined in environmental cases will, of

---

[24] *Scenic Hudson Preservation Conference v. Federal Power Commission, supra* n. 13; *Udall v. Federal Power Commission,* 387 U.S. 428 (1967).

course, be physical scientists, economists, bridge builders or others whose field does not embrace any of the broad resource use issues. There is no special technique known to this writer, peculiar to environmental litigations, in cross examining such experts. A special problem does exist: money. The conservationists' attorney will more often than not be unable to afford to have his expert alongside him as the testimony is given, or with him that evening.

The principal solution lies, again, in securing as much information as possible in the discovery proceedings. While deposition on oral examination of the expert himself may not be permitted, by the use of interrogatories and inspection of documents most of the factual information which will be given and discussed in the testimony will be secured. The task of the conservationists' attorney is not unlike that of the attorney for the stockholder-plaintiff in a derivative action and many of such attorneys' techniques may be borrowed for use in the even more uphill struggle against "progress."

CONCLUSION

The task assigned to this writer with respect to the subject matter is to initiate consideration and discussion. It is sincerely hoped that the way is pointed toward evolving techniques and theories that will serve the protectors in environmental litigations.

DISCUSSION

Joseph Sax, CHAIRMAN   David Sive
Russell E. Brenneman   Victor J. Yannacone
Norman K. Sanders

MR. SAX: As someone who has been the victim of conferences that turn out to be nothing more than a lot of chitchat, it is my feeling that our discussion should be a prototype of a strategy session among lawyers trying to decide what to do when confronted with a problem like Santa Barbara. We have available to us the history of this particular event, the statutes and the regulations, and a series of questions.

First, what if anything ought lawyers to do if a client comes to them with this potential problem? Ought there to be some kind of intervention? If so, at what point in the various processes of decision-making, leasing authorization, granting of permits, and so forth?

Second, what expert scientific knowledge do we need and where do we look for it?

And third, what are the long-range effects of some kind of legal intervention? That is, what are we going to buy for the rather considerable expenditure of time and money that would go into it?

I hope that we will also discuss the question of whether and to what extent the existing legal structure is inadequate, in order to highlight what kinds of reforms are needed—statutory or regulatory.

Obviously, the Santa Barbara situation doesn't conform perfectly to the problems that each environmental lawyer faces. It doesn't have all the difficulties of a highway, pipeline, wetlands, or a Forest Service case. But I think that this is as good a prototype as we are likely to find.

Obviously, one of the things that a lawsuit does, if it gets anywhere, is to bring out information that simply does not get to the public without the kind of tough-minded, equalized give-and-take that is so much the hallmark of the litigation process. As an indication of the difficulties of the citizen trying to know what is going on, I am going to read to you the first paragraph from each of two documents that came to my office on the same day.

The Wall Street Journal said on August 24: " 'You will like Santa Barbara like it is today,' gushes the newspaper ad. 'Cool, sunny Santa Barbara is every bit as delightful as it was last year and the year before. Sun worshippers are basking on our beaches, children are playing in the sands.' Take a long stroll down Santa Barbara's beach front, however, and you are likely to gather some rather different impressions. Even on a weekend sun bathers are less than abundant. There are even fewer children and before long you discover the reason. Though the sand on the beach looks reasonably clean, your feet are soon coated with a black sticky gunk. The gunk is crude oil and despite the cheery optimism of the ad," et cetera.

Air and Water News said on August 25: "Seven months after the nation's most highly publicized oil 'disaster,' the beaches of this resort community are teeming with summer visitors. The city is enjoying the busiest tourist season ever. Property values are at an all time high and it is difficult to prove that the occasional small blobs of oil on the beach aren't anything more substantial than what has been found there for centuries. The petroleum industry, however, will never be the same."

Well, what is a poor fellow like me in Washington supposed to believe?

Now, without further comment, what do we do? Where do we go? File a lawsuit? If so, when, what kind, how? What are we going to be able to prove and what are we going to try to accomplish?

MR. SANDERS: Well, frankly I don't think anything could have been done in the past. The climate was not right for an environmental lawsuit of this nature; it wasn't right until the shock of the spill. It was a creeping thing. The channel was being taken up bit by bit.

In fact, the people did manage to get the Shell-Cunningham Act in 1955 to establish a state sanctuary. At that time they should have pushed for a channelwide sanctuary, but the state controlled the channel and it wasn't until the 1965 Supreme Court decision that the feds actually got control of the Outer Continental Shelf. So, in effect, the people of Santa Barbara thought they had a sanctuary in the channel but they did not.

MR. SIVE: I can supplement that from some personal experience. I studied the possibilities of lawsuits in the Santa Barbara situation about a year before the spill and developed a couple of theories that I think were very long shots. Phil Berry and I and others of the Sierra Club considered some action, but we determined that we couldn't—I think properly so— because the chances of success were very small and because we came up against the overwhelming problem we always have: no money to support a major litigation. And no money would come in the absence of a disaster. Had we studied this the day after the disaster, the matter might have been different. In environmental litigation we don't have the money and we usually don't start litigating until the bulldozer is outside. Santa Barbara is, I think, the best example that I know of.

MR. YANNACONE: Mr. Sive and the Sierra Club considered the possibility of handling the purely aesthetic damage of filling Santa Barbara Channel with oil derricks and they did it a year before the blowout. If someone had had the foresight, they might have started the action. Foresight, unfortunately, must be coupled with money.

In February, 1969, while the oil was still gushing, the Environmental Defense Fund went to Santa Barbara to investigate the possibility of bringing a lawsuit, and Dr. Sanders and I ran into the problem that is most appropros for discussion here. The disaster was four or five weeks old. Multimillion-dollar damage suits had already been filed.

Now there is nothing wrong with damage suits except that the burden of proof is on the plaintiff and you have to prove a number of things, including damage and negligence and proximate cause.

But the Environmental Defense Fund went out on a different tack. The Fund is an organization largely of scientists designed to take whatever legal action is necessary to, euphemistically, prevent environmental degradation.

We are interested in only one question. Is the particular act we are complaining about going to cause serious, permanent and irreparable damage? If so, we "invent" a cause of action. I use the word "invent" as a word of art because there are no conventional causes of action that either have any real probability of demonstrating to the world, through testimony subject to cross examination in the litigation process, any of the facts you need to disseminate to the public, or have a reasonable probability of securing the drastic relief—usually an injunction—that you want.

In the Santa Barbara case the first thing we tried to find out was whether there was any scientific evidence of damage—serious, permanent, irreparable ecological damage. We spent a day questioning biologists and discovered that the biological damage to the marine ecosystem was not serious, permanent, or irreparable. In fact, there was considerably less damage than in the *Torrey Canyon* disaster, primarily because fewer detergents were used. And when we investigated the biological damage in the *Torrey Canyon* disaster, we found that in a year and a half the seashores had come back.

We then went to the problem of aesthetic damage. I saw no real way to handle the question of aesthetic damage if the defendants could prove it was in fact an accident, and if they (the defendants) had all the evidence we needed to prove there was negligence. So, we cross-examined a group of seismologists and discovered that no seismologist who didn't work for an oil company knew anything about the seismic potentialities of drilling in Santa Barbara Channel.

So we conceived of a lawsuit, the lawsuit that we thought had the greatest chance of any kind of success. We had a group of seismologists, characterized by one single factor: None of them were currently working for oil companies or had access to the seismic data of oil companies with respect to Santa Barbara Channel. So we asked them: "Can you, doctor, on the basis of published, available information, state with a reasonable degree of scientific certainty that the continued drilling or pumping of oil from the reserves under the Santa Barbara Channel is safe from the point of view of seismic hazard?" All they had to do was say they didn't have enough information to form an independent professional opinion. We asked them to give us affidavits with respect to that.

The general reaction was, "We can't say that."

"Why?"

"Well, then we would admit we don't know anything."

After we convinced them that it wasn't such a shameful thing to admit that if you didn't work for an oil company you didn't know anything, we prepared an action that said in effect: The people of the State of California have a right to know what the seismic hazard is from this continued activity. So, we were going to demand that the oil companies show cause that there was no seismic hazard before they be permitted to continue drilling.

Now if they said there was no seismic hazard, they would have to come forward with some kind of scientific evidence to support this statement. Our scientists had listed all the missing evidence they needed to render this opinion, so we would then demand from the defendants this evidence as the price of going forward.

I also advised them that if indeed the oil companies could come forward with this evidence and it did satisfy them that there was no seismic hazard, the only cause of action left was one for aesthetic damage. I did not think there was much chance of success in that one.

A major problem at this time was the one Dave Sive pointed out: raising money. It costs an enormous amount to sue the major oil companies, which represent a major part of the assets in *Fortune*'s "five hundred." The problem of getting money is what stopped our lawsuit. Another problem is the strategic question: What do you do if the oil companies come forward and show that it *is* safe?

MR. SAX: Vic, let me raise a new question here related to your point on the absence of substantive law. Would the new regulations of the

Department of the Interior, announced *after* the spill, have affected your decision not to litigate if these regulations had existed *before* the spill?

In the regulations, 43 C.F.R. § 3381.4, it now says that "The Director, prior to the final selection of tracts of leasing, . . . shall evaluate fully the potential effect of the leasing program on the total environment, aquatic resources, aesthetics, recreation, and other resources in the entire area during exploration, development and operational phases. To aid him in his evaluation and determinations he shall request and consider the views and recommendations of appropriate Federal agencies, may hold public hearings after appropriate notice, and may consult with state agencies, organizations, industries, and individuals. The Director shall develop special leasing stipulations and conditions when necessary to protect the environment and all other resources, and such special stipulations and conditions shall be contained in the proposed notice of lease offer."

Are these regulations an invitation for lawyers to bring some kind of action before the tracts are actually offered for leasing?

MR. SIVE: I can tell you what the problems would seem to me. Aside from the one we have mentioned—money, and in the absence of peril (so you don't have the money), it is still not altogether clear that the promulgation of a regulation is an act reviewable by the courts, despite the Supreme Court's decision in *Abbott Laboratories v. Gardner.* I have not studied that fine point beyond reading *Abbott.*

Assuming that such promulgation does give rise to judicial review, I don't know whether the standing of conservation organizations and interested citizens pertains to that type of suit. As far as I know, there is still no case that says a single citizen may go into court. The law we have stemming primarily from *Scenic Hudson* deals with organizations.

The cases that have occurred have been mainly those in which concerned organizations brought suit and in which administrative decisions were involved where there was something you could peg the standing on, such as the "aggrieved" party in *Scenic Hudson.*

I think the really overwhelming problem underlying almost all of the environmental actions that take the form of a review of an administrative determination (and I think most of them do) is this: The basic rule of review states that where there is any rational basis for administrative decision, the decision is upheld. The ultimate problem is that the bulk of information and the so-called record that go into the decision are so vast and difficult to pin down that the task of presenting a case to have the administrative determination overruled is stupendous. It is even more difficult, I think, to overrule a decision that is a regulation, rather than a decision applying a regulation to one particular act.

So, those are the difficulties Mr. Sax mentioned.

MR. SAX: I take it we are talking about a particular application. What I am suggesting to you is that you attack not the regulation but the application, which is the decision that certain specific tracts be offered for lease. Such a decision implies that the potential effects have been fully evaluated. So, I guess that at this point you are a counsel of hopelessness. If you can't get in at a time like this and produce the evidence, doesn't it say something terribly discouraging about the whole future of environmental litigation?

MR. BRENNEMAN: Doesn't *Scenic Hudson* help you in dealing with a regulation like that, at least insofar as it places the burden on the agency and establishes the criteria that must be found?

MR. SIVE: It helps you in that an organization has standing, and it helps you with its references to the administrative agency not being simply an umpire calling balls and strikes. But where you don't have a carefully developed record within the pages of proceedings, it becomes extremely difficult to find out the basis of the decision.

MR. SAX: But we have that because the preceding provision of the regulations say that the Director, Bureau of Land Management, "shall request the Director, Geological Survey, to prepare a summary report describing the general geology and potential mineral resources of the area and shall request other interested Federal agencies to prepare reports describing to the extent known any other valuable resources contained within the general area and the potential effect of mineral operations upon the resources or upon the total environment." So I take it that, even under the regulations, reports on these subjects are required.

Now, aren't those going to be available to you?

MR. SANDERS: No, they are not at all.

MR. SIVE: That raises different problems. One is that of governmental privilege—the withholding of proprietary information during your discovery process.

I think I might list here what I think are the particular features of environmental litigation that differ from other kinds of litigation, viewed from the standpoint of the ordinary lawyer with some litigation experience but who is new in the environmental field, as everybody in it is new.

First, you virtually never have a jury trial, because your relief usually is equitable. And, of course, it is a fundamental difference to the trial lawyer whether he will be arguing before a judge or a jury.

Second, the inequality of monies. This also is fundamental in any action, commercial actions or others.

Third, the inequality of information, and this comes very close to the point Joe Sax just mentioned that highlights the importance of the discovery process.

Fourth, we are generally in a plaintiff position, which usually means we have the burden of proof. Also the plaintiff position creates a particular tactical problem under most procedural codes where the defendant has the relief in the discovery process: 20-day relief, generally, under the federal rules or rules fashioned after the federal rules. Thus the plaintiff must try to work out of that priority problem.

Fifth, an extra-legal matter: You have highly emotional clients who will put a great deal into it—for example, a tremendous amount of volunteer help—but sometimes create extra problems.

Sixth, there is the public nature of the controversy. The fact that it is public can hinder you and it can aid you. It can aid you in getting witnesses who may want to be before the public. It aids you in getting the press, which can definitely be used as an instrument in litigation; sometimes you can get a friend in the press to smoke out information from the opposite party that you may not get in the discovery process.

Then finally you have an absence of substantive law and the elusiveness of the existing substantive law. How many hours can you spend in the libraries? Can you get your cases just by phoning your friends or others, instead of looking in the books?

Then one concluding point: If I were asked to compare environmental litigation to other types of litigation, the one closest to it, I think, is the stockholders' derivative action where you represent the stockholder. In all of this, the central question is how you discover the information and what the problems are in discovering it under the applicable procedural rules.

MR. YANNACONE: Joe has pointed out in the regulations that there is a selection qualification criteria imposed upon the Secretary with the leasing authority. Now, there is a very appropriate, modern, well-founded lawsuit that can be brought: A declaratory judgment action to impose on the Secretary ecologically sophisticated standards for lease selection. This regulation, for example, says he has got to be basically good. He has got to evaluate fully the potential effect of the leasing program on the total environment, aquatic resources, asthetics, and other resources in the entire area during exploration, development and operational phases.

Now, the AEC has a similar imposition on it, and when we brought the Project Rulison action in August, 1969, again, it was a crisis, a disaster—do it yesterday! We had no time for discovery, so we went on a fishing expedition and when we put the AEC witnesses on the st and (since we didn't have any witnesses of our own) we asked them just one simple question: What were your criteria for measuring, or what were your standards of evaluating, the statutory requirement that you consider and protect the entire environment?

The answer we got—quite shocking—was that they were interested in knowing whether or not the seismic disturbance from the blast would have any ecological consequences. To this end they hired the Battelle Research Institute to count the number of cows in the area, measure the yield of milk before the blast and measure the yield of milk following the blast to see whether the shock frightened the cows into giving any less milk.

When asked if they had done radiation-monitoring studies on any of the animals in the area before the test and if they were going to do any afterwards, the answer was "No, this was not part of our assignment."

When the Director was put on the witness stand and was asked what were his standards for conforming to the regulations (which under the AEC law is very close to this regulation), he said the criterion was the opinion of the director of the project.

"Well, what standards and criteria do you use, Mr. Director? You are the Director?"

"I compare it to the other 200 shots."

"Well, what measurements do you use?"

"The data from the other 200 shots."

"Would you summarize the ecological data?"

"Yes. There was no effect from the shockwave."

You then have a squarely raised constitutional question. Are these proper standards under this regulation?

We can sit around here when there is nothing pressing, with our feet up on the desk and speculate as to why we shouldn't bring that lawsuit. Basically, because it is too much trouble, there isn't enough money, and it is after all, a moot point. But when somebody wants to stop the leasing of the next tract, as in Santa Barbara, you are going to have to go to court and the only question you are going to be able to raise is what were these standards? You are going to be told by the Secretary of the Interior, as we were by the AEC, "We have spent vast numbers of dollars advertising for bids and now you want to stop us. Where were you a year ago?"

I suggest that we seriously consider bringing an action for the definition or the imposition of standards under Reg. 3381.4. If that action is properly conceived, properly brought, and properly representative of the interests of all the people of the United States I think we will get a decision.

As to the subject of standing, the first example of a citizen bringing an environmental action in a representative capacity with no allegation of personal damage was Carol A. Yannacone individually and on behalf of all those entitled to full benefit, use, and enjoyment of the Suffolk County

Regional ecosystem without degradation from the effects of DDT used by the Suffolk County (New York) Mosquito Control Commission for mosquito control.

All the environmental litigation brought by my office is brought on behalf of all those entitled to the full benefit, use and enjoyment of whatever national natural resource treasure is involved without degradation from the action of the plaintiff complained of.

This is, in our opinion, the classic confrontation. Every time it has been tried so far by us, from the first DDT case in New York in 1966, to the Project Rulison underground nuclear gas stimulation case last month the standing question has been either avoided by the court or affirmed in the sense that the plaintiffs are properly representative of the group we claim to represent. There is a reason for that. It is a tautological definition. If you are not in the class that wants to be defended by the plaintiff you are not a party plaintiff, so, therefore, you are not being bound by the decision of the Court.

I would hope that the discussion today, would get down to the practical problems that I know every scientist in this room has, and most of the lawyers will have if they don't have already. That is, not what do you do when you have all the time to think about the problem theoretically, but what do you do when you know one year from now the Secretary's defense in some leasing case will be, "Why didn't you do something when the pressure of time was not so great?" For purposes of discussion, let's try a declaratory judgment action to impose or discover the standards that the Secretary should apply in order to properly conform to 3381.4.

MR. SAX: What do you say, Mr. Sanders? Could we talk about standards that—what is the problem?

MR. SANDERS: One problem I find right now is trying to compete against four lawyers for speaking time. (Laughter) As a university professor, I usually have a captive audience.

First, you will find that no ecologist at this time will say that he knows enough to establish what the ecology of an area is or should be. Ecology itself is too new a science, and I think that you will get the same argument we are getting now. A few of our ecologists say, yes, there has been great damage in the Santa Barbara oil spill. Others say no, there has not been any damage, and many say they don't know yet, it is too early. If you are going to start dealing now with academic scientists, I think you will have a difficult time getting them to participate in laying down ground rules that will be acceptable to all parties.

MR. SAX: Of course in every case we characterize as environmental, the problem of future uncertainties exists. But is it your conclusion that there is really nothing we can do?

MR. SANDERS: No. No. Not nothing. Probably my view is too colored by the Santa Barbara oil issue, which is, of course—

MR. SAX: Black.

MR. SANDERS: Yes. Color it black. So all I see is my own trials and tribulations trying to get somebody to say something about it scientifically. I know the ecologists; I know that some would very much like to help us and they just can't say anything about it. But you are talking about establishing criteria right now: If you have 10 years, you can get a whole bunch of academicians to study this thing.

MR. BRENNEMAN: You may not have 10 years. Aren't there at least some minimal criteria that the scientists can come up with? They can't fashion the whole thing, perhaps, but let's say we agree that we are not going to have radioactivity in our atmosphere. We can agree on certain things, can't we?

MR. SANDERS: We should, but, you see, they also come back and say it has never been established that this is really dangerous.

MR. SIVE: In addition to this problem I think you have a fundamental legal problem. I don't believe that a court, even if we expand the standing of the case in controversy definition, is going to issue a set of regulations. It simply is not the judicial process.

Also, substantively, the basic problem in Santa Barbara is philosophical; how much danger are you willing to take to get a certain benefit?

Now, dismissing the aesthetics of the oil wells, you are getting oil, which we all want and need, and nobody will say that there isn't some danger. The question is how much danger are you willing to take in order to get the oil? And I don't think this is a judicially determinable question.

MR. SANDERS: But how do you determine that there is a danger?

MR. SAX: Is what you are saying in essence, translated into legalese, that whoever has the burden of proof in these cases is going to lose?

MR. YANNACONE: Absolutely right.

MR. SIVE: That is fundamental. It is one of the basic problems that goes with being the plaintiff. We generally have the burden of proof.

Now, I can suggest there are two possible routes around this problem. One is if the proceeding is in the nature of a review of an administrative determination. The body that made the determination may be charged with the burden of proof because it is supposed to develop all of the facts, and this goes back to the umpire and balls and strikes language in *Scenic Hudson.*

Secondly, despite the rule requiring that in order to overrule the administrative determination you must prove there is no rational basis for it, if you can show that particular factors were not duly considered, then you can at least get the proceeding remanded to the administrative agency.

Once you get a remand, the agency will probably come up again with the same determination. Thus you get down to the ultimate problem that has to be attacked in the legislature: Somehow we have to get a different rule that the one that applies to most administrative reviews wherein a decision is upheld whenever you can find a rational basis for it. Now, all an agency has to do in court is bring in the thousands of papers they always have and build up a record as to how many man-hours they worked and how well they applied Parkinson's law.

MR. SANDERS: You said perhaps we will have to go to legislation to solve this, and I think that is the key. Maybe what you lawyers are trying to do is actually a legislative function. Perhaps as lawyers you should concentrate on closing the substantive gap that exists now until legislation can catch up to close it permanently. Somehow you have to force new legislation.

MR. YANNACONE: There is a time at this conference for discussing legislation and I take umbrage at using this session to discuss legislation.

I want to point out one thing. Every piece of enlightened social legislation that has come down in the past 50 or 60 years has been preceded by a history of litigation (applause) in which trial lawyers somewhere around the country have forcibly focused the attention of the legislature on the inadequacies of existing legislation.

Now, I submit there is today a forum. The forum doesn't particularly want to be used, but it is there; it is the courtroom. In the courtroom you have ground rules that make it possible to resolve certain conflicts in environmental issues.

I notice Dave Sive keeps talking about administrative agencies. I think the administrative agency is the classic, bastard, aborted offspring of modern legislation. It combines in one agency the judge, jury and executioner, and limits the power of the citizen to challenge the result. Of course, you have got an insurmountable problem when an agency comes in, as the AEC does all the time, with reams of classified data and says you can't see it but on this data we say it is safe.

Now, our task as litigators is to focus this problem in a way that a court of equity can deal with it—a court that exists solely to see that "justice" (whatever that is) can be done under a particular set of facts and circumstances.

Environmental litigation is amenable to equitable judgment and equitable relief, but it will never be amenable to that relief as long as scientists don't come up with the answer to the question. How much damage to beauty or how much inconvenience in the terms of oil on the soles of your feet are you willing to take for developing the oil reserves in the Santa Barbara Channel?

Dave pointed out that you can't get any agreement from the marine ecologists as to how much oil constitutes damage to the marine ecosystem. I agree. I spent all day out in Santa Barbara after the spill. I talked to their marine biologists and none of them will say how much oil is bad. But they will tell you that there are, in some instances, certain demonstrable biological, ecological effects that are bad for the system. This is the criteria.

MR. SAX: Would it be wrong to say that if everything had been done right in the Santa Barbara leasing, in the operations, and so forth, that what happened wouldn't have happened?

MR. YANNACONE: No. You can't say that.

MR. SAX: What mistakes were made?

MR. YANNACONE: There is not one shred of evidence admittable in any court that I have seen that indicates that any mistakes were made. There is only gross circumstantial speculation. There is no scientific evidence that indicates either negligence or anything other than real accident in the classic tort sense of accident. That is why I think it is the wrong case for us to be discussing. There isn't an overwhelming body of scientific opinion that says somebody did something wrong. But we do know, for instance, that the continued use of DDT will cause serious, permanent and irreparable ecological damage and we can line up the top 50 ecologists in the country, all of whom will agree that it will cause damage. The only thing they might disagree on is how much.

We go to court, we present that information, then we let the arbiters determine, from this carefully presented evidence that the scientists can give us, whether they want to accept this much damage. But in the Department of Agriculture hearings you never get the chance to present information on damage to birds, damage to wildlife, damage to anything except the target insect.

MR. SANDERS: Now we are talking about something that you people as lawyers can get your teeth into. You mentioned that we have no data. There is data. There are reams of data on the channel oil spill and exactly how it happened. We cannot get to it. Can you people as lawyers force this—the AEC data, the channel oil data—out into the open?

MR. SIVE: This is the key question, getting the data, and it comes down to the problem of discovery, in court action and in administrative proceedings. We have to find a legal vehicle that overcomes the usual rule of governmental privilege and the privilege against discovery of the opinions of experts in your discovery proceedings. You generally cannot ask the adverse party's experts to testify in a deposition and give you his opinion.

MR. SAX: Dave, isn't that what makes Santa Barbara a good case in the sense that you have a requirement that government agencies do a thoroughgoing study, that it be made available to the Director of Bureau of Land Management before he makes a decision, and that the Director is supposed to consult with interested parties? And isn't the obvious question for interested parties, "What is the point of consulting with us and giving us a public hearing if you don't give us access to any of the information on which we can take an intelligent position?" Isn't that an easy case?

MR. SIVE: Right.

MR. SAX: And we are not talking here about proprietary data. We are not talking about data acquired by the oil companies for their own purposes.

MR. SANDERS: But the trouble is, you see, the U.S. Geological Survey generates none of its own data in this particular case. The Union Oil Company, or other companies interested in the lease tract, tell the U.S. government how much the tract is worth. The government says groovy, OK, and they assign the value. The information comes from them and is all proprietary. You can't get any geological information out of them.

MR. YANNACONE: Let me give you a nuts and bolts answer to the question of how one can get this kind of information. The Environmental Defense Fund has met the problem in every case in which we have dealt with the Department of Agriculture. The USDA says the pesticide registration statements are classified and not subject to production under any one of the known rules.

There is a very simple, practical way to respond. You sit there in court with no information, no case, except the gut feeling that somewhere in that administrative agency is the data you want. You call the director of the administrative agency and put him on the witness stand:

"Doctor, in the course of your regular professional activities, have you reviewed, examined and prepared reports on which you base your professional opinions?"

"Yes."

"Doctor, where are those reports?"

"Back in my office."

"Which reports did you require to base your opinion on?"

He will give you some names.

"Doctor, produce the reports."

"I can't, I am precluded under Regulation 4 of the Federal Insecticide

Fungicide and Rodenticide Act. I can't give you the data."

"Well, Doctor, I don't want the actual hard data. I want you to summarize it for us."

Now, if he summarizes it for you you have got the information. If he doesn't summarize it for you, you sit back and when he is all finished you say, "Now I move to strike his opinion as being unfounded on any evidence."

MR. SIVE: That is a partial solution but it doesn't get us the same benefit in preparation that we have in the ordinary commercial action. The point of discovering the information is so that you can then go to your expert and prepare your case. When you can't discover the information, the next best thing, with a lot of tactical disadvantages, is to call the opposing party's expert or agent as your witness.

Now, to my mind, environmental cases are especially appropriate situations in which to change the rule that you can't discover the opinions of the other party's experts. In my paper I mentioned one quote from a case involving federal condemnation and discovery from the government's expert appraiser.

I would also suggest that perhaps we can refashion the law here by doing something that is a bit drastic. Ordinarily, in the federal courts and in many states, you can't appeal from an interlocutory judgment. You can't appeal from the denial from some order in the discovery proceeding. But there are a few extraordinary cases where you bring a writ of prohibition proceeding against the judge or against the court and then get some kind of review in the circuit court. *Hickman v. Taylor* was such a case.

If information is so important that you are completely disabled from trying the case, you may make a constitutional point and thus get the information in the discovery process. Beyond that, if any of us, and certainly many of us will, lose a case because we don't have the expert testimony, because we didn't have the preparation, because we couldn't get the information in the discovery process, maybe that can be reversible error in the appeal from the final judgment. But we have to work somehow to beat down this rule that bars discovery other than dealing with it at the trial, which isn't as satisfactory as getting the information earlier.

MR. YANNACONE: There is another way of doing it. When you litigate enough cases and you don't have any data, but only a feeling that there is something hidden away, all you have to show is some probability of serious, permanent and irreparable damage to justify an application for a temporary restraining order.

The judge calls a hearing. You subpoena as witnesses all your defendants. They don't tell you anything. You present only one piece of datum, your client's or your experts' testimony that there will be serious, permanent and irreparable damage if something happens unless somebody tells him otherwise.

If the court decides to rely on the unsupported opinion of the defendant's experts, the decision is subject to an immediate appeal. We have done this now three times in the past year.

You take your appeal to the Circuit Court of Appeals and immediately the judge will ask on what data presented by the defendant did the judge deny the plaintiff's application? If there isn't any, it goes back down to the District Court for the production of that data. If you get that data, you adjourn your application for a temporary restraining order long enough to read it. Then when you come back in on your application for a preliminary injunction you have had your discovery.

To give you one little ray of hope, *Parker v. U.S.*, the Forest Service case involving the leasing of some lands in Colorado supported by the Colorado Open Space Council, has established now that the Forest Service and its records are subject to discovery.

Now, in the Santa Barbara oil case the only way you are ever going to get your hands on those proprietary geological records is to threaten seismic damage if the drilling continues, and thereby compel the defendants to show cause why there won't be seismic damage. At this point, defendants are going to have to release the proprietary information. Or you may want to bring an action under the Freedom of Information Act, stretching this regulation to compel the Secretary to release his information to the public, and his answer will be, "It is proprietary, it is the work product of the defendants, and, if you want a public record, go to Congress and get the Geological Survey enough money to do it themselves." That is what you are going to meet with.

MR. SAX: Let me attempt to clarify something. A few minutes ago we were saying that in a situation like Santa Barbara, even if you had all the information in the world, you wouldn't be able to establish satisfactorily, even after the fact, that any mistakes had been made. Now we are saying that there is information to which we can't get access.

MR. SANDERS: But I am saying that if we had the data after the spill we could prove negligence, and I think that is one of the reasons we are not getting the data.

CONGRESSMAN MCCLOSKEY: I would like to comment on this discovery difficulty, particularly with respect to the Santa Barbara situation after the spill. The practicing lawyer should be aware that congressional committees recently held hearings on both Santa Barbara and the Hudson River Expressway. But in such hearings, unfortunately, congressmen are not always staffed to ask the penetrating questions that an attorney would in cross-examination or by discovery. Nevertheless the objective of these hearings is often to obtain the same kind of information sought by lawyers in litigation.

I don't think that any congressman is going to abuse his privilege of congressional inquiry to make somebody a lawsuit, but when, as Professor Sanders has indicated, Union Oil Company has the crucial data, it is perfectly permissible in my judgment, for the Congress to insist that, as one of the conditions for granting a lease, the Secretary of the Interior be furnished with that data; that we have the ability to analyze it; that we have all the data necessary to determine whether the conditions and the regulations are going to be adequate. I would suggest the possibility that the environmental attorney trying to get "privileged" information might contact the congressman engaged in a hearing and even furnish him with a list of precise questions or requests for precise data. If these questions do fit within the purview of the congressional inquiry, this is perhaps the best way to get the data.

I sat on the committee that investigated the Santa Barbara oil spill. There was a fellow sitting next to me from Michigan who sat on two committees and heard conflicting testimony from Geological Survey regarding what the regulations and lease conditions were. Here was a wonderful chance for cross-examination. I suggest that lawyers involved in litigation consider this cooperation with congressional staffs to bring out the necessary facts.

MR. SIVE: It is a good suggestion, but there is a hazard. It depends on the judge. Suppose you are trying a case and you know a congressional hearing is going on that you believe, just as you said, is just as good and valid a way of getting the facts as the adverse proceeding. You may incur the wrath of the judge if he knows that you are somehow participating in a congressional hearing. However, that is just one of the risks you have to evaluate.

But you know, getting the information even before a spill or other disaster may not always be the key to success. Even assuming citizens had gone in before the Santa Barbara accident and had the information, I don't believe that they could have obtained an injunction or anything that would have prevented what happened. The outcome would, in the final analysis, depend on how much danger we would risk to get the promised benefits.

This question has a reverse twist. In *Scenic Hudson*, the conservationists are arguing if there is one ten-millionth of a chance that the city aqueducts will be damaged by the power project that is enough. New York City's water supply should not be threatened. New York City is also making that argument.

The exact reverse is true in the cases I am handling now, involving the Hudson River Expressway—*Citizens Committee v. Volpe.* The state and its witnesses say if there is a chance that one child could be killed on this two-lane road, how can you sit there and prevent the building of the six-lane expressway? You can't answer it logically other than by saying that everything in life has a certain amount of risk and a certain amount of risk, even to a child, is worth assuming for the sake of saving the beauty of the Hudson.

The danger versus benefit thing is something that works against as well as for us.

MR. YANNACONE: That argument has got to be stopped. This is the problem with a great many conservation organizations. They capitulate in advance because they can't answer this "one child" argument. Here is one answer.

You claim that a highway route is going to destroy a scenic vista. To prove your case, all you have to do is produce some expert, a psychologist, a psychiatrist, or whatnot, who says a certain amount of open space and beauty is needed, then point out that this particular beauty or this open space in this area is somewhat unique in terms of location with respect to high-density population areas. Then you say that the destruction of this open space will mean that it is unavailable and has to be replaced, or there is cause to get the highway through another place. If it has to be replaced you have started to prove the basis of the destruction of the cost-benefit argument. If you force the highway department or the Army Engineers to talk in terms of replacement of the natural resource, you begin to shift the burden. Well, they say, how do you evaluate a view? Evaluation of the view is very simple. What does it cost to replace the view? As one woman in Pennsylvania says, "How do you replace a valley where it took a million years for the river to wind its way through, and a 1000-year-old forest and a mountain top?" It is very simple. You prove the dollar value of that replacement cost. The trouble with the conservation organizations is they are accustomed to dealing with cheap labor, the mighty hand of God. (Laughter)

Now, you want to build a valley! You measure the valley, you get some earth-moving equipment in, you move umpteen billion cubic yards of dirt at $3.30 a yard. That is the cost of making the valley. Divert a river? There is a finite cost to that.

Well, how do you replace a 1000-year-old forest? Only God can make a tree, but if you wait for God you might never get your forest. So we move a forest from the other side of the mountain where nobody complains. How much does it cost? So many dollars a tree.

When you have added it all up, the replacement cost is considerably higher than the potential benefit of that highway.

MR. LEVINE: May we interrupt in the case of egregious error? (Laughter) First of all, in economic terms replacement cost is certainly not the only cost measure. In fact, the principal measure is opportunity cost; which means what do you lose by saving that valley? What is that valley worth to you in terms of other things that could be done with it, whether it is saving children's lives or producing enough goods and services that might be distributed to the poor, or a wide variety of other causes? The point is that most resources have alternative uses and the problem is somehow to measure the value of alternative uses.

Admittedly there are problems in constructing a social calculus. To have a rational outcome you must have some rational hierarchy of preferences and some sort of indifference map; that is, some way in which you can choose between alternatives and values. But to talk simply about replacement cost is to obscure the issue: on that basis you would simply never change any natural feature and in fact, it would be impossible to accomplish a great many other goals that we seem to regard as valuable.

MR. YANNACONE: Mr. Levine raised the economic issue very nicely. He immediately rose to the bait. I put an egregious affront to everybody's intelligence by talking about replacement costs, and he immediately met it by countering there are a dozen other cost-benefit analyses that have to go into it.

This is just why you might raise that defense in court. You force the Army Engineers, who can't meet the replacement cost argument in terms of dollars, to shift grounds immediately and let in all the things you really want to prove—things like the economic arguments of least social cost, maximum social benefits. But until you get the Army Engineers off their own very pat cost-benefit ratios, you can't do that.

The only way I have seen in court to back off the Army Engineers is to come up with a dramatic affront such as replacement cost. And that is a technique that marks the difference, I think, between trial strategies and theoretical strategies.

My trial stratagem worked. Mr. Levine rose to the bait. So do the Army Engineers. So would any intelligent economist.

MR. LEVINE: I am delighted to have been so useful to you, Mr. Yannacone.

MR. SAX: I think the panel has given us some sense of the scope of views that are possible. It is now appropriate to open up the discussion more generally.

MR. TIPPY: I am a little confused about the financial problem. The papers and discussion indicate to me that there is a lot of volunteer work in the matter of expert witnesses. Their own time is probably made available at bargain rates. And yet you cite tremendous costs involved.

If we were citizens of Santa Barbara coming in and asking you to prepare a suit, it would be your responsibility to say it is going to cost, say, $50,000 for the following items. What are they? And to what extent are they susceptible to foundation financing or tax deductible contributions.

MR. BRENNEMAN: I think the problem is that you are not going to find the type of expert you need in a case like Santa Barbara on a volunteer basis. Certainly this would be true of a case involving the Atomic Energy Commission. Such experts are highly trained and hard to come by. So, I think that in my experience, a very large portion of that $50,000 would go toward the expert help.

MR. SIVE: Just to give you what I think are the financial problems— more than anything else I am an expert on this—in any law office these days a lawyer must gross upwards of $50,000 a year to pay his expenses and to receive the salary of a highly qualified plumber.

Now, that means if he spends a half year on a litigation, he needs $25,000. If it is a major litigation, he will be facing two to five attorneys from the adverse party, whether it be a big utility company or the U.S. Attorney or some other government agency. So you can assume that a major litigation, if you are going to carry it on, needs at least $25,000 for six months and, if it is appealed, $50,000 for one lawyer. If he is going to have half as many people as the opposition, multiply that by two.

Then there is the cost of the expert witnesses, and you divide them into two categories. Witnesses testifying on planning or scenic beauty issues or on conservation per se you can generally get free, or at very little expense, because we are all brethren.

If you need scientific experts, you must pay close to their arm's length fees, averaging between $300 and $700 per day of work, plus expenses.

For carrying on the major litigation, to have anything approaching equality with the opposition, you will have to get daily copy at $250 a day.

Before the trial you will need depositions, and they may be upwards of 500 pages at a $1.50 per page, at least in the New York area. Now, those are the basic financial burdens and some of them are insoluble except by money. Some are soluble in other ways. The lawyer contributes his time, and so do some of the experts. If the case doesn't involve a trial of issues of fact, but only writing briefs, the lawyer and the volunteers can do it at night in their spare time and they can handle their commercial work during the day. But if you are going to have trial of issues of fact and it is a major case, figure no less than $100,000 to get half the quality that you would ordinarily have in the commercial case.

MR. YANNACONE: The technical or scientific witness, if he works for a university, should be motivated enough to testify without recompense other than expenses. This is the rule in all the environmental litigation in which I am involved.

As to attorneys' fees, the lawyers involved in environmental litigation are of two types, and this is something that very few laymen recognize. There are trial lawyers who equate with the English barrister and there are what we call paperwork or general lawyers who tend to equate with the English solicitor.

A trial lawyer's living in the United States is based entirely on the number of days he can spend in court. He doesn't get paid an hourly rate for preparation, but only for the end result.

If a trial lawyer is involved in conventional plaintiff's damage litigation, he is only paid for winning. This knocks his potential income down by a factor of losing anything from 10 to 30 per cent. If you start losing more than that, you go bankrupt.

The office expense overhead for the trial lawyer, as for any other lawyer, is roughly 50 per cent. In some very well managed offices, it goes down to 40, in others, up to 60.

You must pay the trial lawyer a reasonable per diem in court. The going rate for good trial counsel is between $500 and a $1,000 a day. The National Agricultural Chemical Association, which defended the DDT hearings in Wisconsin, had four top flight trial lawyers on the other side of the table, all making that much. The NACA told the press they spent half a million dollars on the defense of that hearing. The total expenditures by the Environmental Defense Fund, including a $5,000 fee at the very end of the hearing for me, amounted to approximately $47,000 for 29 days of trial.

As for daily transcripts, in a hotly contested four-hour, five-hour day, the cost in all of our litigation averages about $300 to $500 a day. I have never seen a day go as low as $250. For examinations before trial or depositions, we pay a dollar and a quarter per page and if you estimate at least 200 pages per expert, that is roughly $220 to $250.

Now, you have the problem of printing and reproduction that very few people think about. In order to properly testify in an environmental lawsuit, the expert witness you produce must have read all the relevant portions of the transcripts that have gone before. And another caveat: he must have spent at least the prior half-day in that court room watching what happened. If he does less than that, if you insist on less than that, you are doing your expert scientist a terrible disservice. He will get killed, in the vernacular. Our witnesses have been put on only under those rules and have survived.

You have got to add lodging for your witnesses, meals, and conferences. Lunch, dinner, breakfast is when we prepare our witnesses, and the average food bill involves at least 20 people.

You have to spend over $100,000 when your defendant is big enough to put on a good defense.

MR. BENNETT: You fellows have been telling us you can't get any money for these cases and now you are telling us you are spending about $100,000 and up per case.

How do you get this money? I would like to know about fund raising and how it is accomplished.

MR. SIVE: I can just tell you my own experience in the Hudson River Expressway case going on now. The money raised has been just a small fraction of what we contemplate as necessary. What has made it up is the donation of time by both attorneys and expert witnesses, and the fact that the critical issue was in large part legal, and the case didn't involve a trial of complex issues of fact.

Now, in the other case in which I have had experience, *Scenic Hudson*, the amount spent by Consolidated Edison is many millions. The amount spent by the *Scenic Hudson* people, who have been unique in forming a national organization, is several hundred thousand dollars. But I am certain that the amounts paid to Lloyd Garrison and his firm are no more than one-third of their time charges. The answer to how you can carry on these cases is that the attorneys and others contribute their service.

MR. SAX: We are at the stage where many firms have been carrying on environmental cases on a one- or two-time basis rather than regularly, and have been taking such fees as their clients can raise. Just the other day I heard of a situation in which a woman acting as money raiser for a citizens' group had literally gone around knocking on doors, seeing citizen organizations, and so forth, and the group raised something like $15,000. It hired a very prestigous firm who did the job for them. Their billing time ran approximately $60,000 but they accepted the $15,000. Obviously, few firms want to be in this kind of situation permanently.

MR. DURNING: In some environmental suits, fears have been expressed of countersuits by the developers of proposed projects. One such countersuit has actually been launched with a gigantic claim for damages against the organizers and participants in the group that brought the original suit seeking an injunction. Fear of such countersuits is rampant. In one such case persons were reluctant to make a financial contribution because it would make a record of their participation in the suit that might stop the project and bring about a damage action. Consequently, a national organization was asked to receive funds almost in trust, almost surreptitiously, in order to shield those who were going to make a contribution.

Is this a recurring problem, and if so how do we get around it? Someone is going to say incorporate, but as I read *Scenic Hudson* and the other pending cases, I found unincorporated associations with a favorable precedent, with standing. I found the incorporated Sierra Club also permitted standing, but it has been specifically stated to have had a long existing dedicated interest in these types of matters.

When you are forming a new group should you incorporate or not? What is the standing problem, and what is the value of it as a shelter against liability?

MR. SIVE: First as to the standing: In my view, if you are a very new organization, that wouldn't knock you out. I don't think it is a problem.

Secondly, whether you are incorporated or not, I think there is no problem in the standing.

Third, it is a very good technique to have your monies go to a national organization, so that there will be no claim against a contributor and because you may get tax deductibility. It is perfectly proper and lawful to donate monies to any one of several organizations engaged in the environmental field and for them in turn to make contributions to support a particular litigation. That is judicial and not legislative activity. I can get you the memoranda sustaining that.

I don't know the answer to the question of countersuit. You can try to reduce it to the absurd—when they start a countersuit, have your people start another countersuit against them for starting the countersuit. Maybe that will wipe it out.

MR. MICHAEL MCCLOSKEY: One of the problems that hasn't been mentioned that is related to this is the problem of injunction bonds. In the Mineral King case, *Sierra Club v. Hickel,* the Government asked for $75,000 bonds. We were fortunate enough to get away without any. But in the Colorado case, *Parker v. United States,* the Government asked and got $10,000 bond, and there was some reason to fear that they might have asked for a great deal more. This is becoming a standard response every time we deal with them in an injunction. And they are asking for collateral—securities or cash on deposit. You have a few days suddenly to raise $10,000 or $50,000 or whatever it is going to be. This is another very real financial deterrent, in addition to your attorneys' fees and other costs, along with the problem of damages even if the bond is not required. I think this is a very challenging financial difficulty in all these cases.

MR. SIVE: The bond issue is one that I have raised in one case and others will have to raise. The ordinary rule is that the amount of the bond is the forseeable damages to the defendant, and if that is applied literally in any of these cases, we are wiped out of court and we have no standing, practically speaking. Somebody has to work out an amendment to the usual rule. Otherwise, the only solution is to get an early trial—an important aspect in all of these litigations. There is almost always an early trial because you have an injunction motion. You can lower the amount of the bond if you accept and even plead for an early or immediate trial.

MR. YANNACONE: There is an answer to both of those questions and it is wrapped up again in the basic difference between Dave Sive's approach and my approach.

If you take the approach of getting into court, trying the case, having the hearing, developing the record, framing the issues, you are interested in a speedy, public trial and the presentation of the most available evidence at the lowest possible cost.

We have met the problem of posting security and being challenged with potential damage suits in this way. It is all solved in the framing of the pleadings. This is why all the Environmental Defense Fund litigation is framed in the same way.

Some of you who are not lawyers may not enjoy this nuts and bolts answer to the question. If you bring a declaratory judgment action, you are bringing a non-adversary proceeding for practical litigation purposes. This is the first technique. Bring it in terms of a declaratory judgment. Seek judgment declaring the rights of the people in and to the full benefits, use and enjoyment of the national and natural resource you wish to protect.

Then, after the establishment of this right, ask for judgment declaring that the particular complaint of action of the defendant will cause serious, permanent, and irreparable damage to the national and natural resource treasure that is the subject matter of the complaint. Then ask the court for equitable relief by way of preliminary or temporary injunction to sustain the right that they have just upheld.

MR. BENNETT: What happens to this declaratory judgment case you just explained to us? Where has this argument of yours prevailed?

MR. YANNACONE: The most recent is the Defenders of Florissant, Incorporated, against Park Land Company and other developers. The case literally involved the protection of the Florissant Fossil Beds in Colorado from a bulldozer. It was brought on the eve of the destruction of the fossil beds.

The lower court denied our application for a temporary restraining order. The Circuit Court of Appeals for the Tenth Circuit granted our application for a temporary restraining order, reversing the lower court judge. We then went back for a trial 10 days later. The defendants demanded a $4,000,000 bond. Our argument was: "You have two choices: A bond or an immediate trial. We can't post the bond. You must give us an immediate trial. If you can't give us an immediate trial because of the defendant's need to delay (which was the case) or the court's need to delay, the court cannot impose a bond."

MR. BENNETT: But is there a decision or a judgment that we are entitled to this clean air or whatever?

MR. YANNACONE: Of course not yet.

MR. BENNETT: Then, what happened to the declaratory relief you sought? You sought it, asked the court to declare you were entitled to these things. What happened to that?

MR. YANNACONE: In this particular case the court decided that they were going to grant the injunction without answering that question, neatly side-stepping the problem.

MR. BENNETT: So then, these declaratory judgment actions don't really work quite the way it first appears.

MR. YANNACONE: They work theoretically, and you bring them to avoid the possibility of being set up for a prima facie tort case.

All it takes to start a lawsuit is a typewriter and a lawyer and you can be counter-sued on any one of a number of unsubstantiated grounds, be put to a great deal of expense defending it and wind up winning with only $200 in costs coming to you after having spent thousands for defense. This is a matter your clients always ask you about.

Now, what I advise my clients is to structure the action in such a way that you can never be challenged for prima facie tort—maliciously intending to interfere with the defendant's activities. If you bring the declaratory judgment action and bring it properly, and if you go into court with just the format I presented—give us an immediate trial in lieu of a bond—you have avoided most of the major problems.

MR. BERRY: But calling it a suit for declaratory relief doesn't suffice. You must still allege that you have no other way of doing this in law.

MR. SIVE: And it is just as adversary as any other action whether the relief is a declaratory judgment or an injunction or damage. It is adverse.

MR. YANNACONE: But it is not adverse for the purpose of being sued in prima facie tort.

MR. STEVENS: I would like to hear some more discussion about the period before the filing of a suit and before its contemplation—about adequate legislative hearings in the first place. I can't believe that a problem cannot be just as well focused by a well-run, well-staffed and well-informed legislative committee as it can by a well-run trial.

Also, I would like to jump one step further, to the administrative agency. There might be many cases in which, for good reasons, the administrative agency as a remedy has been rejected, but I think there is a danger of a judicial attitude to the effect that you had a chance to go to the agency a year ago and make these arguments. You had a chance to present your case and evaluate the agency evidence. Why didn't you do it? And this attitude is coupled with traditional judicial presumptions favoring administrative decisions and the exhaustion of administrative remedies.

With regard to the information problem—obtaining the data on which the agency decisions depend, if the Public Disclosure Act is not a proper remedy, and it may not be in the case of proprietary information, I think that in an administrative hearing itself some consideration has to be given to this problem. If the information is sought but is denied, then the extent to which an agency decision relies on the proprietary privilege and other privileges might raise serious questions of due process.

MR. SANDERS: First off, in Santa Barbara we just weren't getting the hearings. People weren't interested. There was a Corps of Engineers hearing on the channel oil leasing, but the problem was only vaguely understood at the time. These exploitative operations like the channel oil leasing are creeping things. Their environmental damage isn't evident all at once. It occurs over a period of time. People get used to it and the industry really counts on this.

Until we had the crisis, we really didn't have the local interest in a hearing. In any event, the people didn't have enough facts before the spill to get in there and do too much.

Now after the spill we can see that the hearing we did have didn't protect us. And today we wonder whether we will have hearings before more oil operations in the channel are approved.

Right now the Corps of Engineers is considering granting permits for oil operations in the sea lanes in Santa Barbara Channel and we are saying, "My God, what about a super-tanker colliding with an active oil platform? What will happen then?" And the Corps of Engineers is not sure they are going to give us hearings. If they do, the hearings may be on navigation and national security only without regard to the environment. Now that we have had the tragedy to make us aware, we have a chance to have meaningful hearings and to profit from them, but still the administrative bodies may not permit hearings.

So first off, you can't get the people uptight until there is a catastrophe, after which they are only useful if another catastrophe can be prevented. Secondly, the provision for administrative hearings is, in any case, not universal.

MR. YANNACONE: Mr. Stevens, there is one problem with legislative hearings that Representative McCloskey pointed out. How do you get the right questions to the legislator in a position to ask them? Let's take the classic example of hearings that have been held literally *ad nauseam* and face it with litigation on the other side, and compare the results.

In 1962 Rachel Carson wrote a book, *Silent Spring*. In 1963 the President's Science Advisory Committee recommended the discontinuance of the use of the chlorinated hydrocarbon pesticides, DDT in particular. In 1963 there was another Senate committee hearing, and there was a House hearing.

These hearings were conducted by agriculture committees. There was no cross-examination. Instead each side read prepared statements. Certain very competent environmental scientists were badly abused by certain congressmen.

Senator Ribicoff ran a set of hearings, but by himself was not able to meet the effect of the agriculture forces on his committee. Again some more scientists were treated very, very shabbily.

Finally,—well, finally my wife brought a lawsuit. The state of New York had been conducting legislative hearings on DDT for 11 years, all of which found that DDT was perfectly safe, based on the testimony of Dr. James E. Dewey, head of the pesticide control section at the Cornell University School of Agriculture.

Dr. Dewey appeared on a witness stand. All his prior legislative testimony was let in, all of which said DDT is safe. Dr. Dewey was cross examined. At the end of 45 minutes of cross examination, Dr. Dewey admitted he had no data to support any of the claims he had made. The judge in that case ruled, several years later, that we did have standing and we did prove that DDT was a contaminant that had serious ecological consequences.

Only in that courtroom did Dewey get pinned down.

Then the Environmental Defense Fund went to Michigan, and this is one Professor Sax helped on. We again found the Department of Agriculture referring to these very same congressional hearings as evidence that DDT was safe. Yet, when the director of the department got up on the witness stand, he didn't have any data in support.

So last year the EDF went to Wisconsin and the end of the line. There, arrayed on the other side, was the National Agricultural Chemical Association, four PR men, attorneys, a couple of miscellaneous flunkies, all of whom waved the *Congressional Record*, the Ribicoff hearings, the new National Science Foundation/National Research Council report, none of which were subject to cross examination, and none of which were admitted. So the NACA went down to Washington and produced the Director of the pesticide legislation section, Dr. Whalen Hayes, the famous toxicologist who said DDT was safe because he tried to poison convicts with it.

On cross examination he and other eminent scientists admitted they had no data. Not only that, all they had to do, because of the narrow mission of their department to wipe out pest insects (denominated "pests" like officers and gentlemen by Act of Congress), was to see whether the pesticide killed the pest. They had no burden, they had no duty, and they refused to consider other evidence.

In that courtroom all the evidence finally came out. Two hundred and nine scientific papers, most of which never made it into the Ribicoff committee report, or into the President's Science Advisory Council report.

The legislative process is fine so long as both sides have the opportunity to cross-examine. With cross-examination it becomes a battle of titles.

For 20 years, Whalen Hayes stood up on a testimonial platform given him by various agricultural congressmen and said, "I fed DDT to convicts and none of them got sick. Therefore, DDT is safe because I fed them 35 times the dose you receive in your food."

Finally, on a witness stand in Wisconsin, Whalen Hayes admitted that he did none of the conventional clinical tests other than gross neurological, gross blood, gross urine. He admitted that he had done none of the neurological, blood or other body function tests any competent intern would do for you today.

There is a difference between the legislative process and the judicial process. The legislative process is designed to focus on broad public policy points like the ABM or taxes or national defense. It is not designed subject to conflicting expert opinion or scientific data to cross-examination in individual cases.

In the hands of a good committee with good counsel where every committee member is basically without bias, it is possible to ferret out information. But the very committee structure of Congress and the mission orientation of the Department of Agriculture or the Department of the Interior involves jockeying the question of whether we will have DDT hearings before the Department of Agriculture Committee, which is pro-agriculture and doesn't want to hear about birds, fish or people, or the Interior Department, which doesn't want to hear about the problems of the farmer.

Until we get rid of that problem, the Congressional hearing will not focus on the issue the way a courtroom will.

MR. STEVENS: Haven't you ever had occasion to see some jockeying for choices of judges? Haven't you also been denied adequate cross examination in court, too? It seems to me these are matters of misuse of the hearing process, not a condemnation of the process itself.

MR. SAX: It has certainly been my experience that there are very few lawyers who would take the position that one ought to reach for judicial action and ignore either administrative routes or efforts to see interested Congressmen. All three routes are usually taken, and rarely does litigation come about as a result of any kind of a decision not to try the other routes. Just the opposite. It is usually only after some pretty back-breaking efforts to reach administrative and legislative efforts that the decision is made to go forward with litigation. Look at this Hudson River Expressway case. They had many different agencies in there. They had the Hudson River Commission and Transportation and Interior and everybody running around.

MR. SIVE: You are absolutely right. You can't take one and exclude the other. It is important to remember that a lawsuit is one of the greatest ways of serving a political purpose because a lawsuit has inherent drama. When you bring a lawsuit, you can really spur the legislators. But there is a problem somebody has to check in the books, and that is the ethical problem of the attorney.

If an attorney brings a lawsuit not for a judicial purpose but admittedly to serve a political purpose, there may be an ethics problem. This is something that has been a very serious difficulty with a number of suits I have considered and suits in which the Sierra Club has been engaged. To what extent can you use the court for a political process?

MR. YANNACONE: With all due deference to Dave, that is a gross affront to the judicial process. The common law, which began many years ago as the civilized answer to trial by combat, exists for the purpose of opening the door to the courthouse in order to close the door to the streets. There is no case so new or so novel and no theory so far-fetched that it cannot be heard in court. There are summary ways to dispose of the frivolous or the worthless lawsuit. And to bring a lawsuit with the avowed purpose of focusing issues and disseminating public information is the highest and best use of the courts of this country. The court system was not established to solve corporate stockholder problems, small claims, or personal injury actions. They are designed to answer the basic life and death moral questions of today.

MR. SIVE: I think there is a confusion of issues there. It is your ethical right to go into court on any claim no matter what the chances are against you. The client, be it a private person or a conservation group, says go, whether it is 100 to 1 against you or not. You have the ethical right to litigate. But if the motivation is to secure publicity and serve a purely political purpose, then you do have a problem under the canons of ethics, which somebody has to study a good deal more than I have had the time to do.

MR. SAX: There is also a somewhat more sophisticated strategic issue buried here when you talk in very sharp terms about whether it is a lawsuit or a political act. A good deal of environmental litigation, even some of the older cases, is actually a situation in which people say to the court: A different political or a different administrative constituency should have a role or the last word on this issue. It isn't enough to let this decision be made by a local municipality, for example. It must be made by a statewide constituency.

We have seen some of that in the San Francisco Bay litigation, and a lot in the Wisconsin Public Trust cases. There is a perfectly legitimate and often extremely important aspect of these cases that goes to the heart of the issue: that is, who ought really to be deciding these questions and what are the interests that ought to be taken into account? One should never lose sight of litigation as a technique that legitimately feeds into the political process. This is a matter that we haven't talked about at all in terms of strategies for situations like that in Santa Barbara.

If, for example, the focus of leasing opposition was in a local community rather than a nationwide constituency, or whatever constituency USGS represents, it may be that one of the ways you deal with it is to say, despite all the usual arguments about fragmentation of authority, let another institution or another agency get into the act. We are seeing the Congress deal with this question too, in new environmental legislation, and in debating whether Interior should have veto power over Corps permits or whether the Corps should itself go into the ecological business.

Lawyers have a role to play in helping to focus on some of these issues, you know. We ought not to get too diffuse in our thinking about what these problems are.

MR. McCLOSKEY: There is another basic distinction that hasn't been made here. In the Santa Barbara case it may well be that a legislative remedy is the best one ultimately, but in a number of other cases that the Sierra Club has been involved in, the conservationists were satisfied with the existing statute. They don't want Congress to change the statute. They only want the administrative agency to uphold that statute.

That is the case in the Mineral King and the Hudson River Expressway cases, and it is our contention in the Forest Service case in Colorado. There the court really is our only remedy.

MR. YANNACONE: What about the problem of toxic insults to the environment? A lot of you people are confusing the aesthetic problem with the direct toxic insult. The fact that you are getting a dose of DDT whether you want it or not is an invasion of your fundamental human rights. It requires a different kind of law than that which decides how much oil we want to take or whether we have got a proper use of Scenic Hudson.

There is one piece of testimony from the first DDT case that all of you ought to remember. When the medical entomologist for the state of New York was asked what he would do if he discovered that DDT had thalidomide-like effects? His answer was, "I would report it to my superior."

Q. "What would he do?"

A. "He would investigate."

Q. "What would happen if the investigation showed you were right?"

A. "We would report it to the Governor."

Q. "What would he do?"

A. "He would appoint a committee and continue the investigation."

Q. "What would happen if the investigation supported you?"

A. "He would report it to the legislature."

Q. "What would they do?"

A. "Appoint two committees and investigate."

Q. "How long would this take?"

A. "Two years."

What would happen to all the babies during that two years?

That is the question the courts would answer.

MR. HAIK: The lawsuit is a vehicle to focus sharply on the inequities in the resource decision process. What we are really saying is that, under the present political system in this country, the resource decision is made by regulatory bodies, whether they are state agencies or federal agencies. We are, as a society, really saying one thing: regulatory bodies as constituted are completely inadequate to make an intelligent resource decision.

A good share of the data that they rely on is produced by the resource user. We have laws on our books that encourage the use of resources. We can't, as conservationists, just say no. I couldn't agree with Victor Yannacone that it would be wise to bring a lawsuit in Minnesota, for example, on the use of chlorinated hydrocarbons in the face of a state law that says it is in the public interest to encourage agricultural production. This same problem is illustrated again by the laws that give the power of eminent domain to private corporations and permit them, and others, to destroy wetlands because they act in the public interest.

What we have to do, in my judgment, is figure out how the lawsuit can be the means to call attention to the complete inadequacy of these governmental regulatory bodies. We are questioning their analysis, and we are questioning their criteria in making a resource decision. If we should have any objective as lawyers, it should be to get into the regulatory process at the early stage. We should be right on hand when a resource user is just beginning a new nuclear plant or whatever else.

I have sat as an attorney in the governmental area and tried to say the state law does not allow you to destroy wetlands. The trouble is another state law says you can. And in the long run the judges epitomize the establishment. They are not necessarily going to be the dramatic leaders that we might wish them to be. I wouldn't want to see us put all our faith in that wish.

We have to put our faith in the regulatory bodies and we have to concentrate on staffing them adequately. That can be done only by forcing them to rewrite the standards—for example to require them to determine the toxicity of some chemical product and make a specific finding. To make these agencies do these things requires a legislative act, not talk in generalities.

MR. BRENNEMAN: It seems to me that we cannot rely on agencies that are directed to profit from or encourage development to end up limiting this development on the grounds that environmental harm might result. The Santa Barbara oil spill provides a classic example of this problem. A local, state or federal agency that is directed to derive direct economic benefit from a government resource cannot be expected to take a strong position where environmental values collide with that development. I would suggest that at the federal level there is a vital need for an agency, perhaps analogous to the General Accounting Office, to influence and limit the decisions of the Executive Department and its regulatory agencies.

MR. DURNING: Without disagreeing, I want to shift the focus in a legalistic way. We have talked a lot about the burden of proof. Earlier it was suggested that perhaps he who has the burden of proof in an ecological case loses it, due to the difficulty of obtaining the evidence when you are on the non-governmental, non-user side, or the total lack of any evidence one way or the other. When Mr. Yannacone referred to the toxic insult to the environment, it triggered a thought in my mind. As lawyers trying to develop legal theories and getting cases by analogy, could we in the environmental field go by analogy to absolute liability, which is growing so rapidly in the field of tort—the field of product liability? How do we in the environmental field shift the risk to the producer or the doer absolutely? What effect would this have if suits were brought trying to analogize to absolute liability? What effect might that have on what kind of evidence the other side would have to produce?

MR. BALDWIN: The absolute liability concept has, of course, been applied to the Santa Barbara situation. Secretary Hickel announced in February, 1969, that he would impose absolute liability for cleanup costs caused by spills from offshore drilling. He intended the liability to apply to leases already granted as well as to leases granted subsequently. The

Pauley Petroleum Company and several other oil companies have objected that the Secretary is changing the rules for existing lessors. They've said this is not what they originally bargained for, and they have now asked for damages, a recision of their own offshore lease, and a return of the bonus. It so happens that the American Civil Liberties Union has come down on the side of Pauley Petroleum, alleging that this is a violation of due process—a taking without compensation—and also an unconstitutional breach of contract.

MR. BERLIN: The Secretary's order that there will be strict accountability had an unusual side effect I don't think he intended. If you read the allegations of the Pauley complaint, they state some facts that are diametrically opposed to what the oil companies said about the safety of this entire operation prior to the leasing. It is interesting because, if those facts are true, I think on simple tort grounds of negligence there would be a case for holding the companies responsible. Certainly if they had the lack of knowledge that they allege in that complaint, they should never have gone ahead.

MR. SIVE: The problem is that the liability in damages would be so vast that even Sinclair, for example, might be judgment-proof.

MR. LEVINE: I would like to raise a point about absolute liability that may be overlooked. Under the present system of the granting of leases, the income redistribution that would result from making oil companies absolutely liable would be an income redistribution from the government to injured citizens, not from oil companies to injured citizens. You may be perfectly happy with that, but you ought not to delude yourselves that what you are doing is somehow making the oil companies pay.

The value of the lease to an oil company is based on the terms of liability that the lease carries with it. If, as was suggested, the potential damage under the lease is so great that Sinclair would be judgment-proof, we can expect that Sinclair will not bid on leases knowing that it will be absolutely liable.

That may also be a good thing because it may mean that oil resources won't be exploited that cost more to exploit than they are worth to the public.

But at any rate you ought to be very clear, when you discuss absolute liability, about where the liability will fall and what the remaining income redistribution will be. If you believe the government puts the money to uses that are more valuable to us as a nation than the uses to which the damaged individuals could put them, then you should not favor absolute liability in those terms. If you believe otherwise, you should.

MR. KRIER: I think it is worth emphasizing that the Hickel regulation would impose strict liability only for cleanup costs.

MR. LEVINE: That would leave you in an intermediate position, so that certain kinds of injuries would be paid for by the injured and certain kinds would be paid for by the government.

MR. SIVE: May I make one comment about the point that Raymond Haik made earlier with respect to regulatory agencies? I agree thoroughly with what he said. There is one possibility that I would like to ask those of you who are better students of constitutional law than I. If it is correct that the resources-using agency is weighted in favor of the user, whether it is the Federal Power Commission or the Agriculture Department or the Atomic Energy Commission, is that bias a denial of equal protection because the determination of the use of a very significant resource is inevitably placed with those who consciously or unconsciously have a very parochial interest? The thought has occurred to me that maybe this can be the basis of a constitutional argument involving unequal protection of the law.

MR. BENNETT: Dave, how would you prove that a member of the Federal Power Commission is biased in favor of industry? It is almost impossible, even though you may know it.

MR. SIVE: I don't think you could prove that as a matter of fact with evidence. That would be something that the court would have to judge.

MR. BENNETT: You can only seek to impeach him through the Senate or whatever body would have the authority to impeach him, but you can't prove these regulators are biased. I have tried it. It is impossible.

MR. YANNACONE: Of course the agency is biased. The statutory mission of the agency is what has to be challenged. The Agriculture Department can look only at killing insects. The Federal Power Commission can look only at generating cheap power.

MR. SIVE: The answer to Mr. Bennett's query is that it is not an issue of fact. The agency bias is a point of law that has to be argued, the law that sets up the issues.

MR. YANNACONE: You *can* prove it as an issue of fact. It has been proven time and again. You call the head of the agency and ask him what his statutory mission is and then you ask him whether he is permitted under the statutory mission to include the data from your list of all the ancillary things he should include. He will answer no. Then you've got your fact basis and then you take your appeal on whether this is a denial of equal protection.

MR. SAX: I would say with confidence that that is one case you can't win.

MR. YANNACONE: Try it first before you say it.

MR. PLAGER: Let us concede for the moment that in fact the agency is biased as a matter of legislative policy, that is, in its weighing of the competing interests for the utilization of certain of the public resources. The legislature has come down on the side of one grouping of interests rather than another.

You ask if that raises an equal protection question. If you would look at the substantive side it seems to me that you are then saying that in the ultimate analysis the weighing of competing interests ought not to be made by the legislature but ought to be made by the judiciary. Really what you are then doing is shifting the forum for decision making.

MR. SIVE: No. The answer to my argument, if it is valid, is that it is not right and maybe unconstitutional to have the shoreline of the river determined only by the road department. The same goes for a power project.

MR. YANNACONE: You might also agree that the legislative duty is to impose standards on the agency that everybody can understand, not a vague amorphous concept coupled with or interpreted against a statutory mission of limited vision. If you are going to give an agency a limited vision mission, give it standards that its conduct can be measured against.

MR. LEVINE: That is not an equal protection argument. Now you are making a sort of shotgun constitutional attack—a little bit of due process, a little bit of equal protection, a little bit of unreasonable use of the police power and a few other things.

MR. YANNACONE: So what is wrong with that?

MR. LEVINE: There is nothing wrong with it, but we ought to isolate the arguments. I think the problem raised by Sheldon Plager is that, fundamentally, in our constitutional system, the legislature is given the function of weighing interests and making some people richer and some people poorer, not only in the financial sense, but also in terms of satisfaction and otherwise. If it is the judgment of the legislature that roads are sufficiently important or that the highway department is sufficiently expert or whatever, that they are willing to give discretion to that department, I think it will be very difficult to challenge it on constitutional grounds.

MR. SAX: Yes, the point that is now an issue is one that many objectors have won. They won not on constitutional grounds but by putting before the judge the feel of the case, and getting the courts to move the decision-making power someplace else—sometimes back to the legislature, sometimes to another agency. And, they are not confronting this very stark question of what the legislature wanted but saying, "Sure, the legislature wanted roads but that doesn't mean they wanted every road exactly in the place where the highway department said they wanted it." This has gone on in very significant ways in a series of Massachusetts cases, and in some other states.

All I was saying earlier is that it is a serious mistake, and it is certain to be disastrous, to try to argue on constitutional grounds. But the courts are not so dumb that they don't know what is going on. In *Robbins v. Department of Public Works*,[1] the Highway Department came in with a condemnation statute that said, "Look, we have authority to improve the lands in the Commonwealth." And the court said, "Yes, but it was not our understanding that the legislature said improving lands in the Commonwealth meant taking pieces of park land to build a highway, God damn you people." (Laughter) We ought to face up to the fact that courts are responsible to these realities as long as they are treated subliminally.

MR. YANNACONE: It has got to be decided once and for all that we don't talk about an equal protection argument or due process argument, or a Ninth Amendment argument. My God, the Constitution and the common law are a seamless web. It is about time the legal profession got some ecological sophistication. Ecologists have been spending the past 55 years trying to convince the specialists in various sciences to stop looking down a narrow tunnel and relate their data to the world around them. Maybe this is the difference between the specialist and the scholar and the trial lawyer. We have to go in right now and find a forum to do something about a great many pressing toxic insults to the environment or there isn't going to be any environment that we can do anything about. It's inappropriate to say, "Well, you can't make that an equal protection argument, that is a mixed argument covering due process, equal protection, Ninth Amendment." The Constitution is one big document.

MR. BENNETT: Maybe we had better face the reality that the judicial system is not equipped to deal with these problems.

MR. SANDERS: Well, it must be.

I am one of 17 ACLU plaintiffs in Santa Barbara declaring that my environmental right has been abridged, that I am deprived of the right of sailing my boat in unpolluted waters, and other very valuable considerations.

We were not treated very well before the District Court. The judge said, "I am not going to grant your injunction," before our counsel, Mr. Wirin, started to speak. And then he heard our counsel and then he heard the Government for three minutes and said, "I need to hear no more. You don't get your injunction." So now, we are going into court again.

Also there is the county-city case that challenges the constitutionality of the whole Outer Continental Shelf Lands Act, saying that Secretary Hickel has too much power, that he does not have to give hearings and that he has control over an area approximately one-third of the entire

---

[1] 244 N.E. 2d 577 (1969).

United States, that he can actually control foreign policy by the way the Continental Shelf butts up against Russia and the Arctic Ocean. This is unconstitutional, we claim.

So we are going into court again. We haven't gotten the relief we wanted in court yet, but where else can we go? So far at least the court is serving as a forum, keeping this issue alive, and it may ultimately get us the relief that we want.

I don't know if the channel can be saved. I do know that the courts are the only means at our disposal right now. Hopefully, we may win our constitutional issue, but we may not save the channel.

NEEDED
DEVELOPMENTS
IN THE LAW

Environmental Litigation
and the Burden of Proof

James E. Krier

Only in the last few years has "environmental" litigation come into its own. There have, of course, been decades of air pollution cases, water pollution cases, and poison spray cases, but these were not environmental lawsuits as we use the term today. Generally their focus was narrow; they were proprietary lawsuits, brought by injured persons on their own behalf and to protect their own economic interests. Environmental lawsuits, on the other hand, involve the presentation of broader issues beyond the scope of "property rights" and "personal injury." They are brought, in large measure, to realize something more than narrow, immediate, economic ends—the preservation of natural resources, scenic beauty, pure air and water. They are distinctly nonproprietary, often initiated by persons whose only interest is in a clean and pleasant environment.

The number of environmental lawsuits will undoubtedly multiply rapidly over the course of the next few years. There is a new interest in the environment, a new concern about the broad, ecological effects of air pollution, water pollution, and poison sprays. This is "the year of ecology," *Time* magazine says in its new section on "Environment."[1] Interest groups of citizens concerned about the activities of the environmental "manipulators"[2] are forming in increasing numbers. They are reform-minded people, willing to lobby and litigate in pursuit of a better, more pleasant and healthful environment. Moreover, they are becoming impatient with the political forum, and their earnest litigiousness assures

---

[1] *Time,* Aug. 15, 1969, at 38.
[2] The term was suggested to me by a reference in Senate Comm. on Interior and Insular Affairs & House Comm. on Science and Astronautics, 90th Cong., 2d Sess., *Congressional White Paper on a National Policy for the Environment* (Comm. Print 1968).

that they will not hesitate to ask relief in the courts. As the science writer for the *Los Angeles Times* stated in a recent editorial:

> What to do about our environment? Our system of government is one of checks and balances among its executive, legislative and judicial branches. Rightly or wrongly, the public feels that in environmental matters both the executive and legislative branches have let them down. And so, they have turned to the judiciary in their grievance for a cleaner environment—there will be more and more petitions, initiatives . . . and lawsuits.[3]

The promised surge of environmental litigation calls for rethinking much of our substantive and procedural law. Much of that law was made during the prime of the old, proprietary lawsuit, which it suited well enough; it fits poorly, however, the frame of the new lawsuit brought to protect environmental (not economic) values[4] in the public (not private) interest. The common-law concepts of nuisance and waste, for example, are not responsive to the needs of environmental litigation. Because those doctrines formed at a time when natural resources seemed inexhaustible, they reflect a far too narrow and myopic view to be helpful guides to the solution of many contemporary problems.[5] The same can be said of much of our procedural law. Much of it was shaped for essentially private disputes. Much of it reflects outmoded policy. As a result, there has been a call to "establish judicial procedures so that the individual rights to a productive and high-quality environment can be assured."[6]

Perhaps more than any other procedural rules, those relating to burden of proof[7] deserve the attention of anyone concerned with making the

---

[3] Bengelsdorf, "That Breathing by the People Shall Not Perish From the Smog," *Los Angeles Times*, Aug. 14, 1969, §2, at 7, col. 3.

[4] For the purposes of this essay, the phrase "environmental values" means the interest in protecting natural resources, scenic beauty, wildlife, clean air and water, and so forth. Such values or interests are often nonquantifiable (by any present measure) and are in this sense noneconomic. Environmental values are adhered to with varying degrees of intensity. The pure conservationist tends to favor them over all competing values; other men tend to take them into some lesser degree of account.

[5] *See* J.W. Hurst, *Law and Social Process in United States History* at 153-54 (1960); J.W. Hurst, *Law and the Conditions of Freedom* at 52 (1956). Judge J. Skelly Wright has put this point in broader context. *See* Wright, "The Federal Courts and the Nature and Quality of State Law," 13 Wayne L. Rev. 317, 331 (1967): "Poor old nuisance has been the common law's meager response to the crowdedness of society. The doctrine is pathetically inadequate to deal with the social realities of this half-century, which indisputably call for comprehensive legislative planning."

[6] White Paper, *supra* note 2 at 2.

[7] I use the label "burden of proof" broadly to cover all those rules dealing with the allocation of the burdens of persuasion and of going forward with the evidence, with the weight of the burdens and the amount of evidence necessary to meet them, and with the "shifting" (or alleviating) of the burdens by presumptions and by such doctrines as *res ipsa loquitur* and negligence *per se*.

courts a more responsive force in the efforts to curb environmental abuse. This is so for several reasons.

First, burden of proof rules at present have an inevitable bias against protection of the environment and preservation of natural resources. This is the case for the following reasons. Essentially two classes of demands can be made on such resources as air, land, water, wildlife and so on: (1) demands which consume or deteriorate those resources (water pollution, the slaughter of wildlife, the harvesting of forests) (2) demands which *do not* consume or deteriorate them (swimming, birdwatching, hiking and camping). In a world without laws, those who wish to use resources for consumptive or deteriorating ends will *always* prevail over those who wish to use them for nonconsumptive or nondeteriorating ends. This is simply because consuming users, by exercising their demands, can foreclose nonconsuming users from exercising theirs, while the contrary cannot hold true. In short, the polluter's use can stop the swimmer from using and enjoying a lake, but the swimmer's use *cannot* stop the polluter from polluting the lake.

Of course, we live in a system with laws, but it is a loaded system. And it is loaded precisely because of the point I have just made. For even in a world with rules against resource consumption (against, for example, pollution), the leverage inherent in resource consumers means that they can continue their conduct until sued. In short, they will almost inevitably be *defendants*, and those whose uses preserve rather than deteriorate will ineluctably be *plaintiffs*. And it is one of the simple facts of our present system that (for a host of reasons) plaintiffs most generally carry the major burden of providing most of the basic issues in a lawsuit. The result is striking: Even with a system of substantive rules *against* resource consumption, our present rules ensure that in cases of doubt about any facet of those rules, resource consumption will prevail.[7a]

At one point in our history, such a result was by no means intolerable. For example:

> The common law embodied a general preference for the initiator of economically productive action, by casting the burden of persuasion on an aggrieved person to show cause why law should intervene to shift a loss from where it fell as a consequence of the initiative taken.[8]

This common-law preference reflected a broad policy favoring industrial expansion and economic growth at the expense of natural resource conservation. In those days when expansion and settlement of the vast

---

[7a] This observation about the relationship between burden rules and resource conservation grew out of my reading of an excellent monograph by J. H. Dales, *Pollution, Property and Prices* (1968).

[8] J. W. Hurst, *Law and Economic Growth* at 224 (1964). *See also id.* at 213.

American frontier was essential, that policy made good sense; in any event, it reflected an understandable shortsightedness, for our natural resources were then so abundant that it was almost impossible to think in terms of their eventual scarcity.

Today, however, conditions are radically different. Yet the burden rule, the justifications for its existence largely dead and gone, lives on to govern the allocation of the obligation of persuasion in a large number of suits. The rule is a serious obstacle to successful environmental litigation, especially because the framework of substantive law in which it operates is cast in such narrow terms. Under it, the environmentalist must generally prove not only that certain activities caused (or threaten to cause) specified damage, but in addition that those activities are not legally justified by rules which often are cast in favor of the activities themselves (again reflecting, perhaps, some outmoded policy). It is one thing to provide that an enterprise causing environmental damage is liable only for fault; it may be quite another to place the burden of proof on the issue of fault on the complainant rather than the enterprise.

A second reason why environmentalists and their lawyers might wisely focus close attention on burden-of-proof rules grows from the argument that judges traditionally have felt least restrained about law-making activity when they could operate through the medium of burden of proof. As Julius Stone has pointed out, the burden rules seldom touch "the major prejudices of the age."[9] They are quiet, bland, unspectacular. As a result, juggling them in favor of one interest or another tends to go unheeded—and uncriticized.[10] Policies can be promoted or stifled smoothly, quietly, and without controversy. This befits judicial decorum, lends the appearance of restraint, and enhances the judge's security—and his actual power. Hence burden-of-proof rules can be effective levers for law reform, operating with both little friction and little greasing.

Related to this second reason is a third, the fact that the judiciary has formed a habit of showing favor or disfavor for various allegations and interests by resort to the broad array of burden rules.[11] There are familiar illustrations which suggest this habit at work. Allegations of fraud, for example, have traditionally been disfavored by the courts,[12] and this is probably reflected today in the requirements that fraud must be pleaded with particularity and proved by clear and convincing evidence.[13] The

---

[9] Stone, "Burden of Proof and the Judicial Process," 60 *L. Q. Rev.* 262, 279 (1944).

[10] *Cf.* Cleary, "Presuming and Pleading: An Essay on Juristic Immaturity," 12 *Stan. L. Rev.* 5, 24 (1959).

[11] *See e.g.* J.W. Hurst, *Law and Economic Growth* at 207, 210-11, 213, 224 (1964).

[12] *See* C. Clark, *Code Pleading* §48 at 311-13, §96 at 609 (1947).

[13] *See e.g.* Fed. R. Civ. P. 9(b); C. McCormick, *Evidence* §320.

presumption of legitimacy of children born during wedlock may be, at least in part, a case of the courts promoting a desired policy, or undercutting an unfavored policy, by manipulation of burden-of-proof rules. The development of the law of injured employees is rich with examples. During the reign of the fellow-servant rule, some courts required the employee-plaintiff to prove he was not injured by a co-worker,[14] thus apparently honoring Chief Justice Shaw's dialectic[15] with a vengeance. Today our policy regarding compensation for workmen injured on the job has changed radically, and the Supreme Court reflects the new attitude in the burden-of-proof rules it has created to favor the F.E.L.A. plaintiff, who may be unique in his right to reach a jury on a scintilla of evidence.[16] Probably one of the clearest examples of judicial use of burden-of-proof rules to favor and promote selected interests and policies is found in those few jurisdictions which place on the plaintiff the burden of proving freedom from contributory negligence. The judges of one age may have been expressing by this rule a stubborn determination to restrain recoveries for mere negligence;[17] the judges of a later age softened the hard effects of this rule and favored a new interest by reliance on presumptions of plaintiffs' due care and other burden-of-proof tools.[18]

This penchant for recourse to burden rules to mother favored interests is an important point in a time when we can sense an emerging awareness and worry about deteriorating environmental quality. Official expressions of our growing apprehension are becoming common: statutes and their preambles express broad concern about abuse of natural resources and about environmental corruption. Yet there are still signs of ambivalence and worse. We give allowances for mineral depletion and we subsidize the sonic boom; we establish "standards" and then grant "variances."[19] True, in some ways these acts reflect balanced judgments about what is good national policy. They also reflect, however, "politics" and the efforts of the hobnobbing lobbyist. And they suggest a lingering ambivalence and uncertainty about what our national environmental

---

[14] See e.g. Chicago City Ry. Co. v. Leach, 208 Ill. 198, 200-201, 70 N.E. 2d 222, 223 (1904).
[15] Shaw's dialectic was set out in his decision for the court in Farwell v. Boston & W.R.R., 45 Mass. (4 Met.) 49 (1842). See generally, Friedman & Ladinsky, "Social Change and the Law of Industrial Accidents," 67 Colum. L. Rev. 50 (1967).
[16] See e.g. Note, "FELA, Negligence, and Jury Trials—Speculation Upon a Scintilla," 11 W. Res. L. Rev. 123 (1959); "Supreme Court, 1951 Term," 66 Harv. L. Rev. 89, 162-64 (1952).
[17] See Cleary, supra note 10 at 11.
[18] See W. Prosser, Torts §64 at 426 (3d ed. 1964).
[19] On variances and the Santa Barbara oil spills, see e.g. "The Big Oil Leak Leaves a Messy Legal Residue," Business Week, Feb. 15, 1969, at 30-31. On variances and air pollution control, see e.g. Getze, "Mothers Charge Laxity in Smog-Control Fight (Stationary Sources Granted Variances, State Board Told)," Los Angeles Times, July 17, 1969, §2 at 1, col. 5.

policy is, or ought to be. There are other examples. At this very moment Congress is considering giving tax relief to polluters to encourage their use of pollution control devices. Perhaps this is smart administration: if the carrot works better than the stick, use it.[20] But the fact remains that the carrot is a price paid to someone with no just claim to it; the air does not belong to the polluters. At least, this conclusion appears to be the assumption underlying much of our legislation.

Nevertheless, a widely shared concern is finally emerging in this "year of ecology." National indifference and ambivalence are slowly being replaced by a broadening consensus that environmental values are important and must be taken into account, insofar as practicable, in public and private decision making about all activities which touch on environmental quality, in order that those likely to impair and debilitate the environment will not be undertaken without careful and informed consideration and planning. As it was put in a statement submitted to the recent House-Senate Colloquium on a National Policy for the Environment:

> The issue is not whether technology is useful. It underlies our entire civilization, but we must insure that it is serving the ends of civilization rather than subverting them. There are ample precedents. With food and drugs that have dramatic and immediate effects on health, for example, we require a demonstration of compatibility with the natural system. We must expand this concept to include those technologies which have indirect, cumulative, and long-term effects on the environment. . . .
>
> There should be established mechanisms to assess and predict the effects of technology on the environment prior to its introduction into the public domain.
>
> These methods must certainly include detailed ecological analysis and must, of course, be complemented by sociological, engineering, and economic analysis so that each perspective can be evaluated within the context of human fulfillment. Additionally, these devices must be available at all decision making levels, government and private.[21]

The courts can and should make some effort to respond to the needs expressed in this statement, to the needs of emerging environmental concern.

Courts are called into the environmental decision-making process in essentially two contexts—either before or after some particular occasion

---

[20]For a discussion of the merits and demerits of tax relief and other positive incentives as a means of pollution control, *see* Gerhardt, "Incentives to Air Pollution Control," 33 *Law & Contemp. Prob.* 358 (1968).

[21]*Hearings Before the Senate Comm. on Interior and Insular Affairs and the House Comm. on Science and Astronautics,* 90th Cong., 2d Sess., No. 8, at 213 (1968).

of alleged environmental damage. In both contexts, however, they should have some common objectives. They should hope to make some improvements in *their own* abilities to reach well-informed decisions in environmental cases; they should also take steps to encourage *other* decision makers (industry, for example, or federal, state and local agencies) both to consider the impact of their activities and decisions on environmental quality and to act to avoid any undue or unnecessary impact. Courts could take steps toward simultaneously realizing both of these objectives through the medium of burden-of-proof rules. The rules themselves, however, would differ in the "before" and "after" context.

THE "BEFORE" CASE

Much of what I have termed environmental litigation arises out of allegations of some threatened damage to the environment: a proposed power plant will flood a scenic area; an easement sought by condemnation will damage a wildlife preserve; off-shore oil-well drilling will pollute water and beaches. The relief sought in each case is a judicial decree which limits or forbids the allegedly threatening activity. Each case, of course, may pose different questions of substantive law, and that substantive law itself may be narrow-minded or outmoded from the standpoint of environmental values. That problem, however, is beyond the scope of this paper. Burden-of-proof rules can, within the limitations of substantive law, be applied to promote environmental values and to encourage decision-makers to give careful consideration to the impact of their decisions on the environment.

A recent New Jersey decision illustrates these points. The case grew out of the attempt by a natural gas company to condemn a pipeline right of way through the Troy Meadows Preserve in New Jersey. The Preserve, located "just 20 miles from Times Square," was "considered by ecologists to be the finest natural inland fresh-water wetland in the Northeastern United States."[22] It was owned by Wildlife Preserves, Inc., a private nonprofit corporation, which took the position in contesting condemnation that the lands were devoted to a prior public use more necessary than the pipeline right of way. The Preserve alleged that the damage to its lands in their present use would outweigh any loss suffered by the gas company through denial of the right of way. It also claimed that an alternate route was at the gas company's disposal and that, therefore, no public purpose would be served by condemnation. The trial court rejected all of these contentions on the grounds that they did not

[22]McCarter, "The Case That Almost Was," 54 *A.B.A.J.* 1076 (1968).

constitute valid defenses to the condemnation as a matter of law.[23]

The Supreme Court of New Jersey reversed.[24] It agreed with the trial judge that the Preserve was not qualified to claim the benefits of the prior public use doctrine as such because it was a private enterprise, albeit "public-spirited." But, the court added, this was not dispositive, since "even a private property owner may present the issue of arbitrariness of a taking."[25] The Preserve claimed arbitrariness because the chosen route would have a "devastating and irreparable effect" which would be avoided by the alternate route offered to the gas company but which the latter refused to consider.

The court sent the arbitrariness issue back for a trial to be governed by a special burden-of-proof rule:

> Defendant's devotion of its land to a purpose which is encouraged and often engaged in by government itself gives it a somewhat more potent claim to judicial protection against taking of its preserve or a portion of it by arbitrary action of a condemnor. In such unique cases courts realize that more than a dollar valuation is involved. The public service being rendered must be considered and it cannot be evaluated adequately only in dollars and cents. . . . The difference is not in the principle but in its application; that is, the quantum of proof required of this defendant to show arbitrariness against it should not be as substantial as that to be assumed by the ordinary property owner who devotes his land to conventional uses.[26]

The court left on the Preserve the ultimate burden of proving arbitrariness, but implemented its new rule by holding that if the Preserve

> introduces reasonable proof of (1) the serious damage claimed to result from installation of the pipeline on the path chosen by plaintiff, and (2) an apparently reasonably available alternate route or routes which will avoid the serious damage referred to, the burden of going forward with the evidence will shift to plaintiff. A *prima facie* case of arbitrariness having been made out, Texas Eastern may present its evidence to the contrary, which it claims indicates that the location of the right of way selected represented a reasonable and not capricious choice. . . .[27]

In short, the court favored the condemnee with a special, reduced burden

---

[23] *Texas East. Trans. Corp. v. Wildlife Preserves, Inc.*, 89 N.J. *Super.* 1, 213 A.2d 193 (Law Div. 1965).

[24] *Texas East. Trans. Corp. v. Wildlife Preserves, Inc.*, 48 N.J. 261 , 225 A.2d 130, 137 (1966). The decision is noted in Tarlock, "Recent Natural Resources Case," 8 *Natural Resources J.* 1 (1968); Note, 52 *Iowa L. Rev.* 1209 (1967).

[25] *Texas East. Trans. Corp. v. Wildlife Preserves, Inc.*, 48 N.J. 261, 273, 225 A.2d 130, 137 (1966).

[26] *Id.* at 273, 225 A.2d at 137.

[27] *Id.* at 275-76, 225 A.2d at 138.

of proof on the issue of arbitrariness because it was "a private enterprise carried on by a public-spirited nonprofit organization for the purpose of preserving our natural wildlife resources" and because "at both planes of government a sympathetic concern has been shown for such preserves. . . ."[28]

On remand the trial court, after hearing all of the evidence, "concluded that plaintiff's action was not arbitrary or capricious, and that the right of way sought by plaintiff represented a reasonable exercise of judgment."[29] This conclusion was affirmed; the evidence was "ample."[30]

One might fairly ask, in light of this ultimate result, whether *Wildlife Preserves* accomplished anything at all with its special burden-of-proof rules. The indications are that, in terms of improved environmental decision-making processes, it did indeed. As a result of the decision, once the Preserve introduced evidence that the gas company's chosen site would have serious effects in environmental and ecological terms and that alternative sites were available, the gas company was obliged as a practical matter to disprove the feasibility of those alternatives.[31] This led to a hearing at which there was "much expert testimony and seven days of trial."[32] Whether or not the company had studied the feasibility of other sites or attempted to justify its selection of the chosen site before, it was required to do so after the Supreme Court's decision. It was required to think through its proposed course of conduct and, perhaps more important, it was required to do so publicly, to make a public record

---

[28] *Id.* at 267-68, 225 A.2d at 134. Actually, the court probably extended favorable burden-of-proof treatment even beyond this. *See* Note, 52 *Iowa L. Rev.* 1209, 1211 (1967): "[T]he defendant-condemnee has the burden of proving arbitrariness as an affirmative defense, and merely showing a viable alternative route generally has not been sufficient to carry condemnee's burden of proof. . . . In the instant case, the New Jersey Supreme Court held that condemnee's affidavits of an alternative route constituted a sufficient showing of arbitrariness to merit a jury trial on this issue. In addition, the court extended preferential treatment to a private, charitable condemnee by reducing the quantum of proof necessary for such a party to show an arbitrary and capricious condemnation. The court reasoned that the nature of the activity performed by the condemnee was essentially the same as that performed by many governmental units, and, therefore, the condemnee should enjoy a favored status. Several recent cases and statutes were cited as indicative of society's interest in promoting and maintaining game preserves and conservation projects." It appears that, under the guise of burden of proof, *Wildlife Preserves* actually made some new substantive condemnation law. *See* Tarlock, *supra* note 24 at 2; Note, 52 *Iowa L. Rev.* 1209, 1210-11 (1967). This tends to illustrate the point that burden-of-proof rules can be effective levers of law reform.

[29] *Texas East. Trans. Corp. v. Wildlife Preserves, Inc.*, 49 N.J. 403, 404-05, 230 A.2d 505, 506 (1967).

[30] *Id.* at 405, 230 A.2d at 506.

[31] Tarlock, *supra* note 24 at 5.

[32] McCarter, *supra* note 22 at 1080.

in a public forum where its planning processes could be viewed, criticized, and improved upon. This sort of ventilation of decision-making processes can of itself make the decision maker more conscientious; its public image, reputation and security are put at stake. Moreover, inducing prior planning and discouraging shortcuts to selfish ends increases the chance that acceptable solutions will be found.[33]

The record produced at the hearing also helped the trial court improve its environmental decision-making processes:

> The judge, an ordinary trial court magistrate like thousands of others across the nation, could and did do a perfectly competent and knowledgeable job of evaluating and sifting the evidence offered by each party. His expertise at problem solving served him well in the pipeline case and he found a solution which was a compromise between the proposals of both parties, but which minimized the environmental damage without preventing the pipeline company from getting its job done.[34]

In short, by means of burden-of-proof rules, the court in *Wildlife Preserves* shaped decision-making processes which forced the gas company to think about its proposed course of action in terms of environmental values and which improved the court's own ability to reach an informed decision. The case is interesting because it both illustrates so explicitly the court's favoring the emerging environmental interest through burden-of-proof rules and shows how much of value can be accomplished by means of those rules.

The "before" case, of course, can come up in a myriad of substantive contexts. Each of those contexts can bring with it different substantive law restrictions within which burden-of-proof rules must work. There is no apparent reason, however, why the approach taken in *Wildlife Preserves* could not serve as at least a general model for most of them.[35]

---

[33] *See* the comment in *Scenic Hudson Preservation Conference v. Federal Power Commission*, 354 F.2d 608, 612 (2d Cir. 1965), *cert. denied*, 384 U.S. 941 (1966): "While the courts have no authority to concern themselves with the policies of the Commission, it is their duty to see to it that the Commission's decisions receive that careful consideration which the statute contemplates." *Scenic Hudson* itself is in many ways a case which employed burden-of-proof techniques to improve the decision-making process. *See* Tarlock, *supra* note 24 at 5: "The court, in effect, placed an affirmative burden on the Commission to protect the scenic beauty of an area when it is threatened by an FPC licensee and provided that this burden could only be discharged by seriously considering alternative development proposals which would be less destructive of an area's scenic beauty."

[34] Explanatory Memorandum by Joseph L. Sax on Proposed Natural Resource Conservation and Environmental Protection Act of 1969 (Michigan), at 6.

[35] The court in *Wildlife Preserves*, of course, had a standard of arbitrariness against which it could and did work. It has been suggested to me, however, that most of the significant

Once a reasonable showing is made that a proposed course of action poses a probable threat of significant environmental damage, the body desiring to initiate that action should be required to come forward with evidence on the likelihood of such damage, the unavailability or unfeasibility of alternatives, and the justification for its activities. Proposed Michigan legislation[36] appears to substantially incorporate the *Wildlife Preserves* schema and make it applicable to *any* "before" case. That legislation provides for the maintenance of actions by state officials or citizens for declaratory and equitable relief in the name of the state

> against any person, including any governmental instrumentality or agency, for the protection of the public trust in the natural resources of the State.

The Act would provide that in any such action,

> whenever the plaintiff shall have made a prima facie case showing that the conduct of the defendant has, or is reasonably likely to impair, pollute or destroy the air, water or other natural resources or the public trust of the state, the defendant shall have the burden of establishing that there is no feasible and prudent alternative and that the conduct, program or product at issue is consistent with and reasonably required for the promotion of the public health, safety and welfare in light of the state's paramount concern for the protection of its natural resources from pollution, impairment or destruction.

The purpose of this provision has been well stated:

> To put the burden of establishing alternatives on the proponent of action is a simple matter of common sense, for we expect the proponent of any activity to have considered all reasonable alternatives and to have chosen the best of those available; to ask him to support his decision is merely to ask that he reveal the process which he must—if he operates rationally and with the public interest in mind—already have undertaken.[37]

Much would be gained if the courts would apply this common sense broadly.

"before" cases in the realm of environmental law will involve judicial review of the decisions of public or quasi-public bodies. Most of these bodies, since they must operate in the "public interest," probably have an obligation to refrain from arbitrary action. Indeed, as the power of purely private decision makers (for example, industry) to damage the environment expands, no doubt their power to act arbitrarily will come to be limited by the courts, at least *sub silentio*. In any event, most "before" cases will present some element to which a reduced burden of proof can be applied, just as in *Wildlife Preserves* a reduced burden was applied to the element of arbitrariness. And, even where the body proposing to take action is purely private, the courts can follow the model of *Wildlife Preserves* in terms of requiring that body to make a record. *See* note 38, *infra.*

[36] *See* note 34, *supra.*

[37] Sax, *supra* note 34 at 7.

THE "AFTER" CASE

In the "after" case, damage is a *fait accompli* rather than a threat; the suit seeks a money award for injuries allegedly caused by the defendant's activities.[38] In terms of protecting environmental interests, however, the objectives of burden-of-proof rules should be the same: decision-making processes (judicial and otherwise) that take environmental values into account.

Pollution, noise, destruction of scenic areas and other incidents of environmental damage and debilitation are costs imposed in the first instance on society by the enterprises whose operations and activities cause them. If these costs remain external to their source, if the enterprises responsible for them are not made to bear them, then those enterprises will not be likely to take the costs into account in deciding about the social and economic "wisdom" of their activities. If, on the other hand, the responsible bodies are made to bear those costs through the imposition of damage awards, they will be encouraged either to forego the activities altogether or to carry them out in ways likely to prevent or minimize the damage. They will have an incentive, that is, to take into account in planning their operations the likely impact of those operations

---

[38]Of course, the plaintiff may in this situation seek injunctive relief against the threat of continuing damage, on the ground that legal relief is inadequate in that a multiplicity of suits would be required to recover damages. *See* "Developments in the Law—Injunctions," 78 *Harv. L. Rev.* 994, 1001 (1965); *Renken v. Harvey Aluminum, Inc.*, 226 F. Supp. 169, 173-74 (D. Oregon 1963). The "after" case in this framework becomes essentially a "before" case and should be approached as such: if a reasonable likelihood of future environmental damage can be made out, the defendant should have the burden of airing his decision-making processes—past and present. The courts on occasion appear to have adopted this approach. *See Renken, supra,* 226 F. Supp. at 174: "Once the plaintiff established that fluorides were deposited on their lands from the plant of the defendant, the burden of going forward with the evidence was on the defendant to show that the use of its property, which caused the injury, was unavoidable or that it could not be prevented except by the expenditure of such vast sums of money as would substantially deprive it of the use of its property." *See also Herring v. H. W. Walker Company,* 409 Pa. 126, 132-33, 185 A.2d 565, 568 (1962): "The court below *erroneously* assumed . . . that it was the duty of the plaintiff to come forward with convincing testimony or evidence which established as a fact the defendant had not taken every reasonable means to prevent the conditions of which he complains." (Emphasis added.) Of course, these cases differ from "pure" "before" cases in that a substantial investment may already have been made—for instance, in a factory. The decree, however, can easily take this fact into account by giving something less than complete relief. Here, just as in *Wildlife Preserves,* the interests of both parties can be accommodated. *See e.g. Renken, supra,* 226 F. Supp. at 176; "Developments," *supra,* 78 *Harv. L. Rev.* at 996, 1063-64.

on the environment and the means by which any damaging impact can be avoided.[38a]

Our law does not at present *systematically* encourage enterprises likely to cause environmental injury to take that likelihood into account other than to impose liability for fault. Fault liability, however, is not an effective means by which to internalize the costs of environmental damage. Probably many instances of environmental damage occur without fault.[39] Moreover, fault can be difficult and expensive to prove. The result can be that the environmental damage costs are borne by persons unable to take effective measures to prevent them.

It is this problem of proof, of course, to which the courts can quietly respond through burden rules. To some extent there has been a response, but it has been erratic rather than systematic. Thus, in order to promote other than environmental values the courts have created burden-shifting (and burden-alleviating) doctrines which at times aid in internalizing the costs of environmental damage.

There are, for example, instances in which environmental damage has been caused under circumstances which may give rise to application of the doctrine of *res ipsa loquitur*.[40] The doctrine eases the plaintiff's burden of proving fault and increases the likelihood that external costs

---

[38a] This analysis horribly simplifies the problem of social cost in implying that damage awards should more or less automatically be imposed on polluters and other manufacturers whose activities debilitate the physical and aesthetic environment, as opposed to leaving the costs of those activities lie where they fall. As has been admirably demonstrated, that conclusion does not follow *perforce*. *See* Coase, "The Problem of Social Cost," 3 *J. Law & Econ.* 1 (1960); Calabresi, "Transaction Costs, Resource Allocation and Liability Rules —A Comment," 11 *J. Law & Econ.* 67 (1968). I believe, however, that the analysis suggested by those articles leads to an almost axiomatic conclusion that in the case of environmental damage the polluter or manufacturer is the proper target for the imposition of damages, essentially because of the high ratio of receptors (or "victims") to polluters and manufacturers, the fact that the latter have greater command of relevant information and technology, and the fact that most environmental problems center around essentially common property resources. *See id.* at 69 n. 7 and Note, "The Cost-Internalization Case for Class Actions," 21 *Stan. L. Rev.* 383, 385-98, 403-04 (1969).

[39] For example, the sonic boom. *See* Baxter, "The SST: From Watts to Harlem in Two Hours," 21 *Stan. L. Rev.* 1, 47-48 (1968). Another provocative current example of this point is the Santa Barbara oil spill. The oil companies have taken the position, with some apparent foundation, "that no operator could guarantee that, even with the greatest degree of care, its exploration and production in the area would be free of well blowouts or of other events which would give rise to the unintended discharge of oil into the surrounding waters." Petition in *Pauley Petroleum, Inc., et al v. United States*, U. S. Court of Claims, April 9, 1969, at p. 5. This would seem to suggest, however, that perhaps reasonable men would have elected not to drill in such an area in the first place.

[40] *See e.g. Reynolds Metals Co. v. Yturbide*, 258 F.2d 321 (9th Cir. 1958). *See generally* Sweeney, "Oil Pollution of the Oceans," 37 *Fordham L. Rev.* 155, 180-81 (1968).

will be imposed upon the enterprises causing them. It is obvious, however, that *res ipsa* will have no application at all to many instances of environmental damage.[41] By the same token, statutes, regulations or ordinances may proscribe activity producing environmental damage. Violations of such legislative proscriptions would ease the burden of proving fault since they may constitute negligence per se, or at least evidence of negligence.[42] While this doctrine can be of occasional aid,[43] it will not have systematic application.

Finally, the doctrine of strict liability for abnormally dangerous activities can be of assistance in many cases of environmental damage. Strict liability is, of course, more than a burden-shifting doctrine, since it not only relieves the plaintiff of the obligation to prove fault but forecloses the defendant from proving the absence of fault. The doctrine of strict liability can be of great aid and comfort in environmental litigation because many of the activities which experience has shown to be frequent causes of injury to the environment have been held to be ultrahazardous for purposes of application of a rule of liability without fault.[44]

This might suggest that the doctrine is the best tool for internalizing the costs of environmental damage by any cause; it has, for example, been suggested as the best means of accomplishing this objective in regard to

---

[41]For example, if the event causing damage is one that occurs even in the absence of negligence. *See* James, "Proof of the Breach in Negligence Cases, (Including *Res Ipsa Loquitur*)," 37 *Va. L. Rev.* 179, 200 (1951). As I have suggested, this might be the case more than occasionally. It might, for example, make the doctrine inapplicable to the Santa Barbara spills. *See* note 39, *supra*. Whether *res ipsa* applies there may be of little importance since the case law applicable appears to impose strict liability on oil well drilling on the theory that it is ultrahazardous activity. *See Green v. General Petroleum Corp.*, 205 Cal. 328, 270 P. 952 (1928). *See also Luthringer v. Moore*, 31 Cal. 2d 489, 499-500, 190 P.2d 1, 7-8 (1948). *But see* note 44, *infra*. The problem could, however, arise in jurisdictions not following the *Green* rule. Indeed, the existence of *Green* itself would seem to suggest logically that *res ipsa loquitur* should never apply to oil well drilling. *See Beck v. Bel Air Properties, Inc.*, 134 Cal. App. 2d 834, 841, 286 P.2d 503, 509 (1955), stating that an activity is ultrahazardous if it involves risk of harm which cannot be eliminated even by exercise of the utmost care.
[42]*See generally* W. Prosser, *Torts* §35 (3d ed. 1964).
[43]*See e.g. Gulf Oil Corporation v. Alexander*, 291 S.W.2d 792 (Texas Civil Appeals), *aff'd per curiam*, 156 Texas 455, 295 S.W. 2d 901 (1956); *Comanche Drilling Co. v. Shamrock Oil & Gas Co.*, 122 Okla. 253, 254 P. 20 (1926).
[44]*See e.g.* W. Prosser, *Torts* §77 at 525-26 (3d ed. 1964) and cases there cited, indicating that the rule has been applied to the following conditions and activities, among others: "Crop dusting with a dangerous chemical likely to drift; drilling oil wells or operating refineries in thickly settled communities; an excavation letting in the sea; factories emitting smoke, dust or noxious gases in the midst of a town. . . ." *See also* Juergensmeyer, "Control of Air Pollution Through the Assertion of Private Rights," 1967 *Duke L.J.* 1126, 1148-52. Query whether Prosser's reading of *Green* makes it inapplicable to the Santa Barbara spills.

the sonic boom.[45] The step from fault liability to strict liability, however, is a large one doctrinally, and although the rule can be classified in some senses as a burden-of-proof device, surely it is the most difficult of such devices to successfully convince a court to impose; experience suggests that courts would be more likely to respond to the needs of environmental litigation by blander means.[46] Moreover, a rather large body of law has developed to determine those activities which are abnormally dangerous for purposes of strict liability.[47] Some activities may pose occasional or even frequent threats of environmental damage and yet not fit within this existing rubric. Finally, existing strict liability doctrine is concerned with protecting far more than simply environmental interests. This suggests that an expanded application of the doctrine, while perhaps good policy, is not the environmentalist's battle to fight, especially since he may be able to obtain his particular objective in more limited ways.

What might be urged upon the courts short of a rule of strict liability is one providing that, once plaintiff has shown by a reduced burden of proof that the defendant's activity caused broad environmental damage, the burden of proof shifts to the defendant to show that the highest degree of care was in fact used.[48] The point could be carried a step further by requiring that if environmental damage was reasonably foreseeable, then the highest degree of care has not been exercised unless the defendant can show that its decision-making processes took the possibility of environmental damage into account and made such provision for it as would a man exercising the highest degree of care. While such a rule would still leave some costs external to their source, it would at the same time both internalize many of those costs and encourage the kind of planning which would eliminate many others. It would also tend to produce records facilitating well-informed judicial decisions in the realm of environmental law.

---

[45] See Baxter, *supra* note 39 at 50-53. See also Malley, "The Supersonic Transport's Sonic Boom Costs: A Common Law Approach," 37 *Geo. Wash. L. Rev.* 683 (1969).

[46] See the discussion *supra* and Professor Jaffe's discussion of *Escola v. Coca Cola Bottling Co.*, 24 Cal. 2d 453, 150 p.2d 436 (1944) in "*Res Ipsa Loquitur* Vindicated," 1 *Buff. L. Rev.* 1, 12-13 (1951).

[47] See e.g. Restatement (Second) of Torts §§ 519, 520 (Tent. Draft No. 10, 1964).

[48] Others have suggested this rule as an alternative to strict liability. See Smith, "Liability for Substantial Physical Damage to Land By Blasting—The Rule of the Future," 33 *Harv. L. Rev.* 542, 554 (1920): "The adoption by the courts of another rule favorable to plaintiff is not impossible; *viz.*, shifting upon the defendant the burden of proof as to care. Sir Frederick Pollock, in his draft of an Indian Civil Wrongs Bill, Section 68, proposed a provision that a person keeping dangerous things is bound to take all reasonably practicable care to prevent harm, and is liable as for negligence to make compensation for harm, unless he proves that all reasonable practicable care and caution were in fact used."

CONCLUSIONS

Any effort to talk about burden of proof outside of the context of substantive law in which burden-of-proof rules work is doomed to be somewhat abstract. Within that limitation, I have tried to suggest some sense of the meaning that burden-of-proof rules can have for the objectives of environmental litigation. I have sketched in the most general terms two burden-of-proof models that would be responsive to what I see as two important objectives of environmental litigation—the creation of a system which encourages activities and enterprises likely to cause environmental damage to take that damage and the means to prevent it into their decision-making processes and, just as important, the creation of a system in which courts can make the best informed decisions in regard to the environmental issues that come before them. The idea is simply to encourage responsible thought before decision and action. I have made no effort at rigor in my discussion; my purpose has not been to outline a system but to suggest a relevant line of inquiry about the role of burden-of-proof rules in environmental litigation. To the extent that it lends traditional support to the feasibility and fairness of the models I have suggested, it is worth pointing out that both of them meet, at least in broad terms, one of the traditional criteria governing allocation of burden of proof—namely, the consideration suggesting that the burden should be placed on that party within whose control lies the greater ability to produce evidence on a given point.[49] On the question of the extent to which the decision-making process did and could take environmental values into consideration in any particular case (that is, on the question of the presence of thought before action), the environmental manipulator obviously has the greater ability to produce evidence.

I have suggested that burden of proof is an important focus for the environmental lawyer because law reform here is more obtainable than in the case of other, more spectacular reforms and because the courts have demonstrated an inclination to promote emerging policies with burden rules. If this is the case, it would appear that one strategy for environmental litigation should be to assist in the formulation of responsible policies about natural resources. The effort in any one case should not be limited simply to proving the case for relief under the existing rules, but should extend to proving the case for new rules as well. Legislative facts relevant not simply to existing law but to what law and policy ought to be should be discovered, assembled, and offered into evidence at every practical opportunity. As Kenneth Culp Davis has said,

---

[49] *See e.g.* Cleary, *supra* note 10 at 12.

Legislative facts are those which help the tribunal to determine the content of law and policy and to exercise its judgment or discretion in determining what course of action to take. . . . In the great mass of cases decided by courts and by agencies, the legislative element is either absent, unimportant, or interstitial, because in most cases the applicable law and policy have been previously established. But whenever a tribunal is engaged in the creation of law or of policy, it may need to resort to legislative facts, whether or not those facts have been developed on the record[50]

The importance of these remarks to the environmental lawyer should be obvious. We are entering a period when emerging issues are calling for, and producing, new law. That law must be responsive to and must itself be good policy, yet our policy stand on environmental matters is at best inarticulate and ambivalent. Legislative facts can suggest the need for new rules and attitudes. Interestingly, such facts need not be "proved" by any fixed burden.[51]

Of course, the impact that burden-of-proof rules can have on the problems of our environment is bound in some respects to be minimal. In the first place, the courts can play only a secondary role in the solution of environmental ills; the diffuse impact of environmental damage, the fine and important lines of policy which must be drawn in coping with it, the need for large public expenditures and elaborate administrative machinery, these and other considerations[52] all suggest that the job is primarily one cut out for the executive, legislative, and administrative arms of government and that the courts can perform only a back-up

---

[50] Davis, "Judicial Notice," 55 *Colum. L. Rev.* 945, 952 (1955).

[51] *Id.* at 952-53.

[52] The constraints—especially the necessity of drawing fine lines of policy—might suggest that the courts are by no means competently equipped to handle cases that pit environmental against other values (or one set of environmental values against another set). Subjective judgments open to great differences of opinion will ordinarily be involved in deciding the importance of nonquantifiable environmental values, and the consequences of any decision are often quite likely to be potentially large (forbidding, for example, the construction of an industrial park that would bring with it thousands of jobs, or permitting the construction and causing the loss of, say, a rare pine forest). Yet we can be sure that in the American context the courts generally will continue to be recognized as competent to make decisions in this complex, subjective and essentially political area. Some particular court might solve the obvious dilemmas involved by working out a wise compromise, as in the *Wildlife Preserves* case. Another particular court might simply opt out of the decision-making process altogether. A California trial judge, for example, recently dismissed a $500,000,-000,000 class action filed on behalf of residents of Los Angeles County against 291 corporations allegedly responsible for smog. The judge lamented that "the court would have to balance interests already vested in other branches of government" and concluded that "it is an impossible job for any court to try to abate smog in Los Angeles County. . . . The problem is much too complex for any court to solve." *Los Angeles Times*, Aug. 21, 1969, §1, at 32, col. 1.

function. And within this constraint is the fact that burden-of-proof rules can have only so much bearing on any case, especially since they must work within the limitations of the applicable substantive law. Much of that law makes the problems of proof of cause and damage intractable even if "fault" or its equivalent can be established.[53]

Within all of these limitations, however, burden-of-proof rules can nevertheless perform a valuable service by stimulating thoughtful decision making about the environment, even if they cannot reach the more ideal goal of ensuring perfect decisions.[54]

[53] See e.g., Baxter, *supra* note 39 at 44-46; Malley, *supra* note 45 at 692-96. *But see id.* at 694, n. 44.

[54] Since the time of the conference in September, 1969, several interesting articles have appeared which develop, more extensively and in a broader setting, the themes of cost internalization and decision ventilation outlined in this paper. They are important reading for anyone who wishes to pursue the ideas I have sketched. *See* Katz, "The Function of Tort Liability in Technology Assessment," 38 *U. Cin. L. Rev.* 587 (1969); Sax, "The Public Trust Doctrine in Natural Resource Law: Effective Judicial Intervention," 68 *Mich. L. Rev.* 471 (1970).

Standing to Sue
in Conservation Suits

Louis L. Jaffe

I have been asked to examine this question: who can initiate or participate in proceedings to preserve or improve environmental amenities?
These proceedings may be administrative or judicial or a combination of
both. The proceeding may begin before an official or a board with powers,
let us say, to abate pollution, to license a power plant or set aside an area
for recreation. The action of the board may then be challenged in a court
on the ground that it is inconsistent with law or inadequately considered.
Though all such proceedings may be concerned in one way or another
with the quality of the environment, there are differences which may
have procedural significance.

Broadly we might divide them into two rough and ready classes. One
class would comprise what the Courts denominate nuisances. These are
cases in which private individuals, for example, are polluting the atmosphere or increasing the noise level or otherwise offending the sensibilities to a degree where their actions interfere seriously with the customary
private and public use or enjoyment of the environment. The quarrel here
has been traditionally with private individuals rather than government.
If an individual's property or health is particularly affected by a nuisance,
he may bring an action against the private individual to abate it or for
damages. But it has been the conventional rule that the public's right to
abate a nuisance may be enforced only by public authorities. If the
authorities fail or refuse to take action, the question then rises whether
a citizen or taxpayer or a resident may initiate the action, and if so,
against whom he brings the action—the offending individual or the lag-
gard public official or both. In recent years we have become familiar with
governmental action having the physical, if not the legal characteristics

of public nuisances, and these cases present special legal problems.

The other class of actions would be simply those which do not fall into the class of nuisances. They deal with conditions or projected actions which do not violate common law standards governing the use and protection of the physical environment, but which by reason of policies, usually of statutory origin, are subject to control by administrative officials. Examples are the power to set aside or preserve an area as a national park or wilderness area, the power to permit or not permit the erection of an electrical generating plant which will diminish the beauty of the landscape, the power to zone land uses and control development. In the absence of statutes, such uses and developments might not be so offensive to accepted standards as to constitute a nuisance. But a statute may empower an administrative officer to prohibit or condition a development, to apply a different calculus of utility than is customary in the common law.

In administrative theory, as expounded until recently, the official himself has been looked to as the guardian of the totality of interests represented by the statutory calculus of utilities. But it has become a commonplace—and like so many commonplaces, it is only partly valid —that the official position may become distorted in one or another direction. Put neutrally, this may mean simply that because some interests are over-represented and others under-represented, the official may give inadequate consideration to certain utilities. The commonest form of the criticism today is that administrative agencies are over-responsive to the interests of industry at the expense of the interest of consumers of goods or public amenities. This has led to the contention, now being accepted by the courts, that the consumer interest is entitled to independent representation in legal proceedings. The purpose of this paper is to canvass the available devices and forms for such representation.

There stands at the threshold a veritable Cerberus against intruders into the sacred precincts of the halls of justice, a constitutional doctrine most prominently derived from the Third Article of the Constitution of the United States. That is the Article which establishes the judicial power of the United States. It provides, among other things, that the judicial power shall extend to certain kinds of "cases and controversies." Very early in the history of the federal judiciary, the Supreme Court was asked by Thomas Jefferson, then Secretary of State, a series of questions as to the construction of certain treaties between the United States and France. The Court replied in effect that it would be inconsistent with the distribution of governmental powers and the judicial role of the courts to give advisory opinions.

The basic concept underlying its response is that the essence of the

judicial function is the decision of actual concrete cases, specific demands
for remedies, by those claiming they have been wronged, rather than
abstract hypotheticals. This is a concept based in part on notions of
competence, in part on the promptings of caution. The special competence of a court is to apply accepted rules, standards, and principles to
the solution of controversies, or to put it in another way, to do justice
as between parties according to law. This may require the making of
relatively new law, but a court's warrant for making a new rule is its
consistency with some already accepted principle. Where no rule can be
derived on that basis, the solution is more mete for a legislature than a
court.

If this concept is one of competence, it is also one of caution. A court
strives to maintain its independence to apply the law as it sees it and to
command the respect needed to make its judgments, however unpopular,
acceptable. The theory is that it can better achieve this objective if it
confines itself to its central function of deciding cases and refuses merely
to advise Congress, the President, or the public on abstract questions of
law or fact. There is a risk that if it allows itself too freely to give advice
it is liable to cross the uncertain line of law into politics and thus open
itself to legitimate politic attack with consequent impairment of its independence in administering justice.

It has been the official position of the Supreme Court that in order to
satisfy the case or controversy requirement the party seeking relief must
have "such a personal stake in the outcome of the controversy as to
assure the concrete adverseness which sharpens the presentation of issues upon which the Court so largely depends for illumination." *Flast v.
Cohen.* [1] This requirement of a "proper" plaintiff can be viewed in two
ways. It can be argued that as a matter of strict legal analysis there is no
"legal" case unless the plaintiff seeks protection for a right granted to him
by statute, the Constitution, or the common law. A notion demanding
a less rigid approach to the requirement is that the plaintiff have sufficient
interest to assure proper presentation of the case.

Not all of the judges of the Supreme Court agree that a proper plaintiff,
at least in any strict technical sense, is a constitutionally required element
of a case or controversy. In *Flast v. Cohen,* the Court allowed a federal
taxpayer to protest the constitutionality of a federal subsidy of church-
related activities. The majority of the Court reached its result by manipulation of the traditional formula. Every taxpayer it argued has a right not
to have payments made that violate the prohibition against the establishment of a religion; therefore the taxpayer was asserting his own personal

---

[1] 392 U.S. 83, 99 (1968).

claim. But this logic is infinitely expansible. A statute establishing conservation objectives, fair slum clearance practices, responsible broadcasting, etc., can be read—and the lower Federal Courts are so reading such statutes—as endowing with rights whoever can realistically assert a claim to enjoyment or protection. This still recognizes a limit somewhat short of Everyman but not a very significant limit.

A majority of the state courts do not accept even this limit. They, too, have constitutions that limit the judicial power to cases and controversies, but at least a majority of them allow what I find it useful to call a "public action." There is some dispute between Professor Davis and myself as to the exact number of states which do allow these actions. I have concluded that approximately 29 states allow a citizen—any citizen —to test the legality of official conduct by an action of mandamus, an action which in form requires the officer to perform an act which it is alleged he illegally refuses to do. In most all jurisdictions a taxpayer may enjoin local actions, and in at least 27 states and it may be nine more, a taxpayer may enjoin state actions that he alleges to be illegal and that involve the expenditure of funds, though the effect on expenditure may be incidental and (in many states at least) quite nominal. I would conclude that the constitutional obstacles to suits by interested citizens, taxpayers, residents, etc., are becoming less and less significant. There may still remain, however, obstacles deriving from common law or statute and from the exercise of judicial discretion pursuant to such concepts. A court may be reluctant in a particular case to entertain a "public action" brought by a person whose interests appeared to be remote or factitious or whose capacity to proceed is open to serious question. In a public action a court, in my opinion, has a discretion whether to entertain jurisdiction that it would not have if a plaintiff asserted a claim to legal protection peculiar to himself.

In the last few years there have been extremely important federal law developments in the concepts relevant to our concern. I have already spoken of *Flast v. Cohen*, which allows a taxpayer to raise the constitutionality of public expenditure allegedly in violation of the prohibition against the establishment of religion. This case rests in turn on the earlier line of cases holding that a voter may complain of improper election districting. But more to our purposes are the recent decisions in *Scenic Hudson Preservation Conference v. FPC,*[2] and *Office of Communication of United Church of Christ v. FCC.*[3]

In *Scenic Hudson*, the Federal Power Commission had granted Consolidated Edison a permit to erect a power plant on Storm King Moun-

[2]354 F. 2d 608 (2d Cir. 1965).
[3]359 F. 2d 994 (D.C. Cir. 1966).

tain. Scenic Hudson Preservation Conference, an unincorporated conservation association, petitioned the court to set aside the permit on the ground that the Commission had not satisfied its statutory duty to consider the impact of the power plant on the scenery of Storm King Mountain. The Court held that Scenic Hudson was a proper party to make such a claim. "In order to insure that the Federal Power Commission will adequately protect the public interest in the asthetic, conservational, and recreational aspects of power development, those who by their activities and conduct have exhibited a special interest in such areas must be held to be in the class of 'aggrieved parties,' that is to say, parties who under the statute are entitled to seek review of agency action by a court." The Court noted that Scenic Hudson had an economic interest as well. The New York–New Jersey Trail Conference, one of the two conservation groups that organized Scenic Hudson, had some 17 miles of trailways in the area of Storm King Mountain. Portions of these trails would be inundated by the construction of the project's reservoirs. I believe that this, however, was simply a convenient make-weight for the decision and was not necessary to it.

In the *United Church of Christ* case, the question was whether in a proceeding seeking to renew a broadcast license of a Jackson, Mississippi, station, representatives of the "listener interest" were entitled to participate in the administrative hearing and to seek review of an allegedly invalid order. The objection to renewal of the license came from Negro listeners and institutions in the community claiming that the broadcaster had not given fair representation to issues and activities of concern to them. Those seeking to participate in the proceeding were a local church, a national church organization, the Negro president of the NAACP of Mississippi and one other prominent Negro, both of whom were owners of television sets in the Jackson area. The Court decided that representatives of the listener interest were entitled to participate. It did not, however, decide the standing of any one of the actual plaintiffs. "The Commission," said the Court, speaking through Judge (now Chief Justice) Burger, "should be accorded broad discretion in establishing and applying rules for such public participation, including rules for determining which community representatives ought to be allowed to participate and how many are reasonably required to give the Commission the assistance it needs in vindicating the public interest. The usefulness of any particular petitioner for intervention must be judged in relation to other petitioners and the nature of the claims it asserts as basis for standing. Moreover, it is no novelty in the administrative process to require consolidation of petitions and briefs to avoid multiplicity of parties and duplication of effort."

It will be noticed that the approach of the Court in this case is not—as it was in *Flast v. Cohen*—solely or specifically in terms of the rights of particular plaintiffs but rather in terms of the value to the public qua-listeners in having effective representation. The Court is thus adopting the concept that I have advanced of a "public action" as opposed to a private action. This may mean that both at the administrative and judicial levels particular plaintiffs may be refused participation as non-representative or redundant. There is no reason, however, to predict that courts or agencies will impose strict or unsympathetic standards. They will probably demand no more than to be assured that there is a legitimate controversy of general public interest and that the plaintiffs are responsible parties, able effectively to present the case.

An important decision building upon *Scenic Hudson* is that of Federal District Judge McLean in *Road Review League, Town of Bedford v. Boyd*.[4] In this case the Court reviewed the legality of a decision locating an interstate highway. The decision, made by the Federal Bureau of Public Roads, was the final action in a controversy lasting six years. Each of the two alternative routes had supporters whose claims were both of an economic and conservation character. The Court reviewed the Bureau's action at the suit of a town, a civic association of the same town, two wildlife sanctuaries whose property was adversely affected, and a so-called road review league, a non-profit association concerned with the location of highways. The Court was prepared to hold that all of these were proper plaintiffs. The Highway Act declared that it was the national policy in carrying out the provisions of the Act to preserve park lands and historic sites and the Court held that any or all of these plaintiffs had a sufficient interest to make the claim that the Bureau's action gave legally insufficient consideration to these criteria. The decision is important because it could be thought to go a step beyond *Scenic Hudson*. In that case the statutes specifically provided that an "aggrieved person" is entitled to bring an action for judicial review. There is no comparable provision in the statutes establishing the powers of the Bureau to locate roads, that is, no provision for judicial review. The decision thus opens up to judicial review at the instance of representative persons any official action alleged to have ignored or violated statutory standards governing the action.

Recently the Federal District Court of Colorado has decided a case entitled *Parker v. United States*[5] involving similar questions. The suit concerns a decision of the Forestry Service to sell timber on lands immediately adjacent to a so-called "primitive area." These lands are poten-

---

[4] 270 F. Supp. 650 (S.D. N.Y. 1967).
[5] 309 F. Supp. 593 (D. Colo. 1970).

tially subject to presidential recommendation to Congress for inclusion in a "wilderness area," and it is claimed that the status quo cannot be changed until the Secretary of Agriculture has first considered whether or not to recommend the inclusion of these lands in a proposed wilderness area and noticed his recommendation for hearing. The Court has upheld this claim. The plaintiffs are a variegated group, the *Colorado Magazine*, the Sierra Club, and the Colorado Open Space Coordinating Council. The Court ruled against a motion to dismiss the action. The motion was based in part on the alleged lack of standing of the plaintiffs. It is, I think, significant that of all the issues in the case the judge was least concerned about the standing issue.

In a recent case *South Hill Neighborhood Association v. Romney* 421 F2d 454 (1969), the court interpreted *Scenic Hudson* as requiring the citizen group to have "been actively engaged in the administrative process and [have] thereby shown a special interest in the area in controversy." It may well be that most plaintiff associations will be able to meet this requirement, though that was not true in the *Romney* case itself. The moral is that associations should build up a record of participation in "the area of controversy" by various activities, pronouncements, etc.

One disturbing development at the hearing of the *Parker* case was the Court's ruling that the plaintiffs, if they demanded a temporary injunction, must put up a bond to indemnify the defendant against damage from delay should the defendants ultimately win the suit. The Court, on the suggestion of counsel for the lumber company to which the government had sold the timber, set the bond at $10,000. A condition of that sort on securing a temporary injunction in a case where such an injunction is necessary if the lawsuit is to be effective could be a serious obstacle to a public action. Counsel for the plaintiffs cited *Powelton Civic Home Owners' Association v. Department of HUD*[6] in support of the proposition that in a representative action of this sort against government officials it would defeat the purpose of the suit to require a bond. That was a suit by presumptively poor persons to enjoin a relocation project. The government, as a price of a temporary injunction, suggested a bond of $20,000,000! The *Parker* case, of course, may be thought different. The amount of the bond is comparatively modest. The plaintiffs are, perhaps, not impecunious. There is a private party defendant who may suffer damages as a result of the delay. It would, nevertheless, not be too out of line with the competing equities of such situations to grant at least short delays without requiring a bond. Attempts should be made to convince courts of the justice of this position. However, conservation

---

[6] 284 F. Supp. 809 (E.D. Tenn. 1968).

associations should also explore the possibilities of financing bonds as part of their budgeted litigation expense.

An alternative approach to conservation suits employs the common law concept of nuisance. Broadly defined, a nuisance is a pattern of conduct, usually involving the exploitation of land or space by the defendant which works a deterioration in the utilities and amenities of adjacent lands and spaces to a degree which the law is prepared to prohibit. As the definition implies, it is the court which in each case must make a judgment as to the relative utilities of the offending uses and the affected uses. It is obvious that in a society so committed to rapid change not every disturbance of the status quo detrimental to existing values and utilities will be enjoined—or even taxed by a payment of damages calculated to compensate those owners and users adversely affected. There is no formula for making these judgments beyond a rough calculation of the respective equities of the parties and the broader social interest in their respective uses.

Nuisance actions are traditionally divided into private and public. A nuisance is private insofar as the plaintiff is able to prove that the value (including, of course, the amenities) of his land has suffered. A nuisance is public insofar as it interferes with the uses and amenities to which the citizenry is entitled. It has been and continues to be the rule that a private individual—citizen, taxpayer, resident or what you will—does not have standing to bring action as a member of the public to enjoin or abate a nuisance. This power—and duty—attaches to public offices alone, be it the Attorney General or some county or city official. What then are the potentialities for standing in nuisance cases from the point of view of conservation groups?

The most obvious tactic is to prevail upon individuals who are particularly affected to bring action. Furthermore, such individuals may under recent decisions of the Supreme Court[7] be given financial assistance provided that those who give assistance do not stand to profit financially from the lawsuit. The type of case in which conservation groups will be interested will usually be such that there are many potential plaintiffs, many individuals, that is, whose property is affected. Indeed there are certain types of cases, e.g. air pollution, where the line between private and public injury may be insubstantial. A court might be prepared to hold that everyone within a certain radius of such a nuisance is particularly affected. If so, there should be no difficulty in having a suit brought in the name of one or more of these individuals.

There has recently been a very great development of the so-called

[7] *NAACP v. Button*, 371 U.S. 415 (1965).

"class action." This is a suit in which one or more persons of a class whose rights are more or less similarly invaded can sue as representatives of the class. There are certain limiting conditions for such an action. There must be a common question of fact or law and all of those in the class must be entitled to common relief. Of course, were the object of the suit to secure damages the latter condition would not be satisfied, since the amount of damages among the members of the class would differ depending on the amount and location of the property of each. But insofar as the relief asked for is an injunction the condition would be satisfied. A class action is analytically, I suppose, no more useful than one limited to the named plaintiffs, but psychologically it may carry greater weight and substance. It may in a sense go further in implicating the public interest and in this way increase the appeal of the case.

As far as I can discover, citizens or taxpayers have not to date been permitted to bring an action against a public nuisance as such (though a few states have statutes allowing such suits), and it has been held, for example, that the device of a class action will not permit them to bring a suit which they could not bring as individuals.[8] I have already noted that in many states citizens or taxpayers may sue to require public officers to perform their duties or to stop violating the law in such a way as improperly to expend public money. Attempts have been made by citizens to bring a suit (mandamus) to order the Attorney General to proceed against a public nuisance. To date (as far as I can find out) suits of this sort have failed, e.g. *Warner v. Mayor of Taunton.*[9] The notion behind these decisions seems to be that whether to take action against an alleged public nuisance is within the discretion of the public authority. Arguably the concept of representative plaintiffs now being developed in cases such as *Scenic Hudson* may play a role in a revision of party concepts in nuisance cases. It could be urged that representative plaintiffs be allowed to take direct action against a public nuisance (after, perhaps, seeking without success to induce the public authorities to act), or it could be urged that, in a citizen mandamus suit against the public authorities for their failure to act, the public authorities at least be required to justify their refusal and their action be subjected by the court to a test of reasonableness. It would probably be worth pressing for such a development. Nothing, for example, would be lost in having conservation groups, citizens, etc., join with clearly qualified persons in a private nuisance action, and perhaps eliciting a favorable ruling.

---

[8] *Pacific Interclub Yacht Association v Morris,* 197 F. Supp. 218 (N.D. Calif. 1960).
[9] 253 Mass. 116, 148 N.E. 377 (1925).

ADDENDUM

Since writing and delivering this paper the Supreme Court has decided *Association of Data Processing Service v. Camp.*[10] Does this decision significantly modify the conclusions arrived at in this paper? The question is not easy to answer. The case was one by an association of data processors against the Comptroller-General's ruling that banks could legally engage in data processing. The opinion for the Court by Mr. Justice Douglas is not as clear as it might be. The Court below held that the plaintiff did not have standing because he did not have "a legal interest by reason of statutory protection." This, said the Supreme Court, was wrong. Whether or not he has a legal interest goes not to standing but to "the merits." It is enough if (a) he is injured in fact and (b) "the interest sought to be protected is arguably within the zone of interests to be protected by the statute or constitutional guarantee in question."

I would have thought that this is not very different from the requirement as stated in earlier cases that the plaintiff have a legally protected interest in the sense that his interest was at least one that must be considered in arriving at a decision. And perhaps the formula set out by Mr. Justice Douglas in *Data Processing* means precisely that, as may be indicated by the citation of *Hardin v. Kentucky Utilities Co.*, 390 U.S. 1. Apparently the Court read the decision of the lower court as equating standing with success on the merits. That, of course, would be wrong since in *Hardin* itself the plaintiff ultimately lost on the merits. It has been clear for a long time that it is enough to ground standing that the plaintiff's interest is merely one of a complex of interests which the statute seeks to protect.

However, this criterion is perhaps somewhat relaxed by the Court in *Data Processing*. According to Mr. Justice Douglas the formula requires only that the plaintiff's interest is "arguably" within the area of protection. This would account for the actual decision that the plaintiff in *Data Processing* does have standing, because the argument that the statute means to protect the plaintiff is not too strong. The Court indicates that the basic purpose of the statute in question is to limit the entry of banks into extra-banking activities in order to maintain their soundness as banks rather than to protect non-banking competitors. However, it is no doubt "arguable" that Congress intended to give some protection to competitors from the powerful competition of banking forays into non-banking interests.

The effect of this relaxation (if it is one) is to assure the plaintiffs a more

---

[10]38 *Law Week* 4193, March 3 (1970). See also the companion case of *Barlow v. Collins,* 38 *Law Week* 4193, March 3 (1970).

thorough consideration of the merits than might be given if the case is decided on the preliminary issue of standing. Ultimately the plaintiff, if he is to win, must show that the statute meant to protect him and that he has been improperly deprived of that protection. It may be, however, that if the decision of the agency or officer appears bad enough on the merits this will move the Court to find that the plaintiff's "rights" have been violated or that, quite apart from his rights, the public should be protected.

The opinion reflects and confirms the growing disposition to grant standing to non-economic interests. The Court cites with approval *Scenic Hudson* and *United Church of Christ.* In sum, it is difficult to say that the decision carries the law beyond what has already been stated in this paper, but it quite clearly gives its blessing to the trends noted here.

The Right to a Decent Environment: Progress Along a Constitutional Avenue

E. F. Roberts

> As soon as April pierces to the root
> The drought of March, and bathes each bud
>   and shoot . . .
> Life stirs their hearts and tingles in them so
> On pilgrimages people long to go. . . .
> CHAUCER, *The Canterbury Tales*
>
> April is the cruellest month. . . .
> T. S. ELIOT, *The Waste Land*

THE CIVIL LIBERTARIAN'S TALE

Sitting in his air-conditioned office in an Ivy League university, a law professor long involved in civil rights litigation pauses to reflect upon the state of his intellectual affairs. Fresh from a swim in the enclosed, atmospherically-controlled pool just across the street, he peruses the latest tracts, brought to him by a research assistant, and discovers that they are filled with hosannas about equal rights, justice, privacy and participatory democracy. Why should the reverie of this perennial optimist be so self-satisfied?

Since the end of the Korean War the Supreme Court of these United States has seemed tempted to create a "right of privacy." The word create is apropos because privacy is not included in the list of rights inventoried in the traditional Bill of Rights. Whether the Court would have to manufacture this new right out of whole cloth or whether this right represents merely the shortly to be rendered explicit lintel capping an arch of rights already imminent in constitutional lore remains to be seen.

It is common knowledge that the Bill of Rights was designed to checkmate the new federal government. Originally the Fourth Amendment's "right of the people to be secure in their persons, houses, papers, and effects, against unreasonable searches and seizures" applied only against the central government. The content of the people's rights *vis à vis* their own state governments depended upon their local constitutions. This simple state of affairs was altered when the Fourteenth Amendment was adopted in 1868. This amendment postscripted to the Constitution the additional warning: "nor shall any State deprive any person of life, liberty, or property, without due process of law." With time this due process clause came to mean that the several states likewise had to accord to their citizens at least the fundamental rights guaranteed in the Bill of Rights. That is, while the states did not necessarily have to use a grand jury as the instrument to decide whether a person should stand trial,[1] a method required of the Federal system by a clause in the Fifth Amendment, they did have to respect those key rights "implicit in the concept of ordered liberty."[2]

Remarkable to us today, perhaps, was the fact that civil liberties-wise these constitutional provisions reflected only hollow rhetoric during the 19th and the first half of the 20th centuries. The police regularly burst through doors and ransacked premises without bothering to obtain a warrant and people were sent to jail on the basis of the incriminating data thereby discovered.[3] True enough, the invading police officers might be sued for trespassing on private property, but this was little solace for the imprisoned victim of their invasion.[4]

It was not until 1914, in *Weeks v. United States*,[5] that the Supreme Court clearly held that the product of an unreasonable search by federal officers could not be used as evidence in a federal court. This was done because the Court could no longer countenance a "direct violation of the constitutional rights of the defendant." It would appear, therefore, that the state courts would then have had to take the same view locally because the Fourteenth Amendment ordered the states to respect the fundamental rights guaranteed by the Bill of Rights. Indeed, when the question was faced squarely in 1949, the opening paragraphs of the opin-

---

[1] *Hurtado v. California*, 110 U.S. 516 (1884).
[2] *Palko v. Connecticut*, 302 U.S. 319, 325 (1937).
[3] Mr. Justice Brennan was still wringing his hands over police excesses in 1961. See his "The Bill of Rights and the States," 36 *N.Y.U.L.* Rev. 761, 778 (1961): "Far too many cases come from the states to the Supreme Court presenting dismal pictures of official lawlessness . . . and downright brutality." To catch a glimpse of "law and order" from the black perspective, see Miller, *The Cool World* (1959).
[4] "The truth is that trespass actions against officers who make unlawful searches and seizures are mainly illusory remedies." *Mapp v. Ohio*, 367 U.S. 643, 670 (1961) (concurring opinion).
[5] 232 U.S. 383 (1914).

ion delivered by Mr. Justice Frankfurter tended to this end.[6] He said, for example, "The security of one's privacy against arbitrary intrusion by the police—which is at the core of the Fourth Amendment—is basic to a free society." The question before the Court was, however, whether privacy was so sacrosanct that ill-gotten evidence could not be entertained in the state courts. His response to his question was no. That is, while privacy was basic to a free society, it was not such a fundamental element of the Bill of Rights that the due process clause required the states to follow the federal example!

Interestingly enough, the Court executed a complete turnabout in 1961 and held that the Fourth Amendment's right of privacy was such a fundamental right that state courts had no business using evidence acquired by violating this right.[7] In so doing Mr. Justice Clark observed that "we can no longer permit that right to remain an empty promise" and that the Court was simply giving "to the individual no more than that which the Constitution guarantees him."

What are we to make of all of this? First, that until Hitler's war at least, we were more of a class society than we care to admit. That is to say, the homes of the middle class were most likely secure from unreasonable searches simply because the local constabulary knew their place in the community. A sense of propriety still counted for something when a Norman Rockwell cover on *The Saturday Evening Post* typified a small-town-oriented culture. The lower orders who resided in rows of tenement houses were in no position to register any effective protest if they were victimized by the police because they had little real access to law and lawyers. The citizenry as a whole probably saw nothing untoward in jailing some culprit should a police raid "get the goods on him" because, after all, the poor bugger was guilty. While rough notions of frontier justice may have mellowed, folk heroes like Dashiel Hammet's Sam Spade illustrate that the crowd had little concern for constitutional niceties. In retrospect, therefore, the *Weeks* decision in 1914 may have been ahead of its time. This seems to be confirmed by the fact that for years thereafter the Court countenanced the "silver platter" doctrine whereby federal prosecutors were able to use evidence purloined by local as opposed to federal law enforcement officers.[8]

Second, Mr. Justice Frankfurter's refusal in 1949 to expand the *Weeks* rule and force it upon the state courts is quite understandable if we only

---

[6] *Wolf v. Colorado*, 338 U.S. 25 (1949).

[7] *Mapp v. Ohio*, 367 U.S. 643 (1961).

[8] This practice was not halted until *Elkins v. United States*, 364 U.S. 206 (1960). According to the Court then, the silver platter doctrine even "went unquestioned for . . . thirty-five years" after *Weeks. Id.* at 210.

pause to recall that "judicial restraint" was then *the* prime virtue of enlightened judges. The Court was still fresh from the intellectual wars of the New Deal period which had seen the rout of hyper-active judges bent upon imposing their own particular brand of truth upon the constitutional fabric. The year 1947 was a still point in the history of the Court, but new ideas of "justice" were already abroad in the land. Whether because of the idealism engendered by the war against Hitler, or because the Cold War required the nation to live up to its own rhetoric, or because nine decent men simply happened to believe that it was the fitting and proper thing to do, the Court under Earl Warren, C. J., was shortly to crystallize into effective rules a number of civil rights exhorted about in the Bill of Rights. What may not have been propitious in 1947 became so in 1961.

Whatever the merits of various theories about the decisional process of the Court, one thing is clear in terms of practical empiricism about the function performed by the Court when it makes constitutional law decisions. The Court provides a device by which the Constitution is interpreted in light of each succeeding generation. Cases having become the means by which the otherwise fairly inflexible written Constitution has been injected with the requisite flexibility, it has been possible to alter the *grundnorms* therein piece-meal without, at the same time, destroying the apparent continuity of the whole fabric. The measure of the Court's work is that, apart from the Civil War, the same ideal of a government of laws maintains today in an urban industrialized society as did in a rural, agricultural one 180 years ago.

Having become, in Max Lerner's phrase, "the keepers of the covenant,"[9] the Court exercises tremendous power on the American scene. According to its decisions, the Congress may or may not regulate a particular activity, the executive may or may not do a particular act, and at the same time, the balance of federal and state authority is demarcated. Still, the Court is not free willy-nilly to reinterpret the Constitution at its whim; its authority does not exist in a vacuum. Without funds of its own, without the concrete means of enforcing its orders, its decisions in the ultimate analysis depend upon the national conscience and the esteem in which the Court is held.

Thus, as Professor Carl Brent Swisher has observed:

The Supreme Court is able to lead in constitutional development, then, only by virtue of the fact that its leadership is of such a character that the people and their representatives are willing to follow. To put the matter more simply, the Supreme Court succeeds in leading largely to the extent of its skill not

---

[9] Lerner, *America as a Civilization,* at 442 (1957).

merely as a leader but as a follower. Since the medium of its leadership is the law, or the decision of cases in terms of the law, we can go further and say that the effectiveness of the Court's leadership is measured by its ability to articulate deep convictions of need and deep patterns of desire on the part of the people in such a way that the people, who might not have been able to be similarly articulate, will recognize the judicial statement as essentially their own. The Court must sense the synthesis of desire for both continuity and change and make the desired synthesis the express pattern of each decision.

The function of the Court is to make articulate that body of idealism and demonstrate the capacity for the merging of the each in the all, to the extent of the performance of nine men selected for that purpose, of nine men out of millions who make up our total population.[10]

Yet Max Lerner had a point when he compared the Justices of the Court to a "sacerdotal group. . . . [T]hey alone are privy to the mysteries on which the destiny of the tribe depends."[11] As we have observed, the Court's authority ultimately is rooted in the esteem in which it is held by the electorate, yet it seems clear that its decisions are held in such esteem because the Court's interpretation of the Constitution appears to be law, not judicial legislation. Thus, the Court operates in a field of considerable friction, at once being a legislative device by which the constitution is remolded in contemporary terms and at the same time not a legislature but a court discovering, according to hallowed principle, the law that always was. Professor McCloskey has demonstrated this phenomenon vividly:

For the fascinating thing about the Supreme Court has been that it blends orthodox judicial functions with policy-making functions in a complex mixture. And the Court's power is accounted for by the fact that the mixture is maintained in nice balance; but the fact that [the mixture is] . . . maintained in . . . the Court's claim on the American mind derives from the myth of an impartial, judicious tribunal whose duty it is to preserve our sense of continuity with fundamental law. Because that law was initially stated in ambiguous terms, it has been the duty of the Court to make "policy decisions" about it, that is, to decide what it means in the circumstances existing when the question is presented. But though the judges do enter this realm of policy-making, they enter with their robes on, and they can never (or at any rate seldom) take them off; they are both empowered and restricted by their "courtly" attributes.[12]

And, lest we tend to think that the judges simply use legal concepts to mask uninhibited political actions, it pays to remember that the justices

[10]Swisher, *The Supreme Court in Its Modern Role*, at 179–81 (1958).
[11]*See* Lerner, *supra* n. 9, at 442.
[12]McCloskey, *The American Supreme Court*, at 20 (1966).

themselves are products of the common law system, trained "to think like lawyers," *i.e.*, to think policy in a legal context and within legal rules.

Even saying this much fails really to illuminate the concept of privacy because all we have said so far could be reduced to the bald assertion that in 1961 the law finally put an effective halt to police invasions of a premises unless they were armed with a warrant or exceptional circumstances obtained. This would simply ratify the notion that the police should not trespass on private property. Such a reading of the law, however, would leave us totally unprepared to respond to the contemporary environment in which the police could simply resort to electronic gear and listen to conversations without the need for any physical invasion of premises whatsoever.

The Court has been responding, not without difficulty, to the problems posed by our technological era. In 1942, for example, the Court did hold that the Fourth Amendment had not been violated when police officers listened to conversations in an adjoining room by placing a "detecta-phone" against a wall.[13] In 1961, however, the Court found a Fourth Amendment violation when officers put a "spike-mike" into a party wall to accomplish the same result.[14] The case could be read as one holding that there had been an "unauthorized physical penetration" into the premises next door, but, then again, the Court gave an explicit warning that the decision did "not turn upon the technicality of a trespass."

More recently the Court had to deal with the conviction of an alleged bookmaker obtained when police officers attached an electronic listening and recording device to the outside of a public telephone booth from which he placed his calls. This was in *Katz v. United States*, decided at the end of 1967.[15] The prosecution and the defense both argued the case on two points. First, was a telephone booth so much like a home or an apartment that it too was an area deserving of protection from unreason-able searches and seizures? Second, even if one could equate the booth with a home, was there a violation of the Fourth Amendment when the listening device did not actually penetrate into the booth? The Court immediately made it clear that this easy formulation of the problem was not acceptable. The offer to debate whether a telephone booth was a "constitutionally protected area" was rejected, the Court noting that the incantation of talismanic phrases did not necessarily promote correct solutions to real problems. The real point, said the Court, was that "the Fourth Amendment protects people, not places." Similarly, the proferred debate whether a physical intrusion was necessary was also rejected

---

[13] *Goldman v. United States*, 316 U.S. 129 (1942).
[14] *Silverman v. United States*, 365 U.S. 505 (1961).
[15] 389 U.S. 347 (1967).

because "once it is recognized that the Fourth Amendment protects people—and not simply 'areas'—against unreasonable searches and seizures, it becomes clear that the reach of that Amendment cannot turn upon the presence or absence of a physical intrusion into any given enclosure." Manifestly, therefore, privacy is a personal right, not something keyed to the happenstance of one's geographical location in a house, or even a telephone booth. Indeed, a person cannot claim Fourth Amendment protection for what he knowingly exhibits to the public in his house, but might claim it for a private conversation conducted in a place accessible to the public.

While policing the police, the Court was faced with a knotty problem of privacy which arose in an entirely different context in *Griswold v. Connecticut*.[16] Two defendants, one an officer of the Planned Parenthood League and the other a licensed physician and Yale professor, were convicted of violating Connecticut statutes which made it a crime to prescribe instructions on birth control techniques even to married couples. According to the conventional wisdom which obtained when Mr. Justice Frankfurter refused to impose the *Weeks* rule on the state courts, there was little the Court could do to change the Connecticut result. The right to disseminate birth control information was not rendered explicit in the Bill of Rights and, perforce, there was no right to prescribe such information channeled *via* the due process clause of the Fourteenth Amendment into Connecticut jurisprudence. Judicial restraint, moreover, indicated that the Court had no business striking down a state measure regulating health, safety or morals simply because the Court did not agree with the wisdom behind the legislation. This was precisely the tack taken by Mr. Justice Black when the case came before the Court.[17] His opinion, however, was a dissenting one. In the majority opinion Mr. Justice Douglas held that the Connecticut statutes did transgress a zone of privacy protected by the Constitution.

Finding a zone of privacy protected by the Bill of Rights was no easy task since privacy nowhere is mentioned therein. Then again, while the First Amendment guarantees freedom of speech and religion, it does not explicitly guarantee anyone the right to send his children to parochial instead of public schools. Even so, the Court has struck down as an invasion of First Amendment rights an effort by a state to coerce children into the public school system.[18] Thus it must be understood that each of

---

[16] 381 U.S. 479 (1965).
[17] *E.g.;* "I do not believe that we are granted power by the Due Process clause ... to measure constitutionality by our belief that legislation is arbitrary. . . . Such an appraisal of the wisdom of legislation is an attribute of the power to make laws, not of the power to interpret them." 381 U.S. 479, 513.
[18] *Pierce v. Society of Sisters,* 268 U.S. 510 (1925).

the specific rights inventoried in the Bill of Rights may have "penumbras . . . that give them life and substance." Similarly, the First Amendment guarantees of free speech, press and religion implicitly guaranteed a further "freedom of association" so that a state cannot demand membership lists from legitimate groups.[19] This example, moreover, also illustrates that the First Amendment protects "the privacy" of one's associations. The Third Amendment's clause prohibiting the unconsented-to quartering of soldiers in any house during peacetime reflects "another facet of . . . privacy." As we have already seen, the Fourth Amendment protects privacy and so does the Fifth Amendment when it forbids self-incrimination. Finally, the Ninth Amendment tells us that the very act of listing certain rights in the Bill of Rights must not be construed to deny the existence of "others retained by the people." Privacy, therefore, is imminent within the penumbras surrounding several Amendments and, within the interstices wherein these several penumbras overlap, there is authority for the proposition that the Bill of Rights did create a right of marital privacy so fundamental that the statutes involved herein had to be declared unconstitutional for infringing thereupon.

Lawyers have often insisted that "hard cases make bad law" and *Griswold v. Connecticut* may very well be an example of this phemonenon. That is, the Connecticut statutes, while abhorrent to most of us, may still have been constitutional. The trouble was not law but politics: namely, the fear in the Connecticut legislature that it did not make political good sense to repeal these old statutes in light of the heavy Roman Catholic voting strength in the state. When the Connecticut courts failed to act, the Court solved the problem for them. To do so, however, the Court could not simply attack the wisdom of the legislation, but had to discover a right in the Bill of Rights which dictated the result. Arguably the ploy about intersecting penumbras really translates into a discovery of certain almost natural law–style higher rights, inferrable either from the several explicit rights or contained in the unstated body of Ninth Amendment rights retained by the people.[20] Interestingly enough, this is one of the very few cases wherein these "other rights" ever figured.[21] More interesting still, this decision could come to dog the

---

[19] *NAACP v. Alabama,* 357 U.S. 449 (1958).

[20] *See e.g.* Bork, "The Supreme Court Needs a New Philosophy," *Fortune,* at 138, 170 (December 1968): "One suspects that the new right of privacy is not a concept to be taken seriously but simply one more slogan that some Justices will use or not as convenient in the process of writing their own tastes into law."

[21] *See e.g.* Kutner, "The Neglected Ninth Amendment: The Other Rights Retained By The People," 51 *Marq. L. Rev.* 121 (1968). While Mr. Justice Douglas used the Ninth Amendment as one of the pieces in his opinion, it was Mr. Justice Goldberg's concurring opinion which relied almost exclusively on the amendment. He pointed out that the amendment was

Court when government someday attempts to make birth control mandatory since this likewise would appear to be an invasion of "notions of privacy surrounding the marriage relationship."

We must, however, immediately return to an examination of the *Katz* case which was decided *after Griswold*. If there are natural law-style rights retained by the people, and if the concatenation of isolated concern with various aspects of privacy in the Bill of Rights is added up, it could be argued that the sum of all this *is* that there is such a concept as *a* constitutional right of privacy. Significantly, however, Mr. Justice Stewart in *Katz* served warning that the Court was not translating the Fourth Amendment into any "general constitutional 'right of privacy,'" which he then defined in terms of the pioneering Warren and Brandeis study[22] of the problem as the "right to be let alone by other people." Should a landlord bug a tenant's bedroom for sheer erotic kicks, for example, it would appear that no federal rights would have been invaded. Instead the question would turn to what remedies are available locally to inhibit such behavior. Thus the scope of any general right of privacy equals the sum total of all legal rights available to a person to hold safe a secure enclave for himself, which at the moment means that most of this inventory consists of local law rules.

What then is the right of "privacy and repose" with which we have been dealing? Seemingly, there is no all-encompassing right to privacy, witness the warning in *Katz*, and it may be inevitable that there can never be such a thing as a claim to absolute privacy. "Virtually every governmental action interferes with personal privacy in some degree."[23] Indeed, if we participate at all in the credit-oriented private sector of our society, there is very little information about us that is not recorded somewhere these days on a computer tape. In *lieu* then of any far-reaching philosophic concept, we are dealing here with a set of *ad hoc* responses to the precise issue, raised each time in a different context, to what extent can we demand that the *instrumentalities of government* leave us alone? "For . . . fundamental is the right to be free, except in very limited circumstances, from unwanted government intrusions into one's privacy."[24] It

---

almost entirely the work of James Madison. Professor Bork has suggested that if the Ninth Amendment is construed to mean that the Bill of Rights is an "incomplete, open-ended document" that "it has revolutionary implications for the practice of judicial review, extending the range of individual freedoms far beyond the text of the Constitution." He admits, however, that there is "some historical evidence that this is substantially what Madison intended."

[22] "The Right to Privacy," 4 *Harv. L. Rev.* 193 (1890).

[23] *Katz v. United States*, 389 U.S. 347, 351 n. 5 (1967).

[24] *Stanley v. Georgia*, 394 U.S. 557 (1969). The right of privacy *vis à vis* non-governmental agencies is, of course, another issue which must eventually involve the Supreme Court.

remains to be seen why this question has become so vital in these times.

What has happened is that the Warren Court became aware that the citizen was powerless against the power of the burgeoning state. The talk of privacy and penumbras disguises the fact that the Court was restructuring the law to protect the citizen from the all-powerful state. Thus, out of the language available in various Amendments, the Court carved out a set of ground rules which immunized the citizen from overreaching by the police or even legislators reacting to a particular philosophy about sex. This right to be let alone transcends the home, and is rooted, not in the idea that one's home is a castle, but in the notion that the person, in certain private postures, has rights peculiarly his own. The fact that the "place" counts for less than the person—that constitutional law "protects people, not places"—is crucial because it signals the phenomenon underlying these recent developments.

It was Coke who said that "the house of every one is to him as his castle and fortress. . . ."[25] Observe, however, that this characterization was made not only at a time when old feudal ideas were fading away and political philosophy was being recast in modern terms, but also when the language and ideas of the times were still partly feudal and only partly modern. In opposition to the theory of divine right, for example, Locke had propounded his equally mystical doctrine of natural rights and had not spoken in terms of pure expediency or utilitarianism simply because his abstractions were "the accepted method of political reasoning."[26] Coke seized upon a medieval idea, the sacrosanct castle, and transferred the emotional charge of that idea from castles to houses. "Just as Magna Carta had been transformed from a baronial charter of privileges into a declaration of the rights of all free Englishmen: so Coke gave a new significance to a highly feudal principle when he argued that 'the house of an Englishman is to him as his castle.' "[27]

Before *Katz*, for example, arguments existed to elevate privacy to a constitutional issue. *E.g.* Ezer, "Intrusion on Solitude: Herein Civil Rights and Civil Wrongs," 21 *Law in Transition* 63 (1961). The latest and best study of the problem dares to question whether "the legal profession is ready to come to grips with the ramifications of the computer." Miller, "Personal Privacy in the Computer Age: The Challenge of a New Technology in an Information Oriented Society," 67 *Mich L. Rev.* 1089, 1246 (1969). Akin to the right to environment, this problem is achieving a high level of visibility. *See e.g.* Editorial, *The Times* (London), July 21, 1969, at 9, col. 2; Farson, "A Bill of Rights for 1984," *New Society*, June 12, 1969, at 908. An interesting twist to the problem of privacy was experienced by the author of this piece when his name was neatly purged from the official directory of law teachers. The only explanation has been that unidentified gremlins in the computer apparently decided that he should be "sent to Coventry" American-style.

[25] *Semayne's Case*, 5 Co. Rep. 91a, 91b, 77 Eng. Rep. 194, 195 (K.B. 1604).
[26] 6 Holdsworth, *A History of English Law*, at 293 (2d ed. 1937).
[27] Hill, *Intellectual Origins of the English Revolution*, at 237 (1965).

The Glorious Revolution, of course, was a triumph for the Whigs, and "[t]he great merit of Locke's political theories is the clear manner in which they state the ideals of the Whig party—the freedom of the individual from arbitrary interferences with person and property. . . ."[28] The real point was that the Revolution, "by diminishing the power of the crown, gave a larger measure of economic freedom."[29] The Whigs set about to consolidate this new area of economic freedom and did, in fact, lay the groundwork of *laissez-faire* society. "At the time of the Civil War, English industry was but little developed and English agriculture was very backward. When the *Wealth of Nations* was published, both had advanced enormously."[30] We are dealing in reality with a period when an ideology was propounded, an ideology which became the conventional wisdom in both England and America until the middle of the present century.

Within the context of the Revolution, the idea that a home was a castle had little enough to do with civil liberties of privacy in any personal sense. It was an economic idea in the sense that the castle syndrome was part of a particular ideology structuring the society upon incipient *laissez-faire* lines. Thus, houses had a role to play in the new economic *Weltanshauung*.

> For in the sixteenth and seventeenth centuries more and more Englishmen whose houses were also workshops became rich enough to be able to wage law; and at the same time governments strove more and more to enforce a regulation of industry and agriculture which could only be made effective by extending inspection into private houses.[31]

Thus it is that the house was sacrosanct, not in terms of privacy *per se*, but as an island of unregulated industry which formed the nucleus of the incipient Industrial Revolution then brewing.

This obsession with "property," of course, carried over to the American Revolution, for Daniel Webster could insist that:

> [T]he English Revolution of 1688 was a revolution in favor of property, as well as of other rights. It was brought about by men of property for their security; and our own immortal Revolution was undertaken, not to shake or plunder property, but to protect it. The acts which the country complained of were such as violated the rights of property.[32]

---

[28]6 Holdsworth, *supra* n. 26, at 288.

[29] *Id.*, at 341.

[30] *Id.*

[31]Hill, *supra* n. 27, at 237.

[32]Quoted in Beard, *The Economic Basis of Politics,* at 22 (1947).

The obsession with property, moreover, was to color the result of adopting the Fourteenth Amendment after the Civil War. Corporations were said to be "persons" within the eyes of the law,[33] and it was the corporations which received the benefits of "due process" when the Court protected them from all manner of state governmental interference.[34] Thus the battle to draw an intellectual moat between economics and politics shifted from Silas Marner's cottage to the abstractions of constitutional law. In the meantime, however, the civil rights of human persons went untended.

The very success of the business community between the Civil War and the New Deal era created a certain increment of ideological backlash which undermined their "private property" citadel. This development was best adumbrated by Schumpeter:

> The capitalist process, by substituting a mere parcel of shares for the walls of and the machines in a factory, takes the life out of the idea of property. It loosens the grip that once was so strong—the grip in the sense of the legal right and the actual ability to do as one pleases with one's own; the grip also in the sense that the holder of the title loses the will to fight, economically, physically, politically, for "his" factory and his control over it, to die if necessary on its steps. And this evaporation of what we may term the material substance of property—its visible and touchable reality—affects not only the attitude of holders but also that of the workmen and of the public in general. Dematerialized, defunctionalized and absentee ownership does not impress and call forth

---

[33] *Santa Clara County v. Southern Pac. R. R.*, 118 U.S. 394 (1886).

[34] One can date the era when the ideology of *laissez-faire* captivated the law from the *Slaughter House Cases*, 16 Wall. 83 U.S. 36 (1873), to *West Coast Hotel Co. v. Parrish*, 300 U.S. 379 (1937). *See e.g.* Tresolini, *American Constitutional Law*, at 330–31 (2d ed. 1965): "The majority of Court appointees had been influenced greatly by the propaganda campaign conducted by the American Bar Association in behalf of *laissez-faire* doctrine. The Association, which had been founded in 1878, 'became a sort of juristic sewing circle for mutual education in the gospel of laissez-faire.' " Of course, compared to the alleged autocracy advanced by George III, Whig *laissez faire's* emphasis upon individualism could be said to have been liberal. Thus, one commentator reflected conventional wisdom when, noting the trend since the New Deal era to place property rights second to social welfare, "that the liberalism of the past had become the conservatism of the present." Fenn, *The Development of the Constitution*, at 63 (1948). Observe also that the Court in *Griswold v. Connecticut* reflected the palpable fact that civil rights predominate today over traditional property rights. "We do not sit as a super-legislature to determine the wisdom, need, and propriety of laws which touch economic problems, business affairs, or social conditions." 381 U.S. 479, 482. Arguably this is just another prejudice as strong as that which obsessed the Court during the 19th Century. *See e.g.* Bork, *supra* n. 20, at 170. "[The Court] does not protect economic freedoms. . . . This arbitrary inequality cannot be justified. Rigorous extrapolation of the valid reasons for the Court's protection of nonpolitical speech would require the protection of freedoms in these other areas as well."

moral allegiance as the vital form of property did. Eventually there will be *nobody* left who really cares to stand for it—nobody within and nobody without the precincts of the big concerns.[35]

Interestingly enough, ever since the New Deal we now live in an epoch dominated by corporations controlled by a managerial collective and in an age enthralled by an ideology of partnership between government and business.

In the 19th century, when Horatio Alger was the centerpiece in the national hagiography, one achieved his due according to his place in the economy. An Andrew Carnegie enjoyed more practical freedom than a steelmill worker, but then again the worker was free to invent a better mousetrap or go "West" in search of riches. The parameters of freedom were fixed in terms of the choices money could buy because, in a day when government was supposed barely to govern, government did not threaten freedoms of this sort, such as they were. With the advent of active government and its partnership with even more coagulated business empires in a society planned by informal consensus, the idea that freedom measured in terms of market choices counted for much was destroyed. In *lieu* of economic freedom to boom or bust on one's own, we tend to think that there is no freedom unless there first exists economic security either in a salaried position or even on the dole.[36] In pursuit of this security, politics has replaced economics as the focal point of our concern simply because this security depends largely upon government largesse. Better mousetraps are invented today by salaried *apparatchiks* in corporate "R and D" units. There is no escape West: suburbia is everywhere. Increasingly, therefore, in a status society freedom has come to be internalized in the consciousness of the person in terms of his sense of freedom to be let alone to enjoy in his own way the fruits of his security.

We must, therefore, increasingly expect status to become a "right" and see a line of cases evolve relevant to it. More immediately, however, a person's right to do "his own thing" has already been the subject of the Court's scrutiny. We are free, after all, to take birth control advice before we enjoy the marital pleasures, as indeed we are free to enjoy obscenity in our own homes if we get our kicks that way.[37] Even poor womenfolk on the dole are immune from midnight raids which are designed to get the men out of their bedrooms.[38] More constructively, we are free from

---

[35] Schumpeter, *Capitalism, Socialism, and Democracy,* at 142 (3d ed. 1950).
[36] *See e.g.* Reich, 'The New Property," 73 *Yale L. J.* 733 (1964).
[37] *Stanley v. Georgia,* 394 U.S. 557 (1969).
[38] *Parrish v. Civil Service Commission,* 66 Cal. 2d. 260, 425 P.2d 223, 57 Cal. Rptr. 623 (1967). The recent decision by the Court which outlawed residential waiting periods as a precedent to receiving welfare in effect made the dole a right. That is, the more generous industrial

the government meddling in our intellectual, social and private lives and we owe this freedom to the Court's willingness to stand as a bulwark between our private lives and the potenitally all-pervasive nation-state.

EVERYMAN'S TALE

Let us posit a man sitting at the picture window of the library in his house on a hill overlooking a lake. Contemplating the recent work of the Court, he too takes solace in his "right to be free from state inquiry into the contents of his library." Not only is the "sacred precinct" of his marital bedroom off limits to the authorities, "what he seeks to preserve as private, even in an area accessible to the public, may be constitutionally protected." When he pauses from his ruminations to look out through the window, however, he must gaze through a maze of electric utility pylons in order to enjoy his view of the lake. The lake water no longer shines blue, its color having been changed by sewer effluents superheated by the water's use as a coolant for a nearby atomic power plant. He then rises to turn up the volume of his hi-fi set in order to drown out the noise of a jet aircraft, taking time to brush away the dust on the top of the set which has wafted in from a newly opened cement factory. This only causes him to remember that the cement is being poured into the foundations of new high-rise apartment houses being built in the midst of the last remaining natural spot still abutting the lake.

Inspiration suddenly strikes our hypothetical homeowner and he begins to question the value of his newly guaranteed zone of privacy. Privacy may be personal, but in a very real sense his home is being turned into a Cokelike castle all over again. That is, it is his last refuge from the war being waged against nature all around him. Arguably, his right to privacy is really a sop thrown him in order better to let him enjoy his coming imprisonment in the castle soon to be besieged all around by an uninhabitable environment![39]

---

states must accept the rest of the country's welfare cases or they must persuade the federal government to set a national standard. Politics can be counted upon to insure the eventual creation of a minimum income via federal sources in one form or another. *See Shapiro v. Thompson*, 394 U.S. 618 (1969). The Court's indulgence in dirty movies, however, should not be overinterpreted as a "new freedom" à la D.H. Lawrence. Sex in America has extraordinary commercial overtones and is a key factor in the mystique of consumption which is part and parcel of conventional wisdom. *See e.g.* "Notes From the Underground," *Cornell Law Forum*, Spring 1969, at 14.

[39]This may not be so fanciful as it sounds. In England, the Airports Authority Act of 1965 authorized the Minister [of Aviation] to "make a scheme requiring the Authority to make grants toward the cost of insulating . . . dwellings [near aerodromes]." For those who are

Apart from celestial maneuvers engaged in by astronauts, the platform for human activity is the earth, or, more precisely, land. The problem of environment can, therefore, be viewed from the perspective of land-use controls. That is, if each one of us, located on our particular terrestrial situs, did the appropriate thing, we could maintain an ecological balance. If what we do on land is not controlled, all hell can, nay, has broken loose. Thus we must investigate what controls we have over the use to which land is put.

The oldest device controlling land-use which concerns us is the law-suit known as the action for nuisance. In brief, the idea behind nuisance is that, if *B* next door, without trespassing onto *A*'s parcel, uses his property in such a way as to destroy *A*'s enjoyment of his parcel, *A* can petition a judge to enjoin *B* from continuing the noxious activity. Thus *A may* be able to put a stop to *B*'s all night jam sessions, noisy machinery, belching furnaces, and stink-making processes. The "may" is a necessary *caveat* because whether the irritating activity amounts to an actionable nuisance depends upon whether the behavior complained of is appropriate in light of the neighborhood where it is carried on. Should someone build a coke manufacturing plant in a residential area, inundating the neighbors with soot and smell, an injunction would shortly put an end to the activity. Should someone build a home in a manufacturing district next door to a coke manufacturing plant, he should not expect much relief from the law. Just as in modern day morals, rights and wrongs are relative to the circumstances in which the question arises.

Nuisance cases are really a form of zoning in which, after the event, the judges try to resolve discordant land uses. The judges play the role of referees, a role which forces them to apply their own value scale as to what are appropriate uses in the particular area which is the scene of the dispute. A bottling plant was once enjoined from using soft coal in the outskirts of Saratoga Springs, New York, for example, because the

---

still frightened by George Orwell, the functions of the Ministry of Aviation were transferred to the possibly ominous sounding Ministry of Technology. The Ministry of Aviation (Dissolution) Order 1967, 1 Stat. Instr. No. 155 (1967). In February, 1968, moreover, *House and Home*, at 8, reported that the Los Angeles International Airport was financing experiments with the construction of sound-proofed homes. Consider the very fact that the following questions were put: "What are the basic rights of an American citizen in the remaining third of the 20th century? Does he have a right to be exposed to nature's own weather? The right not to be exposed to man-made environmental contaminants injurious to health? The right not to be subjected to . . . life-shortening influences? The right not to be subjected to extraordinary noise?" Green, "The New Technological Era: A View From The Law," *Bull. Atomic Scientists*, Nov. 1967, at 12, 17–18.

judges decided that the area involved was a "country district suitable for country homes."[40] More recently, however, New York judges refused to enjoin a cement plant which was inundating a number of homes in the outskirts of Albany with large quantities of dust because the plant contributed to the "Capital District's economy."[41]

This last example, by the way, illustrates how a form of private eminent domain operates in this country. That is, where the perceived public-need causes the judges to refuse to enjoin certain activity, they may also recognize that the activity is nonetheless a nuisance which has improperly destroyed neighboring property values. In this event the judges can refuse to grant an injunction, because that remedy is said to be discretionary with them, and leave the injured party with a claim for money damages. The classic example of this "balancing of interests" arose in *Madison v. Ducktown Sulphur, Copper & Iron Co.*[42] There the plaintiffs had farms with an aggregate assessed value of less than $1,000. Defendants were "two great mining and manufacturing enterprises" worth the then immense sum of nearly $2,000,000, representing half of the taxable values in the county. Defendants reduced their copper ore by cooking it over open-air wood fires, thereby producing large volumes of sulphur dioxide smoke which very nicely turned the valley into a wasteland. The Tennessee court held that the plaintiffs were not entitled to injunctive relief because "the law must make the best arrangement it can between the contending parties, with a view to preserving to each one the largest measure of liberty possible under the circumstances." "Liberty" here meant that the companies were free to create a wasteland if they paid for it, whereas the farmers were free to take jobs with the industry and continue to reside in a valley totally polluted with chemicals.

Some writers admit that nuisance cases are a species of judicial zoning carried out on a sporadic, hit-or-miss basis but purport to see "a definite increase in judicial sensitivity to the character of the neighborhood."[43] This sensitivity remains to be seen. Consider, for example, two cases which arose in Washington.

In *Powell v. Superior Portland Cement, Inc.*,[44] plaintiff-homeowner sought to enjoin the creation of dust by defendant's plant. Plaintiff had resided in Concrete since 1907, had purchased his house in 1934, and had

[40] *McCarty v. Natural Carbonic Gas Co.*, 189 N.Y. 40, 81 N.E. 549 (1907).

[41] *Boomer v. Atlantic Cement Co.*, 55 Misc. 2d 1023, 287 N.Y.S. 2d 112 (Sup. Ct. 1967), *aff'd*, 294 N.Y.S.2d 452 (App. Div. 1968).

[42] 113 Tenn. 331, 83 S.W. 658 (1904).

[43] Beuscher & Morrison, "Judicial Zoning Through Recent Nuisance Cases," 1955 *Wis. L. Rev.* 440, 443.

[44] 15 Wash. 2d 14, 129 P.2d 536 (1942).

lived in it until 1938 when he began to rent it. The cement plant had been in town since 1908. Indeed, it appears that the town grew because of the plant, and that the local economy was dependent on it. The installation of newly devised dust-catching machinery would have alleviated the problem, but the costs would theon have been enormous, requiring total reconstruction of the plant. The trial court refused plaintiff an injunction, but awarded him $500 damages. The Washington Supreme Court reversed even the award of damages lest the principle established thereby "encourage litigation which would unreasonably harass industry . . . which it is the policy of the law to protect within reason."

Ten years later, the same court decided *Riblet v. Spokane-Portland Cement Co.*[45] This time plaintiffs sued to recover for damage to their residential property caused by cement dust. Here, however, the same supreme court reversed the trial judge who relied on *Powell,* and announced modestly that "rights as to the usage of land are relative" and that the "crux of the matter appears to be reasonableness." Again the company had arrived in 1910, the town had grown up around the plant, and the plaintiffs had arrived later. This time, however, plaintiff's property was located on a plateau some 3,000 feet away, and perhaps significantly, the plaintiff husband was an "official" of a tramway construction company and an "investor." Illustrative of their independent suburban status, moreover, were the facts that plaintiffs owned a vista house, a garage, a swimming pool, a croquet court which could be flooded in the winter to serve as a skating rink, and an outdoor checkerboard with giant-sized checkers. On these facts, the high court found the case distinguishable from *Powell.* The neighborhood, after all, was not devoted solely to industrial activity, "that is, the production of cement."

It seems fairly safe to assert that a suburban dream house has become part of the contemporary concept of utopia, which makes all the more interesting the Riblets' testimony that their home was "the culmination of their dreams." As a tentative hypothesis, therefore, the nuisance cases thus far examined can all be organized around the rule that a home in a suitable suburban locale has become sacrosanct in American thought. Inhabitants of areas adaptable to "country-style living" merit protection against the inroads of tranquility-upsetting industrialization. The poor dirt farmer and the city dweller, however, must grin and bear it amidst the grime and stench of "progress."

Zoning, in its original World War I format, was a legislative solution to the problems caused by discordant land-use decisions. It was, in substance, simply a verbal prophylaxis custom tailored by municipal govern-

---

[45] 41 Wash. 2d 249, 248 P.2d 380 (1952).

ments to prevent the spread of the nuisance contagion. If every village and town was carved up into several distinct industrial, commercial and residential zones, theory had it that the land uses within each district would inevitably be harmonious and, perforce, nuisances would disappear. The whole idea that a use-map could be dropped down over a given community and that the districts drawn thereon would solve the problem presupposed a static community in which the only movement would involve the internal migration of existing users into the appropriate districts. This was not the case because communities persisted in expanding. Thus zoning has only been a success if success is measured in terms of preserving middle-class and expensive (pronounced "white") bedroom communities around urban centers. In center city, zoning seems only to have slowed inevitable change, or merely necessitated that change should require an illicit tithe; be that as it may, zoning has not appreciably altered the market-dictated development of center city.

Modern zoning enthusiasts claim that zoning has become dynamic in the sense that it is merely one tool in the planners' kit. This, however, has necessitated a return to nuisance-style thinking. The now much vaunted "planned unit developments," for example, envisage an entrepreneur installing a succotash of stores, apartment units and single-family homes in mini-villages of sorts if the planners approve of the site. Thus the static district map has given way to districts custom tailored to the felt needs of the moment. Uniformity within the district, moreover, has been replaced by any mixture which will pass muster as not likely to cause nuisances among themselves. Significantly, the decision whether and what to develop still depends upon the market so that planning, so-called, really entails the planners playing the role of *ad hoc* prophylaxers.

Legal responses to the problem of ordering land use, therefore, are not decisions how to use land but rather umpire decisions resolving or avoiding discordant market-dictated uses. The results of this system are not hard to see. Suburbia tends to form a white noose around center city, a phenomenon which has only exacerbated the race problem.[46] Developers, moreover, only want to improve flat land in order to keep costs down, but these flat lands are apt to be viable agricultural land. However high the value of the land for agriculture, agriculture is nonetheless quickly priced out of the land market once the suburban sprawl arrives.[47] So

---

[46] *See e.g.* Sager, "Tight Little Islands: Exclusionary Zoning, Equal Protection, and the Indigent," 21 *Stan. L. Rev.* 767 (1969).
[47] Ciriacy-Wantrup, "The 'New' Competition For Land and Some Implications for Public Policy," 4 *Nat. Res. J.* 252 (1964).

avaricious indeed are the locustlike suburbanites that this process may promise us a food shortage in the none too distant future.[48] What these developments have done to the water table, by way of extraction, and to the rivers, by way of sewage, does not even bear repeating.[49]

After the suburban exodus, of course, center city's population level has been maintained by the migration from the South, victims of mechanization, and from Puerto Rico. The city increasingly has become a car-filled, manufacturing and commercial high-rise site of feverish daytime activity. After dark, however, there is little real difference between Lincoln Center and the Dakota Bad Lands: both are desolate wastelands, and hostiles abound. Indeed, this after-dark phenomenon has generated the greatest political force with which we must now contend as the whites too poor to move, or too rich to want to move, to suburbia have become obsessed with the law and order syndrome.

The city, moreover, with its high-rise architecture, factory chimneys, incinerators, apartment house boilers and automobiles, has achieved a remarkable break-through; that is, the city can do something about the weather![50] The city warms up quicker in the morning and cools more slowly in the evening, its high-rises baffling any breezes so that it creates its own heat island around and above it. This, in turn, causes a dust dome to form over the city, replete with its own noxious gasses and particles. London has, of course, already suffered 3,500 to 4,000 dead in one losing battle with smog, but this record is bound to be broken.

In a real sense, therefore, a reflective citizen must begin to sense that he is trapped in a deteriorating environment. A future in which he is condemned to live indoors and travel in air-conditioned corridors, subject at the same time to food rationing, is not totally impossible. This is all the more absurd because the economy holds the promise of increasing leisure, what with a forty-week, four-day work cycle. His potential right to privacy turns out, therefore, to be the right to enjoy his coming encapsulation away from the wasteland that once was his natural environment.

CONSENSUSMAN'S TALE

A political columnist for a national newspaper likewise is engaged in

---

[48] Allee, "American Agriculture—Its Resource Issues for the Coming Years," *Daedalus* 1071 (1967); Gould, "Urban Sprawl and Its Spatial Implications," 9 *Curr. Mun. Prob.* 219 (1967).
[49] *See e.g.* Dickinson, "The Process of Urbanization," in *Future Environments of North America*, at 463, 471 (1966); Gottmann, *Megalopolis*, at 729-35 (1961); Warne, "The Water Crisis Is Present," 9 *Nat. Res. J.* 53 (1969).
[50] *The New York Times*, July 30, 1967, Sec. IV, at 10, col. 1.

contemplating the apparent decline in the environment around him. He can recall, however, that the nation went through a similar period of despondency during the Great Depression, yet the Republic survived. True enough, the use of federal credit *à la* Keynes may not have worked immediately because the new economics frightened the business community, and it did take the 1941–45 war to get the economy going again. The war, however, also got government and business used to working together and created the psychological basis for contemporary Keynesian conventional wisdom. Since the war business depends upon the government's tax and spending policies to encourage growth without untoward inflation. In its turn the government's tax and spending policies encourage growth without untoward inflation. In its turn the government is dependent upon a healthy business climate because, taxing the profits of business at roughly 50 percent, the government has become the single largest investor and beneficiary of the so-called free enterprise system. In large measure, therefore, the corporations finance the central government, while the central government is committed to maintain an economy conducive to the corporations.

This new society has become so complex that the man in the street cannot hope to formulate a grasp of it. In 19th century England it may have been possible to follow Hansard and take a position on some clear-cut issue, but in our complex society clear-cut issues are all but nonexistent because of the interdependent variables involved. Conventional wisdom now tends to be filtered through the particular group to which one belongs, be it the ACLU, ADA, the Birch Society or CORE. Any consensus, therefore, is not so much the meeting of minds of the masses but the general agreement of these intermediate bodies. Ours, then, is an era of the collective, and the collectives' thinking is influenced in turn by the consensuses hammered out among them by federal and state executives. In large measure the constructive thinking which leads to the accommodations among these collectives is done not only in the governmental agencies and at the top echelons of these interest groups, but in the foundations and universities. We are ruled by consensuses arrived at among the leaders of these collectives, who themselves are on the verge of constituting themselves an interchangeable establishment: witness Ted Sorensen representing General Motors, McGeorge Bundy at the Ford Foundation, and Professor Haar in Washington.

In our era the idea about using the ballot box to achieve change ignores the facts that the several collectives have cancelled each other out and that legislative change is possible only if the collectives can be brought together into a consensus presided over by the executive department. In point of fact it could be seriously argued that parliamentary democracy is losing its significance in England, and that it is only as a check upon the executive that Congress remains significant in this country.

Although the solution to the Great Depression was to use federal credit to stimulate private spending, the post-World War II conventional wisdom focused on production and, necessarily, consumption. If sheer production will keep everyone employed and in the long run filter purchasing power down to the poor, it becomes essential to sustain consumer demand for products. People must not cease to desire; and no eccentric bauble, be it an electric toothbrush or an electric knife, is to be denigrated if consumer demand for it can be stimulated by the advertising media. It is within this context, moreover, that suburban housing has been carefully nurtured as the keystone to consumption of all the paraphernalia of the affluent society.

The keystone in this whole structure has been the assumption that resulting full employment and increased personal income will seep down to the lower orders and thus remove poverty. Presupposing that the industrial revolution is alive in the United States, and that the problem of the poor involves only a lack of income, the rationale would appear sound. The fates, however, have undercut the assumptions supporting this Keynesian world. The United States is no longer involved in the Industrial Era, for the country has broken through into a new epoch, the Technological Revolution. The computer, automation, systems analysis, consumer research, cybernetics, and planning have replaced the old axioms of raw production and natural resources exploitation.

This Technological Revolution has left innumerable people ineligible to join the projected march to prosperity. Unskilled labor has become an irrelevant segment of society. Putting the unskilled to pasture, however, has had a profound impact on the cities. Just as suburbia lured away the successful, the cities have drawn these itinerant "misfits." Integration, to say nothing of assimilation, into the normal patterns of society has been barred by racial prejudice and educational deprivations. Thus, we have with us the unsolved problem of the poor. At the same time, the affluence achieved by their betters has proved somewhat illusory. Of what value is material affluence if, as John Kenneth Galbraith suggests, the air itself is too dirty to breathe, and the water too polluted to drink?

The poor, however, have one advantage. As they crowd more and more in the cities, they create the spectre of revolt. The image of a gutted Wall Street or a second torch being put to the White House can set the various members of the new government-business collective to work on methods of placating the poor. Evidence of this can be found in the very fact that some form of negative income tax is no longer an unthinkable expedient. Indeed, conventional wisdom is tending toward the notion of some kind of guaranteed minimum standard of living which will purchase society a time-frame during which education and training can be applied to bring the poor back into productive participation in a technologically oriented society. Thus an admixture of *Realpolitik* and a belief in contemporary wisdom may blend readily enough to afford some hope that the problem of the poor can be solved by conventional political action.

Solving the problem of the poor is really a long-term investment in even more affluence in the future as more self-supporting consumers are brought into the system and the burden of welfare correspondingly decreases. Note carefully, however, that this emerging consensus reflects a built-in predilection for not merely maintaining the economy, but to filter all reforms through the litmus test of affluent society economics. If we are bent on fixing a high standard of living as the *alpha* and *omega* of progress, then anyone interested in the quality of the so-called good life must pause to wonder, Why? Because the production of pollutants and an increasing need for pollution management are an inevitable concomitant of a technological society with a high standard of living. Pollution problems will increase in importance as our technology and standard of living continue to grow.

THE POLITICAL PHILOSOPHER'S TALE

A political philosopher riding on an airplane between Syracuse and Chicago spends his time looking out through the window. Over Buffalo he views the inspiring panorama of Niagara Falls. At the same time he cannot escape noticing the voluminous smoke emitting from the Buffalo mills as the pall wends its way eastward over the green countryside. A few minutes later, after enjoying what appeared to be the clear blue waters of Lake Erie, he observes that Detroit is almost totally obscured in a dense cloud of red-tinged smoke. Still later, as the aircraft begins its gradual descent over Lake Michigan, he is surprised to see a cone of smoke working its way northwards parallel to the lake's surface for some 40 miles from Gary. Then, as the plane banks into the final approach pattern near Chicago, he notices that the lake water there is not really blue but slate gray, its dullness highlighted here and there by all manner of flourescent oil slicks and coagulating effluents. For just a moment he wonders whether, like Cleveland's river, these waters will actually support a fire, our technological era's equivalent of the miracle of walking on water.[51]

The aging accumulation of case lore involving nuisance, the later legislation authorizing zoning, and the contemporary concern over land-use

---

[51] *The New York Times*, June 29, 1969, at 38, col. 3.

planning still boil down to a single axiom: "Each use in its proper place." The difficulty with this axiom is that, relative to strip mining, coke manufacture and jet airports, it naturally invites the accompanying corollary that a pig in its proper place is a proper pig. That is to say, if all of the mills in Buffalo and the plants in Detroit can be segregated into an "industrial use" district, then all will be right with the world. A fan of McLuhan might be able to make something of this phenomenon because the neat segregation of colors on a use-map seems sufficient in itself to satisfy the planners' urge for order. Still, these maps do not depict the clouds of soot emitted by coke-ovens, the exhaust uttered by automobiles and the sewage dumped into rivers which, in a real world, illustrate that land users are not so neatly to be segregated.

True enough, there has lately appeared in these United States and in the United Kingdom an awareness that some kind of environmental quality control has to be superimposed upon the land-use grid. Both countries have, for example, enacted Clean Air Acts.[52] The federal government here will match local appropriations for air pollution programs, but this program remains exhortatory rather than mandatory at the national level and largely academic at the local level. Anyone who has lived in the Midlands or tasted the air in Detroit, to say nothing of Los Angeles, must retain a certain amount of skepticism about the immediate efficacy of these schemes.

If, as we have suggested, the United States is ruled by consensus, and politics have assumed the primacy once held by *laisser-faire* economics, we can expect that an enlightened public over the long haul will demand that something be done about its environment. Nevertheless, as Keynes observed, in the long run we are all dead. In this context, however, the Keynesian dictum is not funny at all: rather than a witty aside it may all too accurately depict the future awaiting all of us. Concomitantly, if we are indeed ruled by the ultimate consensus arrived at among the various collectives which make up our society, given the race to make outer space safe for the "free" world, the need to maintain the capacity for limited wars on the fringes of the empire, and the immediate need to pacify the more militant poor at home, the political viability of a campaign to render the environment secure by legislative action remains a dubious bet at best. Hence, the most attractive route leading toward concrete results may be along the constitutional avenue.

But why a constitutional tack? Because, as we have said, the Court has been the device by which questions of fundamental structure have been resolved in this country and, if the nation is going to be put in a posture

---

[52]Clean Air Act, Public Law 88–206, 77 Stat. 392 (1965), later amended by the Air Quality Act of 1967, P.L. 90–148, 81 Stat. 485; Clean Air Act, 1956, 4 & 5 Eliz. 2 c. 52.

where it must face the question of environment, some heady restructuring has got to be done. Given the contemporary participation in the conventional wisdom of affluence which afflicts most of our collective social groups, the legislature has ceased to be an effective originator of ideas because the legislature, unlike the executive, lacks the ruthless democratic centralism necessary in order to adopt a clear-cut posture with which to take the initiative in consensus building. Classic notions of democracy notwithstanding, it is the executive which rules, if any rule there is, and this rule is successful only to the extent that the executive's policies crystallize the consensus possible among the various collectives.

Consensus does not necessarily reflect justice. It was the Court, after all, which decided *Brown v. Board of Education,*[53] the classic recognition that the Republic has to be reconstituted if it is not to wallow in a racism more suitable to South Africa. It was the Court, moreover, which decided *Baker v. Carr,*[54] the case which necessitated that electoral districts be redrawn in order to reflect more accurately the one-man one-vote axiom fundamental to the democratic process. The Supreme Court of the United States has not been alone in re-adjusting traditional rules in order to re-structure the ground rules of the nation in order to make possible necessary social responses to contemporary problems. In an environment where consumption outweighs saving for a rainy day, the several state courts have created an *ersatz* system of social insurance for the victims of accident by making manufacturers strictly liable for injuries occasioned by their products.[55] Indeed, several state courts have even begun to treat new houses just like any other manufactured product in this regard, notwithstanding the traditional lawyer's obsession that anything to do with real property was at once removed from any changes occurring in the rest of the *corpus juris.*[56]

Thus there is a certain intellectual awareness abroad in the land that changes must be made in the decisional law to make it more responsive to the needs of contemporary society. Concomitantly, there is a growing awareness that something needs to be done about the deteriorating environment. In London, *The Times* has reported that "planning and application of pollution control lag far behind what is needed,"[57] and that the problem cannot be solved "simply by the production of greater

---

[53] 347 U.S. 483 (1954).

[54] 369 U.S. 186 (1962).

[55] *See e.g.* Roberts, "Negligence: Blackstone to Shaw to? An Intellectual Escapade in a Tory Vein," 50 *Cornell L. Q.* 191 (1965).

[56] *See e.g.* Roberts, "A Eulogy for the Old Property," 20 *Me. L. Rev.* 15 (1968).

[57] Smith, "Stronger Powers Needed to Control Industrial Waste," *The Times* (London), July 3, 1969, at 9, col. 5.

wealth."[58] *The New York Times* complains that American "rivers are cesspools and the cities slums."[59] Interestingly enough, the paper's same editorial writers have suggested that it would require nothing less than "the redirecting of all [of the country's] priorities to restore what has been spoiled." Implicit in the intellectual milieu of the day, therefore, is the felt need to restructure the society in order to encourage the necessary responses to this growing crisis.

Of great significance, moreover, is the growing recognition that people have a right to be heard when administrative decisions affecting their environment are made. Thus the Federal Power Commission recently licensed the Consolidated Edison Company of New York to construct a pumped storage hydroelectric project at Storm King Mountain along the Hudson River. The site chosen happened to be "an area of unique beauty and major historical significance." Subsequent litigation established two important points.[60] First, that a conservation group and two towns in the area had sufficient interest in the affair to enter the courts to seek a reversal of the administrative decision. Second, that the Commission had to rethink the grant of the license, not merely in terms of cost-accounting, but in such a way that they included in their judgmental scales "a basic concern for the preservation of natural beauty and of national historic shrines." Indeed, the federal court explained that one of the reasons for its decision on the standing to sue question had been "to insure that the Federal Power Commission will adequately protect the public interest in the aesthetic, conservational, and recreational aspects of power development."

The case, however, only established that the agency should have taken the environment problem more seriously into account in the process of making a decision. Even if administrators are ordered to worry about environment, a decision still may have a deleterious impact upon an individual's environment. Consider, for example, a story recently related by Mr. Tom Wicker in *The New York Times*.[61] Ten New England power companies are financing the construction of a nuclear power plant along the Connecticut River in Vermont. Simply to pour the river water used as a coolant back into the river would heat the water downstream to a point whereat even the warm-water fish would be exterminated. The local Water Resources Board responded to this threat by setting a limit

[58]Editorial, *The Times* (London), July 21, 1969, at 9, col. 2.
[59] *The New York Times*, July 23, 1969, at 40, col. 1.
[60]*Scenic Hudson Preservation Conference v. Federal Power Commission*, 354 F. 2d 608 (2d Cir. 1965).
[61]Tom Wicker, "In the Nation: Paying A Price in New England," *The New York Times*, July 20, 1969, Sec. IV, at 13, col. 4–7.

on the temperature of the water poured back into the river. This resulted in saving the fish, but it means that two massive cooling towers will have to be built, the costs of which will be passed onto the users of electricity. The cooling towers in their turn will threaten to become two giant humidifiers capable of creating mist and fog immediately around them. What happens, however, if several homeowners in the vicinity are not particularly happy to find that now they live in the midst of a man-made environment more typical of an English Gothic novel than of their native Vermont? This is the same problem encountered earlier by the several homeowners in the Albany area when a cement plant opened nearby and inundated them with dust. The court, as we noted, refused to enjoin the plant but allowed the homeowners to collect the depreciation in the value of their homes by way of a money judgment. Presumably the Vermont courts would not shut down a power plant and would adopt the same approach.

In theory, of course, the authority to seize private property belongs to the instrumentalities of government, whether federal, state or local, and they can exercise this authority only when they intend to put the land to a public purpose. Until recently condemnation involved the seizure of a whole parcel or a strip thereof. It was possible to distinguish nuisance-style damages, which left the owner in possession of his whole but possibly worthless tract, and condemnation, which saw the government take the whole or a part of the parcel away from him. More recently, courts have come to recognize that condemnation may involve the seizure of more intangible interests in a parcel which leaves the owner in possession of the same horizontal area as before just as in the instance of nuisance. An Air Force glide path over a farm house has been likened to the seizure of a path across the property.[62] A county airport, the jet noise from which made homes uninhabitable, has been held to have amounted to condemnation in fact of an interest in land.[63] If a noise vector across land amounts to condemnation, why doesn't the seizure of a right to lay cement dust on it amount to a similar seizure? Looking at the scene itself, a home made uninhabitable because one goes crazy from the noise or because one chokes to death on dust appears to be one and the same thing in the sense that the enjoyment of the home has been destroyed. Adopting this empirical approach, however, leads to a startling result! Only government and its instrumentalities are authorized to condemn property. Hence, in this day and age, the ancient notion that courts sitting in nuisance actions can balance interests and refuse to enjoin what amount to private exercises

[62] United States v. Causby, 328 U.S. 256 (1946).
[63] Thornburg v. Port of Portland, 233 Ore. 178, 376 P.2d 100 (1962).

of the power of eminent domain is manifestly unconstitutional.

This need not bring an instant halt to every cement plant and power station in the country. As Professor Leach has suggested, there is no reason why the courts should not make such a ruling prospective, leaving it to legislative initiative to attack the already existent problems of pollution.[64] The point is that such a ruling would block the creation of new environment-poisoning operations in built-up areas. The reality imposed by transportation costs from rural areas would seem to insure that any new industrial users in these built-up areas will have to employ the technological imagination prerequisite to avoid causing pollution. Such a prospective embargo would, therefore, prevent the situation from getting any worse.

THE RIGHT TO ENVIRONMENT

All the great revolutions of our contemporary world had their origin round the North Atlantic.

> Barbara Ward, *The Rich Nations and the Poor Nations*

There has been much talk about the lack of any discernible order in our present environment. I think this largely nonsense. Is not the common denominator capital gain and material accumulation? Is not the pattern of our environment very largely that of real estate interests and advertising maniacs? . . . Our task—as professional people and as citizens—is to formulate standards; to set forth as a conference ten or twelve propositions on which we are willing to stand up. Let us begin this, here and now.
C. Wright Mills, *The Big City: Private Troubles and Public Issues*

A man's land, or merchandise, or money is called his property. [But] a man has property in his opinions. . . . He has property very dear to him in the safety and liberty of his person. . . .
If the United States mean to obtain or deserve the full praise due to wise and just governments, they will equally respect the rights of property, and the property in rights.
James Madison, *Property and Liberty*

---

[64] Leach, *Property Law Indicted!*, at 14–24 (1967).

Thus far we have only come up with a tentative and modest change in the law of property and the rules of procedure which might help to alleviate the situation. The gravity of the situation is such, however, that these are not appropriate times during which to temporize. We must face squarely the ultimate concern whether or not there exists a personal right to a decent environment.

A careful reader of all that has gone before might have observed that the Storm King hydroelectric project came a cropper because organized interests took the field to oppose it. Similarly, the New England electric companies had to temporize with Vermont authorities who reflected the mood of sundry conservationist forces interested in the Connecticut Valley, to say nothing of Vermont's own interest in the tourist industry. The individual homeowners outside Albany, however, lost. Where collectives are involved fighting to protect a recognized area, therefore, there is some hope for a decent environment; the individual homeowner is at the mercy of politico-economic *apparat*, the mutations of which transcend and overpower him. Hereat, however, we reach the nub of the matter because, to rest content with the countervailing force of collectives is to leave Everyman at the mercy of the system of affluence which has exacerbated his plight. We need, after all is said and done, to fashion some new viable foothold from which the common man can assert that, as a free individual, he has some personal claim to a decent environment in which to live.

Our hypothesis has been that there no longer exists an independently functioning economy subject to its own internal laws: business and government have merged into an interlocking whole which runs the gamut from local zoning ordinances to national economic policies which influence business decisions. In short, the several governments are the effective partners in the decisional workings of the market-place. If, however, government is a partner in the market-place, we have actually retreated from the idyll depicted by Pitt when he declared that

> [t]he poorest man may in his cottage bid defiance to all the force of the Crown. It may be frail—its roof may shake—the wind may blow through it—the storm may enter, the rain may enter—but the King of England may not enter—all his force dares not cross the threshold of the ruined tenement![65]

Fine rhetoric this may be, but the fact of the matter is that the wind caused by jet aircraft does blow through cottages, the pollution of artificial weather besets them, and the ruin is occasioned as much by these

---

[65] Quoted by Mr. Justice Douglas in one of the early privacy cases, *Frank v. Maryland*, 359 U.S. 360, 378–79 (1959) (dissenting opinion). The dissent ultimately became law. *Camara v. Municipal Court of City & County of San Francisco*, 387 U.S. 523 (1967).

uncared for external forces as by any internal neglect. True, the police may not be responsible for these invasions, but "the Crown" cannot escape its own responsibility for the deliberate creation of these by-products of affluence which undercut and make a mockery of the manufactured creature comforts occasioned by this era of government assured affluence.

Obviously the conventional wisdom held dear in the business sector of the economy foresees an eventual end to pollution when business is able to attack the problem at no expense when efforts are given the requisite tax-abatement treatment. This pat solution ignores the fact that the real *owner* of business in this allegedly non-socialist society is the federal government, recipient as it is of the largest single share of the earnings of business through the taxes levied thereupon.[66] Thus, like any earner or owner of a vested interest, government is willing to attack the pollution problem with an increment of future increased earnings, not out of current income. We are again locked into the conventional wisdom which dictates that only increasing affluence solves problems. This thesis, however, must give one chance to pause because the very deterioration of the environment which concerns us has been the inevitable by-product of our expanding affluence! The public is faced, therefore, with a monolithic combine against which various constituent collectives may be able to function as countervailing forces, but in the face of which the individual is powerless. Somehow "environment" has to be interpolated into the decision-making processes of this business-government goliath. The process of elimination dictates that the courts remain the only avenue through which the intellectual adrenalin necessary to enable a process of value restructuring to begin can be interpolated into the national *Weltanschauung.*

Is there then the "legal" basis for a right to an environment conducive to human survival? This is a horse soon curried. The Constitution was adopted, after all, in order to "promote the general Welfare." The Fifth Amendment was adopted to guarantee that no one should be "deprived of life . . . without due process of law." Still, the framers of the Constitution may have had in mind a general welfare guaranteed by untrammeled *laisser-faire,* whereas the proponents of the Fifth Amendment may only have anticipated the despotic State as the threat to human life. Notwithstanding the historicism which can be used to limit these clauses to the protection of rights then contemporaneously seen to be in jeopardy, it is

---

[66] *Quaere:* who "owns" a large corporation? There has been a lot of talk about the reality of managerial control and the myth of stockholders' ownership. Still, if ownership equals the right to a cash share of income, there is a lot to be said for viewing the taxing authorities as the real partners in interest in the business world.

the Ninth Amendment which affords the growth principle prerequisite to modifying old *grundnorms* to suit today's environment. That is, the "enumeration in the Constitution, of certain rights, shall not be construed to deny or disparage others retained by the people." What use are these other rights, however, if life itself ceases to be worth living? Indeed, if the Ninth Amendment affords even partial support for a right to receive birth control data, certainly it sustains the right to live to enjoy the fruits of that in information. Such a conclusion is actually a conservative one since it does no more than mandate a return to adherence to the "self-evident" truth that any populace is entitled not merely to "Liberty" but to "Life . . . and the pursuit of Happiness."

Given the technique rehearsed in *Griswold v. Connecticut*, there is no need to belabor the language with which such a right could be rendered articulate. The problem is to suggest the impact that such a promulgation should have upon practical affairs. The enunciation of such a right would require every agency of government, whether a local zoning board or a federal home mortgage lending agency, to review their plans to make certain that their activities did not actually exacerbate the deteriorating environment. A strip mining operation could not be certified as safe unless the entrepreneur had begun to implement plans to restore the area destroyed by his operations. An off-shore drilling operation could not be licensed unless it was manifest that immediate steps could be taken to remedy any accident which threatened neighboring shores. No oil tanker could enter territorial waters unless its owners could guarantee to set right any damage to nature that a navigational accident might occasion. Indeed, it is impossible to adumbrate in detail the day by day impact to be caused by such a declaration. The avenue envisaged here must perforce remain a formidable "thicket" which would produce a considerable load of new cases and controversies.[67]

If citizens could contest zoning laws which did not include environmental prophylaxis and could object to any agency ruling which allowed any further deterioration of the environment, notwithstanding how much

---

[67]In *Colgrove v. Green*, 328 U.S. 549 (1946), the Court refused to get involved in the reapportionment controversy because that question was "of a peculiarly political nature and therefore not meet for judicial determination." Indeed, Mr. Justice Frankfurter characterized the whole area as a "political thicket." As we have seen, the Court reversed itself in *Baker v. Carr* and seems to have survived the political quicksand hidden in the thicket in so far as the public is concerned. Interestingly enough, Senator Dirksen had been quietly working upon a proposed constitution which would undo *Baker v. Carr*. More interesting still, this plan has not received much public attention and the amazing progress achieved thus far has been the work of state legislators who are notoriously interested in the machinery as opposed to the democratic dogma of both political parties. *See e.g. Time*, August 8, 1969, at 18.

these decisions promised to increase abundance and affluence as measured in market terms, such a declaration would have a profound impact upon the course of this nation's development.[68] In substance, we should all be poorer in things and yet richer in terms of the environment in which to enjoy the things that we have got. That is, future expansion would be rendered more expensive and perforce slow down when new industrial development had to be pollutant free, when certain sites were closed to development in order to preserve their unique naturalness and when the overhead to finance the requisite planning considerations had to be interpolated into the everyday decision-making process. In short, such a declaration would compel a restructuring of our conventional wisdom in favor of the pursuit of a quality environment rather than the contemporary involvement in quantity consumption which is undercutting that environment. Thus, it was the Court which forced the nation finally to face the fact that blacks are equal in the eyes of the law, and it was likewise the Court which forced the nation to live up to its ideal that each man's vote should be equal. These decisions recast the concerns of society into a mode consonant with the existing politicosociological environment. The society, however, is not structurally postured to respond to the threat to its environment. To insure that the people whose rights were recognized earlier can exist in a milieu where those rights are worth exercising, the challenge of a deteriorating environment must be quickly met. In point of fact, the recognition of the right to a decent environment does not merely right wrongs done to a segment of society, it can save the whole society. Whereas earlier decisions finally redeemed nineteenth century ideals, the recognition of a right to environment would make certain that the nation was ready to enter the technologically oriented 21st century. A nation not postured to respond to the challenges of that century, moreover, may not be fortunate enough to survive long enough to rectify the error of its ways.[69]

---

[68] Inevitably, of course, the Court is going to have to broaden the classic notion of "standing to sue." This idea, however, is similarly abroad in the intellectual environment of the day, witness *Scenic Hudson Preservation Conference v. Federal Power Commission, supra* n. 60; *Office of Communication of United Church of Christ v. FCC*, 359 F.2d 994 (D.C. Cir. 1966). *See*, particularly, Reich, "The Law of a Planned Society," 75 *Yale L. J.* 1227, 1251–1255 (1966); and Jaffe, "The Citizen as Litigant in Public Actions: The Non-Hohfeldian or Ideological Plaintiff," 116 *U. Pa. L. Rev.* 1033 (1968).

[69] "It is as if all the jokes about the rich Texans were abruptly to be replaced by tales of the shifts the Texan beggars were compelled to by their poverty. The analogy is not an inept one. . . . No one who has even a dilettante's interest in archeology and ancient history can avoid being struck by the multitude of ruined cities stretching throughout North Africa and western Asia. . . . The cause of that land's desiccation has probably been more the result of land use than any alteration in climate. . . . By exploiting without regard for replacement or survival resources originally abundantly present, the men of the area built first greatness and wealth for their societies and later poverty and, in most cases, oblivion." Murphy, "The

We suggested earlier that the Court is only able to lead in constitutional development when the people will recognize a constitutional restatement as essentially their own. The intellectual environment is now propitious in which to promulgate new doctrine. Various amendments to both the federal and state constitutions have been drafted relative to the right to environment.[70] Senator Henry Jackson's bill would have the Congress and every federal agency interpret all "laws, policies and regulations in terms of a new national goal—safeguarding and enhancing the physical environment."[71] The editorial writers of *The New York Times* have applauded the idea of a judicial ruling which would "arrest the continued destruction of the environment, surely where it is done with government sanction."[72] Indeed, to the extent that constitutional pronouncements reflect the distillation of considered wisdom relevant to necessary restructuring of our basic law to keep its tenor consonant with our evolving society's needs, there already exists a constitutional right to a decent environment. We merely need a ringing decision to ratify this existential fact of life.

Necessity to Change Man's Traditional View of Nature," 48 *Neb. L. Rev.* 299, 306–307, 311–12 (1969).

[70] *See also*, Ferry, "Must We Rewrite the Constitution?," *Saturday Review*, March 2, 1968, at 50. The existence of these several amendment plans are a good omen in the sense that they create the atmosphere of felt need in which the Court can act to restructure the constitutional matrix to respond to these needs. The amendment route as an actual solution to the problem is dubious at best. The several state legislatures are remarkably subject to lobbyists from commercial interests and, ignored for the most part by their constituents except when they increase taxes, are conversely immune from felt needs of any esoteric variety. Indeed, the success of the "Dirksen amendment" illustrates that these state legislatures by and large still remain strongholds of party power politics and cannot be counted upon to respond to anything which might upset the affluent society approach to life.

[71] *Time*, August 1, 1969, at 42.

[72] *The New York Times*, July 15, 1969, at 34, col. 2.

Law in Action:
The Trust Doctrine

Edward Berlin · *Gladys Kessler*
Anthony Z. Roisman

In the June, 1969, *Sierra Club Bulletin*, W. Lloyd Tupling wrote these depressing words:

> If you want to see it like it is, stop reading now and call for an airline reservation to Alaska.
> Tomorrow it will be a different place. And by this time next year, if indications from Washington discussions prove valid, construction crews will have built nearly half of an 800-mile oil pipeline from Prudhoe Bay on the Arctic Ocean to Valdez on the Pacific. Nothing man can do will alter the fact that this 48-inch siphon from the oil-rich North Slope and its accompanying activity will change the ecology of vast wilderness areas.

Unfortunately, the same can be said for virtually every area of land, every stream, river and ocean, every species of wildlife, every breath of air— even the moon. The march of "progress" must inevitably, so we are told, adversely affect man's environment. Conservationists have been moving to stem the tide, to seek compromise, to save something, to make technological progress progressive technology. How did it happen that economic and industrial progress were presumed to be paramount to legitimate conservation objectives? The answer is the industrial revolution, "manifest destiny," special interest politics, *laissez-faire* government, a lack of vision, and laxity attributable to a failure to appreciate the magnitude of the threat. However, this paper is not intended to lament the environment losses already suffered, but to explore steps which may be taken to prevent further unwarranted and detrimental encroachment. This can be done only by taking the initiative and refusing to be content with a responsive or reactive position.

This paper is about one of the weapons that can be used in the offensive

—the trust doctrine. For years conservationists have written and talked about the "trust doctrine."[1] Although the theory, to the extent that it has been developed, has for the most part been applied in the case of submerged lands, its rationale and effect have broad application to conservation problems in general. The doctrine was summarized by the Supreme Court in 1892 in a case concerned with the power of the sovereign to relinquish, irrevocably, control over submerged lands subject to this trust. The Court said

> That the State holds the title to the lands under navigable waters of Lake Michigan, within its limits, in the same manner that the State holds title to soils under tide water by the common law, we have already shown, and that title necessarily carries with it control over the waters above them whenever the lands are subjected to use. But it is a title different in character from that which the State holds in lands intended for sale. It is different from the title which the United States hold in the public lands which are open to pre-emption and sale. It is a title held in trust for the people of the State that they may enjoy the navigation of the waters, carry on commerce over them, and have liberty of fishing therein freed from the obstruction or interference of private parties. The interest of the people in the navigation of the waters and in commerce over them may be improved in many instances by the erection of wharves, docks and piers therein, for which purpose the State may grant parcels of the submerged lands; and, so long as their disposition is made for such purposes, no valid objections can be made to the grants. It is grants of parcels of lands under navigable waters, that may afford foundation for wharves, piers, docks, and other structures in aid of commerce, and grants of parcels which, being occupied, do not substantially impair the public interest in the lands and water remaining, that are chiefly considered and sustained in the adjudged cases as a valid exercise of legislative power consistently with the trust to the public upon which such lands are held by the State. But that is a very different doctrine from the one which would sanction the abdication of the general control of the State over lands under the navigable waters of an entire harbor or bay, or of a sea or lake. Such abdication is not consistent with the exercise of that trust which requires the government of the State to preserve such waters for the use of the public. The trust devolving upon the State for the public, and which can only be discharged by the management and control of property in which the public has an interest, cannot be relinquished by a transfer of the property. The control of the State for the purposes of the trust can never be lost except as to such parcels as are used in promoting the interests of the public

---

[1]Professor Joseph Sax of the University of Michigan Law School has written a comprehensive analysis of the trust doctrine and its application by the courts. *See* 68 *Mich. L. Rev.* 478 (1970). The analysis is not only replete with citations and discussion of cases but provides a rational theory for tying together many diverse trust cases. For anyone planning to invoke the trust doctrine, the analysis is an absolute necessity both for the availability of precedents and to facilitate an understanding of the doctrine.

therein, or can be disposed of without any substantial impairment of the public interest in the lands and waters remaining. It is only by observing the distinction between a grant of such parcels for the improvement of the public interest, or which when occupied do not substantially impair the public interest in the lands and waters remaining, and a grant of the whole property in which the public is interested, that the language of the adjudged cases can be reconciled. General language sometimes found in opinions of the courts, expressive of absolute ownership and control by the State of lands under navigable waters, irrespective of any trust as to their use and disposition, must be read and construed with reference to the special facts of the particular cases. A grant of all the lands under the navigable waters of a State has never been adjudged to be within the legislative power; and any attempted grant of the kind would be held, if not absolutely void on its face, as subject to revocation. The State can no more abdicate its trust over property in which the whole people are interested, like navigable waters and soils under them, so as to leave them entirely under the use and control of private parties, except in the instance of parcels mentioned for the improvement of the navigation and use of the waters, or when parcels can be disposed of without impairment of the public interest in what remains, than it can abdicate its police powers in the administration of government and the preservation of the peace. In the administration of government the use of such powers may for a limited period be delegated to a municipality or other body, but there always remains with the State the right to revoke those powers and exercise them in a more direct manner, and one more conformable to its wishes.[2]

This was not the first application of the doctrine. Long before the revolution it was recognized that initially title to all land (whether dry or submerged), reposed with the king

who held it as trustee in his official and representative capacity, with no private interest. The dry land, and the soil under fresh rivers, brooks, and small ponds, was convertible by his grant into private property, for settlement, and for the advancement of the common welfare. The seashore, arms of the sea, and large ponds, by reason of their special adaptation to public uses, was set apart and reserved as public waters. They could not be converted into private estates or subject to a private easement by the trustee's grant, or by any act of the executive branch of the government.[3]

This idea, that the sovereign at one time owned all of the land, is not limited to kings. It applies to the land in this country and the federal government's ownership or right to ownership of all the land. In *Fairfax's Devisee v. Hunter's Lessee*,[4] the Supreme Court was faced with the problem of competing claims to certain Virginia land. Fairfax's devisee

---

[2] *Illinois Central R.A. v. Illinois*, 146 U.S. 387 at 452–454, 13 S. Ct. 110, 36 L.Ed. 1018 (1892).
[3] *Concord Mfg. Co. v. Robertson*, 66 N.H.1, 25 A. 718 (1889).
[4] 11 U.S. (7 Cranch) 602 (1813).

claimed ownership based on the title that Fairfax had from the king in pre-revolutionary times. Hunter's lessee claimed that Hunter had title from the State of Virginia. The Court ruled that Fairfax's devisee had title but noted that it was within the authority of the State to take title to the property by enactment of a statute. This residual power of the new states to take title to all land even if held by a private individual with a deed from the king suggests that all land, even land owned by private individuals, is subject to a prior right of the government. Of course, the Fifth Amendment to the Constitution gives the government the right to take property for a public use upon the payment of just compensation. But beyond this an argument can be made that all property is owned subject to certain pre-existing rights in the government to limit its use and that those limitations do not constitute a taking which requires payment of compensation. (See subsequent discussion of this point.)

In *McCulloch v. Maryland*[5] the Court declared:

> The Government of the Union, then . . . is, emphatically, and truly, a government of the people. In form and in substance it emanates from them. Its powers are granted by them and are to be exercised directly on them, *and for their benefit.* [Emphasis added][6]

The thrust of this decision for our purposes is that whatever interest citizens may have had in the land they transferred to the government in exchange for the government's promise to deal with that property for the benefit of the people. This obligation of the government to act for the benefit of the people is what the trust doctrine is all about.

Of course the public benefit, or as it is more commonly known, the public interest, is not always the same. For instance, why were the submerged lands, the lands under navigable waterways, the subject of so much trust litigation? Simply because the public interest required open channels of navigation and free access to partake of the resources of the water, namely the liberty to fish. Those were the special characteristics of the submerged lands that required rejection of any notion of absolute private dominion. Fishing and navigation were too critical in the 18th and 19th centuries to run the risk of interference or destruction by private interests.

Today, other characteristics have assumed positions of peculiar prominence. We are concerned about other resources that are threatened and *that the public interest requires be retained and protected by the trust for the public use and enjoyment:* clean air, clean water, wilderness areas, unique recreational sites. The responsibility of the sovereign should be

---

[5] 17 U.S. (4 Wheat) 316, at 404–405 (1819).
[6] *Id.*

no less emphatic. In short, the trust doctrine is the device by which the government can use and preserve land for the benefit of the people.

The trust is perpetual and the public interest that it protects is constant. That public interest requires that man's environment be utilized in a manner that permits the maximum number of people to obtain the benefits of their environment. Those benefits are viewed in light of the future generations of man and not merely as benefits for today.

However, as noted before, the most beneficial use of the property will change with time. For an emerging nation stretching its frontiers with little population, problems of air and water pollution would be virtually nonexistent; nature's own cleansing processes would preserve the environment.

Today, however, in this country of exploding population and incredible output of waste products, protection of the air and water has become essential for survival. The expanding population has also made protection of wildlife species and open spaces a necessity if man is to retain some portion of his environment in its natural state. Thus, application of the broad public interest, protected by the trust, to a particular case will require a specific determination of how the land is to be used. This decision will be made in light of the way in which the environment has been changed by pressures of population and technology, and in such a case the public welfare demands the impression of a trust.

While the courts have not spelled out the reach of the trust doctrine, they have clearly recognized that the trust applies to all property.

In *United States v. California*[7] involving the ownership, as between the federal and state governments, of offshore lands, the Supreme Court, in responding to the suggestion that an official of the United States had waived that sovereign's claim to ownership, stated

> The Government, *which holds its interests here as elsewhere in trust for all the people*, is not to be deprived of those interests by the ordinary court rules designed particularly for private disputes over individually-owned pieces of property; and officers who have no authority at all to dispose of Government property cannot by their conduct cause the Government to lose its valuable rights by their acquiescence, laches, or failure to act.[8] [Emphasis added.]

The trust not only attaches to land owned by the government, but also to land that was owned by the government and has passed to private ownership. That the trust reaches such property is clear from the Supreme Court's decision in the *Illinois Central* case where the Court said

So with trusts connected with public property, *or property of a special charac-*

---

[7]332 U.S. 19 (1947).
[8]*Id.*, at 40.

ter, like lands under navigable waters, they cannot be placed entirely beyond the direction and control of the State.[9] [Emphasis added.]

At any given time any property may take on this special character when conditions that exist in society, such as urban sprawl or technological advance, raise a serious threat to the public interest values of the land. The trust is the assurance to the people that, at that time, the uses to which the property will be put must be consistent with the public interest. We shall discuss later how that public interest is established and what are some of the basic elements that make up the public interest.

The traditional use to which the trust doctrine has been put does not really go beyond forcing the government to recognize and consider conservation values in making decisions about public lands. In this regard, it has served a valuable function by placing these environmental concerns on a par with the concerns for industrial and economic progress. But this is only the beginning. To say that the government holds property in trust for the people is not merely to say that when making a decision about the environment, the general public concern with preservation should be considered. A trust imposes an affirmative duty upon the trustee to hold and use the property for the exclusive benefit of the beneficiary, and where that benefit involves conservation objectives, the government must act affirmatively to achieve its realization.

A trust is a specialized legal form and to invoke its protection properly it is necessary to talk in terms of trustees, trust property, beneficiaries, and trust duties. By developing each of these elements it is possible to increase materially the effectiveness of the trust doctrine. With specifically defined trust duties and an identifiable trustee, those who seek to protect the property will have a much firmer basis for arguing that a governmental agency has specific duties with respect to the property and has an affirmative duty to preserve the trust property and to avoid a wasting of its assets.

In this paper we will attempt to explore certain basic aspects of the trust doctrine that apply to all situations. We will not, except in a specific example, explore the nuances of those basic trust aspects as they apply to particular problem areas. Furthermore, because the complexity of the subject makes any attempt at specific answers in this short paper impossible, we shall confine our discussion to an exploration of some fundamental questions that need to be resolved in applying the trust doctrine to particular problems. Our major thesis is that the trust doctrine, expanded to its logical boundaries, can be utilized as a highly effective affirmative weapon in the war against environmental deterioration. Our purpose is

---

[9]146 U.S. at 454.

to make a most cursory examination of those outer boundaries and to take a specific example and explore in depth how the trust doctrine can be adapted to it. Although we know that a trust protects all property, it is another matter to determine how that protection should operate. To understand this process, we look to three different types of property:

1. Property owned by the government.
2. Property owned by private individuals and presently used in a manner consistent with the public interest.
3. Property owned by private individuals and used in a manner which is inconsistent with the public interest.

GOVERNMENT PROPERTY

The trust doctrine may be applicable to this type of property in a fairly traditional manner. Where the government intends to use property that it owns in a manner inconsistent with the public interest—for instance, by a sale of the property—the beneficiaries of the trust, *i.e.*, the people, may, having exhausted any administrative remedies, seek a writ of mandamus or other relief to prevent the sale of the property or to compel the appropriate governmental agency to dispose of the property with limitations on its use that will protect the public interest.

This relief might involve the imposition of a requirement in any deed of sale subjecting the purchaser and all future owners to certain restrictions in their use of the land or that any use would have to be approved in advance by the government.[10] Even if the transfer were intra- or inter-governmental, imposition of conditions at the time of the transfer would reduce the need for future litigation. Theoretically, of course, all property is subject to the trust even after the sale by the government, and special restrictions at the time of transfer should not be necessary. But as we shall see later, the failure to impose clear restrictions based on the trust may fail to place the landowner on adequate notice and may require more drastic remedies later. Also, it will be much easier to protect property where the deed itself spells out the conditions and limitations on its use.

Where the government retains the property but its use of the property now or its intended use are not consistent with the public interest, the same mandamus or similar remedy will have to be utilized. The litigation will be more difficult because generally in these cases the relief sought will be to compel the government to take affirmative action with respect

---

[10] *See e.g. Petition of Pauley Petroleum, Inc. v. United States*, No. 197–69 (Ct. Cl., filed April 9, 1969), where the government is being sued for attempting to impose conditions subsequent in petroleum leases.

to the property, such as maintenance, providing public access, excluding certain uses, etc. In the extreme case, a suit might seek discontinuance of an existing use, such as a military installation, from an area that should be returned to its natural condition. The theory, *i.e.* the obligation of the trustee to use the property for the public interest, would be the same but the suit would most vividly represent the conflict between the government's judgment regarding the public interest and the judgment of the public itself. At a minimum the government's obligation with respect to the trust property should require that public hearings be held to determine what use should be made of the property.

As in any mandamus proceeding, the issue in these cases involving government-owned property would be either to establish an abuse of discretion or to establish that the action sought is a ministerial act that the agency is obligated to perform. In the context of the trust doctrine, this litigation will afford the conservationist an opportunity to pursue the argument that in today's world, environmental concerns are of paramount importance and outweigh other legitimate government interests. Growing public and governmental awareness of this fact makes this a most propitious time for conservationists to take the initiative. Of course, in such a mandamus action the burden of proof will be on the public to establish that the government's action, presumably legal, was not in fact in the public interest.

While reliance on a statute will bolster the argument, it is not essential. The trust is in the nature of a common law duty that the government assumes as a condition of its lawful authority to govern. However, where a government dictate specifically requires or even permits the objectionable use of land, more difficult problems arise. Normally any action specifically approved by the legislature is beyond question except on constitutional grounds. An argument can be made that the Fifth Amendment to the Constitution, which requires that the taking of private property be by due process of law and that it be for a public purpose, has imposed a substantive constitutional requirement that property held by the government must be used, just as the power to govern must be used, for the people and only for the public interest and that even a legislative determination that property be used for a particular purpose does not foreclose the inquiry into whether the use is consistent with the public interest.

As a practical matter, this argument will not have to be made in many cases because most legislation is so broad that the public interest question with respect to particular property is wide open. Only where the legislature identifies a particular piece of property for a particular use will the constitutional problem be unavoidable.

Thus, in the case of property owned by the government, the trust doctrine is the vehicle for the conservationist to present the public interest issue to the governmental agency. The existence of the trust is also the basis for the use of mandamus even in the absence of a statutory requirement. Fortunately, government agencies possess fairly broad statutory authority and there should be no problem establishing that the agency in question possesses the necessary authority to act. Occasionally, more than one agency may be the subject of the suit.

PRIVATE PROPERTY—USED IN THE PUBLIC INTEREST

Property owned by a private individual and being used in a manner consistent with the public interest is also subject to the application of the trust. The doctrine will come into play when the owner contemplates using the land for a purpose inconsistent with the public interest or where the land is subject to a change in use due to action taken against the will of the landowner, such as by condemnation.

The first case presents the most difficult situation for application of the trust doctrine, for here the private property rights of landowners are in direct conflict with the public interest terms of the trust. However, for the trust doctrine to have any viability, it must be established that the trust has been in existence from the beginning of our constitutional government and that every transfer of property includes with it, as an implicit condition, the obligation that the property be used for the public interest. Such a theory is presumably the basis for the current legislation that imposes water and air pollution standards on landowners (the standards that necessarily restrict the use of their property), without providing any compensation for this "taking." It is true that the overriding public interest in clean air and water was the impetus for the legislation, but nonetheless, the requirement of costly antipollution devices constitutes a "taking" without compensation. Whether called an exercise of the police power, a health and welfare measure, or application of the trust doctrine, the fact remains that the interest of a landowner in his property is limited by certain pre-existing, unwritten conditions that, in effect, require that the land not be used for a purpose inconsistent with the public interest.[11]

---

[11]The idea that the government can take property without paying compensation is not new. In *Euclid v. Ambler*, 272 U.S. 365 (1926), the Supreme Court held that a city council could restrict the uses to which land could be put by zoning ordinances without paying the landowner for the loss of value to his land. The Court noted that the zoning restrictions could only be upset by a showing of arbitrary and capricious action.

In the case of air and water pollution legislation, the legislature, by enacting the law, created a very strong presumption that the public interest required that these restrictions be imposed on the land use.[12]

But in the absence of a legislative enactment, the general public through a class action suit should also be able to impose restrictions on the uses to which a private landowner may put his property. The suit would require the public to carry a very substantial burden of proof in order to establish that the restrictions sought were clearly necessary for the public interest.

Inevitably, an element of the public interest is the presumption that private property may be used for any purpose not specifically declared illegal by the government. This is the rebuttable presumption that the public must overcome in order to win its class action. As we shall see later, if the government were to condemn the land the burden of proof would be on the landowner to overcome the presumption that there was a valid public purpose and to show that the taking was arbitrary. But in that case, the government would have to pay for the land and would obtain an interest in the land. Here the general public does not obtain an interest in the land, but merely restricts its use. Thus the fact that no interest is taken and that the public, unlike the government in a condemnation suit, bears the burden of proof, balances the equities sufficiently to permit the restriction to be imposed by private citizens through a class action without the payment of compensation to the landowner.

Where the use to which land is to be put is against the will of the landowner, *i.e.* where his land is about to be condemned, he may, of course, resist the condemnation on the usual theory that the taking is not for a public purpose but rather is for a private purpose.[13] In this case the trust doctrine does not really come into play unless the condemnor is viewed as the trustee seizing land for the public interest.

The more interesting case is where the landowner's present or contemplated use of the land is itself beneficial to the public interest. Then an entirely different line of argument is available. For even assuming that the taking is for a public purpose, if the landowner can establish that the proposed taking would seriously impair a beneficial public use and that the condemnor can reasonably achieve his objective by using some other

---

[12]An alternative line of argument against the pollution problem is an extension of the nuisance doctrine of *sic utere tuo ut alienum non laedas* (so use your own property as not to injure the right of another). This doctrine is arguably another form of the trust doctrine representing an imposition of restrictions on all land. The "rights" referred to in the doctrine should include the right to a clean environment for all people. *See* E. Roberts, "The Right to a Decent Environment: Progress Along a Constitutional Avenue," in this volume.

[13]*See West River Bridge v. Dix, et al.*, 47 U.S. (6 How.) 507 (1848).

land, then the landowner can prevent the condemnation.[14] The land-owner is, in effect, relying on trust doctrine and is raising the public interest as his defense. If there is a public trust then it requires a balancing of conflicting public interest goals, and finding alternatives[15] that allow both goals to be achieved is the essence of sound administration of the trust.

It is unfortunate that litigation is necessary to force those who have the power to condemn to use that power in a manner designed to protect the broadest possible public interest. Intervention of a public organization will lend some moral and evidentiary support to this case, but it is not necessary for raising the argument.[16] We shall discuss later a specific case in which the trust doctrine can be used to create a situation in which most objectionable condemnation by private utilities, railroads, etc., can be prevented.

Where the condemnation is by the government, the problem is some-what different because the government is presumed to act in the public interest. In his analysis, Professor Sax suggests that this presumption can be overcome if it can be shown that little or no effort was made by the government to give the public genuine opportunity to be heard on the public interest issue. However, if the condemnor is a private corporation to whom condemnation authority has been delegated, but over whom there is virtually no public control, it is very doubtful that the "public interest" determination should be presumed correct. In such a case, the burden should be on the private corporation to establish that the pro-posed taking is in the public interest and that no apparent public interest is being harmed by the taking.[17] Although this is not the law today, there is very little reason to support the current theory. The possible delay in public utility construction caused by imposing a burden of proof on the private condemnor is more than offset by the opportunity for a full

---

[14] See Texas Eastern Transmission Corp. v. Wildlife Preserves, Inc., 48 N.J. 261, 225 A.2d. 130. (Sup. Ct. 1966).

[15] Some values are of sufficient importance that even the failure to find an alternative for a power plant, for instance, is not a justification for destroying the value. Today, with the real spectre of total annihilation of all life through pollution of the environment, it is a valid argument that even a critical source of needed electric power or a military installation is not sufficiently important to allow more air or water pollution. By the same token it is no longer possible to weigh the ecological benefits of the alternative that prevents the pollution against the dollar and cents cost of the alternative.

[16] The presence of a scenic easement held by a conservation trust will bolster the land-owner's argument about the uses to which the land is dedicated but will not prevent condemnation.

[17] In West Virginia, for instance, the law requires the condemnor to establish that it is a company entitled to condemn and that the taking is for a purpose specified in the statute. What is not required is that the company establish that the purpose, a power line, is required by the public.

consideration of all aspects of the public interest. To avoid such delays, private condemnors would be forced to bring the public into the early planning stages and to fully recognize the conservation interests—a development that is long overdue. The corporation would then have some impetus to seek land that has no special values and to design its projects in such a way as to minimize the damage caused. For instance, there might be a material increase in the research and development of high voltage underground cables, once power companies are compelled to carry the burden of proving in open court that any proposed power line and the route and design selected are necessary and in the public interest. This line of argument can probably best be presented in a case where the private landowner is resisting the taking on the grounds that a public value will be destroyed, and in which suit he is joined by a class of defendants, represented by a conservation organization, arguing the trust doctrine.

PRIVATE PROPERTY—NOT USED IN THE PUBLIC INTEREST

A third kind of land to which the trust doctrine applies is private property already being used in a manner inconsistent with the public interest. Here, the public and the government have failed to act to prevent this use. It hardly seems justifiable now to require the landowner to tear down his factory or power line. In such a case, the public and the government should be equitably estopped from forcing the landowner to discontinue the improper use.[18] However, it may still be possible to stop the harmful use and to preserve the land. Such action can be taken by a traditional condemnation suit by the government in which the landowner is compensated for his property. Where the government is unwilling to act, a mandamus action based upon the trust doctrine can be instituted to require that the land be taken for the public purpose. To avoid conflicting decisions, the landowner should be joined in the suit so that one final determination on the public interest questions will be made.

SOME DETAILS

We have explored how the trust would operate in various types of land ownership situations. The next question: What are some of the more important details of the trust? We have discussed government respon-

[18] In case of air and water pollution standards, there is in effect a "taking" which limits present uses, but apparently the failure to force the landowners to cease operations coupled with the fact that the "taking" is by direct legislation, has been sufficient to avoid any equitable estoppel argument or constitutional objection.

sibilities as the trustee, but have not said which government is meant. Actually it is probably conceptually preferable to speak in terms of many trusts and therefore of many trustees.

For instance, it is reasonable that the trust protecting a national park should be different from the trust prohibiting unnecessary and harmful air pollution in a large metropolitan area. Not only is the subject matter diverse, but those charged with the responsibility of carrying out the trust —the trustees—are different. A national park is protected by the National Park Service of the Department of the Interior. Responsibility for clean air in urban areas is shared by state and local governments and by the Department of Health, Education and Welfare.

The trustee to whom the public should look in any given case is that government (federal, state, or local) or department within the government that has the clearest responsibility and authority for taking the action desired. The safest course to follow when there is any doubt is to bring in all relevant government agencies as joint trustees, any one of whom, it will be alleged, has authority to act.

There are a whole series of questions concerning the detailed terms of the protection afforded by the trust that need careful analysis, particularly with the assistance of expert ecologists, foresters, etc. Fortunately, conservation groups across the country are keenly aware of the conservation interest in most areas. These groups can assist in developing a survey of property and a catalog of essential values throughout the nation that must be protected.[19] Skilled land use and trust lawyers can then prepare the basic terms of the trust applicable to each land or water area and, in time, can relate the responsibilities for preservation to the appropriate governments and departments. These surveys and trust instruments would be invaluable aids to those who are fighting the battles in the courts.

Even those lands held in private trust, such as property held by the Nature Conservancy, are and should be, subject to the public trust. As will be discussed later, the inability to condemn a property interest held by the government makes its interest in all lands a critical weapon for resisting so-called "public" corporations such as power companies, railroads, and the like, in their attempts to condemn land without regard for broader public values.

One area of trust law that relates to the terms of the trusts but is not a term itself concerns the applicable rules of construction. These rules— for example, a trust is to be construed in light of the purposes of the grantor, and amendments by implication are to be avoided—may be used

---

[19]Such an outline of conservation values was taken by many local groups participating in the Environmental Teach-In on April 22, 1970.

to preserve the status quo and to resist tenuous arguments put forth by government agencies or others in an attempt to avoid the terms of the trust. Other doctrines such as *cy pres* can be used to preserve the basic objective of the trust even if the original purpose no longer exists. This latter doctrine may be a useful tool where land has already been partially and irrevocably despoiled and efforts are being made to prevent further desecration.

A SPECIFIC EXAMPLE

In the next few pages, we attempt to apply these concepts to a concrete problem dealing with federal responsibility to protect land. The problem and analysis do not touch all aspects of the trust doctrine explored above, but hopefully they demonstrate the practical use to which these ideas can be put.

Let us assume that we are endeavoring to protect from condemnation property that has unique scenic and recreational values. The condemnor is a public utility that intends to build a power line on the property. The landowner is willing to dedicate his land for use in a manner consistent with environmental objectives. Let us further assume that state law is "stacked" in favor of the utility, whose power line will destroy the scenic and recreational value of the land. Our assumption regarding state law is certainly sound in most jurisdictions, with the only real justiciable issue being that of compensation.[20]

---

[20]It is possible to argue, as a constitutional prerequisite, that before there can be a taking, when there is an allegation of a competing public purpose that would be substantially destroyed or materially interfered with by the taking, there must be a full comparative hearing on the question of which use would be more consistent with the public interest. It is already settled that where condemnation is sought of property already dedicated to a public use, the taking will be denied unless specifically authorized by the sovereign. *See City of Norton v. Lowden*, 84 F. 2d. 663 at 665 (CA.10, 1936); *United States v. Certain Parcels of Land, Etc.* 196 F.2d. 657 at 661 (C.A. 4, 1952). But it must be noted that except for the excellent innovative decision of one enlightened court (*Texas Eastern Transmission Corp. v. Wildlife Preserves, Inc.*, 48 N.J. 261, 225 A.2d. 130 [Sup. Ct. 19]), private property owners have received little if any comfort from the competing public use doctrine. It must also be remembered that the property with which we are concerned may not yet have been developed for public purposes. In speaking of "public purposes" it must be clear that we are convinced that private developments of property can, in appropriate circumstances, equate with development for public purposes—for example, the private development, whether or not for profit, of a recreational center on property uniquely suited for that purpose.

Consideration should still be given to contending for a broadening of the *Texas Eastern* rationale, but in the absence of one's presence in a sensitive, activist court, the likelihood of success would have to be viewed as remote. In fact, even the *Texas Eastern* case fails to acknowledge that a general public interest (a wildlife preserve) represents a true compet-

We have earlier discussed the use of the trust doctrine as a basis for the landowner or a class of intervenors to argue that the proposed taking is not in the public interest. However, if the federal government has an interest in the land, then no condemnation can occur because of the doctrine of sovereign immunity. If the property is subject to protection by the trust, then in effect the government has an interest in the property as trustee. But to put teeth in this argument, why not have the landowner reconfirm this trust protection by granting the federal government, or rather the agency of the government that has responsibility for the kind of environmental concerns involved (*i.e.* the Interior Department) an easement on the property that would require government approval of any use of the land other than certain clearly defined environmentally desirable uses? In short, no power line may be built upon the property without government approval.

A problem may arise if the Department of the Interior refuses to accept the easement. In such a case, it is subject to a mandamus to compel it to fulfill its trust responsibility and accept the easement. This argument will be materially assisted by reference to specific statutes that appear to us to be examples of delegation of trust responsibilities by Congress to the Interior Department.

The Outdoor Recreation Act provides:

> The Congress finds and declares it to be desirable that all American people of present and future generations be assured adequate outdoor recreation resources, and that it is desirable *for all levels of government and private interests* to take prompt and coordinated action to the extent practicable without diminishing or affecting their respective powers and functions to conserve, develop, and utilize such resources for the benefit and enjoyment of the American people.[21]

To facilitate the realization of those objectives, the Secretary is authorized to[22]

> accept and use donations of money, property, personal services, or facilities for the purposes of [the Act].

A scenic easement is a donation of property.[23] Once accepted by the Secretary, he becomes the trustee charged with the furtherance of the

---

ing interest with a gas transmission line which is specified in the condemnation statute. Such a view is far too restrictive. Thus, the dilemma is how to immunize the property from condemnation.

[21] 16 U.S.C. §4601 (Emphasis added); *see also* 16 U.S.C. §4601–4, 16 U.S.C. §742 and 16 U.S.C. §661.

[22] 16 U.S.C. §4601.1 (h).

[23] We assume the easement is given without cost, thus also giving the landowner a charitable tax deduction based upon the value of the interest given.

objectives of the easement, his obligation running both to the private grantor and the public at large.[24] Where there is any doubt that the Interior Department will accept the easement, the best course to follow is to record the easement. The condemnation would then be resisted on the ground that an indispensable party, the Department of the Interior, has not been joined and cannot be joined.

Alternatively, litigation can be considered to settle the Secretary's status. The statute only *permits* the Secretary to accept donations of property, but where the property involved has unique scenic and recreational values that the Department can protect, it would be our position that there is no discretion to decline acceptance. To decline would be inconsistent with the Department's overall trust responsibilities for recreational and scenic land development and preservation. In effect, if we assume that recreational development is a governmental responsibility, it follows that the Secretary's rejection of a free donation would necessitate public expenditure some time in the future in order to condemn property to provide the scenic and recreational values now lost.

In our hypothetical case, the public at large is the intended beneficiary of the exercise by the Department of its fiduciary responsibility. Hence, equitable relief should lie to compel discharge of that responsibility, to compel, in short, acceptance of the easement that would cloak the property with the government's immunity and preserve and protect it for the enjoyment of future generations.

CONCLUSION

Many of the ideas and theories expressed are admittedly radical. They are possible arguments and approaches offered for speculation and rumination—not fully developed final theories. They are intended to stimulate a new approach to the problem of saving a deteriorating world. To many, the theories of law that have reshaped civil and individual rights in the past 25 years must also have seemed too radical for serious consideration. The fact is that by a constant barrage on a new front there is a real possibility for advancement—if not today, then in the future. The imaginative use of class action suits to fight pesticide problems, which the Environmental Defense Fund has undertaken, are the kinds of new vistas that must be opened. The expanded concept of the traditional trust doctrine discussed here hopefully will be such a new vista.

[24]If the Department attempts to misuse the property, such as granting the right to build a power line, it is still possible to challenge the action procedurally (demand a public hearing) and substantively (charge an abuse of discretion).

Outline of Federal Environmental Law for the Practicing Lawyer

James Watt Moorman

I. Procedure
  A. Jurisdiction and related subjects
    1. Standing to sue
      a. Review of administrative decisions
      b. Taxpayers suits to enjoin improper expenditures
      c. Mandamus
    2. Sovereign immunity
    3. Administrative Procedure Act
    4. Venue
  B. Discovery, The Freedom of Information Act and the Executive Privilege
  C. Other procedural matters
    1. Burden of proof
    2. Evidence
      a. Natural beauty
      b. Cost-benefit ratios
II. Substantive Environmental Matters
  A. Pollution
    1. Water pollution
      a. Federal Water Pollution Control Act
      b. The Refuse Act
      c. The Oil Pollution Act
      d. Interstate Compacts
      e. Federal activities
      f. Thermal pollution
    2. Air pollution
      a. Air Quality Act of 1967
      b. Federal installations

c. Emergency powers
d. Vehicle exhaust emission standards
3. Pesticides
4. Noise pollution
a. Tucker Act
b. Federal preemption
c. Federal Aviation Administration
d. Civil Aeronautics Board
5. Aesthetic or visual pollution
B. Land and water use
1. Rivers, estuaries and coastal waters
a. Basis of federal control: the navigational servitude
b. Basis of federal control: reserved rights
c. Exercise of federal control: The Rivers and Harbor Act of 1897
d. Exercise of federal control: The Federal Power Act
e. Exercise of federal control: federal projects
2. Strip mining
a. State scheme
b. Federal legislation
c. Public domain
3. Right-of-Way Planning and Routing and Plant Siting
a. Federal transportation projects
b. Pipe line and power line rights of way
4. Fish and wildlife
a. Federal power: constitutional source
b. Federal power: exercise
C. The public domain
1. The recreation concept
2. National forests
3. National parks
4. Bureau of Land Management
a. The Classification and Multiple Use Act of 1964
b. The Sales of Public Lands Act of 1964
c. The Taylor Grazing Act
d. Mining laws
e. O & C Lands
5. Wildlife refuges
6. Wilderness
7. Alaska
a. State selection
b. North slope oil strike
8. Outer Continental Shelf

a. Jurisdiction and laws
b. Santa Barbara

We are witnessing an uneasy awakening to the dismal destruction of our environment by our culture. Hundreds of groups are forming to protect this wild area, to stop that "parkway," to fight the pollution of some stream or lake. Alarms go out from the Sierra Club and thousands respond with a torrent of telegrams and letters. Congress is responding with programs and prohibitions; with bureaucracies and money to spend. Yet the mindless machine grinds out: a thousand laws seem not to have delayed ultimate destruction by much more than a day.

Part of the problem lies in the refusal of the Executive Branch to take Congress seriously. For this reason, the concerned citizen often finds himself in a frustrating position. After waging and winning a tough legislative battle, nothing happens in the administration. It seems pointless to go back to Congress. Instead, he goes to a lawyer.

The problems facing this lawyer can be formidable. The law may be a new, unfamiliar and technical statute. Again, it may be a vast collection of miscellaneous unfamiliar precedents. Worst of all, it may be nonexistent. If the suit is to be against the United States, the prestige and resources of the Department of Justice must be faced. More than likely, the action will promise to be long and expensive, involving lengthy discovery, expert witnesses and serious legal research. On top of this, the client will probably be a poorly organized and financially weak citizens' group. Some lawyers understandably reject the environmental case; others simply plunge in and pray they can make the far shore.

As it happens, more and more lawyers are taking the plunge, and things have begun to happen. *Scenic Hudson*,[1] discussed on later pages, was not only a landmark in the law of standing to sue; it marks a new era of environmental law. Now there is a good chance that the judiciary will force the executive to follow legislative mandates to protect the environment.

Because things have begun to happen and lawyers are taking the plunge, the need for an outline of the law from the viewpoint of the "environmental lawyer" is obvious. This is a first attempt at such an outline. As such, it is not an outline primarily for the participants in the Conference on Law and the Environment, who, presumably, have a greater depth of knowledge than is presented here. Rather, it is primarily an outline for the attorney who is just getting into the environmental "thing."

This outline is primarily concerned with federal law, the federal gov-

---

[1] *Scenic Hudson Preservation Conference v. Federal Power Commission*, 354 F.2d 608 (C.A. 2, 1965).

ernment and the federal courts. This is, however, only because of the interests of the author and the time limits under which the outline was written. The role of state and local law, government and courts in environmental matters is, of course, enormous and no treatment of environmental law can be considered complete without including them. Nevertheless, the federal government could play a pivotal role in the fight to save our environment. In some fields, recent federal legislation holds forth great, but yet unrealized promise. The federal government's role in the scheme of American government gives it powers that are both preeminent and nationwide if they can be harnessed. In fact, the misuse of these powers is the very cause of certain environmental problems.

The topics with which the environmental lawyer is concerned break themselves, as one would expect, into procedure and substance.[2] We will turn first to procedural matters.

PROCEDURE: INTRODUCTION

Before beginning an environmental action, any lawyer would take many procedural matters into account. No attempt is made here to systematically cover the whole subject. Only the few problems which, from the author's experience, seem of particular concern to the environmental lawyer are included.

JURISDICTION AND RELATED SUBJECTS

The first, and perhaps the greatest hurdle in a suit with the federal government is the motion to dismiss for lack of jurisdiction. Because the government puts so much of its litigation effort into such motions, he who defeats one may consider himself to have won a major victory. In fact, establishing the right of the citizen to sue to protect the environment by defeating such motions is of the first priority. Precedents in the field are trophies to be sought after.

Standing to sue.

The environmental lawyer will often be met by the argument that his client does not have standing to sue. He is not alone with this problem, however. Because of numerous emerging problems, the doctrine of standing has been subjected to quite a bit of scholarly attention of late.[3]

---

[2] The author recognizes two shortcomings with the discussion which follows, and its organization. First, it is incomplete and, second, many problems will lie in several categories as listed.

[3] Jaffe, *Judicial Control of Administrative Action*, at 459–500 (1965); Berger, "Standing to

This outline, therefore, will simply note developments in three areas: review of administrative decisions, taxpayers' suits and mandamus.

Office of Communication of the United Church of Christ v. Federal Communications Commission[4] and *Scenic Hudson Preservation Conference v. FPC* represent an exciting breakthrough in the law of standing to review the actions of the administrator. In *United Church of Christ,* the church, as a representative of the listening public, sought to intervene in an FCC television license renewal proceeding to present evidence and arguments opposing renewal. The Commission denied the petition to intervene for lack of standing, under section 309(d) of the Federal Communications Act,[5] on the grounds that no greater injury was claimed than would occur to the general public and that standing in such circumstances would cause a great administrative burden. The court held that the listener had an obvious and acute interest in broadcasting, though it was neither economic nor involved injury.[6] The court then observed that:

> The theory that the Commission can always effectively represent the listener interests in a renewal proceeding without the aid and participation of legitimate listener representatives fulfilling the role of private attorneys general is one of those assumptions we collectively try to work with so long as they are reasonably adequate. When it becomes clear, as it does to us now, that it is no longer a valid assumption which stands up under the realities of actual experience, neither we nor the commission can continue to rely on it. The gradual expansion and evaluation of concepts of standing in administrative law attests that experience rather than logic or fixed rules has been accepted as the guide.[7]

In addition, the court was unimpressed by the plea of administrative inconvenience, pointing out that the Commission already used *ad hoc* criteria for identifying "responsible spokesmen for representative groups having significant roots in the listening community" and that such groups

---

Sue in Public Actions: Is it a Constitutional Requirement?," 78 *Yale L.J.* 816 (1969); Rogers, "The Need for Meaningful Control in the Management of Federally Owned Timberlands," 4 *Land & Water L. Rev.* 121 (1969); Allen, "The Congressional Intent to Protect Test: A Judicial Lowering of the Standing Barrier, 41 *Colo. L. Rev.* 96 (1969); Jaffe, "The Citizen as Litigant in Public Actions: The Non-Hohfeldian or Ideological Plaintiff," 116 *U. of Pa. L. Rev.* 1033 (1968); Reich, "The Law of the Planned Society," 75 *Yale L. J.* 1227 (1966); Jaffe, "Standing to Secure Judicial Review: Private Actions," 75 *Harv. L. Rev.* 255 (1961); Jaffe, "Standing to Secure Judicial Review: Public Actions," 74 *Harv. L. Rev.* 1265 (1961).
[4] 359 F.2d 994 (C.A.D.C., 1966).
[5] 78 Stat. 193 (1964), 47 USC 309(e) (1962).
[6] 359 F.2d at 1002. 47 USC 309 (e) provides for intervention by "parties in interest." 47 USC 402(b) (6) provides for appeals from the Commission to the U.S. Court of Appeals for the District of Columbia "by any other person who is aggrieved or whose interests are adversely affected" by an FCC decision.
[7] 359 F.2d at 1003–1004.

appear in every community. The court noted the economic barrier to the imagined flood of suits and its confidence in the FCC's ability to identify spurious claims.[8] As a final word, we wish to invite attention to the following language of the court:

> ... intervention on behalf of the public is not allowed to press private interest but only to vindicate the broad public interest relating to a licensee's performance of the public trust inherent in every license.[9]

In *Scenic Hudson Preservation Conference v. FPC,* conservationists sought to intervene in an FPC proceeding concerning the application of the Consolidated Edison Company of New York for a license to construct a pumped storage hydroelectric project on Storm King Mountain. The Commission argued that applicants did not have standing to obtain judicial review because they claimed no economic injury. The court observed that the case or controversy requirement of Article III, section 2, of the Constitution does not require an "aggrieved" or adversely affected party to have a personal economic interest.[10] The court also observed that the Federal Power Act seeks to protect noneconomic as well as economic interests.[11] The court said:

> In order to insure that the Federal Power Commission will adequately protect the public interest in the aesthetic, conservational, and recreational aspects of power development, those who by their activities and conduct have exhibited a special interest in such areas, must be held to be included in the class of "aggrieved" parties under §313(b). We hold that the Federal Power Act gives petitioners a legal right to protect their special interests.[12]

In addition, this court was also unimpressed by the Commission's fear of a flood of interventions.

Several recent decisions have extended *Scenic Hudson* and *United Church of Christ* to grant standing to citizens who wish to be heard in the making of decisions with an environmental impact[13] or with some

---

[8]359 F.2d at 1004–1006.

[9]359 F.2d at 1006.

[10]354 F.2d at 615. 16 USC 825 1. (b) states: "Any party to a proceeding under this chapter aggrieved by an order issued by the commission may obtain a review . . ."

[11]The court suggested the broad public interests in recreation protected by 16 USC Sec. 803 (a) (354 F.2d at 613–615) included natural resources and beauty and historic sites. The author would suggest that the section protects, and that the court implied that it protects, the whole public interest, whatever it is, in the licensing of hydro projects.

[12]The court also noted certain applicants in intervention had a sufficient economic interest to intervene. 354 F.2d at 616.

[13]*Nashville I–40 Steering Committee v. Ellington,* 387 F.2d 179, 182 (C.A. 6, 1967) (Federal Aid Highway Act of 1956); *Road Review League, Town of Bedford v. Boyd,* 270 F. Supp. 650, 660 (S.D.N.Y., 1967) (Federal Highway Act, 23 USC 101(b), 109(a), 134 and 138);

other similar public interest impact.[14] These cases, either explicitly or by logical implication, find standing and jurisdiction under the Administrative Procedure Act, which provides:

> A person suffering legal wrong because of agency action, or adversely affected or aggrieved by agency action within the meaning of a relevant statute, is entitled to judicial review thereof.[15]

For example, in *Road Review League,* the court assigned the same meaning to the word "aggrieved" under 5 USC 702 as the court in *Scenic Hudson* assigned to that word in the Federal Power Act. This is certainly correct for the purposes of standing. (The question of jurisdiction is discussed later in this section.) There are other cases,[16] however, where the court looks to the "relevant statute" to determine whether that relevant statute recognizes "aggrieved" parties with standing.

As Professor Jaffe has pointed out, most states recognize the taxpayers suit to some extent.[17] Unfortunately, *Frothingham v. Mellon*[18] and its progeny[19] have stifled such suits at the Federal level. The recent case of *Flast v. Cohen*[20] has revived hope that such suits may yet be possible. In *Flast,* the court noted that the question of standing only raises the issue of whether the "dispute sought to be adjudicated will be presented in an

---

Citizens' Committee for the Hudson Valley v. Volpe,. 302 F. Supp. 1083 (69 Civ. 295 S.D.N.Y., July 11, 1969) standing to challenge unauthorized conduct of Army Corps of Engineers and Department of Transportation in granting license to fill in navigable water under Rivers and Harbor Act of 1899, 33 USC 401 *et seq.,* the General Bridge Act of 1946, 33 USC 526 *et seq.,* and the Department of Transportation Act of 1966, 49 Stat. 1651); *Parker v. United States,* Civ. Act. No. C–1368, U.S. Dist. Ct. for the Dist. of Colo. (The District Court denied a motion of United States to dismiss for lack of standing and jurisdiction without opinion on July 26, 1969. Plaintiffs brought suit to enjoin timber cut of *de facto* wilderness area within a National Forest under the Sustained Yield and Multiple Use Act of 1960, 16 USC 528 *et seq.*)

[14] *Norwalk Core v. Norwalk Redevelopment Agency,* 395 F.2d 920 (C.A.2, 1968) (National Housing Act, 42 USC 1455 (c)); *Powelton Civic Home Owners Ass'n v. Department of Housing and Urban Development,* 284 F. Supp. 809, 821–828 (E.D. Penn., 1968). (National Housing Act, 42 USC 1455 (c).)

[15] 5 USC 702.

[16] See *REA v Northern States Power Co.,* 373 F.2d 868 (C.A. 8, 1967) (Rural Electrification Act); *Association of Data Processing Service Organizations, Inc. v. Camp,* 406 F.2d 837 (C.A. 8, 1969) (National Bank Act); *Johnson v. Redevelopment Agency of the City of Oakland,* 317 F.2d 872 (C.A. 9, 1963); *Braude v. Wirtz,* 350 F.2d 702 (C.A. 9, 1965); *Turner v. Kings River Conservation District,* 360 F.2d 184 (C.A. 9, 1966) (Reclamation Laws).

[17] Jaffe, *Judicial Control of Administrative Action,* 470–472 (1965).

[18] 262 U.S. 447 (1923)

[19] *E.G. Perkins v. Lukens Steel Co.,* 310 U.S. 113 (1940).

[20] 392 U.S. 83 (1968).

adversary context and in a form historically viewed as capable of judicial resolution." For that reason, standing requires a personal stake in the outcome of a particular case. The court said: "A taxpayer may or may not have the requisite personal stake in the outcome, depending upon the circumstances of the particular case." To demonstrate this stake, a logical nexus between the status asserted (*e.g.*, taxpayer) and the claim sought to be adjudicated must be shown. It was suggested that the taxpayers are logical parties to challenge an unconstitutional exercise of taxing and spending powers, but not to challenge an essentially regulatory statute.

The court also said a logical nexus between the status asserted and the constitutional infringement asserted must be shown by alleging the specific limitation on power allegedly abused.

Hopefully, the principle of *Flast* may apply to the unauthorized expenditure of money by an executive officer. Admittedly, it is difficult to stretch the language of *Flast* to this result. However, it is a far more serious act of judicial control to declare an act of Congress unlawful than to declare executive spending unlawful. It is, however, of equal seriousness to the taxpayers who would, along with the courts, we hope, consider expenditures made contrary to Congressional instructions as unconstitutional as those made in *Flast.*

28 USC §1361[21] provides:

> The district courts shall have original jurisdiction of any action in the nature of mandamus to compel an officer or employee of the United States or an agency thereof to perform a duty owed to the plaintiff.

The question is whether "a duty owed to the plaintiff" embraces the right of the public interest litigant to obtain mandamus relief against a public officer requiring performance of a public duty he is neglecting.

By way of background, 28 USC §1361 was passed by Act of October 5, 1962. Prior to that date, the United States District Courts were without mandamus jurisdiction. The District Court for the District of Columbia, however, deriving jurisdiction not only from Title 28, but also from the law of the State of Maryland as of 1801, when the District was ceded, could assert such jurisdiction.[22] The purpose of 28 USC was to extend the mandamus jurisdiction of the District Court for the District of Columbia to all the other District Courts.[23]

---

[21] 76 Stat. 744.

[22] *See Kendall v. United States,* 12 Pet. (37 U.S.) 524 (1838).

[23] 1962 U.S. Code *Cong & Adm. News,* 2784–2790, Sen. Rep. No. 1992, 87th Cong., 2d sess., 1962. The best discussion the author has found on 28 U.S.C. §1361 is in Byse & Fiocca, Section 1361 of the Mandamus and Venue Act of 1962 and "nonstatutory" Judicial Review

The mandamus jurisdiction contemplated by Section 1361 is:

... to issue orders compelling Government officials to perform their duties and to make decisions in matters involving the exercise of discretion, but not to direct or influence the exercise of the officer or agency in the making of the decision.[24]

Again:

... the court can only compel the official or agency to act where there is a duty, which the committee construes as an obligation, to act or, where the official or agency has failed to make any decision in a matter involving the exercise of discretion, but only to order that a decision be made and with no control over the substance off the decision.[25]

Where a statute does not specifically provide for review of the actions of a Government official, the aggrieved party may obtain judicial review through invoking one of several nonstatutory proceedings. Which of these he chooses turns upon the relief sought. In certain cases, the relief desired can only be obtained by compelling a Government official to perform an act which he is required to do by statute but which he nevertheless failed to do. Traditionally, the appropriate remedy in that case has been a writ of mandamus. . . . [26]

The District of Columbia precedents have, unfortunately, been rather narrow on the subject of standing. For example, the court held in *Laughlin v. Reynolds*[27] that the plaintiff did not have standing as a member of the bar or as a taxpayer[28] to bring a mandamus action to require the Commissioner of Public Buildings to evict the bar association library from the court house. Again, in *United States v. Dern,*[29] mandamus standing was denied on the ground that plaintiff was representing the public (also citing *Massachusetts v. Mellon*). The court said, "Their

---

of Federal Administrative Action, 81 *Harv. L. Rev.* 308 (1967).

[24]196 2 U.S. Code *Cong. & Adm. News,* 2785.

[25]*Id.* at 2787. This language obviously harks back to the concept that mandamus is strictly for ministerial acts. The recent case of *Harms v. Federal Housing Administration,* 256 F. Supp. 757 (D.C. Md., 1966), is, however, an example where the court was obviously edging close to reviewing a discretionary act, reversing a decision of the Secretary of the Interior disallowing a will. See Professor Jaffe's enlightened comments of how discretion should be treated under mandamus, *Judicial Control of Administrative Action,* at 180–186.

[26]1962 U.S. Code *Cong. and Adm. News,* 2785. One court has gone so far as to say jurisdiction under 1361 can be used to effectuate the Administrative Procedure Act. *Atewooftakewa v. Udall,* 277 F. Supp. 464 (W.D. Okla., 1967).

[27]196 F.2d 863 (C.A.D.C., 1952).

[28]The court cited *Massachusetts vs. Mellon,* 262 U.S. 447 (1923).

[29]68 F.2d 773 (C.A.D.C., 1934).

interest is not personal and direct, but indirect and remote."[30]

This narrow view of mandamus is unfortunate in view of an early Supreme Court case which indicated another approach. In *Union Pacific R.R. v. Hall*[31] an action was brought to compel the railroad to perform its public duty under a special mandamus statute.[32]

The court put the question thus:

> The appellants contend that the court erred in holding that Hall and Morse, on whose petition the alternative writ was issued, could lawfully become relators in this suit on behalf of the public without the assent or direction of the Attorney-General of the United States, or of the district attorney for the district of Iowa. They were merchants in Iowa, having frequent occasion to receive and ship goods over the Company's road; but they had no interest other than such as belonged to others engaged in employments like theirs and the duty they seek to enforce by the writ is a duty to the public generally. The question raised by the objection, therefore, is whether a writ of *mandamus* to compel the performance of a public duty may be issued at the instance of a private relator.

The court believed the answer to the question was yes in England and in the preponderance of American jurisdictions and held that relators "were competent to apply for the writ." Professor Jaffe also points out that "The very considerable weight of authority now supports the citizen-mandamus suit," noting 29 jurisdictions that allow the action, five that are doubtful and 10 that are contra.[33]

Because the court in *Laughlin v. Reynolds* and *United States v. Dern* relied upon *Massachusetts v. Mellon*, it would seem appropriate to reexamine standing under § 1361 in light of *Flast v. Cohen*. Certainly, with the District of Columbia Circuit decisions so far out of line with the Supreme Court's statement in *Hall* and the preponderant American authority, the environmental lawyer should not discount the Federal citizen-mandamus suit.

Sovereign immunity.

The most important jurisdictional bar to an action to enjoin the federal government is the doctrine of sovereign immunity. That doctrine can,

---

[30]68 F.2d at 774. In this case, plaintiff actually had strong personal interest. As a warehouseman, he sought to force the cancellation of a lease of warehouses owned by the United States and leased to a competitor. Also see *United States ex rel. American Silver Producers' Ass'n v. Mellon*, 32 F.2d 415 (C.A.D.C., 1929) and *United States ex rel. Alsop Process Co. v. Wilson*, 33 U.S. App. D.C. 472 (1909).

[31]91 U.S. 343 (1876).

[32]Act of March 3, 1873 (17 Stat. 509, §4).

[33]Jaffe, *Judicial Control of Administrative Action*, at 468–469.

practically speaking, at this time only be skirted by an action against a federal officer to enjoin unauthorized conduct. Such an action, however, often provides an excellent vehicle for a court to define the language of the statute under which the official purports to act on a motion to dismiss. Unfortunately, as the doctrine has developed, the injunction suit is only a useful tool to *prevent* unauthorized action; the courts have shunned ordering the official to do a *positive act*[34] or preventing the officer from doing merely a wrongful act.[35]

In essence, the United States, by reason of its sovereignty, is immune from suit, save as it consents to be sued.[36] Congress alone can waive the immunity of the United States from suit.[37] Unless the United States, through an Act of Congress, has consented to be sued, no court in the land has jurisdiction of an action against the United States.[38] In the words of Chief Justice Marshall:

> As the United States are not suable of common right, the party who institutes such suit must bring his case within the authority of some Act of Congress, or the court cannot exercise jurisdiction over it.[39]

The sovereign, of course, can only act through its agents. Consequently, if an action is brought against an individual who is an employee of the United States to enjoin an act done within the scope of his duties, the action is against the sovereign.[40]

A statement in *Larson*, pp. 701–702, is often quoted as providing the criteria as to when the suit is against the sovereign:

> . . . the action of an officer of the sovereign (be it holding, taking or otherwise legally affecting the plaintiff's property) can be regarded as so "illegal" as to permit a suit for specific relief against the officer as an individual only if it is

---

[34] *See Dugan v. Rank,* 372 U.S. 609 (1963); *City of Fresno v. California,* 372 U.S. 627 (1963), *See dissent of Frankfurter, Larson v. Domestic & Foreign Corp.,* 337 U.S. 682, 705, 711–714 (1949). The magic words are that a suit cannot be had that would "expend itself on the public treasury or domain, or interfere with the public administration." *Land v. Dollar,* 330 U.S. 731, 738 (1947). On the relation of this doctrine to mandamus, see Jaffe, *Judicial Control of Administrative Action,* at 224–225, 227–229 (1965).

[35] *See Larson v. Domestic & Foreign Corp.,* 337 U.S. 682 (1948). Frankfurter's vigorous dissent should not be skipped. *Also see* Jaffe, *Judicial Control of Administrative Action,* at 222–231 (1965). A return to an earlier position allowing certain types of wrongs to be enjoined would be refreshing. See Douglas's dissent in *Malone v. Bowdoin,* 369 U.S. 643, 648 (1962) and Byse, "Proposed Reforms in Federal 'Nonstatutory' Judicial Review: Sovereign Immunity, Indispensable Parties, Mandamus," 75 *Harv. L. Rev.* 1478 (1962).

[36] *United States v. Sherwood,* 312 U.S. 584, 586 (1941).

[37] *Dalehite v. United States,* 346 U.S. 15, 30 (1953).

[38] *United States v. Shaw,* 309 U.S. 495, 500–01 (1940).

[39] *United States v. Clarke,* 8 Pet. (33 U.S.) 436, 444 (1836).

[40] *Land v. Dollar, supra; Larson v. Domestic & Foreign Corp., supra; Dugan v. Rank, supra; Malone v. Bowdoin, supra.*

not within the officer's statutory powers or, if within those powers, only if the powers, or their exercise in the particular case, are constitutionally void.

Thus, one must at this point find lack of statutory authority to enjoin an individual officer and such lack must be alleged.[41]

Whether an officer has acted beyond his authority most likely cannot be determined until after a factual investigation is made of what, exactly, he did or plans to do. Nevertheless, the government will usually try to dismiss on the pleadings. Justice Douglas' observation in *Land v. Dollar* that "this is the type of case where the question of jurisdiction is dependent on the decision of the merits"[42] should be brought to the court's attention on any motion to dismiss.

A case not to be overlooked and which should still be good law is *Ickes v. Fox*.[43] On its facts, it may show that the *Larson* distinction between unauthorized conduct and a wrong may really depend on how a complaint is phrased.

Having avoided the jurisdictional problem of sovereign immunity, on what does one base jurisdiction in the federal courts of the suit against the officer? The problem arises where the bone of contention may be of great value, *e.g.* a National Forest, but it is hard to phrase the interest of the plaintiff in terms of money. Based on the author's experience at the Justice Department, many government attorneys do not believe it is cricket for the United States to raise the question of jurisdictional amount. The Supreme Court, perhaps, feels the same way. In *Harmon v. Brucker*,[44] without being very explicit, it very helpfully said:

> Generally, judicial relief is available to one who has been injured by an act of a government official which is in excess of his express or implied powers. *American School of Magnetic Healing v. McNulty*, 187 U.S. 94, 108; *Philadelphia Co. v. Stimson*, 223 U.S. 605, 621–622; *Stark v. Wickard*, 321 U.S. 288, 310. The District Court had not only jurisdiction to determine its jurisdiction but also power to construe the statutes involved to determine whether the respondent did exceed his powers. If he did so, his actions would not constitute exercises of his administrative discretion, and, in such circumstances as those before us, judicial relief from this illegality would be available. Moreover, the claims presented in these cases may be entertained by the District Court because petitioners have alleged judicially cognizable injuries. Cf., *Joint Anti-Fascist Refugee Committee v. McGrath*, 341 U.S. 123, 159, 160, and see Army Regulation 615–360, par. 7.

The District Court shifted the problem in *Citizens Committee for the Hudson Valley* by putting jurisdiction on the Administrative Procedure

[41] *Malone v. Bowdoin, supra* at 647.
[42] *Supra* at 735.
[43] 300 U.S. 82 (1937).
[44] 355 U.S. 579 (1958).

Act (see below). We may infer that Professor Jaffe would approve of this solution. He states:

> It does seem inapt to make it a condition of a suit against an officer that the right asserted be given a value, if indeed in many cases it is even possible. This being so it would seem to be sound to treat § 10 (of the Administrative Procedure Act) as a source of jurisdiction with respect to any of the questions which that section makes reviewable, and some courts have so held.[45]

Administrative Procedure Act.

A division of opinion has developed over whether or not the Administrative Procedure Act[46] is a jurisdictional statute. The government takes a strong position that it is not and that jurisdiction must be found elsewhere in the "relevant" statute. The author believes the Act itself should settle this matter. Section 701 (a) reads:

> This chapter applies, according to the provisions thereof, except to the extent that—
> (1) statutes preclude judicial review; or
> (2) agency action is committed to agency discretion by law.

The debate is shifted by the government to 5 USC § 702, which reads:

> A person suffering legal wrong because of agency action, or adversely affected or aggrieved by agency action within the meaning of a relevant statute, is entitled to judicial review thereof.

This outline will not attempt to treat the arguments seriously at this point, except to bring to the reader's attention some of the cases pro[47] and con.[48]

---

[45] Jaffe, *Judicial Control of Administrative Action*, at 164–5.

[46] 5 U.S.C. 701, *et seq.*

[47] *Abbott Laboratories v. Gardner*, 387 U.S. 136 (1967) (Review permissible under APA and Declaratory Judgment Act of regulations issued under the Federal Food, Drug and Cosmetic Act, § 701(f)(6); 21 U.S.C. § 371 (f)(6), which provides that: "remedies provided for in this subsection should be in addition to and not in substitution for any other remedies provided by law"): *Converse v. Udall*, 399 F.2d 616 (C.A. 9, 1968) (Appeal from decision of Secy. of the Interior under the Surface Resources Act of 1955, 69 Stat. 367, 30 USC § 601 *et seq.*); *Norwalk Corp. v. Norwalk 'Redevelopment Agency*, 395 F.2d. 920, 932–937 (C.A. 2, 1968) (Review under § 105(c) of the Housing Act of 1949. While right to review found under relevant statute, it is clear that that statute was interpreted in light of APA, 395 F.2d at 932–3. This case also involved standing.); *Brennan v. Udall*, 379 F.2d 803 (C.A. 10, 1967), *cert. den.* 389 U.S. 975 (Decision of Secy of the Interior reserving oil shale under Act of July 17, 1914, 30 USC §§ 121–123, reviewable under APA); *Coleman v. United States*, 363 F.2d 190 (C.A. 9, 1966), *aff'd on reh.*, 379 F.2d 555 (1967), *rev'd on other grounds.* 396 U.S. 599 (1968) (Review of Secy. of the Interior's decision under the Surface Resources Act of 1955, 30 USC 601 *et seq.*, reviewable under APA); *Cappadora v. Celebrezze*, 356 F.2d 1 (C.A. 2, 1966) (Review of decision of Secy of HEW refusing to reopen denial of Social Security benefits, reviewable under APA); *Freeman v. Brown*, 342 F.2d 205 (C.A. 5, 1965) (Action

Professor Davis at Chapter 28, *Administrative Law Treatise,* discusses generally the full range of problems of unreviewable administrative action under the APA. See in particular §28.08.

Venue

The major problem[49] of venue and service of process in suits against Federal officers was solved with the addition of section 1391(e) to Title 28 of the United States Code, which reads:

A civil action in which each defendant is an officer or employee of the United States or any agency thereof acting in his official capacity or under color of legal authority, or an agency of the United States, may, except as otherwise provided by law, be brought in any judicial district in which: (1) a defendant in the action resides, or (2) the cause of action arose, or (3) any real property involved in the action is situated, or (4) the plaintiff resides if no real property is involved in the action.

The summons and complaint in such an action shall be served as provided by the Federal Rules of Civil Procedure except that the delivery of the summons

---

of Secy of Agriculture in fixing crop quotas reviewable under APA where action alleged to be outside the statutory boundaries of Agricultural Adjustment Act of 1938, as amended); *Estrada v. Ahrens,* 296 F.2d 690 (C.A. 5, 1961) (Nonresident alien could obtain review of Immigration and Naturalization officer's decision. "If Estrada's plight resulted from a government official's misconstruction of the statute, the official exceeded his statutory authority. A court of law is the proper place to test 'unauthorized administrative power,'" 296 F.2d at 695); *Adams v. Witmer,* 271 F.2d 29 (C.A. 9, 1958) (Judicial review of BLM order denying mining patent founded on APA); *Powelton Civic Home Owners Ass'n. v. HUD,* 284 F. Supp. 809 (E.D. Pa., 1968) (Jurisdiction found to review decision of Secy of HUD denying plaintiffs hearing under National Housing Act; Standing also involved); *Road Review League, Town of Bedford v. Boyd,* 270 F. Supp. 650 (S.D.N.Y., 1967) (Review of decision of Bureau of Public Roads; standing also involved); cf. *Harmon v. Brucker,* 355 U.S. 579 (1958); *Foster v. Seaton,* 271 F.2d 836 (C.A.D.C., 1959) (Which, though APA jurisdiction not discussed, must have same basis as *Coleman* and *Converse* above). *Also see Shaughnessy v. Pedreiro,* 349 U.S. 48 (1955). *See Byse & Fiocca, supra* n. 20.
[48]*Motah v. United States,* 402 F.2d 1 (C.A. 10, 1968) (Review of decision of Secy of Interior on contest of Indian election and complaints of denial of right to vote denied); *Twin Cities Chippewa Tribal Council v. Minnesota Chippewa Tribe,* 370 F.2d 529 (C.A. 8, 1967) (Decision of Secy to approve election and amendments of tribal constitution and bylaws held unreviewable; 25 USC §476, under which Secretary acted held to be discretionary); *Rural Electrification Administration v. Central Louisiana Electric Co.,* 354 F.2d 859 (C.A. 5, 1966) (No jurisdiction to review grant or denial of loans under §4 of the Rural Electrification Act of 1936, 7 USC §904); *Chournos v. United States,* 335 F.2d 918 (C.A. 10, 1964) (Secy of Interior's decision that mining claims were invalid held unreviewable under APA); *Local 542, International Union of Operating Engineers v. NLRB,* 328 F.2d 850 (C.A. 3, 1964), cert. den. 379 U.S. 826; *Cyrus v. United States,* 226 F.2d 416 (C.A. 5, 1955); *Cf. Blackmar v. Guerre,* 342 U.S. 512 (1951).
[49]*See Blackmar v. Guerre,* 342 U.S. 512 (1957), a wonderful example of pre–1391(e) problems. *See also* 1962 U.S. Code *Cong. & Adm. News,* 2784–2790, Sen. Rep. No. 1992, 87th Cong., 2d sess., 1962.

and complaint to the officer or agency as required by the rules may be made by certified mail beyond the territorial limits of the district in which the action is brought.

A snag remains if *each* defendant is not an officer or an agency of the United States. The District Court for the Eastern District of Pennsylvania, in *Powelton Civic Home Owners Ass'n. v. Department of Housing and Urban Development,*[50] said:

> . . . we conclude that the requirement that "each defendant" be a *federal* defendant refers only to defendants who are *beyond* the forum's territorial limits. Thus the joining of a non-federal defendant located within the forum's territorial limits and adequately served under F. R. Civ. P.4(f) has no effect on the applicability or operation of Section 1391(e). Indeed, any other conclusion would appear illogical.

Powelton was followed by the District Court in Colorado in *Brotherhood of Locomotive Engineers v. Denver & Rio Grande Western R.R.*[51] An earlier Eastern District, Pennsylvania, decision reads the statute literally and comes to the opposite result. *Chase Savings & Loan Ass'n v. Federal Home Loan Bank Bd.,*[52] followed by the District Court in Minnesota, *Benson v. City of Minneapolis.*

DISCOVERY, THE FREEDOM OF INFORMATION ACT AND THE EXECUTIVE PRIVILEGE

Discovery falls logically into two broad categories: (1) discovery during an action under the Federal Rules of Civil Procedure, and (2) discovery under the Freedom of Information Act, 5 USC 552.[54] A third category might be discovery during administrative proceedings which presents special problems if information is desired from another private participant. This outline will be confined to one topic, under both the Freedom of Information Act and the Federal Rules, in discovery against the government: the executive privilege.

The executive privilege as developed in discovery proceedings has been used from time to time to limit discovery in judicial proceedings. The privilege has several branches and its scope has varied a bit from decision to decision. This outline is concerned chiefly with its use to cover intradepartmental documents incident to the formulation of policy decisions.[55] 5 USC § 552(b) (5) of the Freedom of Infor-

---

[50]284 F. Supp. 809 (1968).
[51]290 F. Supp. 612 (1968).
[52]269 F. Supp. 965 (1967).
[53]286 F. Supp. 614 (1968).
[54]Act of June 5, 1967, 81 Stat. 54; Act of July 4, 1966, 80 Stat. 250.
[55]*See United States v. Reynolds,* 345 U.S. 1 (1953); *United States v. Morgan,* 313 U.S. 409 (1940); *Kaiser Aluminum & Chem. Corp. v. United States,* 157 F. Supp. 939 (Ct.Cl., 1958);

mation Act is designed to incorporate the privilege. That section reads:

(b) This section does not apply to matters that are:

* * *

(5) inter-agency or intra-agency memorandums or letters which would not be available by law to a party other than by a party in litigation with the agency; . . .

The purpose of this provision as it appears in legislative history is as follows:

Inter-agency or intra-agency memorandums or letters which would not be available by law to a private party in litigation with the agency: Agency witnesses argued that a full and frank exchange of opinions would be impossible if all internal communications were made public. They contended, and with merit, that advice from staff assistants and the exchange of ideas among agency personnel would not be completely frank if they were forced to "operate in a fishbowl." Moreover, a Government agency cannot always operate effectively if it is required to disclose documents or information which it has received or generated before it completes the process of awarding a contract or issuing an order, decision or regulation. This clause is intended to exempt from disclosure this and other information and records wherever necessary without, at the same time, permitting indiscriminate administrative secrecy. S.1160 exempts from disclosure material "which would not be available by law to a private party in litigation with the agency." Thus, any internal memorandums which would routinely be disclosed to a private party through the discovery process in litigation with the agency would be available to the general public.[56]

The rationale for the privilege is sometimes stated to be the principle that the reasoning process of the administrator should not be probed by the courts.[57] The real underlying reason, though, is the one cited in H.R. Rep. No. 1497, *supra*, to encourage a frank exchange of ideas in office memorandums prior to decisions. The court, in *Kaiser*, made it clear:

Free and open comments on the advantages and disadvantages and of a proposed course of governmental management would be adversely affected if the civil servant or executive assistant were compelled by publicity to bear the blame for errors or bad judgment properly chargeable to the responsible individual with power to decide and act. Government from its nature has necessarily been granted a certain freedom from control beyond that given the citizen. It is true that it now submits itself to suit but it must retain privileges for the good of all.

Carl Zeiss Stiftung v. V.E.B. Zeiss, Jena, 40 F.R.D. 318 (D.D.C., 1966).

[56] 1966 U.S. Code Cong. & Ad. News, 2427-2428; H.R. Rep. No. 1497, 89th Cong., 2d sess., 1966.

[57] *United States v. Morgan, supra; Carl Zeiss, supra.*

There is a public policy involved in this claim of privilege for this advisory opinion—the policy of open, frank discussion between subordinate and chief concerning administrative action.[58]

With all that said, the policy really does not amount to much. In fact, the courts have seen its potential for abuse and have limited it.

The first thing to note is that it is not a privilege which can be raised as a matter of course by the government, but must be formally claimed by the head of the department which is concerned.[59]

Secondly, an observation should be made about *Morgan*. In that case, the Secretary of Agriculture was deposed concerning the weight he gave to various documents in the record. The court's statement that this procedure was improper certainly should never properly be an obstacle to prevent a party from obtaining the entire administrative record upon which a decision was made.

Thirdly, the privilege "is not to be lightly invoked."[60]

Fourth, the court said in *Reynolds*:

The court itself must determine whether the circumstances are appropriate for the claim of privilege.[61]

Whether this is to be done by the court by an examination of the document *in camera* or by accepting the arguments of the government is a matter for judicial discretion. The court is to observe the circumstances of the case and the showing of necessity for the document in order to determine how far to probe and, of course, the propriety of the reasons for claiming the privilege.[62]

The author believes that the *Reynolds* case, representing a claim of national security, should be the hardest for the judge to decide and that in any less important matter, the court should examine the material *in camera*, although the courts refused to make the examination in *Kaiser* and in *Carl Zeiss*.[63]

Should Rule 5–09 of the proposed Federal Rules of Evidence be

---

[58]157 F. Supp. at 945–46.

[59]*United States v. Reynolds*, 345 U.S. 1 (1953).

[60]*United States v. Reynolds, supra* at 7. (The *Reynolds* case actually involved the privilege against revealing military secrets. The court's generalizations, however, fit the less important privilege against furnishing intra-office memos. See *Kaiser Aluminum & Chem. Corp. v. United States, supra*, and *Carl Zeiss, supra*.)

[61]*United States v. Reynolds*, 345 U.S., at 8. See *Kaiser Aluminum & Chem. Corp. v. United States, supra* at 947.

[62]*United States v. Reynolds, supra* at 10–11.

[63]*Carl Zeiss* clearly involved diplomatic secrets, so is on a par with *Reynolds*. *Kaiser* is less clear.

adopted in its present form,[64] the privilege will no longer exist as to intra-office memoranda. The proposed rule limits the privilege to "secrets of state" which are defined to include only matters of "national defense" and "international relations."

OTHER PROCEDURAL MATTERS

Additional subjects will, if they do not already, obtain special significance for the environmental lawyer under the general topics of procedure. Two will be touched briefly in these pages.

Burden of proof.

The assignment of the burden of proof in administrative proceedings and at trials may be the ultimate determinant of many environmental cases. Professor Krier, in this volume, offers a discussion on this topic in which he points the way for the environmental lawyer. I will simply restrict myself to a few observations on some recent cases.

In *Scenic Hudson Preservation Conference v. FPC*,[65] the court placed the burden on the FPC to make the record complete on the criteria defined in its Congressional mandate. The Supreme Court adopted this view as its own in *Udall v. FPC*.[66]

We also note that in the second *United Church of Christ* opinion,[67] Judge Burger stated:

> . . . a "public" intervenor who is seeking no license or private right is, in this context, more nearly like a complaining witness who presents evidence to police or prosecutor whose duty it is to conduct an affirmative and objective investigation of all the facts and to pursue his prosecution or regulatory function if there is probable cause to believe a violation has occurred.

Later, the court observed:

> The Commission and the examiners have an affirmative duty to assist in the development of a meaningful record which can serve as the basis for the evaluation of the licensee's performance of his duty to serve the public interest. The public intervenors, who were performing a public service under a mandate of this court, were entitled to a more hospitable reception in the performance of that function. As we view the record the Examiner tended to impede the exploration of the very issues which we would reasonably expect the Commission itself would have initiated; an ally was regarded as an opponent.

---

[64]Committee on Rules of Practice and Procedure of the Judicial Conference of the United States, *Preliminary Draft of Proposed Rules of Evidence for the United States District Courts and Magistrates*, 8–13.

[65]354 F.2d 608 (C.A. 2, 1965), *cert. den.*, 384 U.S. 941 (1965).

[66]387 U.S. 428 (1967).

[67]*Office of Communication of the United Church of Christ v. FCC*, ____ F.2d ____ (C.A. D.C., No. 19, 409, June 20, 1969).

Thus, the FCC has the burden of insuring a complete investigation and record for the matters which it decides.[68]

These decisions are inherently correct for an administrator who is going to administrate as well as decide. This is obvious when one shifts his view from a regulatory body to an executive agency such as the Forest Service or the Corps of Engineers. The burden is clearly on them to follow the criteria set forth in statutes that authorize their administration. The responsibility should never rest on the citizen to bring one iota of evidence to the administrator's attention. The rule should be that he must search out the relevant facts or act at his peril.

Evidence.

Of the many problems of evidence that will confront the environmental lawyer, I will mention two articles in the *Sierra Club Bulletin* that discuss, respectively, natural beauty and cost-benefit ratios. David Sive's report in this volume, "Securing, Examining and Cross-Examining Expert Witnesses in Environmental Cases," discusses, *inter alia*, the problems of natural beauty. Mr. Sive has dealt with this issue once before in a very fine article in the *Sierra Club Bulletin* for May, 1968, entitled "The Storm King Mountain Case: Natural Beauty and the Law." A few points cribbed from these articles are included here because of their importance to the environmental lawyer.

The question is what type of evidence can be introduced on the subject of natural beauty when it must be weighed against the values of the technocracy? How does one present an objective analyzation of the degree of scenic beauty of a specific place when asking the decision-maker "to elevate rather than fatten mankind."

Among the topics touched on are the type of experts that may be used and the comparative approach available to experts. Of great interest is the evidence and argument used to rebut the claim that a vast project could be disguised so as not to injure visually the scenic beauty of a mountain. Testimony was introduced to establish that the scenic beauty of the mountain depended on the continuance of the mountain's integrity as a mountain and not as a pumped storage project.

Attorneys will often come up against the cost-benefit ratio in struggling with projects destructive of environmental values. A model analysis of

---

[68]If any party had a burden before the Commission, it was the license-seeking station rather than the public interest intervenor. ". . . The conduct of the hearing was not primarily the licensee's responsibility, although as the applicant it had the burden of proof." *Office of Communication of the United Church of Christ v. FCC*, _____ f.2d _____ (C.A.D.C., No. 19, 409, June 20, 1969).

one such cost-benefit ratio is beautifully set forth in the January, 1968, *Sierra Club Bulletin:* Neuzil, "Uses and Abuses of Highway Benefit-Cost Analysis, with Particular Reference to the Red Buffalo Route."

While the article dissects a highway ratio, many of the points discussed, such as interest rates and project life, are applicable to any project. The potential gains from detailed analysis are evident. When confronted with a cost-benefit ratio, the environmental lawyer must make the effort to understand it completely and to secure the expert engineering help necessary to combat it.

SUBSTANTIVE ENVIRONMENTAL MATTERS: INTRODUCTION

Substantive environmental matters are broken into three broad groups in this outline: pollution, land use, and public lands. Within each of these broad groups are several subgroups. Generally, each subgroup is characterized by its own cluster of special statutes. Problems, of course, will often cross lines, falling in several categories. In addition, goals and approaches may be very similar from one category to the next.

Within each category of these problems attorneys will face difficulties of several types:

Information. In many areas, a client's real need may simply be to discover certain facts. For example, what a specific agency is doing to enforce water pollution control or what the status of a proposed project is.

Rule-making. A problem's solution may depend on how an agency interprets its authority. The courts bend over backwards to uphold the administrator's interpretation of the law.[69] Therefore, participation in rule-making and less formal administrative interpretations may be the problem the environmental lawyer faces.

Precedent. The client may have a problem which involves a broad management policy that requires a judicial precedent. This may give the attorney the opportunity to do that which the Justice Department often does: pick the best case on the facts under that policy.

Enforcement. The problem may simply be to get an environmental enforcement agency to do its job under the law or to prevent an agency from engaging in activities contrary to its policy mandate.

The four types of problems exist in each of the environmental topics which will be discussed below. The analysis of each topic in terms of these types is beyond the scope of this outline, but would, of course, be useful for the environmental bar.

---

[69] *Udall v. Talman,* 380 U.S. 1 (1965).

POLLUTION

The earth is being increasingly polluted by both substances and energy levels inimical to life. It has become clear in the last few years that man holds the future of all life on the planet, including his own, in his hands. Pollution control laws are the awakening responses of man to the realization of the problem. These laws must, however, be enforced and extended if their promise is to be fulfilled. This task will fall on the environmental bar.

Water Pollution.

The legal literature on water pollution control has now reached significant size. A good starting survey is Gindler, "Water Pollution and Quality Control."[70] There is a substantial amount of private and state statutory law in this field, which Gindler covers. This outline will be limited to the federal law.

The Federal Water Pollution Control Act[71] is the most important Federal water pollution legislation. Unfortunately, it seems deliberately designed to make it difficult for the person injured by pollution, much less a mere citizen group, to participate in its enforcement proceedings. Serious study should, however, be made by environmental lawyers of ways to participate in the enforcement proceedings.

Section 10 is the key section for our purposes. This section provides procedures for two types of enforcement: pollution abatement procedures, and water quality standard enforcement procedures.

The pollution of "interstate or navigable waters" which endangers the health or welfare of any person is made subject to abatement.[72] Interstate waters, as defined by the Act, are "all rivers, lakes, and other waters that flow across or form a part of State boundaries, including coastal waters." Under this definition, state boundaries include international boundaries; coastal waters include the Great Lakes; and rivers, lakes and other waters include the entire body, regardless of how much of it flows across or forms part of a boundary.[73] "Navigable waters" are not defined, but would seem to embrace the entire authority of Congress under the Commerce clause.

The abatement proceeding under the Act is rather long and cumber-

---

[70]3 Clark (ed), *Water and Water Rights*, 1967.

[71]33 USC 466, *et seq.*

[72]Pollution is not defined, but apparently is matter discharged into interstate or navigable waters or that reaches such water after discharge into a tributary thereof.

[73]U.S. Dep't of the Interior, Federal Water Pollution Control Administration, *Guidelines for Establishing Water Quality Standards for Interstate Waters*, 10,11 (May, 1966).

some, involving three steps: conference, hearing and court action.

The conference is an informal gathering of state and Federal agency representatives. The Secretary of the Interior *must* call a conference if requested by a state governor or state water pollution control agency, and interstate pollution is involved.[74] He *must* also call such a conference whenever he has reason to believe, on the basis of reports, surveys, or studies, that interstate pollution is occurring or that:

> . . . substantial economic injury results from the inability to market shellfish or shellfish products in interstate commerce because of pollution referred to in subsection (a) and action of Federal, State or local authorities.[75]

The Secretary *may* call a conference when requested by a governor and intrastate pollution is involved if, in his judgment, the effect of the pollution is of sufficient significance. He may also call a conference in certain cases of international pollution.

The conferees are essentially the state water pollution control agencies, not polluters or persons injured. The state agencies (but apparently not the federal government) can bring anyone they choose to the conference. However, every person contributing to the alleged pollution or affected by it is to be given an opportunity to make a full statement of his views. The majority of the conferees may request an alleged polluter to file a report "based on existing data, furnishing such information as may reasonably be requested as to the character, kind, and quantity of such [pollution] and the use of faciltiies or other means to prevent or reduce such [pollution]."[76]

Following a conference, the Secretary prepares for the conferees a summary of the discussions, including the occurrence of pollution subject to abatement, the adequacy of measures taken toward abatement, and the nature of the delays being encountered in abating the pollution.

If, at the close of a conference, the Secretary believes progress toward abatement is not being made and that any person's health and welfare is being endangered, he is required to recommend that the appropriate state agency take remedial action. If, after six months following the Secretary's recommendation, appropriate action has not been taken, the Secretary is required to call a public hearing to be held before a board.[77]

---

[74] By interstate pollution is meant "pollution of waters which is endangering the health or welfare of persons in a State other than that in which the discharge or discharges (causing or contributing to such pollution) originates."

[75] 33 U.S.C. 466g(d) (1).

[76] 33 U.S.C. 466g(k) (1).

[77] The Board will have five or more members picked by the Secretary, one by the Secretary of Commerce, one from each state where the pollution originates or which is affected thereby. Majority must not be employees of the Department of the Interior.

In the words of the statute:

> ... It shall be ... the responsibility of the Hearing Board to give every person contributing to the alleged pollution or affected by it an opportunity to make a full statement of his views to the Hearing Board. On the basis of the evidence presented at such hearing, the Hearing Board shall make findings as to whether pollution ... is occurring and whether effective progress toward abatement thereof is being made. If the Hearing Board finds such pollution is occurring and effective progress toward abatement thereof is not being made it shall make recommendations to the Secretary concerning the measures, if any, which it finds to be reasonable and equitable to secure abatement of such pollution. The Secretary shall send such findings and recommendations to the person or persons discharging any matter causing or contributing to such pollution, together with a notice specifying a reasonable time (not less than six months) to secure abatement of such pollution, and shall also send such findings and recommendations and such notice to the State water pollution control agency and to the interstate agency, if any, of the State or States where such discharge or discharges originate.[78]

The Secretary also may, in connection with a hearing, require a polluter to file a report similar to that which may be required at a conference. The report is made under oath and is considered confidential.

If action is not taken in the specified reasonable time required to abate the pollution, the Secretary may request the Attorney General to bring an enforcement suit. (If the pollution is intrastate, the consent of the state governor is required.) In the words of the statute:

> The court shall receive in evidence in any suit a transcript of the proceedings before the Board and a copy of the Board's recommendations and shall receive such further evidence as the court in its discretion deems proper. The court, giving due consideration to the practicability and to the physical and economic feasibility of securing abatement of any pollution proved, shall have jurisdiction to enter such judgement, and orders enforcing such judgment, as the public interest and the equities of the case may require.[79]

The only court action ever filed under these laws was filed against the City of St. Joseph, Missouri, in 1960.[80] That action resulted in a firm order requiring compliance. One is led to wonder, given the amount of pollution in our streams, why the Secretary has not followed up the St. Joseph victory with other actions.

The Water Quality Act of October 2, 1965, provides for the establishment of water quality standards and plans for their implementation and enforcement by the states, or by the Secretary, in regard to interstate

---

[78] 33 U.S.C. 466g(f) (1).
[79] 33 U.S.C. 466g(h).
[80] *United States v. City of St. Joseph*, No. 1077, W.D. Mo., St. Joseph Div.

waters (but not on navigable waters).[81] The standards are to "be such as to protect the public health or welfare, enhance the quality of water and serve the purposes of [this Act]." In establishing standards, "use and value for public water supplies, propagation of fish and wildlife, recreational purposes, and agricultural, industrial, and other legitimate uses" must be considered.

As of this date, the process of enacting standards is substantially complete, although there are some sticking points between the states and the Secretary which may require Secretarial action and review by a special hearing board. The most notorious and important issue has been the "no degradation" policy. The Secretary has required the states to implement a general standard that provides that no water may be degraded below its present quality.[82]

Once standards are set, as they already substantially are, the discharge of matter into the interstate waters which reduced the quality of the water below the water quality standards is subject to abatement by court action. The discharge subject to abatement may be one that reaches interstate waters after discharge into a non-interstate tributary. Any violator must be given 180 days' notice. The statute requires that the court give:

> . . . due consideration to the practicability and to the physical and economic feasibility of complying with such standards.[83]

The question arises as to how the two procedures outlined above mesh. It would seem that pollution abatement proceedings would still be applicable when water quality standards do not apply. The obvious examples are to navigable waters that are not interstate and to interstate waters prior to formal adoption of standards. One would hope that pollution abatement would also apply to any type of pollution in interstate waters not covered by adopted standards.

The Refuse Act, or more properly, section 13 of the Rivers and Harbor Act of 1899, makes it unlawful to discharge "any refuse matter of any kind or description whatever other than that flowing from streets and sewers and passing therefrom in a liquid state" into any navigable water of the United States, except as authorized by the Secretary of the Army.[84] This Act is still fully alive and has in no way been replaced by the Federal Water Pollution Control Act.[85] Section 16 of the Act makes violation of

---

[81]33 U.S.C. 466g(c).

[82]The Secretary's justification is the language of 33 U.S.C. §466g(c) (3).

[83]33 U.S.C. 466g(c) (5).

[84]33 U.S.C. §407.

[85] *United States v. Interlake Steel Corp.*, (No. 68, CR 77, N.D., Ill., March 27, 1969. Memorandum and Order on Defendant's Motion to Dismiss).

Section 13 a misdemeanor.[86] The United States, however, is not limited to the inadequate criminal penalties, but may bring a civil action to enjoin unlawful discharges, although the scope of this remedy is still uncertain.[87]

Sewage under this Act does not include industrial wastes[88] and any type of refuse, such as gasoline, is covered, regardless of its lack of effect on navigation.[89]

The United States Attorney is directed by §17[90] to prosecute vigorously any violators when requested by certain named officers, the most important being the Corps of Engineers through the Secretary of the Army. The United States Attorney, however, may enforce the Act on his own motion if a violation is brought to his attention.[91]

Of great importance is the absence of a scienter requirement.[92]

The Refuse Act is an obvious tool that could eliminate substantial pollution if any real effort to use it were to be made. Clearly good work can be done in reviewing the administrative activities of the Corps of Engineers in granting permission to pollute and in requesting the prosecution of violators. Good work could also be done in reviewing the conduct of the Department of Justice in responding to the requests of the Corps and of others to enforce the Act.

The Oil Pollution Act[93] prohibits the discharge of oil from a vessel into the territorial sea and inland waters navigable in fact. The Act, however, is practically worthless as "discharge" is defined to mean a willful or grossly negligent act. There are, however, presently pending before Congress several bills which may remedy the situation and also cover offshore drilling blow-outs.[94]

When concerned with a pollution problem involving interstate waters, an attorney should always review any existing interstate compacts.[95]

---

[86] 33 U.S.C. §411.
[87] *United States v. Republic Steel Corp.*, 362 U.S. 482 (1960).
[88] *Id.*
[89] *United States v. Standard Oil Co.*, 384 U.S. 224 (1966).
[90] 33 U.S.C. §413.
[91] *United States v. Interlake Steel Corp., supra*, n. 85; *United States v. Burns*, 54 F. 351 (C.A.4, 1893).
[92] *United States v. Interlake Steel Corp., supra*, n. 85. Congressman Ottinger of New York has recently brought an action as a citizen to enforce a very similar statute which applies only to New York Harbor; *Ottinger v. Penn Central Co.* (No. 68Civ.2638, S.D.N.Y.).
[93] 33 U.S.C. 431 *et seq.*
[94] *E.g.* S. 7 and H.R. 4148.
[95] *E.g.* Potomac River Basin Compact, 54 Stat. 748; New England Interstate Water Pollution Control Compact, 61 Stat. 682;Tri-State Compact (N.Y., N.J. and Conn.), 49 Stat. 932; Ohio River Valley Sanitation Compact (ORSANCO), 54 Stat. 752; Tennessee River Basin Water Pollution Control Compact, 72 Stat. 823; Bi-State Metropolitan Compact (Ill. and Mo.), 873

By Executive Order 11288,[96] a significant program is outlined to control pollution emanating from federal installations and federal activities.

Thermal pollution of waters is a particularly aggravated problem of nuclear installations. Unfortunately, the Atomic Energy Commission has washed its hands of the matter and refuses to require its licensees to comply with water quality standards. This position, in which the AEC does not seem to view itself as the "United States" in the broad sense, has been upheld recently in a distressing opinion of the First Circuit.[97]

Air pollution.

The primary Federal air pollution control act is the Air Quality Act of 1967.[98] This Act provides for an enforcement scheme even more elaborate than the Federal Water Pollution Control Act previously discussed. And while no satisfactory text has yet appeared on the Act, there have been several legal articles which give a good description of its requirements.[99]

Under the Act, the Secretary of Health, Education and Welfare is to designate atmospheric areas[100] and air quality control regions.[101] In addition, he is required to publish air quality criteria[102] and control technology data.

Following the designations of the control regions, etc., each state will formulate ambient air quality standards—as opposed to emission standards—and an enforcement plan. The standards and plan are to be based on the air quality criteria and control technology data for the particular air quality control regions. Economic and technological factors are to be considered, as well as health and welfare.

Stat. 582; Red River of the North Compact, 52 Stat. 150; The Arkansas River Compact, 80 Stat. 1405; and Delaware River Basin Compact, 75 Stat. 688; Hudson River Basin Compact, 80 Stat. 847.

[96] 31 Fed. Reg. 9261, July 2, 1966.

[97] *New Hampshire v. AEC,* 406 F.2d 170 (C.A.1, 1969).

[98] 81 Stat. 485, 42 U.S.C. §1857 *et seq.*

[99] Symposium, 33 Law & Contemp. Prob. (1968); Symposium, 10 *Ariz. L. Rev.* (1968); Birmingham, "The Federal Government and Air and Water Pollution," 23 *Bus. Law.* 467, 482 (1968); *Note,* The Air Quality Act of 1967, 54 *Iowa L. Rev.* 115 (1968); *Note,* 55 *Calif. L. Rev.* 702 (1967); Tyler, "Methods for State Level Enforcement of Air and Water Pollution Laws," 31 *Texas B. J.,* 905 (1968); and Cunningham, "A Review of Air Pollution Control Legislation and Some Suggestions," *A.B.A. Law Notes* (1969).

[100] The Secretary has designated eight such areas, 2 CCH, Clean Air News, No. 1, p. 1 (1968), 33 F.R. 16537.

[101] A number of such regions have been designated. Designation is to be completed by July, 1970, and could include up to 100 regions.

[102] Criteria can be described as the effects that can be expected to occur at a given level of pollution.

Enforcement proceedings similar to the Federal Water Pollution Control Act proceedings are provided. The Secretary may, at the request of a governor or, if "he has reason to believe that . . . pollution . . . is endangering the health and welfare of persons" in a state other than that which is discharging the pollutants, *sua sponte*, call a conference of interested pollution control agencies at which all interested parties can present their views. After the conference, the Secretary makes his recommendations to the pollution control agencies for remedial action. If, after six months, no satisfactory remedial action has been taken, the Secretary may call a hearing before a special hearing board. The board's findings and recommendations are sent to the interested and affected agencies and to the various polluters. After another six months have gone by, the Secretary may, if satisfactory action has not been taken to implement the board's recommendations, request the Attorney General to bring an enforcement action.[103] So far, there has been one abatement action. The law was generally upheld in this decision, though no pollution has yet been abated.[104]

President Johnson issued an Executive Order similar to that for water pollution control, providing detailed procedures for the prevention, abatement and control of air pollution caused by Federal installations and activities.[105]

The Air Quality Act of 1967 provides that in cases where pollution is presenting "imminent and substantial endangerment to the health of persons" and state and local authorities have not acted, the Secretary may request the Attorney General to institute judicial action to enjoin any contributor to such pollution.

The Federal air pollution control laws also require, in addition to the matters discussed above, standards for control of pollution emission from gasoline and diesel powered vehicles, which may be set by the Secretary.

Pesticides.

The pesticide problem is a difficult one for the environmental lawyer at the federal level, primarily because there are laws that cover the subject, but they are not fully adequate. The Federal Insecticide, Fungicide and Rodenticide Act,[106] administered by the Department of Agriculture, makes it unlawful to ship in interstate commerce any economic poison (dieldren, DDT, etc.) which is not registered under the Act. The princi-

---

[103]The request of the governor is required for intrastate pollution.
[104] *United States v. Bishop Processing Co.*, 287 F. Supp. 624 (D.Md. 1968), *Also see Bishop Processing Co. v. Gardner*, 275 F.Supp. 780 (D.Md. 1967).
[105]Executive Order No. 11282, 31 F.R. 7663, May 26, 1966.
[106]7 U.S.C. 135 *et seq.*

pal purpose of the Act was to prevent misbranded articles from being sold in interstate commerce. The law, however, contains language that should prevent poisons which cannot be used safely from being registered.[107] The statute also provides for deregistration when articles do not comply[108] with statutory requirements.

A second statute is the Federal Food, Drug and Cosmetic Act, which prohibits the introduction into interstate commerce of adulterated foods, including agricultural commodities which contain unsafe pesticide chemicals.[108a] The statute is administered by the Secretary of Health, Education and Welfare, who prescribes tolerance levels for the chemicals. If a pesticide on a commodity exceeds tolerance levels, it is adulterated. By regulation, the Secretary of HEW is "to set tolerance levels to protect the public health" and may set the level at zero.[109]

Noise.

While pollution of the environment by noise is not restricted to the airplane, most federal law concerning noise concerns airplane noise in particular. This outline, therefore, discusses only airplane noise.

Section 10 of the Air Commerce Act of 1926[110] subjected air space to a public right of freedom of navigation above minimum safe levels.[111] Direct overflights from takeoffs and landings, however, can still result in a compensable taking. The landmark case is *United States v. Causby,*[112] which held the government liable under the Tucker Act[113] on a theory which peculiarly combined tort elements of trespass (overflight) and nuisance (actual injury to use). Under *Causby,* the owner of an airport can also be held liable.[114] The major problem which stems from *Causby* is that of lateral noise. Thus, if airflights are not directly overhead, one cannot collect,[115] although one decision has held the other way.[116]

---

[107] *See also* 7 C.F.R. 362.10(k).
[108] *See also* 7 C.F.R. 362.10(i), (j); 7 C.F.R. 362.106(g).
[108a] 21 U.S.C. 321 *et seq.*
[109] 21 U.S.C. 346a(b). *See also* 21 C.R.F. 120.5.
[110] 44 Stat. 568, 574.
[111] *See* 14 C.F.R. 91.79 (1966) for regulations on minimum safe levels. *Also see* §101(24) of Federal Aviation Act of 1958, 49 U.S.C. 1301(24).
[112] 328 U.S. 256 (1946).
[113] 28 U.S.C. 1346, 1491.
[114] *Griggs v. Allegheny* County, 369 U.S. 84 (1962).
[115] *Batten v. United States,* 306 F. 2d 580 (C.A. 10, 1962), *cert denied* 371 U.S. 955 (1963) (Chief Judge Murrah dissented forcefully); *McKee v. Akron,* 1760. D. 282, 199 N.E. 2d 592 (1964).
[116] See *Thornburg v. Port of Portland,* 376 Pac. 2d 100 (Ore., 1962).

There have been several attempts by local governments to regulate airplane noise by ordinance. The courts have held, however, that the Federal government has preempted the field and that such ordinances are invalid.[117]

By Act of July 21, 1968,[118] Section 611 was added to Title VI of the Federal Aviation Act of 1958.[119] Section 611 is entitled "Control and Abatement of Aircraft Noise and Sonic Boom." Under Section 611 the Administrator of the FAA:

> Shall prescribe and amend standards for the measurement of aircraft noise and sonic boom and shall prescribe and amend such rules and regulations as he may find necessary to provide for the control and abatement of aircraft noise and sonic boom, including the application of such standards, rules and regulations in the issuance, amendment, modification, suspension, or revocation of any certificate authorized by this title.

In prescribing standards, rules and regulations, the Administrator is required to consider relevant available data and research on aircraft noise and sonic boom, the highest degree of safety in the public interest, whether a rule is economically reasonable and technologically practicable, and whether it is appropriate for the equipment in question. In any action to alter a certificate, a certificate holder is given notice and appeal rights which include the right to have the matter heard again by the National Transportation Safety Board.

So far the Administrator has issued regulations for newly certificated airplanes. These regulations do not cover the SST or sonic boom.[120]

It has been suggested in one case, and probably in others, that the Civil Aeronautics Board must consider environmental impact issues in carrying out its regulatory functions.[121] It would seem only logical that a certificate of public necessity and convenience would include the impact of noise and pollution upon the neighborhoods affected.

Aesthetic or Visual Pollution.

There is no general law, state or federal, to protect the aesthetic quality of our environment. The concept of such a law is, in fact, so revolutionary

---

[117]See *American Airlines, Inc. v. Town of Hempstead*, 398 F. 2d 369 (C.A. 2, 1968) *cert denied*, U.S. (1969); *All American Airways v. Village of Cedarhurst*, 106 F.Supp. 521 (E.D.N.Y. 1952), *Aff'd sub nom Allegheny Airlines v. Village of Cedarhurst*, 238 F.2d 812 (C.A. 2, 1956).

[118]P.L. 90-411, 82 Stat 395.

[119]49 U.S.C. 1421 *et seq.*

[120]34 Fed. Reg. 18355 (November 18, 1969).

[121]Brief for Petitioners, *The Palisades Citizens Association, Inc. v. Civil Aeronautics Board*, F.2d (No. 21,422, DC. Cir., Sept. 12, 1969).

that we can be fairly certain that none will be enacted in the foreseeable future. However, enactments crop up from time to time which are directed to the aesthetic or visual aspect of some project, area or type of project. The billboard laws are an example. Serious questions have been raised in the past concerning the propriety of such laws, and will certainly be raised in the future. The correct position to be taken is that such laws, when at the state level, are a proper use of the police power and when at the federal level, fall clearly with in the welfare clause.

Aesthetic statutes are often justified on other grounds, such as safety, under the state police power. Whether the courts stand on aesthetics alone, or combine it with other considerations, several states have given aesthetics a place within the police power.[122]

At the Federal level aesthetics considerations are a proper use of the Welfare Clause. In *Berman v. Parker*[123] Justice Douglas said:

> The concept of the public welfare is broad and inclusive . . . The values it represents are spiritual as well as physical, aesthetic as well as monetary. It is within the power of the legislature to determine that the community should be beautiful as well as healthy, spacious as well as clean, well-balanced as well as carefully patrolled. . . . [124]

The freedom to be left alone has been described as the beginning of all freedom.[125] If the freedom to be free of undesirable aesthetic assault were to be recognized and translated into a freedom from any unwanted and harmful environmental assault, the environmental fight could easily be won. Unfortunately, Justice Douglas spoke in dissent.[126]

Before leaving aesthetics, I wish to invite the reader's attention to the

---

[122] *See e.g. St. Louis Poster Advertising Co. v. St. Louis*, 249 U.S. 269 (1919); *General Outdoor Adv. Co. v. Dept. of Public Works*, 193 N.E. 799, 815–817 (Mass., 1935); *Perlmutter v. Greene*, 182 N.E. 5 (N.Y., 1932); *Farley v. Graney*, 119 S.E. 2d 833 (W.Va., 1960); *Preferred Tires, Inc. v. Hempstead*, 19 N.Y.S. 2d 374 (1940). Florida has produced an unusual number of decisions. *See e.g. Eskind v. Vero Beach*, 150 So. 2d 254 (1963); *Daytona Beach v. Abdo*. 112 So. 2d 398 (1959); *Dade County v. Gould*, 99 So.2d 236 (1957); *Merritt v. Peters*, 65 So. 2d 861 (1953); *Hav-a-Tampa Cigar Co. v. Johnson*, 5 So. 2d 433 (1941); *Standard Oil Co. v. Tallahassee*, 87 F. Supp. 145, N.D. Fla., 1949. *Cf. New York Thruway Authority v. Ashley Motor Court*, 176 N.E. 2d 566 (N.Y.1961); *Murphy v. Westford*, 40 F.2d 177 (Conn., 1944); *People v. Stover*, 191 N.E. 2d 272 (N.Y. 1963); *Contra People v. Dickenson*, 343 P.2d 809 (Cal., 1959); *Town of Vestal v. Bennet*, 104 N.Y.S. 2d 830 (1950); *New Orleans v. Southern Auto Wreckers*, 192 So. 523 (La. 1939); *State v. Brown*, 108 S.E. 2d 74 (N.C., 1959); *Chicago Park Dist. v. Canfield*, 19 N.E. 2d 376 (Ill. 1939).

[123] 348 U.S. 26 (1954). *Also see State v. Wieland*, 69 N.W. 2d 217 (Wis., 1955).

[124] 348 U.S. at 33.

[125] *P.U.C. v. Pollock*, 343 U.S. 451 (1951) (Justice Douglas in dissent, 467–469. The case involved a Muzak type device on a public bus.)

[126] *See* generally the section in this volume by E. Roberts, *"The Right to a Decent Environment, Progress Along a Constitutional Avenue."*

features of the Federal Highway Act concerning billboards[127] and junk-yards, landscaping and other aesthetics[128] and to *Markham Advertising Co. v. State*[129] and *Southeastern Displays, Inc. v. Ward.*[130] *Markham* and *Southeastern Displays,* which generally uphold state billboard control laws, and also hold that the Federal Highway Act did not preempt the field and prohibit a state statute that did not pay just compensation or which was stricter than Federal requirements.

LAND AND WATER USE

The general uses to which land and water resources are put has created broad categories of environmental and conservation problems. Because of the numerous specialized laws which govern the public domain, however, that segment of land-use problems is treated in this outline under a separate heading (with the exception of strip mining on the public domain).

The most important category in this topic will not be discussed in this outline because of the paucity of federal law: the protection of private open space, agricultural land, wetlands and forest land. The foremost priority for new legislative action by environmentalists should be to enact legislation establishing the public stake in the management and use of such private lands.

While federal control over private land use is nonexistent, federal control over water resources is fairly broad. For that reason, water will be taken up first. The author feels impelled to observe that the most important federal control over water stems from the commerce clause and that a large share of present day private land abuse can be directly related to interstate commerce.

Rivers, Estuaries and Coastal Waters.

The federal government, by virtue of a navigation easement or servitude[131] under the commerce clause,[132] controls the use of the navigable waters of the United States. Navigable waters are those which are navigable in fact in their natural condition or susceptible to navigation through reasonable improvements.[133] The power over those waters is not limited to matters related to navigation, but is a plenary power to prevent any

---

[127] 23 U.S.C. 131.

[128] 23 U.S.C. 136.

[129] 439 P. 2d 248 (Wash., 1968).

[130] 414 S.W.2d 573 (Ky., 1967).

[131] *F.P.C. v. Niagara Mohawk Power Corp.*, 347 U.S. 239, 249 (1954). *United States v. Twin City Power Co.*, 350 U.S. 222, 225 (1955).

[132] *Gibbons v. Ogden*, 9 Wheat. 22 U.S. 1 (1824); *Levy v. United States*, 177 U.S. 621 (1900).

[133] *U.S. v. Appalachian Power Co.*, 311 U.S. 377, 407–409 (1940).

structures in navigable waters.[134] Navigable waters are not subject to own
ership,[135] a concept the Supreme Court considers "inconceivable."[136]
The servitude is in the stream bed below ordinary highwater mark,[137] and
to the entire bed, not just that under the navigable part.[138]

In addition to the servitude in navigable waters, the United States has
certain rights in non-navigable streams. The most important, and the
only ones discussed here, are the reserved rights in western streams. The
Supreme Court has recognized that when the United States acquired
ownership of the public domain by cession from foreign sovereigns it
acquired the rights to use the waters thereon within the bundle of rights
which land ownership involves. Without permission of the United States,
no one could acquire any property rights in such waters.[139] The Desert
Land Act of March 3, 1877[140] constitutes permission in thirteen western
states to obtain property rights by appropriation against the United States
under state law or custom.[141] The Desert Land Act, however, was not
a blanket conveyance of the Federal title. The United States retains the
power to reserve unappropriated waters from future appropriations
under state law, to utilize itself or to provide for their utili
zation by others. The reservation need not be explicit, but may be implied
by   the
reservation of public lands for a particular purpose,[142] as well as by
statute.[143]

We have referred previously to Section 13 of the Rivers and Harbor Act
of 1899. That section and other sections of that Act,[144] as amended,
remain as a major exercise of federal control over the nation's water
resources. That act, among other things, regulates the construction of
bridges, dams, dikes and causeways and regulates the general obstructions of structures and fills. Any project built in violation of the Act is
subject to injunction to enforce removal.

---

[134] Id. at 424, 427; United States v. Chandler-Dunbar Co., 229 U.S. 53 (1913).

[135] U.S. v. Appalachian Power Co., supra at 424; United States v. Rands, 389 U.S. 121, 123
(1967); United States v. Twin City Power Co., supra at 227. The power of Congress also
extends to all coastal waters. United States v. California, 381 U.S. 139, 177 (1964).

[136] United States v. Chandler-Dunbar Co., supra at 69.

[137] United States v. Rands, supra; United States v. Vepco, 365 U.S. 624 (1961).

[138] United States v. Chicago, M., StP. & P.RR., 312 U.S. 592, 596 (1941).

[139] See e.g. United States v. Grand River Dam Authority, 363 U.S. 229, 235 (1960).

[140] 19 Stat. 377, has amended, 43 U.S.C. 321 et seq.

[141] California Oregon Power Co. v. Beaver Portland Cement Co., 295 U.S. 142 (1935).

[142] Arizona v. California, 373 U.S. 546 (1963); Federal Power Commission v. Oregon, 349 U.S.
435 (1955); Winters v. United States, 207 U.S. 564 (1908); United States v. Rio Grande
Irrigation Co., 174 U.S. 690 (1898); 1 Kinney, Irrigation and Water Rights, 692 3 (1912).

[143] 43 U.S.C. 300 (waterholes); Sec. 13(c) of the Wild and Scenic Rivers Act of October 2,
1968; Public Law 90–542, 82 Stat. 906.

[144] 33 U.S.C. 401, et seq.

The most recent and perhaps important decision under this Act is the recent *Citizens Committee for the Hudson Valley v. Volpe.*[145] The State of New York had planned and was on the verge of building a six-lane highway on 9,500,000 cubic yards of fill extending 1,300 feet into the Hudson River. The State applied for a permit to fill under 33 USC §403, which was authorized by the Secretary of the Army and issued by the Corps of Engineers as is required by §403. The court held, however, that the project fell under 43 USC §401 which required the additional approval of Congress for dikes and the approval of both Congress and the Secretary of Transportation for the causeways in the project.[146]

It is of interest to note that the Supreme Court has upheld the refusal of the Secretary of the Army to issue a permit under §403 for reasons slightly connected with conservation, but, more importantly, having absolutely nothing to do with navigation.[147]

As in the case of refuse dumping, the Corps is the major funnel for dredge and fill permits. Literally thousands must cross the Corps desk annually. Clearly, work needs to be done by environmental lawyers in the area of review of procedures concerning these permits.

By passage of the Federal Power Act of June 10, 1920, the power to license private dams on navigable waters and federal reservations was shifted to the Federal Power Commission where it resides today.[148] Much of the responsibility for the rapid destruction of our river resources can, where private developments are concerned, be laid to this Commission and its narrow view of the public good. Two recent cases, however, have given hope that the FPC is being forced to take an environmental view of its jurisdiction.

In *Scenic Hudson Preservation Conference v. F.P.C.*[149] the court pointed out that the Commission had a congressional mandate under 16 USC 803 (a) to insure that any project "will be best adapted to a comprehensive plan for improving or developing a waterway or waterways for

---

[145]302 F. Supp. 1083 (69 Civ. 295, S.D.N.Y., July 11, 1969). (Appeal pending.)

[146]Section 401 makes it unlawful to construct any *bridge, dam, dike* or *causeway* in any navigable waters until the builder has obtained (1) consent of Congress, and (2) approval of his plans by the Chief of Engineers, and (3) the Secretary of the Army. The General Bridge Act of 1946, 33 USC 525, *et seq.*, granted general consent to build *bridges.* The Department of Transportation Act. 49 USC 1655 (g) transferred jurisdiction over *bridges* and *causeways* to the Secretary of Transportation. Thus, a *bridge* requires the Chief of Engineers' and the Secretary of Transportation's approval. A dike still requires approval of Congress, the Chief of Engineers and the Secretary of the Army. A causeway requires the approval of Congress, the Chief of Engineers, and the Secretary of Transportation.

[147]*United States v. Dern*, 289 U.S. 352 (1933).

[148]See 16 U.S.C. §797(e).

[149]354 F.2d 608 (2nd Cir., 1965); *see supra*, n.1.

the use or benefit of interstate or foreign commerce, for the improvement and utilization of water power development, and for other beneficial public uses, including recreational purposes."[150] Recreational purposes, according to the Court, encompasses the conservation of natural resources and the preservation of natural beauty. In remanding the case for further proceedings before the Commission, the Court made it clear that the burden was on the Commission to include in its deliberations "as a basic concern the preservation of natural beauty."[151]

In the case of *Udall v. FPC*,[152] the Supreme Court put its stamp of approval on the *Scenic Hudson* approach. The burden was put on the Commission to take into account recreational purposes in a comprehensive river plan, which are to include the preservation of anadromous fish.

Perhaps the saddest fact any concerned person must contemplate is the overwhelming destruction of water resources carried on by the Federal Government. The destruction has now reached a point where we are in danger of having only a memory to save. It is therefore of great importance that handles be found to protect rivers from the federal dam builders and dredgers in much the same way as *Scenic Hudson* and *FPC v. Udall* found a handle to temper FPC licenses.

The worst offenders are reclamation projects constructed under the reclamation laws by the Bureau of Reclamation,[153] flood control projects and dredging projects of the Corps of Engineers built under various Flood Control Acts[154] and Rivers and Harbor Acts,[155] the projects of the Tennessee Valley Authority,[156] and the projects built under the Columbia Basin Project,[157] although these by no means exhaust the list.

Section 460 1–12 of 16 USC sets forth the declaration of policy of the Federal Water Project Recreation Act.[158] This Act comes close to providing the handle:

It is the policy of the Congress and the intent of this Act that (a) in investigating and planning any Federal Navigation, flood control, reclamation, hydroelectric, or multi-purpose water resource project, full consideration shall be given to the opportunities, if any, which the project affords for outdoor recreation and for fish and wildlife enhancement and that, wherever any such project

---

[150]354 F.2d at 620.

[151]354 F.2d at 624.

[152]387 U.S., 428 (1967).

[153]Act of June 17, 1902, 32 Stat. 390, as amended. *See* 43 U.S.C. §371 *et seq.* (1964).

[154]*See e.g.* 33 U.S.C. 701 *et seq.*

[155]*See e.g.* 33 U.S.C. 540 *et seq.*

[156]*See e.g.* 16 USC 831 *et seq.*

[157]16 U.S.C. 835 *et seq.*

[158]Act of July 9, 1965, 79 Stat. 213.

can reasonably serve either or both of these purposes consistently with the provisions of this Act, it shall be constructed, operated and maintained accordingly; . . .

The question arises as to what is to be done when planning reveals a project is utterly destructive of recreational or wildlife values. A literal reading of the Act could mean the project is built anyway; a sane reading would mean the opposite. With federal projects, of course, these considerations are overridden by authorizing acts and the appropriation of construction funds, as such acts can always be read as exceptions to any general policy statement.

In 1968 Congress declared a national policy "of protecting, conserving and restoring the estuaries of the United States."[159] Under this Act the Secretary of the Interior has been ordered to conduct a study and inventory of the nation's estuaries and their problems. The law requires the Secretary to report to Congress no later than January 30, 1970.

At the same time this study has been under way, the Secretary has made a second study of estuarine pollution under Section 5(g) of the Clean Water Restoration Act of 1966[160] The study was completed and submitted to Congress in November, 1969.

Strip Mining.

Unfortunately, there is no general federal law either to prevent strip mining or to repair stripped lands. We will, however, outline briefly the general state regulatory scheme and mention one federal law that may be of some assistance to this distressing problem. In addition, though it is out of order, the federal laws that apply to the public domain will be listed.

Some states, mostly in Appalachia, have established strip mining regulations. Generally speaking, these laws require a permit in order to strip. A performance bond must be posted with, and periodic reports supplied to, a state agency. After the mining is completed, the land must be graded and planted to specifications within set time limits. The state agency must certify compliance. Failure to comply can result in forfeiture of the bond and prohibition against additional permits. Criminal penalties are usually provided for those who strip without a permit.[161] Some states give

---

[159] Estuarine Study Act of August 3, 1968, 82 Stat. 625, 16 U.S.C. 1221 et. seq.

[160] 33 U.S.C. §466(c).

[161] 93 Ill. Ann. Stat. §180 et seq. (1969 Supp.) (eff. July 1, 1968); Ind. Stat. Ann. §46–1501 et seq. (eff. 1941); Ind. Stat. Ann. §46–1517 et seq. (1968 Supp.) (eff. 1967); Ky. Rev. Stat. §350–010 et seq. (eff. 1962); Ann. Code Md., Art. 66C §657 et seq. (eff. 1955); Ohio Rev. Code §1513.01 et seq. (eff. 1959); 52 Penn. Stat. Ann. 681 et seq. (eff. 1947) and 1396.1 et seq. (eff. 1945); 10A Tenn. Code Ann. §58–1522 et seq. (eff. 1967); Code Va. §45.1–162 et seq. (eff. 1966); West Va.

an agency power to deny permits in order to protect exceptional scenic values.[162] Some states, such as Pennsylvania and West Virginia, have active restoration programs.

The Federal water pollution control laws should provide a means of controlling certain strip mining which results in severe acid pollution or siltation that lowers the quality of water below federal water quality standards.[163]

The basic hurdle to controlling strip mining on the public domain is the scheme of the Mining Law of 1872[164] under which patents are made without controls. However, the *laissez-faire* principle of this law has been eroded, and some tools for the control of stripping have been developed.

The Mineral Leasing Act of 1920[165] removed *coal, phosphate,* potassium, oil, *oil shale,* asphalt, bitumen and gas (italics denote important strip minerals) from disposition under the Mining Law of 1872 and established a system of discretionary leasing under the Secretary of the Interior. The Secretary has authority to prescribe mining restoration standards.

The Mineral Leasing Act for Acquired Lands Act of 1947[166] essentially extends the leasing scheme of the Mineral Leasing Act of 1920 to 52 million acres of acquired lands not covered by that Act. The lease, in addition to conditions of the Secretary of the Interior, is subject to such conditions as the head of the department, independent establishment or instrumentality having jurisdiction over the lands wishes to impose. This is clear authority to control strip mining.

Laws have been enacted to provide for mineral leasing on 50 million acres of Indian lands.[167] The Secretary of the Interior has the authority to control the terms of any leases under these laws.

Materials Act of July 31, 1947,[168] gives the Secretary of the Interior the authority to dispose, among other things, of sand, stone and gravel. The Secretary has the authority needed to enforce good conservation practices.

The Act of July 23, 1955,[169] removed sand, stone, gravel and other

---

Code §20–6–1 *et seq.* (1969 Supp.) (eff. 1963, 1967).

[162] West Va. Code §20–6–11 (1969 Supp.).

[163] *See Water pollution, supra.*

[164] *See generally* 30 U.S.C. Sec. 22, *et seq.*

[165] 30 U.S.C. 181–287.

[166] 30 U.S.C. Sec. 351–359.

[167] 25 U.S.C. 396 (allotted lands) and 25 USC 396a (unallotted lands). Other acts apply to specific lands.

[168] 30 U.S.C. 601 *et seq.*

[169] 30 U.S.C. Sec. 611, *et seq.*

materials from the Mining Law of 1872. In addition, the Act gives the United States authority to manage the surface resources of any new mining claim prior to patent, but is somewhat ambiguous as to whether strip mining can be controlled.[170]

Section 402, Reorganization Plan No. 3 of 1946,[171] gives the Secretary of the Interior power to dispose of certain minerals from certain acquired lands under such statutes as the Bankhead-Jones Farm Tenant Act[172] and the Weeks Act.[173] The Secretary of the Interior can regulate the conditions of disposal. (The Secretary of Agriculture also retains certain controls).

Public lands may be used for materials for Public Aid Highways.[174] The head of the agency administering such lands can stop or regulate the use consistent with public interest and the primary purposes for which the lands are reserved.

Right-of-Way Planning and Routing (Highway, Pipeline, Power Line, etc.) and Plant Siting.

Section 4 (f) of the Department of Transportation Act of 1966[175] is of overriding importance in the field of federal transportation projects. This section prohibits approval of any transportation program or project which requires the use of any publicly owned land from a public park, recreation area, or wildlife and waterfowl refuge of national, state, or local significance as determined by the federal, state or local officials having jurisdiction, or any land from an historic site of national, state or local significance as so determined by such officials unless (1) there is no feasible and prudent alternative, and (2) such program includes all possible planning to minimize the harm.

It would seem that Section 4 (f) applies to all Department of Transportation programs, including highway routing, airport location or expansion, bridge or causeway construction over a navigable stream, or the funding of a high-speed railroad.

Lawyers should think imaginatively about what the term "use" could mean in the phrase "require the use of . . . land." Thus a bridge requiring secretarial approval could be looked at as "using" that land which its location forces a non-federal connecting highway to "use." The various impacts of an airport on park land on which the airport is not located

---

[170] 30 U.S.C. Sec. 612 (b).
[171] 5 U.S.C Sec. 133y–16, note.
[172] 7 of U.S.C. Sec. 1010.
[173] 16 U.S.C. Sec. 513–519.
[174] 23 U.S.C. Sec. 317.
[175] 49 U.S.C. 1653 (f) (Supp IV, 1969).

should be examined to determine if they can be considered as requiring the use of the park. Perhaps even a project such as the SST can be examined under 4(f) to determine what it requires the "use" of and whether there is a feasible and prudent alternative.[176]

It should also be born in mind in approaching transportation problems that section 4(f)—and section 2(b) (2), 49 U.S.C. 1651 (b) (2) (Supp. IV, 1969)—provides that:

> It is hereby declared to be the National policy that special effort should be made to preserve the natural beauty of the countryside and public park and recreation lands, wildlife and waterfowl refuges, and historic sites.

The Federal Power Commission is presently considering comments in a rulemaking proceeding (Docket No. R–360) on proposed policy guidelines for the planning, location, construction and maintenance of natural gas rights-of-way and pipelines. These guidelines are primarily concerned with the various aspects of protecting scenic, historic and recreational values. It is to be hoped that the commission will adopt these guidelines in the strongest possible form and that it will follow these up with similar guidelines for electric power lines.

Fish and Wildlife.

The important case of *Missouri v. Holland*[177] is famous for Justice Holmes's elucidation of the treaty powers. It is likewise the starting point in any discussion of federal power to protect wildlife. As the opinion relates, statutory attempts by Congress to protect migratory birds had been declared unconstitutional. The government then entered in a treaty on December 8, 1916, with Great Britain to protect migratory birds, and Congress enacted legislation to implement the treaty.[178] Missouri brought the suit to prevent a federal game warden from enforcing the Act on the ground that the Act and treaty were unconstitutional. Holmes upheld the treaty and Act and observed in passing, "But for the treaty and the statute there soon might be no birds for any powers to deal with."[179]

When federal property is involved, of course, no treaty is required to

---

[176]There are at least three lawsuits pending in which section 4(f) is in issue. *Lukowski v. Volpe* (Civ. No. 20634 D.C.Md.); *Citizens Committee for the Columbia River v. Resor.* (Civ. No. 69–498, D.C.Ore.); *Citizens to Preserve Overton Park, Inc. v. Volpe* (Civ. No. 3396–69, D.C.Tenn).

[177]252 U.S. 416 (1920).

[178]Migratory Bird Treaty Act of July 3, 1918, 40 Stat. 755.

[179]252 U.S. at 435.

control wildlife[180] and, of course, none would be needed to protect wildlife in the conduct of federal projects.

States may also regulate fish and wildlife for purposes of conservation within their police power.[181]

The following paragraphs simply list, with brief comment, the many federal enactments designed to protect fish and wildlife.

The United States entered into a treaty with Great Britain on August 16, 1916, to protect migratory birds[182] and into a treaty with Mexico on February 7, 1936, to protect migratory birds and game mammals.[183] Congress has enacted legislation to implement these treaties.[184] The scheme of protection is elaborate, including hunting restrictions, licensing, refuge systems, etc.

The United States entered, on October 12, 1940, into a convention with several other American Republics to protect nature and wildlife.[185] This treaty also provides for protection of migratory birds and provides:

> The Contracting Governments agree to adopt, or to propose such adoption to their respective appropriate law-making bodies, suitable laws and regulations for the protection and preservation of flora and fauna within their national boundaries, but not included in the national parks, national reserves, nature monuments or strict wilderness reserves referred to in Article II hereof. Such regulations shall contain proper provisions for the taking of specimens of flora and fauna for scientific study and investigation by properly accredited individuals and agencies.[186]

The convention further provides:

> The protection of the species mentioned in the Annex to the present Convention, is declared to be of special urgency and importance. Species included therein shall be protected as completely as possible, and their hunting, killing, capturing, or taking, shall be allowed only with the permission of the appropriate government authorities in the country. Such permission shall be granted only under special circumstances, in order to further scientific purposes, or when essential for the administration of the area in which the animal or plant is found.[187]

---

[180] *Hunt v. United States*, 278 U.S. 96; *New Mexico State Game Commission v. Udall* 410 F.2d 1197 (C.A. 10, May 15, 1969).

[181] *Tommer v. Witsell*, 334 U.S. 385 (1948); *Puyallup Tribe v. Dept. of Game*, 391 U.S. 392 (1968).

[182] 39 Stat. 1702.

[183] 50 Stat. 1311.

[184] 16 U.S.C. 703 *et seq.*

[185] Convention on Nature Protection and Wildlife Preservation in the Western Hemisphere. 56 Stat. 1355.

[186] 56 Stat. 1362–1364. A similar obligation is incurred to protect natural scenery. 56 Stat. 1364.

[187] 56 Stat. 1366. For information concerning the Annex, see Note at 56 Stat. 1366 referencing Treaty Series 981, pp. 27–77.

To what extent the obligations above are enforceable is conjectural. In substance, however, they cover a problem which demands urgent action.

In 1965 Congress passed the Anadromous Fish and Great Lakes Fisheries Act,[188] which on its surface appears rather weak. The Act authorizes the Secretary of the Interior to enter into cooperative agreements with a state "for the purpose of conserving, developing, and enhancing within the several states the anadromous fishery resources of the Nation that are subject to depletion from water resources developments and other causes." The secretary is also authorized to conduct studies and make recommendations "regarding the development and management of any stream or other body of water for conservation and enhancement of anadromous fishery resources and the fish of the Great Lakes that ascend streams to spawn."

While this does not seem very potent, it was enough to stop an FPC License at High Mountain Sheep.[189] In that decision Justice Douglas ruled that the Anadromous Fish Act is in *pari materia* with the Federal Power Act, that the Secretary of the Interior has a special mandate to appear in FPC proceedings to introduce evidence and participate fully in proceedings affecting anadromous fish, and that the issue of whether the proposed project is in the public interest can only be made after an exploration of all issues relevant thereto, including what "the public interest teaches of wild rivers and wilderness areas, the preservation of anadromous fish for commercial and recreational purposes, and the protection of wildlife."[190]

This Act[191] establishes a "national policy"[192] "that wildlife conservation shall receive equal consideration and be coordinated with other features of water-resource development programs."[193] Under that policy, the Act provides for consultation by any agency carrying out or licensing any project affecting water resources with the United States Fish and Wildlife Service.

In a recent decision, a Federal District Court in Florida has held that the Corps of Engineers could not consider fish and wildlife matters when considering a license request to fill navigable waters.[194] The court was clearly wrong and the Government has appealed.[195] If predictions are in order, a strong precedent upholding the Act is forthcoming.

This Act was the subject of a recent report of the House Committee

[188] 79 Stat. 1125, 16 U.S.C. Sec. 757a, *et seq.*
[189] *Udall v. FPC,* 387 U.S. 428 (1967).
[190] 387 U.S. at 438, 439–440, 450.
[191] 16 U.S.C. 661 *et seq.*
[192] *Udall v. FPC, supra* at 443.
[193] 16 U.S.C. 661.
[194] *Zabel v. Tabb* (No. 67–200 Civ. T., M.D. Fla., Feb 17, 1969).
[195] Fifth Circuit, No. 27555.

on Government Operations which analyzes and criticizes as "unlawful" the Interior and Army Departments' failure to follow the procedures of the Act in one specific case.[196]

The Fish and Wildlife Act of 1956[197] establishes the United States Fish and Wildlife Service and the Bureaus of Commercial Fisheries and of Sport Fisheries and Wildlife, and authorizes various functions and programs thereunder. Of general interest in the declaration of policy set forth is 16 U.S.C. 742a.

Other acts of interest include: Wildlife Restoration Act;[198] Military Reservation Conservation Program Act;[199] Act to Preserve Game Birds and Other Wild Birds;[200] Eagle Protection Act;[201] Endangered Species Act;[202] Fur Seal Act of 1966;[203] Northern Pacific Halibut Act;[204] Sockey Salmon Fishery Act;[205] Sponge Taking Laws;[206] Laws regulating Interstate Transportation of Certain Game Fish;[207] *Whaling Convention Act;*[208] *Great Lakes Fisheries Act;*[209] *Tuna Conventions Act;*[210] *Northwest Atlantic Fisheries Act.*[211]

THE PUBLIC DOMAIN

The Federal Public Domain, though much reduced from its original grandeur, is a treasure of hundreds of millions of acres. An elaborate scheme of conservation laws has been built up in this century to govern that domain partly, but not entirely, replacing the *laissez-faire* philosophy of 19th century laws. This outline will not begin to touch the complexities of this law, but will simply mention some of the important laws which govern the Public Domain.

The Recreation Concept.

The word "recreation" has begun to appear with ever increasing fre-

---

[196]H.R. Rep. No. 113, 91st Cong., 1st sess.(1969).
[197]16 U.S.C. Sec. 742a *et seq.*
[198]16 U.S.C. 669, *et seq.*
[199]16 U.S.C. 670a, *et seq.*
[200]16 U.S.C. 701.
[201]16 U.S.C. 668, *et seq.*
[202]16 U.S.C. 668aa, *et seq.*
[203]16 U.S.C. 1151, *et seq.*
[204]16 U.S.C. 772, *et seq.*
[205]16 U.S.C. 776, *et seq.*
[206]16 U.S.C. 781, *et seq.*
[207]16 U.S.C. 851, *et seq.*
[208]16 U.S.C. 916, *et seq.*
[209]16 U.S.C. 931, *et seq.*
[210]16 U.S.C. 951, *et seq.*
[211]19 U.S.C. 981, *et seq.*

quency in laws pertaining to the public domain. A run through Title 16 of the United States Code would probably produce over a hundred references. The meaning of recreation will, it is contended, become an important fulcrum in the management of the public domain.

The author would contend that recreation must include the concepts of natural beauty and resource conservation as suggested in *Scenic Hudson* and the preservation of wildlife as suggested in *Udall v. FPC.* Indeed, the concept must come to include those things that lead to the cultivation and flowering of the human spirit and, hopefully, to eventually exclude certain fatuous, time and money wasting "sports" which make outrageous demands on the land and the economy.

The National Forests.

The overriding policy statement of Congress for the management of the National Forests is found in the Multiple-Use Sustained-Yield Act of 1960.[212] Section 1 of that Act provides, *inter alia,* that:

> It is the policy of the Congress that the national forests are established and shall be administered for outdoor recreation, range, timber, watershed and wildlife and fish purposes. . . .

Section 2 of the Act provides:

> The Secretary of Agriculture is authorized and directed to develop and administer the renewable surface resources of the national forests for multiple use and sustained yield of the several products and services obtained therefrom. In the administration of the national forests due consideration shall be given to the relative values of the various resources in particular areas. The establishment and maintenance of areas of wilderness are consistent [herewith].

Both "multiple use" and "sustained yield" are defined.

How seriously the Forest Service will be required to take these policy guidelines will soon be tested in the case of *Parker v. United States.*[213] In that case the plaintiffs allege, in essence, that the forest service has given no consideration to any factor except timber management in a decision to cut a *de facto* wilderness area.

National Parks.

National Park law presents the lawyer with a great number of statutes. Almost every park is created under its own statute which invariably has a policy guideline in it somewhere.[214] Furthermore, there are various

---

[212] Act of June 12, 1960, 74 Stat. 215, 16 USC 528, *et seq.*
[213] Civ. Act. No. C–1368, U.S. Dist. Ct., Dist. of Colo.
[214] *E.g.* Yellowstone and Sequoia are "dedicated and set apart as public parks or pleasuring

tracts which are administered by the Park Service but have a title other than National Park and, in varying degrees, are not appropriate to administer as a National Park. Thus, there are National Military Parks[215] National Seashores and National Seashore Recreational Areas,[216] National Scenic Riverways,[217] National Recreation Areas,[218] and National Lakeshores.[219] In addition, there are the National Monuments, created under the Antiquities Act of June 8, 1906 by presidential proclamation.[220] Many of these, such as Glacier Bay, are on the scale of a National Park and should be managed as such.

Despite the jumble of several hundred statutory provisions, the overriding mandate of the National Park Service is clear:

> The service thus established shall promote and regulate the use of the Federal areas known as national parks, monuments and reservations hereinafter specified, except such as are under the jurisdiction of the Secretary of the Army, as provided by law, by such means and measures as conform to the fundamental purpose of the said parks, monuments, and reservations, *which purpose is to conserve the scenery and the natural and historic objects and the wildlife therein and to provide for the enjoyment of the same in such a manner and by such means as will leave them unimpaired for the enjoyment of future generations.*[221]

In a later Act, Congress has said:

> ... the Congress hereby finds that the preservation of park values requires that such public accommodations, facilities, and services as have to be provided within those areas should be provided only under carefully controlled safeguards against unregulated and indiscriminate use, so that the heavy visitation will not unduly impair these values and so that development of such facilities can best be limited to locations where the least damage to park values will be

---

grounds for the benefit and enjoyment of the people." 16 U.S.C. 21, 41. Big Bend is established for "recreational park purposes," 16 U.S.C. 156. A long list of prohibited Acts are set forth individually for several parks, 16 U.S.C. 60, 98, 117c, 127, 128, 170, 198c, 204c, 204d, 256b, 256c, 394, 395c, 408k. The Virgin Islands National Park is to be preserved "in its natural condition for public benefit and inspection." 16 U.S.C. 398. The Everglades is to be retained as "wilderness" and the flora, fauna and "essential primitive natural conditions" are to be preserved. 16 U.S.C. 410c.

[215]16 U.S.C. 411, *et seq.*
[216]16 U.S.C. 459, *et seq.*
[217]16 U.S.C. 460m, *et seq.*
[218]16 U.S.C. 460n, *et seq.*, 460 USC, 460v. *et seq.* (Some of these will be administered by the Forest Service. *See e.g.* 16 USC 460p.
[219]16 U.S.C. 460u.
[220]16 U.S.C. 431. See note listing proclamation data and statute at large citation for various monuments.
[221]16 U.S.C. 1 (Emphasis added.)

caused. It is the policy of the Congress that such development shall be limited to those that are necessary and appropriate for public use and enjoyment of the national park area in which they are located and that they are consistent to the highest practicable degree with the preservation and conservation of the areas.[222]

It would seem that under these strong guidelines, the Secretary of the Interior would be loath to permit any use which subordinates the overriding policy to preserve the park to another use. This proposition will soon be tested in the Mineral King litigation[223] where plaintiffs have alleged that the Secretary has authorized construction of a highway in the Park to serve no park purpose.

Bureau of Land Management (BLM).

Far and away the largest part of the public domain is under the jurisdiction of the Bureau of Land Management. The lands are put to many uses and are governed by many diverse laws. We have already mentioned the mining laws (which also apply to National Forests). Anachronistically, much of this land is still subject to entry and patent not only under the mining laws, but also under the Homestead Laws,[224] the Desert Land Laws[225] and miscellaneous other acts. Happily a great portion of these lands is reserved under the Taylor Grazing Laws[226] and other laws.[227]

Periodic raids are made by various resource-using interests from time to time on the public domain. With each assault it seems another part of the public domain is lost. Much still remains, however. Presently another assault is being readied by the Public Land Law Review Commission.[228] The time will shortly be upon us when the question of the final dismemberment of this priceless resource will be before us. The stakes could be so enormous. It is hoped that all concerned will make an effort equal to the task.

The Classification and Multiple Use Act of 1964[229] is one of the most important acts now governing the public domain.

43 U.S.C. 1411 provides, *inter alia:*

Consistent with and supplemental to the Taylor Grazing Act of June 28, 1934, as amended, and pending the implementation of recommendations of the

---

[222]16 U.S.C. 20.
[223]*Sierra Club v. Hickle,* Civil Action No. 468, U.S. Dist. Ct., N.D. Cal.
[224]43 U.S.C. 161–302.
[225]43 U.S.C. 321–339.
[226]43 U.S.C. 315, 315r.
[227]*See e.g.* 43 USC 141-158.
[228]43 U.S.C. 1391, *et seq.*
[229]43 U.S.C. 1411-18. *See* full discussion by Harvey, 2 *Nat. Res. Law.* 229 (1969).

Public Land Law Review Commission

(a) The Secretary of the Interior shall develop and promulgate regulations containing criteria by which he will determine which of the public lands and other Federal lands, including those situated in the State of Alaska exclusively administered by him through the Bureau of Land Management shall be (a) disposed of because they are (1) required for the orderly growth and development of a community, or (2) are chiefly valuable for residential, commercial, agricultural (exclusive of lands chiefly valuable for grazing and raising forage crops), industrial, or public uses or development, or (b) retained, at least during this period, in Federal ownership and managed for (1) domestic livestock grazing, (2) fish and wildlife development and utilization, (3) industrial development, (4) mineral production, (5) occupancy, (6) outdoor recreation, (7) timber production, (8) watershed protection, (9) wilderness preservation, or (10) preservation of public values that would be lost if the land passed from Federal ownership. . . .

(b) The Secretary of the Interior shall, as soon as possible, review the public lands as defined herein, in the light of the criteria contained in the regulation issued with this section to determine which lands shall be classified as suitable for disposal and which lands he considers to contain such values as to make them more suitable for retention in Federal ownership for interim management under the principles enunciated in this section. In making his determinations the Secretary shall give due consideration to all pertinent factors, including, but not limited to, ecology, priorities of use, and the relative values of the various resources in particular areas.

43 U.S.C., Sec. 1413 provides:

The Secretary of the Interior shall develop and administer for multiple use and sustained yield of the several products and services obtainable therefrom those public lands that are determined to be suitable for interim management in accordance with regulations promulgated pursuant to this sub-chapter.

16 U.S.C., Sec. 1415 gives the following definitions:

(a) The term "public lands" means any lands (1) withdrawn or reserved by Executive Order Numbered 6910 of November 26, 1934, as amended, or 6964 of February 5, 1935, as amended, or (2) within a grazing district established pursuant to the Act of June 28, 1934, as amended, or (3) located in the State of Alaska, which are not otherwise withdrawn or reserved for a Federal use or purpose.

(b) "Multiple Use" means the management of the various surface and subsurface resources so that they are utilized in the combination that will best meet the present and future needs of the American people; the most judicious use of land for some or all of these resources or related services over areas large enough to provide sufficient latitude for periodic adjustment in use to conform to changing needs and conditions; the use of some land for less than all of the resources; and harmonious and coordinated management of the various resources, each with the other, without impairment of the productivity of the land, with consideration being given to the relative values of the various resources, and not necessarily the combination of uses that will give the greatest dollar return or the greatest unit output.

(c) "Sustained yield of the several products and services" means the achievement and maintenance of a high level annual or regular periodic output of the various renewable resources of land without impairment of the productivity of the land.

Public notice is required to be given for all proposed classifications over 2,560 acres.[230] Regulations of the criteria required by 43 U.S.C. 1411 were promulgated on October 5, 1965.[231] Classifications are made pursuant to administrative procedures, including hearings, under the criteria regulations.

Although the Act is not clear, the Department of the Interior has decided that classifications for retention will continue indefinitely[232] after the authority to classify expires six months after the Public Land Law Review Commission submits its report.[233]

As of January 31, 1969, about 138,000,000 acres were classified for retention, and about 2,500,000 acres classified for disposal. Another 19,000,000 have been proposed for classification. BLM has estimated about 10,000,000 acres would be classified for disposal.[234]

It seems clear without saying it that there is a great stake not only in what and how much land is classified for disposal, but also for what reasons land is classified for retention. For example, land may be classified for retention as wilderness. Conceivably, more land is involved than under the Wilderness Act.[235]

One important potential of the Act is the power of the Secretary to segregate lands from operation of the mining laws. The Act provides that nothing therein shall restrict prospecting, locating, developing, mining, entering, leasing, or patenting the mineral resources of the lands to which this Act applies under law applicable thereon, pending action inconsistent therewith under this Act.[236]

This section means that the Act itself does not affect the mining laws. However, classification actions taken under the Act can affect mining.[237]

---

[230] 43 U.S.C. 1412.

[231] 30 Fed. Reg. 12912-12922: 43 CFR 2410, et seq.

[232] Memorandum from Associate Solicitor, Division of Lands, to Assistant Secretary, Public Land Management, June 19, 1967.

[233] 43 U.S.C. 1418.

[234] Statement of BLM Director Rasmussen, etc., Hearing Before the Subcommittee on Public Lands, Senate Committee on Interior and Insular Affairs, 90th Cong., 1st sess; (1967).

[235] 16 U.S.C. 1131, et seq.

[236] 43 U.S.C. 1417(a).

[237] This was Interior's position during the legislative process. Hearings on H.R. 5159, H.R. 5498, and H.R. 8070, Subcom. on Publ. Lands, Comm. on Interior and Insular Affairs, 88th Cong., 2d Sess. 43 (1964).

The regulations provide that public lands classified for retention are to be segregated from disposal that could "interfere significantly" with multiple use management or "impair or prevent, to an appreciable extent, realization of public values in the lands. . . ."[238] and that "land shall not be closed to mining location *unless* the nonmineral uses would be inconsistent with and of greater importance to the public interest than the continued search for a deposit of valuable minerals."[239]

Very little land has been segregated by classification from mining. Thus we may be witnessing one of the great missed opportunities of conservation history.

Of interest is the fact that the classifications are not immutable. By regulation, lands classified for retention may be reclassified for disposal.[240] It is hoped that Interior will consider this one-way street at a dead end when its general power to classify expires.

The Sale of Public Land Act of 1964[241] provides for sale of those lands classified for sale under the Classification and Multiple Use Act.

The Taylor Grazing Act of 1934,[242] together with the 1934[243] and 1935[244] executive withdrawal orders, was one of the great conservation events concerning the public domain. By this Act the domain was essentially closed from entry except under the mining laws. Under it grazing districts were set and a Grazing Service was established to protect and administer the districts. The major administrative problem has been controlling overgrazing. At present the controversy has polarized around user fees, which BLM seeks to raise to cover management costs.

Range stock raising has been declining in recent years in favor of feed lot raising. User fees reflecting true costs would shift the competitive advantage further in the direction of the feed lots. This would have the effect of reducing somewhat the pressure on the grazing lands.

It should be noted that the grazing lands are not to be managed solely for grazing. The Classification and Multiple Use Act applies, of course. In addition, the Act indicates that the Secretary is required to take other values into account. Of greatest importance is a mandate to conserve wildlife.[245]

---

[238] 43 C.F.R. Sec. 2410.1-4(b) (1968).
[239] 43 C.F.R., Sec. 2410.1-4(b)(2) (1968).
[240] 43 C.F.R., Sec. 2411.2(d) and (e).
[241] 43 U.S.C. 1421, *et seq.*
[242] 43 U.S.C. 315, *et seq.*
[243] Exec. Order No. 6910, Nov. 26, 1934.
[244] Exec. Order No. 6964, Feb. 5. 1935.
[245] 43 U.S.C. 315h.

The mining laws have been discussed earlier under strip mining. The mining law of 1872,[246] the mineral leasing laws,[247] the Materials Act,[248] the Act of July 23, 1955,[249] and others are primarily the concern of the Bureau of Land Management. Thus it is to BLM we must look to protect the public domain from abuse by the mineral industry. As with the Corps in dredging and refuse permits, so those concerned with the environment must act as watchdog over BLM's handling of mineral leases, etc.

As would be expected, the law of mining and mineral leasing is quite complex. One landmark case for the environment is mentioned as a starting point. *United States v. Coleman*[250] established a strict marketability test for obtaining a patent under the mining law of 1872 and upheld the integrity of the Act of July 23, 1955, removing common building stone from the mining laws and placing its disposal under the Materials Act of 1947.

The revested Oregon and California Railroad and Coos Bay Wagon Road Grant Lands are exceedingly productive and valuable timberlands primarily in Oregon. They are managed by BLM for sustained yield timber production.[251]

National Wildlife Refuge System.

Congress has created by statute many wildlife refuges,[252] and has authorized the creation of the refuges by the executive under specified conditions.[253] In addition, the executive has reserved many refuges on his own initiative.[254] These refuges are under the jurisdiction of the United States Fish and Wildlife Service of the Department of the Interior[255] and, since 1966, administered as the National Wildlife Refuge System.[256]

The policy guides to the refuges are scattered.[257] The purposes of the refuges, it would seem, are so obvious as to need no explanation. Any

---

[246] 30 U.S.C. 22, *et seq.*

[247] 30 U.S.C. 181, *et seq.*

[248] 30 U.S.C. 601, *et seq.*

[249] 30 U.S.C. 611, *et seq.*

[250] 390 U.S. 599 (1968)

[251] 43 U.S.C. 1181a, *et seq.*

[252] *See* 16 U.S.C. 671-697a, 721-731, 1161-1168.

[253] *See* 16 U.S.C. 715-718f.

[254] *See e.g.* Public Land Orders Nos. 2213 and 2214 of Dec. 6, 1960, establishing Kuskokwim National Wildlife Range, 25 FR. 12598, and the Arctic National Wildlife Range, 25 FR. 12598.

[255] *See* 16 U.S.C. 742a, *et seq.*

[256] 16 U.S.C. 688 dd.

[257] *See e.g.* 16 U.S.C. 742f. *Also see* 16 USC 742a.

activity such as hunting should require a Congressional exception. Two recent statutes make it of some interest as to how those purposes would be defined. Section 4 of the Act of October 15, 1966,[258] provides:

> (d) The Secretary is authorized, under such regulations as he may prescribe, to
>
> (1) permit the use of any area within the System for any purpose, including but not limited to hunting, fishing, public recreation and accommodations, and access whenever he determines that such uses are compatible with the major purposes for which such areas were established: *Provided*, that not to exceed 40 percentum at any one time of any area that has been or hereafter may be acquired, reserved or set apart as an inviolate sanctuary for migratory birds, under any law, proclamation, Executive Order, or public land order may be administered by the Secretary as an area within which the taking of migratory game birds may be permitted under such regulation as he may prescribe; and
>
> (2) permit the use of, or grant easements in, over, across, upon, through, or under any areas within the System for purposes such as but not necessarily limited to, powerlines, telephone lines, canals, ditches, pipelines, and roads, including the construction, operation, and maintenance thereof, whenever he determines that such uses are compatible with the purposes for which these areas are established.

The Act of September 28, 1962,[259] reads, in part, as follows:

> In recognition of mounting public demands for recreational opportunities on areas within the National Wildlife Refuge System, national fish hatcheries, and other conservation areas administered by the Secretary of the Interior for fish and wildlife purposes; and in recognition also of the resulting imperative need, if such recreational opportunities are provided, to assure that any present or future recreational use will be compatible with, and will not prevent accomplishment of, the primary purposes for which the said conservation areas were acquired or established, the Secretary of the Interior is authorized, as an appropriate incidental or secondary use, to administer such areas or parts thereof for public recreation unless in his judgment public recreation can be an appropriate incidental or secondary use: *Provided* that such public recreation use shall be permitted only to the extent that is practicable and not inconsistent with other previously authorized Federal operations or with the primary objectives for which each particular area is established . . .

The problems that can arise under this type of statute are illustrated by the Mineral King litigation. There the Sequoia National Game Preserve,[260] which, because of historical accident is administered by the

---

[258]80 Stat. 927, 928, 16 U.S.C. 668dd.
[259]76 Stat. 653, 16 U.S.C. 460k.
[260]16 U.S.C. 688.

Forest Service rather than the Fish and Wildlife Service, is the site of a planned massive recreational ski development. The development seems so utterly contrary to the "primary" or "major" purposes of a refuge that it is hard to imagine why the government is permitting it, yet the fact remains it is.

Wilderness.

In 1964 Congress passed the Wilderness Act.[261] This Act provided congressional protection for a few named wilderness areas and provided an elaborate scheme whereby lands within the National Forests, National Parks and National Wildlife Refuges would be reviewed and appropriate areas set aside within the National Wilderness Preservation System. Of immediate interest to conservationists is the timetable set forth in 16 U.S.C. 1132(c). By that section the Secretary of the Interior is given 10 years to complete his share of the review. One third of the reviews were to be completed in three years and two thirds in seven years. There are indications that Interior is seriously behind in regard to its National Parks.

Alaska.

The conservation of Alaska, our last great wilderness, is highly complicated by two developments: the selection of state lands and by the north slope oil development.

Section 6(b) of the Alaska Statehood Act[262] granted the state 103,-000,000 acres of land, subject to selection. Fortunately Section 4 of that Act protected native lands. Though the courts have ruled that the native title was extinguished by the treaty with Russia,[263] several earlier Acts of Congress have recognized that Alaska natives were not to be disturbed in possession.[264]

To protect the native lands, the Secretary of the Interior put a freeze on state selections on January 17, 1969, to last through 1970.[265] There are also pending cases in the Ninth Circuit to both force and stop selection.[266] The problem may ultimately be solved, however, in Congress rather than in the courts.[267]

---

[261] 78 Stat. 890, 16 U.S.C. 1131, et seq. Wilderness is defined in 16 U.S.C. 1131(c).

[262] Act of July 7, 1958, 72 Stat. 339, as amended by the Act of June 25, 1959, 73 Stat. 141.

[263] Miller v. United States, 159 F.2d 997 (CA 9, 1947).

[264] The Organic Act of May 17, 1884, Sec. 8, 23 Stat. 24-26, Act of June 6, 1900, Sec. 27, 31 Stat. 321, 330.

[265] 34 Fed. Reg. 1025 (1969).

[266] Alaska v. Native Village of Nenna (No. 23997); Alaska v. Udall (No. 23603).

[267] To understand the problem, see Federal Field Committee for Development Planning in Alaska, Alaska: Natives and the Land.

The discovery of oil at Prudhoe Bay on the north slope of Alaska was announced in the summer of 1968. Estimates of the magnitude of the discovery vary widely, from 5,000,000,000 to as much as 100,000,000,000 barrels. Most of the land involved in the exploration is state selected lands. On September 11, 1969, the state held a lease auction for tracts within the area, from which revenue of between $800,000,000 and $900,-000,000 was realized.

In June, 1969, the Department of Interior received an application from a pipeline consortium for an 800-mile right-of-way from Prudhoe Bay to Valdez on the Gulf of Alaska. The following month Interior also received a request from the state of Alaska that the land "freeze" be lifted to allow construction of 53 miles of highway along the proposed pipeline route.

The freeze was lifted for the highway with approval of both the Senate and House Interior Committees and the Federal Power Commission. No restrictive stipulations were attached. But, as of mid-December, 1969, the pipeline permit itself had not been granted. A Federal Task Force held a hearing on the application in Alaska.[268] The Senate and House Interior committees also held extended hearings in Washington, D.C. A proposed set of Interior Department protective stipulations were agreed to by the oil companies.

North slope oil development raises a host of issues: environmental impact of drilling and exploration sites; increased public use of hitherto inaccessible areas; construction of tanker docking and loading facilities; tanker operations and accident potential; and unplanned industrial and commercial development in general.

Outer Continental Shelf.

The continental shelf has had a legal history quite different from that of the fast lands. Unfortunately, the best synopsis of that history is probably unavailable to most members of the bar.[269]

The original states were held to own the lands under their navigable waters as an incident of sovereignty taken over from the crown upon independence.[270] New states likewise obtained ownership of such lands upon admission under the equal footing doctrine.[271]

---

[268]The two-day public hearing was held August 29 and 30, 1969, at the University of Alaska. Records of the hearing are available at Bureau of Land Management offices in Fairbanks, Anchorage, and Washington, D.C.

[269]Swarth, "Offshore Submerged Lands: An Historical Synopsis," 6 *Land & Natural Resources Division Journal* (U.S. Dept. of Justice) (1968), p. 109. *Also see* Swarth, "Offshore Boundary Problems," *L&NRJ* 405 (1968); as a general reference, *see* Shalowitz, *Shore and Sea Boundaries* (1962).

[270]*Martin v. Waddell*, 16 Pet. (41 U.S.) 367 (1842); *Massachusetts v. New York*, 271 U.S. 65 (1926).

[271]*Pollard v. Hagan*, 3 How. (44 U.S.) 212 (1845).

It was long assumed that these rules applied to all lands beneath the territorial sea. The Department of the Interior, for instance, refused to issue mineral leases off the California coast, leaving the field to California.[272] In 1945, however, the Federal government reversed its position, bringing legal action to quiet its title to lands of California within the three-mile limit and by proclaiming on September 28, 1945, ownership in the bed of the continental shelf beyond the three-mile limit.[273] The natural resources of the subsoil and seabed of the continent itself were placed under the administrative jurisdiction of the Secretary of the Interior.[274] In a series of decisions, the Supreme Court confirmed the title of the United States to the bed of the continental shelf beyond, essentially, the line of mean low tide.[275] On January 16, 1953, President Truman set aside the entire continental shelf as a naval petroleum reserve, transferring jurisdiction to the Secretary of the Navy.[276]

On May 22, 1953, Congress upset Federal ownership, giving away a large part of the continental shelf.[277] Essentially the Act gave the States title to the bed of the territorial sea within their boundaries up to three miles in the Atlantic or Pacific or three leagues in the Gulf of Mexico from ordinary low water. The rights of the United States seaward were preserved.

The Submerged Lands Act was upheld as constitutional in a *brief per curium* decision in 1954.[278] The Gulf States boundaries were later held to be three leagues for Texas and Florida and three miles for Louisiana, Mississippi and Alabama.[279]

By Act of August 7, 1953,[280] Congress arranged for the administration of the shelf seaward of the area conveyed to the States. Under this Act the naval petroleum reserve was canceled and provision was made for mineral leasing exclusively under the Act by the Secretary of the Interior. State laws in general, except tax laws, were adopted as federal law for the shelf opposite each state, but are to be administered by federal officials and courts and are not to be a basis for any state claim of inter-

---

[272]Swarth, *supra*, at 112.
[273]Proclamation No. 2667, 59 Stat. 884. The proclamation specifies that it does not affect the character of the high seas of the waters above the continental shelf.
[274]Exec. Ord. 9633, 10 Fed. Reg. 12305 (1945).
[275] *United States v. California*, 332 U.S. 19 (1947), decree at 332 U.S. 804 (1947); *United States v. Texas*, and *United States v. Louisiana*, 339 U.S. 699 (1950), decrees 340 U.S. 899, 900 (1950).
[276]Exec. Order No. 10426, 18 Fed. Reg. 405.
[277]Submerged Lands Act of May 22, 1953, 67 Stat. 29, 43 U.S.C., Secs. 1301-1315.
[278]*Alabama v. Texas; Rhode Island v. Louisiana*, 347 U.S. 272.
[279] *United States v. Louisiana*, 363 U.S. 1 (1960); *United States v. Florida*, 363 U.S. 121 (1960).
[280]The Outer Continental Shelf Lands Act of August 7, 1953, 67 Stat. 462, 43 U.S.C., Sec. 1331-1343.

est or jurisdiction in the outer continental shelf.

There are specific provisions preserving the jurisdiction of federal courts and several federal statutes, including 33 U.S.C. Sec. 403.

Four of the 1958 Geneva conventions on the Sea have been adopted by the United States.[281] The convention on the Territorial Sea and the Contiguous Zone established a method for determining the base line of the territorial sea, adopting what is commonly called the "arcs of circles" or "envelope line" method and adopting a closing line for bays of 24 miles. The Supreme Court in 1965 decided that the method set forth in the Convention should govern the grant in the Submerged Lands Act.[282] The case rejected certain claims of California, of most importance being the "Over All Unit Area" in the Santa Barbara Channel.[283] Overall, this decision is the most comprehensive and definitive statement on the application of the Submerged Lands Act.

The Santa Barbara oil leak has focused everyone's attention on what is at stake on the Outer Continental Shelf, Malcolm Baldwin, in this volume, ties together the various threads. There is no need for further comment here. The future of the OCS, however, may largely be determined by events stemming from this affair.

[281]Convention on the Territorial Sea and the Contiguous Zone, 15 U.S.T. (Pt. 2) 1606; Convention on the High Sea, 13 U.S.T. (Pt. 2) 2312; the Convention on Fishing and Conservation of the Living Resources of the High Seas, 17 U.S.T. (Pt. 1) 138; and Convention on the Continental Shelf, 15 U.S.T. 471.

[282]*United States v. California,* 381 U.S. 139 (1965). Texas boundary of three leagues has been found to be "as it existed at the time the State became a member of the Union" a fixed unmovable line. 389 U.S. 159 (1967).

[283]See Areas in dark red on first map following 381 U.S. at 213.

The Role of Government
in Environmental Conflict

Harold P. Green

I have been asked to prepare this section on the role of the executive branches of our federal and state governments in environmental conflicts and litigation, and to discuss in particular "what is and should be" the role of various components of these executive branches. After considerable reflection, I concluded that literal compliance with this mandate would not be constructive. Even if we were to assume that the executive branch has the constitutional authority to act on its own initiative in defense of the environment,[1] it is obvious that the legislatures have the superior power to shape, control, and restrict such actions by the executive; and, in any event, an effective role by the executive is dependent upon appropriation of funds by the legislature. The more meaningful question is as to the role of *government* in environmental conflicts and litigation. There is further difficulty with the question as to "what is and should be" the role of government. The roles currently played by the federal government and the states are too spotty, diffuse, and amorphous to warrant any form of generalized description. Suffice it to say, whatever government is doing today is not nearly adequate. This paper, therefore,

---

[1] It seems clear that a state attorney general has the right, independent of specific statutory authority, to initiate litigation deemed necessary for the public welfare. See Am. Jur., *States, Territories, and Dependencies* §80 and cases cited therein. On the other hand, the authority of the Federal Government to initiate litigation is more limited. Geneally speaking, the United States may not bring suit unless it has an interest in the relief sought. Where no pecuniary interest exists, the United States may nevertheless bring suit to restrain wrongs which affect the public at large where the subject matter of the litigation is within an area of Federal concern under the Constitution. Thus, even in the absence of a statutory basis for suit, the United States may, for example, initiate litigation to abate a nuisance which impedes interstate or foreign commerce. *In re Debs*, 158 U.S. 564 (1895).

discusses primarily what the role of government *should be* and how this role can be effectively played.

My starting point is the premise that only appropriate government intervention can effectively protect against environmental abuse. Private litigation to vindicate common law environmental interests—although it is to be encouraged and may in some cases be successful—simply cannot be relied on to protect the public interest against environmental abuse in this era of technological affluence and revolutionarily rapid technological advance. This conclusion is based primarily on the fact that our legal system, reflecting the high value that our society places on individual initiative and "progress," imposes on plaintiffs seeking common law relief in cases of environmental abuse a burden of proof that is very substantial and that is extremely difficult to carry.

To begin with, the plaintiff must prove at least that the defendant before the court has engaged in activities which have resulted or which will result in injury to the plaintiff or to the interests represented by the plaintiff. The injury alleged must be actual and demonstrable—something more than mere inconvenience, wounded sensibilities, or speculative or contingent injury. Even if such legally cognizable injury can be shown, the causal relationship between the injury and the defendant's acts may be difficult to establish. This is particularly true in those cases (probably most) in which the environmental abuse does not produce immediate, apparent injury, but is of a more subtle character—a creeping, cumultative injury that is nonspecific and that may become manifest only over a period of many years or perhaps even generations. For example, we know that asbestos particles are discharged into the environment when automobile brakes are applied, and we know that this may result in lung cancer.[2] But how can a plaintiff demonstrate that his lung cancer was caused in this manner, let alone that automobile brakes may significantly jeopardize his health? And the causal link may be even more difficult to forge where the injury results from environmental abuse stemming from multiple sources and is the product of, or exacerbated by, synergistic effects.[3]

Even if injury and the causal link can be demonstrated, still more may be necessary. Again reflecting the premium our society places on private

[2]Report of the Environmental Pollution Panel of the President's Science Advisory Committee, *Restoring the Quality of Our Environment*, 3, 12, 99, (1965).

[3]The Report to the Secretary of Health, Education, and Welfare by the Task Force on Environmental Health and Related Problems, *A Strategy for a Livable Environment* (June, 1967), stresses the problem of the synergistic consequences of the combination of individual pollutants. At page 2 of this report, it is stated: "An individually acceptable amount of water pollution, added to a tolerable amount of air pollution, added to a bearable amount of noise and congestion, can produce a totally unacceptable health environment."

initiative, the legal system uses concepts such as "comparative injury" and "balancing of the equities" to avoid stultifying socially useful activities unless the adverse consequences to members of the public clearly outweigh their social utility.[4] Indeed, even the phrases "negligent," "at fault," and "reasonable" are given content in specific cases through an explicit or implicit form of cost-benefit analysis as the courts weigh the social utility of the defendant's activity against the degree of adverse impact on the complaining party.[5] Defendants usually fare much better than plaintiffs in these respects, primarily because the defendant usually has a clear, well-defined economic interest that is obviously socially useful, while typically the plaintiff's interest is subjective and amorphous.

Finally, these complex dimensions of environmental litigation discourage initiation of environmental litigation by even the most public spirited potential plaintiffs. This is clearly shown in Malcolm Baldwin's "The Santa Barbara Oil Spill," in this volume. The complexities of environmental litigation make such litigation extremely expensive, and the unhappy fact of the matter is that members of the public generally do not feel sufficiently threatened by environmental insults to join, morally and financially, in resisting them at a sufficiently early date. Even where plaintiffs do emerge, the litigation is a *David v. Goliath* affair, with dubious prospects for success since the meager resources of the plaintiffs are pitted against the powerful economic and political interests which seek to use the environment for their own purposes. In my own experience I have been approached by a number of citizens' groups reflecting broad-based public concern over the environmental effects of nuclear power plants. Invariably, their treasuries have only a few thousand dollars which is, of course, only a small fraction of the costs that must be incurred in a complex, lengthy hearing, where effective participation requires skilled counsel and a battery of technical experts.

If private litigation cannot successfully defend the environment, only governmental action of some kind can effectively protect against environmental abuse. Moreover, government action is clearly appropriate since environmental abuse is more a matter of public rather than private concern. But it is not enough merely to recognize the appropriate role of government and to wish for appropriate governmental action. There

[4]This is particularly the case when injunctive relief is sought, and especially where only threatened or anticipated injury is alleged. See Am. Jur., *Nuisances* §161 and cases cited therein.

[5]For example, in 1931 the Wisconsin Supreme Court held that a driver who splashes muddy water on a pedestrian on a rainy day was not liable to the pedestrian, saying, "The benefit of allowing people to travel under such circumstances so far outweighs the probable injuries to bystanders that such conduct is not disapproving." *Osborne v. Montgomery*, 203 Wis. 223, 233, 234 N.W. 372 (1931).

must be a commitment to effective and timely governmental intervention.

If government is to play a role, what should that role be? Immediate and vigorous action is required lest America be smothered in its own technological affluence and effluents. There are three basic forms that governmental action may take. These are non-exclusive, and they all should be pursued.

At the most elementary level, the attorney general of a state or the Attorney General of the United States may initiate litigation in defense of the environment or join in private litigation as *amicus* or intervenor. Such action would be helpful in at least two respects. It could serve to convince the courts that there is an important public interest at stake in the litigation, counterbalancing the defendant's economic interests and the social utility of his activities. It is apparent, however, that if the gravamen of the litigation is vindication of a common law right, the plaintiffs must establish their case through presentation of effective evidence. The plaintiff, whether the attorney general or a private litigant supported by the attorney general, is still faced with the necessity of demonstrating at the very least that there is *unwarranted* activity by *this* defendant that results or will result in *actual injury* to the public. Government participation in the litigation would also be helpful in providing the financial wherewithal to make the case. But, as pointed out above, effective litigation is not an inexpensive exercise, and there must be a commitment on the part of the legislature to provide the necessary funds.

At the next level, governmental action may take the form of enactment of legislation establishing environmental standards or prohibiting or restricting certain activities which detrimentally affect the environment. The legislation might provide for enforcement through private civil litigation, through civil or criminal litigation initiated by the attorney general, or through both. With the substitution of a statutory standard for civil or criminal liability for the common law standard, both private litigation and litigation initiated or supported by the attorney general would in all probability become less complex and expensive.

Finally, governmental action may take the form of regulatory legislation administered by an administrative agency charged with responsibility for establishing and enforcing environmental standards. Such an approach is undoubtedly the most comprehensive and effective means for defending the environment. It is not a panacea, however, as shall be discussed.

The first of these approaches requires at least the tacit acquiescence of the legislature as well as the appropriation of funds. The second and third require affirmative, substantive legislation. The basic problem, then, is to induce our legislative bodies to take cognizance of the need for a stronger governmental role in environmental conflict.

Unfortunately, there is no button which can be pushed to obtain appropriate legislative action. The fact that a problem desperately cries for legislative action does not mean that legislation will be forthcoming. Our legislatures are intrinsically political bodies, melting pots in which diverse views and interests are fused and usually compromised. Considerable inertia must be overcome before a legislature will even begin to give serious consideration to a problem. Unfortunately also, the difficulties in moving a legislature to take appropriate action in the area of environmental protection are particularly acute.[6] They are substantially the same difficulties which detract from the effectiveness of environmental litigation. Those who are disturbing the environment usually have strong, immediate, and obvious economic interests and, arguably at least, are engaged in socially useful endeavors. They are usually well-financed and constitute an effective lobby, and legislators are disposed to pay heed to their arguments. On the other hand, those members of the public who contend for protective environmental legislation typically do not represent important economic interests, and the social detriments on which their contentions are bottomed are typically more subjective. The injuries which they claim will result from the environmental abuses which they allege are frequently ill-defined, vague, and speculative. Moreover, relatively few members of the public feel sufficiently threatened by environmental abuse to exert pressures on the legislature. Usually the legislatures will not act until the environmental injury, and concomitant injury to society, is obvious—and frequently even then they will not act until the public is aroused by a Ralph Nader or Rachel Carson or by a Santa Barbara catastrophe—and by that time powerful vested interests in the environmental abuse have become entrenched to complicate the task of providing effective statutory action.

Unfortunately, the problem of inducing our legislatures to take a benign, let alone positive, attitude towards environmental defense is more than merely a problem of overcoming apathy and inertia. If our legisla-

---

[6] Admiral Hyman Rickover has described the pattern dramatically but overoptimistically: first, efforts are made to confuse the issue by arguing as if a "law of science" were at issue. "If this argument fails, the need for the proposed law is then categorically denied. Warnings of scientists are rejected as 'unproven' or 'exaggerated.' Later . . . the argument shifts . . . to any attack on the legitimacy of any kind of protective legislation. Such legislation would violate basic liberties, it is claimed; it would establish tyranny and subvert free democratic institutions. If all this is futile and legislation is imminent, there will be urgent demands that it be postponed until 'more research' can be undertaken to establish the appositeness of the proposed law." "A Humanistic Technology," address before the British Association for the Advancement of Science, London, October 27, 1965.

tures are not actually inhospitable to the views of those who seek to protect the environment, at least they seem more hospitable to the contrary views, particularly where the development and application of new technology are involved. This is most obvious at the federal level where we have witnessed during the past 25 years the development of an almost obsessive national policy in support of technological advance. At the same time the Congress in various areas has acted to minimize air and water pollution and to protect various other environmental interests, it has permitted, authorized and directed implementation of federal programs which have an impact on the environment and on ecology ranging from highly questionable to obviously detrimental. As the federal government, for example, seeks to reduce pollution caused by fossil-fueled power plants, a key element in this effort is the encouragement and support of nuclear power technology. Nuclear power plants are obviously more aesthetic than conventional plants, and their operation is obviously much cleaner in terms of visible pollution. On the other hand, their normal operation results in thermal pollution of our waters and in the discharge of radioactive effluents, the effects of which on life are not yet fully known or understood,[7] into the atmosphere and waters; and a serious accident could result in environmental catastrophe dwarfing by many orders of magnitude any other catastrophe which can be imagined as resulting from man-made causes.[8] Similarly, the government permits noise pollution from aircraft and is overtly the sponsor of the sonic boom. In still other areas—the creation, storage, and transportation of biological and chemical warfare agents, testing of nuclear weapons, and development and use of nuclear explosives for civil purposes—the government engages in programs whose potential consequences to the environment range from uncertain to potentially catastrophic. And, on a more mundane level, many programs of the Corps of Engineers are seemingly

---

[7]Thirteen years ago it was authoritatively stated that "it is abundantly clear that radiation is by far the best understood environmental hazard." National Academy of Sciences— National Research Council, *The Biological Effects of Atomic Radiation* 34 (1956). Still in 1969, with nuclear technology under rapid development, it can be stated, as was stated by the Federal Radiation Council in 1960: "There are insufficient data to provide a firm basis for evaluating radiation effects for all types and levels of irradiation. There is particular uncertainty with respect to biological effects at very low dose and low-dose rates. It is not prudent therefore to assume that there is a level of radiation exposure below which there is absolute certainty that no effect may occur." 1 CCH At. En. L. Rep. ¶4046.

[8]In 1957, an AEC study concluded, on pessimistic assumptions, that a major nuclear power accident (the probability of which was stated to be "exceedingly low") could result in property damages of $7,000,000,000. See H.R. Rep. No. 435, 85th Cong., 1st Sess. 31-34 (1957). Since that time technological advance makes the probability of such an accident even more remote but increases the potential destruction in the event the accident does occur.

conducted in blatant disregard of environmental considerations.

I do not suggest that in implementing these programs the government totally ignores or casually or haphazardly disregards environmental considerations. These considerations are usually recognized, but are factored out on the basis of a cost/benefit calculus that concludes that the public should be subjected to some environmental detriment or risk which the experts conclude is "tolerable" in exchange for obvious and more substantial benefits.[9] As this calculus is performed, the cost (risk) element tends to be minimized through the following reasoning process: (1) We do not have enough scientific knowledge to tell us whether or not the risks are really significant, but our best present judgment is that the risks are insignificantly small. (2) As the project goes forward, further research will be undertaken to verify our judgment that the risks are insignificantly small. (3) Whatever risks do exist can be reduced to tolerable dimensions through technological devices. (4) If the risks indeed are found to be, and remain, significant, the program will, of course, be abandoned or drastically restricted or controlled to protect the public interest. QED.

It takes no great sophistication to comprehend that the assumptions underlying this calculus are quite dubious. When all is said and done, there is no black or white answer. Rather, the answer always lies in a fuzzy gray area subject to human judgment. Moreover, if there is one axiom which we must regard as controlling, it is that the most conscientious judgments and predictions by scientists and engineers are not infallible. To quote Murphy's Law: "If something can go wrong, it will go wrong." And, finally, it is totally unrealistic as a matter of human and political nature to assume or expect that an activity in which substantial investment has been made and vested interests developed can be turned off when, as will almost always be the case, the cost/benefit analysis produces the fuzzy gray result.[10]

Clearly the federal government is no monolith. At the same time that agencies such as the Department of Defense, the Atomic Energy Commission, the Federal Aviation Administration, and the Corps of Engineers have a congressional mandate to conduct programs with adverse

---

[9] Atomic energy is a good example. The assumption that any radiation exposure may be harmful leads to the basic principle underlying regulation of radiation uses (as stated by the Federal Radiation Council) that "there should not be any man-made radiation exposure without the expectation of benefit resulting from such exposure." 1 CCH At. En. L. Rep. ¶ 4046, at 9115. Part 20 of the AEC's rules and regulations sets forth the maximum amount of radiation exposure to which workers and the public may be subjected in activities regulated by the AEC. Part 20 obviously reflects the judgment that the uncertain risks of radiation must be assumed by the public in exchange for the benefits of atomic energy technology.

[10] Here again the Santa Barbara story is instructive.

environmental implications, other agencies such as the Departments of Interior and Health, Education and Welfare have a congressional mandate to improve and defend the quality of the environment. Not infrequently the conflicting views of these agencies clash in the context of specific issues. It is interesting and instructive to note, however, that both the executive offices of the President and the Congress seem more disposed to authorize programs which involve the likelihood of environmental abuse than to give primacy to protection of the environment.

Malcolm Baldwin's "The Santa Barbara Oil Spill" suggests that a similar situation prevails even in those areas in which the government has a more passive, non-programmatic interest. There the government's interest was in the economic benefits to the public which would result from tapping off-shore oil resources and in the revenues which would flow to the public treasury from leasing of these resources. Drilling was authorized apparently on the assumption that spillage was virtually a technological impossibility.

The fundamental problem seems to be that of an information gap.[11] To state the matter bluntly, technological advance and the government's paternalistic commitment to bestow the benefits of technology on its public have far outpaced man's knowledge of the possible risks and adverse consequences of the application of technology. This information gap permeates every level at which effective action can be taken to defend the environment. Plaintiffs in private litigation cannot develop the kinds of evidence needed to make their case. Legislatures do not have access to information concerning the consequences of environmental abuse sufficient to warrant legislative action in the face of the potential benefits pressed upon them by the vested interests. Indeed, the interested public does not have, and cannot afford to develop, the information necessary to pressure the legislatures into appropriate action. And regulatory agencies may suspect, but have insufficient data adequately to confirm, the existence of adverse factors. These difficulties are exacerbated by the strong tendency of the government to rely on bodies of scientific and technological experts not only to develop relevant facts but to make the actual determinations as to whether costs outweigh benefits.[12] Concomitantly, the carefully nurtured myth that technical issues

---

[11] "At present our knowledge regarding toxicity of air pollutants is not adequate to allow us to know how to safeguard the health of the variety of people making up a community." Report of the Environmental Pollution Panel, *supra* n. 2, at 66.

[12] For example, the AEC's radiation protection standards, *supra* n. 9, are derived from the studies and conclusions reached by the National Committee on Radiation Protection. While this body unquestionably knows more about the effects of radiation on life than any other, the fact that it is composed virtually entirely of scientists and other technical experts (with no lawyers, economists, sociologists, psychiatrists, philosophers, theologians, etc.)

are beyond the comprehension of the public, and even the legislators—coupled with the corollary proposition that Big Brother knows best and the public should not be unduly alarmed—serves to minimize public discussion and debate.[13] To the extent that members of the public become involved as protagonists in defense of the environment in the political arena, they are usually compelled to argue on the basis of less than adequate information, and it is usually not very difficult for the vested interests to prevail through the simple device of exposing the weaknesses of the protagonists' case through a barrage of more authoritative information. Indeed, it is a distressingly frequent occurrence for the vested interests—both private and governmental—to deal with these protagonists *ad hominem*.

Mr. Baldwin has stated the principal problem succinctly: "What mechanism should exist to evaluate new technology and to determine when or whether to employ it when its operation or malfunction could seriously affect the environment?" This is a subject now under intensive discussion as a result of Congressman Daddario's proposal for creation of a Technology Assessment Board. Most discussion of this proposal has centered upon the question as to what kind of mechanism can be created to give Congress and the public an authoritative, balanced presentation of the costs and benefits of technology as a predicate for Congressional action. The assumption is that Congress as a *political assessment* body lacks the competence to make *technology assessment* judgments; therefore, some mechanism must exist to give Congress technology assessments on the basis of which political judgments can be made.[14] The function of technology assessment would, of course, be performed primarily by scientists and engineers.

This approach to technology assessment ignores the fundamental fact that the benefits of technology are always fully articulated and usually overstated, while the costs and risks are rarely adequately discussed. This is so for two reasons. First, in the very nature of new technology, comprehension of potential benefits precedes recognition of risks by a wide time margin. Secondly, as discussed above, the sponsors of the technology

---

makes it dubious at least that it is qualified to deal with the benefit side of the cost/benefit calculus or to reflect the judgment of society as a whole.

[13] Although this is never explicitly articulated, there seems little doubt that a major premise underlying the elaborate AEC administrative procedures in power reactor licensing cases is that all AEC participants should play their role in a manner which will not alarm the public. See e.g. Regulatory Review Panel, *Report to the Atomic Energy Commission*, July 14, 1965.

[14] See e.g. Carpenter, "Technology Assessment and the Congress," published in The George Washington University Program of Policy Studies in Science and Technology, *Technology Assessment—The Proceedings of a Seminar Series*, at 33-46 (July, 1969).

have a unique knowledge of the potential risks, which they tend to understate in order to avoid retarding development of the technology. This approach also ignores a basic premise of a democratic society: since the process of assessment involves the decision as to what costs and risks are to be assumed *by the public* in exchange for benefits to the public, the public itself, acting through its elected representatives in Congress, should have full opportunity to determine for itself what risks it is willing to assume ("tolerate") for what benefits. If an expert agency charged with responsibility for technology assessment is asked to weigh benefits against risks, information reaching Congress and the public will be highly distilled and carefully selected, and decisions will be made on the basis of the judgments of an elite body rather than by the public itself. Worse, the judgments of the elite body will reflect the nonhumanistic biases of its scientific and technologically oriented members.

The Daddario proposal is premised on the view that a new and novel form of government institution is required to assess technology and to provide Congress with "early warning" signals as to technological risks. This premise is unquestionably sound. We know from experience that executive branch departments and administrative agencies have not demonstrated an adequate capacity to evaluate new technology in the light of potential adverse consequences. Such departments and agencies invariably have dual, conflicting obligations; *i.e.* they usually are chartered to regulate without unduly crippling the objects of their regulation. As a matter of fact, their charters frequently specify that regulation is to be imposed in a manner which will *promote* sound development of the technologies they regulate. Fulfilling this mandate requires cost/benefit analysis, and these agencies inevitably make judgments *ex cathedra*, based on expert evaluations, as to what risks the public must assume. Beyond this, they are, of course, subject to the overall economic, social, and political policies of the chief executive. In this connection, Mr. Baldwin's discussion is highly instructive in pointing out the likelihood that no regulatory framework would have resulted in blocking the Santa Barbara drilling activity.

Similarly, it seems unlikely that less than a novel legislative agency could function effectively in assessing technology. Even a special legislative committee, such as has been proposed, to deal with environmental problems would not be adequately effective. It would inevitably be subject to political influences and, to the extent it functioned aggressively, would come into conflict with other legislative standing committees which have more direct and substantive jurisdiction over activities impinging on the environment. Such other committees, with jurisdictional primacy and superior knowledge of and interest in the benefit side of the cost/benefit analysis, would ride roughshod over the environmental committee. Moreover, such an environmental committee, to be effective at all, would require a large, expert staff, and legislative bodies are ill-equipped to create and maintain such a staff.

I do not suggest that any of these thoughts are without merit. They all represent steps in the right direction. If, however, we are really serious about protection of the environment against rampant new technology, it is at least worth considering a more radical solution to redress the balance between technological advance and fundamental human values.

Ideally, a mechanism should be created to assure that the potential costs, risks, and adverse consequences of technology will be articulated as fully and vigorously as the potential benefits are articulated. If such a mechanism existed, we could have a basis for confidence that the ordinary legislative processes would deal effectively and in a timely manner with environmental abuse. What is needed to accomplish this is an agency in the nature of an ombudsman, although an information-oriented rather than action-oriented ombudsman. It should be charged with the sole function, to be performed responsibly, of course, of ferreting out, publicizing, and pressing upon the Congress, the public, and the administrative agencies the potential adverse consequences and risks involved in technological or other activities which affect the environment. The salutary effects of this procedure are obvious. A body of information would be developed indicating the need for further research and development and consideration of risks before irreversible technological commitments are made. Proponents of the questioned activity would be compelled to respond directly, in public and in language the public can understand. The public would be able to make its own judgments as to what benefits it wants in exchange for what costs and risks, and to press its views on the legislature. The judgments of scientists and engineers would, of course, be important elements in the decisions made, but they would not be controlling. The issue would be resolved in the rough and tumble of the political arena where resolution of such issues belongs in a democracy. The information developed by the agency would be available for use not only by the legislature but also by administrative agencies and by litigants.

Where should such an agency be placed in the governmental framework? If it were located in the executive branch, it might become subordinated to the mission objectives of the executive. Accordingly, it should probably be located as an arm of the Congress—an independent agency analogous to the General Accounting Office.

In short, the concept of such an ombudsman-type agency is advanced as a "needed development in the law." It is, I recognize, an extreme solution to the problem of protecting the environment, but the extremity of the proposed solution is, I believe, commensurate with the gravity and complexity of the problem. The need for such an agency is clearly demonstrated in the Santa Barbara discussion. It is easy enough after a Santa Barbara catastrophe occurs to create laws and procedures designed to preclude a repetition. But we may not always be able, considering the exponentially escalating capacity of man to destroy himself, to tolerate a first catastrophe. The real questions to be answered are (1) how the Santa Barbara catastrophe could have been prevented through any means short of giving the remote possibility of a serious oil spill equal time and dignity as the expected benefits of the drilling activity in the process of deciding whether the drilling should be authorized; and (2) how such equal time and dignity could have been provided short of a vigorous articulation of the possibility that the spill might occur and its potential consequences. It is not suggested that even this solution would provide complete assurance that a Santa Barbara catastrophe would not occur. But, if it did occur, clear responsibility for the erroneous judgment would be unambiguously fixed.

It will be suggested by some that this proposal "institutionalizes fear" or "institutionalizes conservatism." This may be true, but to institutionalize fear or conservatism would have the beneficial effect of offsetting the already firmly entrenched institutionalization of technological optimism and of faith in technological gimmicks. It may also be contended that such an agency would unnecessarily, by arousing undue public concern, retard technological "progress."[15] This is not an unlikely result, but why, in a democratic society, should the public not have the full opportunity to decide, rationally or irrationally, whether it wants "progress" and what kinds of "progress" it wants?

The suggestion for creation of such a devil's advocate ombudsman agency was initially advanced last spring in a seminar series on Technology Assessment.[16] There was considerable belief expressed that this paper was a "spoof" or "put-on." Apparently those who have a strong interest in research and development and technological "progress" find it difficult to take seriously any proposal which would impose restraints

---

[15]This was stated much more dramatically when this proposal was first advanced last March in the Seminar Series referred to in note 14. One of the participants in the seminar, a senior staff member of a congressional committee very much interested in science and technology, responded: "His nihilism would undo a million years of evolution for, make no mistake about it, what Professor Green is proposing here is nothing less than the complete destruction of civilization." *Id.*, at 81.

[16]Green, "The Adversary Process in Technology Assessment," published in The George Washington University Program of Policy Studies in Science and Technology, Technology Assessment—The Proceedings of a Seminar Series, at 59–78 (July, 1969).

upon the rate of such progress. Although this proposal is not intended as a "spoof," I recognize that it is probably impractical for two reasons. Most importantly, it would be difficult to staff such an agency with competent scientists and engineers who would find it distasteful to expend their talents on perpetual negativism. Secondly, it seems unlikely that our strong social bias in favor of affluence and "progress" would permit what many would regard as an unnecessary emphasis on negativism. Nevertheless, I believe that the suggestion has some value as an ideal or model against which less extreme mechanisms for technology assessment can be measured.

DISCUSSION

Sheldon J. Plager, CHAIRMAN   James Krier
Anthony Roisman   James Watt Moorman
Harold P. Green   E. F. Roberts

MR. PLAGER: It seems to me that we have before us three classes of problems.

One of them is the general class of policy issues, asking such questions as: Who should be the decision maker? What is the role of the courts relative to the role of Congress or the legislature? What kind of institutional decision making functions are involved? This is hard to deal with in the abstract, of course, but it is a theme that we have seen running through our discussions and one with which lawyers and others are deeply concerned.

A second area is that of substantive law issues. That is, what is the substantive legal right that is being protected or for which protection is being sought, particularly in the litigation field?

And, thirdly, there is the question of procedural aspects of litigation, such as burden of proof and related issues.

I suggest we turn our attention first to the question of the substantive law issues, since our focus on "Needed Developments in the Law" might well begin there.

It seems to me we have identified four independent legal theories upon which legal actions might be brought. The first kind of action is the traditional nuisance action brought by private individuals or conservation groups against a polluter who is charged with violating the common law standard of nuisance.

The second class of actions is the one Professor Jaffe talks about as the public action. I am not sure I fully understand it. It seems to be the idea that when you have a statutory standard—provided by the rules of an agency or by an act of Congress—being violated, and when you have the agency that is charged with enforcing that rule not taking action, there should be a right of intervention by citizen groups or individuals to enforce that standard. Perhaps *Scenic Hudson* is an example of that kind of case.

A third independent theory would be Professor Roberts's suggestion that there is a Ninth Amendment (constitutional) right to a decent environment. And the fourth one is Mr. Roisman's doctrine.

MR. ROBERTS: Let me say a word about the Ninth Amendment approach. I hear constant frustrations with the kind of due process in which an administrative agency shifts some papers around in what purports to be a rational behavior pattern, then if it plays the Parkinsonian game, a judge will not substitute his judgment for the administrative agency's. As a result the environment around us continues to deteriorate.

I think I really agree with the, shall we say, subtle approach of Mr. Yannacone. Certainly we need the shock therapy of some good lawsuits, but I think what we are really talking about is the return to substantive due process. We are sick and tired of this Parkinsonian, solely procedural due process.

I used the Ninth Amendment in my paper. I would have preferred to write it along Mr. Yannacone's lines and say, "All right, here is a copy of the Constitution." Because there is a right to apply a good deal of it, I just staple a copy of the Constitution to my complaint and we have solved the problem.

I admit the Ninth Amendment bit may be a bit of flak, but I also suspect that this kind of conference may be a law generating device by which we throw out a citation and hope that some day some judge finally cites the damn thing for his emotional conclusion because, trained like a lawyer, he has to cite something that says it's authority.

My only reservation about this whole affair is the fact that the environment we are in now, here at Airlie House, is so shocking. Think of the W. C. Fields who must have built this place with his caveat, no children and no dogs. (Laughter) I am taking that sign home and showing it to my children and my dogs.

But what is really so shocking about this environment is that there is actually clean air here, there is a tolerable noise level (other than the noise we make ourselves). It is almost a cloud-cockooland environment that we are enjoying. Watch your colleagues as they wander around the walks almost agape in a kind of mystic trance. (Laughter)

Now, what worries me is that we are really looking at the tip of an iceberg. I think that as lawyers, we are fighting a series of isolated issues. Like lawyers, we stick to facts and narrow issues, but really we are moving into a new society, a technological society in which one little error may blow half of us up. The reason I argue the Ninth Amendment is that I am hoping Mr. Yannacone will take this great case up and, bang, get the right of environment declared. I suspect in the long run we are going to have to go to a political restructuring, whereby we make all of our agencies bring in some kind of ecological litmus test on every single decision they make. But I suspect within the conventional wisdom of our affluent society we are not really prepared to face the problems of a technological era, that we really aren't prepared to take environment into action if it cuts into our rising standard of living.

I, therefore, am going along absolutely with the shock therapy treatment. I have grave doubts about it, but if we are going to get restructured before we are all dead, we can't wait for the administrative or the political solution. So I am asking Mr. Yannacone to ask the Supreme Court to put its neck in the guillotine and come down with a decision that would force every agency to restructure its thinking process. The Burger Court must be so damn activist as to make the Warren Court look like a tea party. Period. (Applause)

MR. MOORMAN: I think we should realize that the environmental problem is fragmented. There are, for example, a lot of standards in the law and, while some people want to talk about constitutional rights, we should have a lot of legal rights. There are a host of legal duties for federal administrators. Rather than attempt to push constitutional rights that the courts are not yet ready to accept, we should concentrate on standards that Congress has written into various acts and try to put some life into them. Often Congress has given us a law that is either adequate or partially adequate on its face, but we can't seem to get anything to happen. Standards are written into the law, administrators are given a duty, but still the environment continues to deteriorate. That, of course, is where most of the environmental lawsuits come in.

MR. GREEN: But this environmental deterioration cannot be arrested solely through litigation, which is, of course, part of the thesis of my paper. The reason I am inclined to place so much emphasis on an improved articulation of negative environmental factors is because, unhappily, when any kind of a cost-benefit analysis of a new technology is performed, the benefits, one may be sure, are always fully articulated. There are always people who have vested interests at stake, and they can be relied upon to do the fullest possible job of articulating the benefits they think will flow from their activities. On the other hand, the cost and risk factors are only rarely adequately identified, because there are relatively few people who have an immediate concern about these costs and risks when the decisions are being made. If they have any such concern, they almost never have the money to do the necessary job of articulating the costs and risks.

It follows that the only way that you can really have cost-benefit analyses and computations made with any kind of validity is to provide some strong artificial stimulus to assure that the decision makers have as strong and full a presentation of costs as they do of the benefits.

MR. LEVINE: One tool available to correct this imbalance, which we haven't used to anywhere near the extent that we could, is the market. We are dealing with problems that have been traditionally classed as external problems. That is, they are not taken into account in market transactions because of their relatively small impact on individuals, or because of large removals in time, with impact on future generations. So when someone decides to build a steel mill or a power plant in a certain place, or to produce widgets somewhere, and among the resources he uses is the environment (by making it ugly or by polluting the air or water), he doesn't take into account the true cost of using those resources, which is their value to other people. The widely discussed device of effluent charges is one way you can make him account for these values. You can attempt to put a value on these resources, make them no longer free goods, because they are no longer free goods in the economist's sense. You put a price on them and make people, through the market, decide whether they want these environmental resources used in this way, whether they would prefer them used in other ways or left alone.

This would require some attempt at valuing scenery, clean air and clean water.

There are obvious empirical effects such as disease or reduction in the fishing industry, and so on, that one would take into account. There are other more subtle things like beauty or recreational values about which we would probably have to be fairly arbitrary, but, of course, we are making those decisions already—and making them badly. There is no reason why we couldn't arrange to make them better by trying to face up to the question, "Since you can't have anything you want, what is it you do want?"

Even with respect to future generations, there are possible methods, some of them fairly involved, that would allow the government to place a price on resources based on its estimate of their future value, and in effect to offer to buy private resources—large tracts of timber, for example—so as to apply a more favorable long-term discount rate. I won't bore you with explaining that.

But it seems to me that we have not even begun to set up structures by which people, by exercising their preferences and doing the things they know how to do, can make intelligent decisions about using the environment. If you say to someone, "You play God for a while, you control the Hudson River," it would be very difficult for him to take into account all preferences, whether that someone is the FPC or Department of the Interior or anyone else. But if you can structure things so that individuals exercising their preferences will take into account all the consequences of their choice, you might end up with a better decision-making system.

As to the carrot and the stick, discussed by Professor Krier in his paper, some recent articles including one by Professor Ronald Coase[1] deal with the problem of social costs. They suggest that from the standpoint of economic efficiency, the carrot or the stick, applied appropriately, are equally effective weapons against externality.[2] The principal consequences of choosing one rather than the other are the political consequences of distribution of income. It makes no difference for resource allocation and the amount of pollution he will choose to create whether we pay a man not to pollute or whether we tax him if he does pollute. We may not like the distribution of income that results from paying him not to pollute, for example. I don't happen to like it much myself. I prefer it, however, to having pollution, and if the tax is impossible, in many cases I would prefer to see the subsidy used.

This problem is one that can be dealt with in part through the use of microscopic, rather than, as Professor Green suggests, macroscopic devices. That is, it can be dealt with by designing structures so that individuals can act to make a difference rather than trying to do it all on a very large scale.

MR. ROISMAN: The problem that I have with Mr. Levine's approach is that it presupposes the environment is bargainable, can be sold, has a price, that the price can be paid and that the purchaser can, therefore, get value for the money received. I think that approach is a presupposition that has put us where we are today.

It seems to me we must start now with some approach, whether it is the Ninth Amendment or a trust doctrine or something else, that really turns the whole thing around. We now know our society has the technological capacity—it has proven it—to do virtually everything that we are really interested in doing. We put men on the moon.

We have got little tiny things the size of your thumb that can run railroad trains and all kinds of other technological advances. We can also build a power plant that will not pollute. We can also build, if we need to, a power line that will not be visible. We can construct an industry that can get rid of its solid wastes without polluting anything around it. We can get rid of vermin that damage crops with-

---

[1] "The Problem of Social Cost," 3 *Journal of Law and Economics* 1.
[2] See also Calabresi, "Transaction Costs, Resource Allocation, and Liability Rules—A Comment," 11 *Journal of Law and Economics* 67.

out also damaging the people who eat the crops.

All of those things are well within the capacity of the technological part of society to accomplish. The question is, do we pay people for doing it? Do we ask them kindly if they would please do it? Or do we, in effect, force them to do it by giving them no reasonable alternative?

Our society seems to function best under the third form, the stick, not the carrot. If you really want the oil industry to figure a way of getting oil out of Alaska without running a pipeline, you can make it illegal for them to use a pipeline. They will find themselves a really good boat that will make the Northwest Passage without polluting the Arctic. They will fly the oil out. Or they will find an alternative source of power.

Now, we—those of us who are interested in the environment exclusively—are the ones who are in a position to put that pressure on. We can start off by saying, "We are going to give you a little bit of money to encourage development" (which is what the power companies, for example, tell us we have to do if we want underground powerlines). "You come up with what you want." But, if we say that, we will not get the results we are after. They have all the answers.

I have a tremendous amount of faith in the ability of Standard Oil of New Jersey to come up with the answers once we make it clear to them that they must do so. I don't blame them for taking the easy way out as long as we give it to them.

An analysis that begins with the premise that we can afford a little bit of pollutant in our water because of some tremendous value that comes from up river, presupposes a technological impasse. I don't really believe such a technological impasse exists in the great bulk of things we are concerned with. If it does, then that is the place where Jim Krier's burden of proof comes in: let's let the industry take its technological abilities and show us that it is a physical impossibility to do what we ask.

MR. KRIER: To take a little different focus on this for a minute, just assume that Mike Levine might be right in believing what the economists say. I think a more important question in a welfare-economics analysis is to accept, as many people will, the idea that everything has its price. But what is going to be the pricing mechanism and who is going to decide?

For instance, I can live on the shores of the ocean in Santa Barbara and I can be approached by Union Oil and they can say we will give you a million dollars if we can pollute your beach and I say fine, and I pack up and go to live in the South Sea Islands, which is good because the women there are even more topless than they are on the shores of Santa Barbara, or practically the same as Berkeley. (Laughter) But my decision affects a lot of other people besides myself. There are other people who might want to use the beach, there are people living away from the beach who fish. There are people who don't have some recognized vested property interest that they can sell. Really the implication of what Mike says is that we must create a better market structure so we can have rational pricing decisions. And I think he is right: everything does have its price.

Mr. Moorman: That very activity is going on today in Chesapeake Bay where power companies are buying up oyster beds so that they may destroy them. I don't suppose it is in order to destroy them, but when thermal pollution does so or when other pollutants from the power plant does, they can say they purchased the oysters and that they are theirs to destroy.

Mr. Plager: In part because they are already polluted by effluent.

Mrs. Strong: I was going to say just what Professor Krier said, but I also would like us to give a little attention to how you establish the pricing mechanism because, obviously, it is not likely that it will be the environmentalist who is in control.

I am concerned with how we establish a more effective voice for the environmentalists than we have today. I don't see how you can argue that you don't have to put a price on everything, because then you are failing to face the reality that this is what we do constantly, whether it is what we say we do or not. Our decision to tax or not to, our decision to offer neither carrot nor stick, is an economic decision.

Mr. Roisman: I think there are two different positions in this and I don't want them to be confused. You are talking about what you think is eventually going to happen.

Mrs. Strong: No. I am talking about what I think does happen now.

Mr. Roisman: Okay. I am talking about what has to be argued in order to get what you want to have happen happen in the best possible light. You cannot go into court and begin with the premise that the other side has half of the ball game already won, that they really could prove that it is better to pollute a stream than it is to clean it up.

Mrs. Strong: Why can't you?

Mr. Roisman: Because if you do that you are going to lose all the streams.

Mrs. Strong: Not necessarily. Look at the Rhine system. There you have a decision that it is better to pollute one stream and keep all the others clean.

Mr. Roisman: But wouldn't it be better not to pollute that one stream?

Mr. Levine: Not necessarily. It depends upon what it costs you in lost goods and services. There are poor people in the country. They might do better if goods were cheaper in money terms. (They might do even better if we ever adopt a redistribution of income system, but that is something else, and doesn't seem likely to happen very soon.)

The problem is that nothing, including these technological miracles you speak of, comes free. To devote effort to creating those technological wonders, you have to give up other things that you would like to have done.

MR. ROISMAN: But, to be as pragmatic as Mrs. Strong wishes me to be, we already do it the other way when it comes to military expenditures. We have no cost-benefit analysis decisions about whether we need to spend money on the war or not. Let's get environment into the same position that military spending is now put into. Let all the assumptions run in favor of protecting the environment, and let the other side fight us, instead of doing the opposite. In other words, load the dice so that you have the presumptions your way by taking some of the Ninth Amendment or trust-doctrine arguments or similar arguments, and shift the emphasis.

MRS. STRONG: You are just trying to put a different value on environmental values.

MR. LEVINE: No. He is trying to put an infinite value on them. The trust doctrine takes them out of the market entirely and then no price is appropriate. Therefore, even if there are possible alternatives uses that would be better in some sense than the natural state, it becomes impossible to take the alternative. That is one problem with common ownership. No one has the right to determine how allocation will be made, so no rational decision can be made about the use of the resource.

MR. ROISMAN: No, no. I don't think that's true at all. The trust as I envision it imposes a public interest blanket over property. Now, the public interest blanket may include many different kinds of uses. I mean cities have a public interest value. It does not mean that everything must remain wilderness. It simply means that you make judgments about how that property is going to be used but that those judgments are made in the context of some environmental concern.

MR. PLAGER: Mr. Yannacone has been very patient.

MR. YANNACONE: I am beginning to feel like Adolph Eichmann at a bar mitzvah. (Laughter)

At the risk of insulting some of the people here, the magnitude of the legal scholarship and the economic crudition is exceeded only by the awesome lack of ecological sophistication. The one thing that the Environmental Defense Fund has done in three years with the scientific community has been to separate the negotiable elements of the environment from the non-negotiable elements.

Since 1960 I have litigated the Ninth Amendment and the trust doctrine with respect to some natural resources and every time I try a highway case, an Army Engineer case, anything that involves aesthetics, natural beauty, highways, construction, zoning, land use planning, I deal exactly the way Mr. Levine does. I try the case to establish the basic issue of what are the costs and benefits and establish Ian McHay's idea of determining the actual social costs so that an intelligent decision can be made.

I only attack an agency when I feel they have not fully evaluated all the social costs. However, there are some air pollution cases that are manageable in the sense of economic balance, but there are some air pollution cases that require the imposition of the trust doctrine. This is what I wanted to discuss this morning, but we got hung up on oil.

In Missoula, Montana, after two years of searching, the Environmental Defense Fund found the perfect air pollution test case: a regional air shed with a single sulphur polluter and a decrease in photosynthetic activity in the green plants of the whole regional ecosystem, directly downwind of the sulphur plume. This is the only demonstrable damage.

So, we go to the ecological systems analysis people—those of you who are economists are probably familiar with systems analysis. We establish that if you reduce photosynthetic activity in a regional ecosystem to the lowest possible level, you will ultimately be reducing the oxygen budget for everything above green plants up to and including man. If there is a trapped regional ecosystem bounded by mountains, as in Missoula, you have a serious hazard.

This is a non-negotiable hazard. Reducing the oxygen-making potential of an area is a non-negotiable question. It is a matter of life and breath, as they say in the ads.

To go one step further. We alleged that the company's pollution resulted from its failure to install state-of-the-art air pollution control devices, and we asked the court to impose the state of the art in pollution control on the company.

So far, by dint of discovery and other procedures, we have gotten the company to admit that it can reduce total sulphur content output considerably but to date it has not done so.

We are saying that we have a right to the best environment that money can buy. We have squarely raised the Ninth Amendment question. We have no other grounds. We are not alleging Air Pollution Control Acts or any other statutes—just the Ninth Amendment and the public's right to the best possible air objectionable thru today's state-of-the-art.

You have got to make a distinction, based on some degree of ecological sophistication. You must go to your scientists, and ask if the actions complained of cause serious, permanent and irreparable damage to a regional ecosystem. If the answer is yes, it is non-negotiable. If the answer is no, as it was in Santa Barbara, it is negotiable. If it is negotiable, all we ask is that they apply social cost theory and modern economics and fully evaluate the costs as well as the benefits.

If it is a non-negotiable affront to the environment you must go to court and assert that the resources that will be permanently, seriously and irreparably damaged by the defendant's actions are held in trust by this generation for the benefit, use and enjoyment of the next generation. This is the essence of the trust doctrine. This is the kind of right that is meant to be protected by the Ninth Amendment.

MR. CURRIE: I would be interested in hearing the contents, first, of the trust doctrine that is proposed, and second, the constitutional right that is proposed. Specifically, I would like to know how either of these new handles help us in a way that is not possible under the law of nuisance. That is, whether we do not run into the same kind of problem of balancing the equities where, again, it will all depend on the judge.

MR. ROBERTS: This is going to be a thicket filled with ad hoc piece by piece. A case that interests me and cited in my paper, is *Boomer v. Atlantic Cement Company*.

A new cement company was built with planning approval. Nuisance action was brought and much to my surprise, the New York judges went back to balancing the interests. I thought the time had come when we could build a cement plant on a piece of ground big enough not to bother its neighbors, or to put in modern equipment and get rid of the dust and the plant's byproducts. But apparently not. The people who live in that neighborhood were given some money damages and told, in effect, that the cement company can inundate your property with pollution as long as it gives you a few dollars. This was a classic nuisance case. I suppose the balancing interest there was that it helped the greater economy of the so-called capital district Gov. Rockefeller is building.

Frankly, it bothers me because if I owned one of those houses I would not be persuaded that any damn cement company has a right to come in and buy the lot next door, flood me out with dust, throw some sheckles on my counter and say, "Toddle along, Free Man." Damn it, I would love to make a constitutional argument in that case: I have a right to a decent environment, and unless that right is respected, an injunction can be issued and the plant closed down until the company makes the necessary technological improvements.

This is what makes me nervous about the market. I am persuaded that my environment is being marketed away by the economists. What worries me in this business of cost-benefit analysis and balancing of interests is that unless we can somehow reinstitute the humanity into this equation, with some very basic right in these nuisance cases to overturn that balancing of the interests, it is going to be a steady chipping away process and a continuation of the current chaos.

MR. ROISMAN: I see the trust doctrine as, if you will, a universal solvent. You apply it to whatever the problem is and it dissolves. (Laughter) That is to suggest it is less substantive than procedural. It is a hook. We've got some old case law that establishes the existence of a trust, something that suggests that all property needs to be utilized for the benefit of the public interest. There is some possibility of arguing, though I evade it in my paper and I am not prepared to argue it at this point, that we can attach the trust concept to all property; the king had the trust that was passed to the Continental Congress, then it went on to the United States as we now have it under the Constitution. It can be argued that it didn't matter whether the property had at one time been in private or public ownership. In point of fact all property has to be used for the public.

Now, what the public interest is at any given moment obviously will depend on what the situation is. When Lewis and Clark took their expedition, there was an entirely different set of considerations that would have gone into determining what was proper use of the land in the country.

Today I think the situation is fairly clear because we are virtually running out of land. I would disagree with Vic Yannacone. I don't think the only damage to be shown has to be a health hazard. There is psychological damage created by the inability to find a peaceful place, one without a highway or power line to disrupt it. It is possible that scientists and medical people who have already developed a pretty good set of arguments regarding damage to health because of lack of oxygen in a given area can do the same thing with the argument that there is a lack of beauty and peace and untrammeled property. These are considerations that now make up a large part of the public interest simply because they are becoming so scarce.

The trust doctrine gives you a basis for presenting these arguments, which, if proved, should allow you to win your case.

MR. ROBERTS: Regardless of the other competing public interests? It seems to me that the public interest standard is exactly what the nuisance doctrine is all about, too, and it comes out wrong in many cases for the conservationist. The same judge is likely to do the same thing with your trust doctrine.

MR. ROISMAN: First of all, as far as the judge is concerned, you are right. We have concrete evidence of that. Sure, if you get the wrong judge it won't matter what theory you have. There are judges today who don't follow the obvious law much less get into the more obscure areas. The difference in the trust doctrine is that, assuming you have a judge who is either neutral or partial to your case but still needs something to hang it on, you can give the court a basis to prohibit a certain act because the public interest dictates that we protect a particular piece of property.

Now, without the trust doctrine there may be a "balancing" of those public interests. *Texas Eastern Transmission*, discussed at length in Jim Krier's paper, suggests that this balancing technique involves a consideration of alternatives. But there are very, very few matters that ecologists or psychologists are concerned about professionally that are really negotiable. That is, as Vic Yannacone pointed out this morning, it is very difficult to figure out how you would replace an ecosystem or a view if someone wants to destroy it. If it is a power line along the Chesapeake & Ohio Canal, you can't ever move the Canal to some other location. As a matter of fact, you will never be able to do that because there is historical significance attached to its present location. In effect, you have what I would consider a non-negotiable situation.

So what do you do with the power line? There are a lot of alternatives. The nuisance doctrine, as I understand it, doesn't really permit consideration of alternatives on the side of the person creating the nuisance. The trust doctrine gives you a basis to force that consideration on the theory that if I am the beneficiary of a trust and the government is my trustee, you must then deal with my trustee. In the ultimate case, if you really need to fight it, you can then try to force the government, by a mandamus action, to perform its fiduciary obligation. If the government will take the property, either an easement or in fee, then it can never be condemned.

That is what the trust doctrine does. It is not necessary in every case to deed your property to the federal government to get the protection, but in an extreme case that would be the remedy.

MR. SIVE: To comment further on the question raised by David Currie, even though we might concede that constitutional rights are really not absolute in character and even though it is true that the trust doctrine eventually does get around to the same sort of weighing process as the nuisance theory, it seems to me that both of these doctrines, the constitutional point and the trust doctrine, are worthy of examination and exploration for several additional reasons. Very often the remedies you seek are not possible under a nuisance theory. And in the case of constitutional principles, you might well have, in some instances, the right of jury trial, which you may wish to accept or reject.

MR. MOORMAN: I don't believe that we have much of a constitutional right today. I think the question of how the environment is used is so politically important, that we are not going to find the court kicking aside the Air Pollution Act and declaring a constitutional right to clean air.

Now, part of this discussion seems to be based on the assumption that there really aren't many standards. But I think Representative McCloskey and his peers have been doing a lot of work—though they need to do a lot more. A lot of good things have been written into the law in recent years. I thank the Sierra Club for being one of the major lobbyists.

MR. BERRY: May I suggest that word be left out of the transcript? (Laughter)

MR. MOORMAN: That is not, incidentally, an opinion of law.

MR. PLAGER: Let the record show that the word "lobbyist" was objected to by the counsel for the Sierra Club.

MR. MOORMAN: What kind of air we are to have is going to be decided by Congress. For better or worse, it has written a law and we are stuck with it.

If it is not good enough, we have to go back to Congress and ask for something better. That is where the weighing is going on. These acts that are passed are the things we have to deal with rather than theory of constitutionally protected environment.

MR. DURNING: I would like to pose a question to Mr. Roisman and others about the public trust doctrine as used in the field in which it originated, the law of submerged land. This is an environmental issue of some great significance around the country. My area, Seattle, is on the shores of Puget Sound and I know of one giant application for land fill in Hood Canal for a high rise hotel, another application for a dredging permit to go in for six to ten miles of fill in Padilla Bay, another on land in Birch Bay. It seems Puget Sound is about to undergo the San Francisco Bay experience.

In this connection, the law in our state is clear, and our Attorney General's office, I hope, will find it so. What are the rights of the public in submerged tidelands already sold by the states to private ownership and, may these lands be bulkheaded and filled on such a huge scale? Is there still a public interest, and if so is it still impressed with the trust? Is there an environmental law strategy about the use of this doctrine that already exists, or can we simply go ahead and assert the trust? Some feel that there is still a lot to be decided about the rights of the tideland owner who got a deed from a state before the state ever heard of the trust doctrine.

MR. COHEN: Several citizen groups currently have a suit pending in the U.S. District Court for the Eastern District of Virginia, right here in Alexandria, involving the Hunting Creek Estuary of the Potomac River.[3] Some developers want to construct a bulkhead and fill 36½ acres of it.

[3] *Fairfax County Federation of Citizens Associations, et. al. v. Hunting Towers Operating Co. et al.* Civ. No. 4963 A, U.S. Dist. Ct. E.D. Va. (filed Oct. 1, 1968).

We filed a suit in Federal Court and alleged as the jurisdictional base the Civil Rights Act of 1871: the suit complained that the state was acting under the color of law in depriving the complainants of their civil rights.

The civil right that I claim they are entitled to is a right under the trust doctrine to submerged lands under navigable waters of the United States. I am arguing the Ninth Amendment, the Fourteenth Amendment due process clause, the Fourteenth Amendment equal protection clause, and the Fourteenth Amendment rights, privileges and immunities clause, using as my tag for the latter the right to navigation established as a federal right under *Crandall v. Nevada* and *Gibbons v. Ogden.* We asked in our pleadings for an injunction but never went to court to have a hearing for the temporary restraining order or a preliminary injunction because we could not put up money for a bond. If you talk about strategies, here is an example where you get the effect of an injunction without ever having a court order, because the developers found that they could not get title insurance to the land once we filed a suit and therefore could not go forward with developing. They were planning to start on October 1, 1968, with filling the land and we filed a suit the same day. Because it was an 11th-hour appeal and took several weeks of research and planning to draw the pleadings, we flooded the area with lots of publicity about the suit being brought.

Since that time, with the help and in combination with a congressional subcommittee that is investigating the matter, we have effectively stopped the developers.

Secretary Hickel asked the Corps of Engineers to revoke the permit that had been granted. The Corps of Engineers suspended it and we hope that after public hearings the permit will be suspended permanently.

If the permit is not revoked, the suit is still pending in court, and I have every intention of going to the Supreme Court with it.[4]

MR. LEFCOE: The lawyers' bent for sharpening issues and creating controversies has obscured one of the implications in Mike Levine's comments.

The presently available legal doctrines in the negotiable cases, to borrow Vic's phrase, have a number of shortcomings for such a case as Professor Roberts' and the concrete factory spraying dust on him. Among them is that Roberts and his neighbors probably could not condemn a negative easement to prevent dust spray even if they are willing to pay a fair price. The legal doctrines we have discussed don't provide this alternative.

We have been concentrating on doctrines that result in an all-or-none

---

[4]The Corps of Engineers revoked the land fill permit in April, 1970.

rule, which often, for better or worse, turns out to mean "none" for the conservationist. Shouldn't we devise some doctrines and remedies more consistent with our traditional market assumptions, when we happen to feel that the market place is not far off?

Another question. There are limited resources available for bringing lawsuits and writing laws. People are always free to initiate legally frivolous actions that can establish a negative precedent. Yet there is rarely a way for people to obtain thoughtful, careful advice on whether they should bring a lawsuit and what issues, in terms of the whole conservation strategy, they should raise. The fact of a lawsuit and the issues litigated are too often the aftermaths of an outrageous event, and not taken as the measured steps in a planned strategy of litigation.

I would hate to have someone type the Ninth Amendment argument in two sentences, in a case with miserable facts and poor briefings, and wind up with something close to a *per curiam* opinion saying: "This is an absolutely absurd notion, it is not worth a minute of anyone's serious thought, but since it has been raised let us put it to rest once and for all." It would be hard to live that down. This is the special hazard of a system that relies so much on precedent.

Can a way be found to work out the priorities for environmental litigation and legislation, given the diversity of interests and the odd ways that money is raised?

MR. YANNACONE: I have had to eat the Robert Cushman Murphy DDT case in every DDT suit we have brought. There is an example of a great deal of money spent to protect three acres of an organic garden on Long Island against $3 million worth of gypsy moth damage to the country with no scientific basis that DDT was harmful. This case made very, very bad law because the court in a long opinion said DDT had been proven beyond all reasonable doubt to be safe and harmless.

Another example,—Project Rulison in Colorado. There is not one shred of scientific evidence that the blast is dangerous. The American Civil Liberties Union action was brought to stop the blast. On the other hand, we went in on behalf of the Colorado Open Space Coordinating Council to prevent the release of radionuclides to the environment. We were not about to tell the Atomic Energy Commission how to detonate their bomb. But we were about to tell them that it must stay underground and encapsulated until some court determines whether we should live with that much tritium and Cesium 137 added to the environment.

These are the questions I have asked the Sierra Club. How do you evaluate when to go to court and when not to go? If it emotionally looks like a good case, have you fully cross-examined your scientists and thoroughly investigated the basis for their opinion? Will there be a potential disaster? Is the subject legally frivolous? As a trial lawyer I will only bring an environmental lawsuit after a great deal of scientific legal and other discussion, and when we do leap into one, as sometimes we do on short notice, we try to couch it in such a way that a dismissal will not preclude another action against the same type of damage.

MR. BALDWIN: The Sierra Club, of course, is probably responsible singlehandedly for more usable precedents in this field than any other organization. But this fact does not detract from the real problem of trying to assess priorities, assess where the law should go and determine what a useful course should be in litigation in, say, the next decade. One of the things I would like to see come out of this conference directly or indirectly is some mechanism and perhaps some new institution to assess these needs and these strategies at a national level.

A number of organizations are doing this individually with varying degrees of success and varying amounts of staff attention. It is nevertheless a very *ad hoc* arrangement at present.

MR. EVANS: I can understand Mr. Yannacone's concern and agree with Mr. Baldwin's suggestion. But there are other kinds of problems. There are wilderness and scenic places you just cannot lose: Hells Canyon, the gorge of the Snake River, some mines in the White Cloud, portions of southeast Alaska, and so forth. You can't save them by the political process. You've got to go to court. That may or may not be to your taste, but you can't let the place go, because if you do it is gone forever. This, I think, is where the philosophy comes in. We may talk about market devices or try to quantify some of these things, but you can't keep philosophy out of it.

I am still not convinced that the fate of the environment is negotiable, whether it involves air, wilderness, parks, wildlife or whatever. I think that our basic premise in all of these things should be at least in the very beginning, that the answer is no. We have lost too much already. We talk about balancing equities, but we should consider what has happened in this country during the last 300 years when the balance has been all the other way. Let's start taking a hard line and try to change the balance.

MR. SANDERS: I am a nonlawyer and I am going to make a nonlawyerly remark. I am going to say, "Look, Vic, who told you when you started out that you had a good case?"

MR. YANNACONE: A bunch of ecologists told me that DDT continually being used the way it was being used would cause serious, permanent, irreparable damage to the regional ecosystem.

MR. SANDERS: When you first started out, everybody told you you were crazy, didn't they?

MR. YANNACONE: No. The lawyers told me I was crazy; the scientists told me it had to be done.

MR. SANDERS: The point I am making is: We have a huge problem and I don't know if we can wait to make sure we've got a good level ground every time we want to.

MR. YANNACONE: We must ask what are the scientific elements of this case. Is this kind of case, the kind that cries out to the court or to heaven or to whoever the higher authority is for retribution; is it so great that it results in reshaping the law?

These are the cases that ought to be looked at first. If somebody is going to put an open pit mine on top of Glacier Peak, I don't care whether there isn't one shred of precedent. This is the kind of environmental rape that cries out to those nine men and says, "Gentlemen, you have a choice here. You close the door to this courthouse and you are opening the door to the streets. You are encouraging conservationists not to turn to the law, but to go out and blow up bulldozers."

These are the kinds of cases you can use to make law, cases when there is such an atrocious affront that you don't get wound up in the problems of economics of the situation.

MR. SIVE: I am glad that someone spoke up earlier for the Sierra Club because this morning my understanding was that we were not adventurous enough. This afternoon it seems we have been too adventurous. When people come to you and say we want you to litigate, it may again be an ethical problem if you tell them you won't represent them because you're afraid you will lose and that will prejudice some unnamed plaintiff in some future action. That would certainly be a breach of legal ethics and a breach of contract.

I don't see how it could be looked upon any differently just because it is environmental litigation.

MR. BERRY: The Sierra Club selects its lawsuits according to three different principles, and we give separate weight to each. First, is the suit within our means? Second, does it involve a piece of real estate or a principle or a problem that is really important? And third, is there some reasonable chance of success?

Most of the suits that are proposed to us we reject. We take maybe one out of ten or perhaps even fewer.

MR. SIVE: I would like to ask Professor Roberts whether he thinks there will be some judicial use possible of the constitutional amendment, which will probably be adopted by New York State in November,[5] that includes a basic declaration of rights in the environment.

[5]The amendment, Article XIV of the New York State Constitution, was adopted in November, 1969.

MR. ROBERTS: Coming from New York State, I suppose the best bet I could make with you is that the court will say that the declaration of an ideal is not self-executing and is an instruction to the legislature in Albany to implement it.

I am willing to bet we will get two judges on the Court of Appeals to dissent and I hope over the next 20 years that case will be reversed. I hope in the meantime that the Supreme Court will come along with a Ninth Amendment and undo the necessity of that 20-year ordeal.

MR. CURRIE: What do you suggest we put in a constitution for a state now having a constitutional convention that would be of use in defining a useful right enforceable in the courts?

I quite agree that the kind of general bill of rights, the kind of general right to a decent environment, is not likely to be much help. What kind of a general statute, for example, would have been useful in dealing with something like the oil spill in Santa Barbara?

MR. ROBERTS: My own feeling is that if I were to have the power of God to start drafting a constitution, I wouldn't want to give an opinion as to the proper language until I had a little more knowledge about ecology and planning.

This whole afternoon's discussion reminds me of Herbert Marcuse's notion of repressive tolerance. You have so many isolated individuals running around like mice through the cheese, I am not really sure whether we are geared up to even attack this problem. Until we somehow coagulate the scientists and the lawyers and the planners so I can avoid my shock treatment and go to another kind of therapy and get some kind of constitutional convention in which we keep the commissars of capitalism—my phrase for lawyers—to a minority, I wouldn't want to give an advisory opinion on that kind of a broad question.

We will have to shoot a few lawyers and get some scientists into this creation of environmental standards. Then we will have to work out new legal processes to impose upon the administrator—the apparatchiks of the technological society.

MR. CURRIE: But the hard work of developing specific substantive standards is one of the big tasks that confronts people like us.

One place we see this in action is in the setting of air quality standards under federal legislation. It seems to me we ought to plump for more of that kind of thing and then get in there at the administrative hearings and argue for strict standards.

MR. LEVINE: When you start talking about standards and when you start talking about wiping the slate clean, I think Mr. Roberts should perhaps reach not for his gun but for a pen to write the kind of tax and subsidy legislation I was suggesting earlier this afternoon. Rather than try to decide what is the correct standard for all time—or at least until the next legislative revision—for this or that activity, you would do a lot better to devote your energy to determine which activity could be operated and continued on a day-to-day basis by administration.

MR. CAVER: Turning to Mr. Green's concept of the technological ombudsman, I have been wondering whether it comes close to the position taken in the recent report of National Academy of Sciences–National Research Council Committee on Technology Assessment.

MR. GREEN: The National Academy panel report deals with the general question posed by Congressman Daddario as to what kind of a technology assessment mechanism ought to be established. I have read the NAS panel report several times. I carry it around with me and I have it here. At odd moments I read it, but I am not sure I understand it.

One of the points that the NAS panel makes is similar to the point that I have made, namely, that some mechanism must be found for bringing the dissenting minority, the unorthodox point of view about the hazards of technology, more forcefully to the attention of the public and the policy makers. It is not clear to me, however, whether the panel provided any formula as to how to do this. On balance, what the Brooks panel seems to be suggesting is the creation of some kind of elite body of experts to perform what is essentially the task that Congress should be performing: that is, the assessment of technology, with the expectation that Congress would then react by legislating along the lines recommended by the technology assessment mechanism.

I really don't think that kind of device is responsive to the need for resolution of these problems in the rough and tumble of the political process. At the political level, arguments should be made in ordinary language of political discourse and not in the esoteric scientific and engineering jargon of the experts. That only tends to obscure what the issues really are and tends to pacify an unsophisticated public and Congress.

MR. TIPPY: Picking up this ombudsman point, Professor Green is probably on sound ground when he suggests that a special environmental worrying agency should be vested in the legislative rather than the executive branch.

Does anyone think a White House Commission on Environmental Quality, under this administration, could seriously look at the North Slope of Alaska and come to any conclusion that would be negative to the early exploitation of the oil resources?

It would have to function more effectively if it were an analogue of the General Accounting office. I worry that the effort now in Congress to create this thing in the Executive Branch will obviate in the legislators' minds the necessity for creating an institution such as Professor Green recommends.

CONGRESSMAN MCCLOSKEY: I don't dispute Professor Green's recommendation. It is absolutely proper and very significant that in the Government Operations Committee, the name of the subcommittee formerly called "Power and Natural Resources" was changed this year to "Conservation and Natural Resources."

This subcommittee, chaired by Henry Reuss of Wisconsin, is holding hearings and practically acting as an ombudsman today for almost anyone who wants to come in and complain about some environmental matter. The whole Daddario concept and the problem the Congress has run into in this field is a lack of adequate staffing and the need in the White House for an Environmental Quality Council. The President created one. He appointed six Cabinet officers and Dr. DuBridge as advisor. We are concerned that of the 15 scientists in the Office of Science and Technology, not one of them was an environmental scientist. OST hitherto has not included any concept of environmental inquiry.

Now, Dr. DuBridge himself, and the White House, proposed this year that they add five full-time ecologists, environmental multi-discipline people, but they wanted them to be under the aegis of OST to advise the President. I don't think these developments are inconsistent with each other; we need them both. But it is interesting to note what happened to the White House proposals. The House Appropriations Committee refused to fund these five new scientists under DuBridge's proposal, saying that this was a half-way measure and that they wanted a separate and independent group of environmental people advising the President.

MR. NADER: When you are in a situation that might be classified as a period of last desperation, oftentimes you have to look at microscopic techniques, fully aware that these are not going to achieve broader objectives but simply are going to escalate the pace toward achieving broader objectives.

One can, for example, treat a certain court case with legitimate condescension because of its limited impact, but quite apart from its declared complaint, it may trigger a disclosure of information that can be used in another context, in another arena, to far greater consequence.

Many of these problems are susceptible to useful distinctions as far as environmental problems are concerned. Rolling back an existing hazard is one type of problem. Stopping one from being generated is another, and trying to head off a hazard coming on the horizon brings distinct problems of its kind.

Perhaps if some of us are questing for a view of the law writ a little larger than it has been thus far, we could look in terms of the purposes of the law beyond the ones that have been discussed here. And I want to suggest a few that draw on many of the bodies of knowledge outside the law, again which have consequences perhaps beyond the narrow channel of the law being used. I want to suggest a few, not for any extended discussion, because I am sure we don't have time, but simply to get them on the record.

First, in the law toward competition for a quality environment, there are antitrust actions. We have had before us a Justice Department action against the auto industry alleging a conspiracy over a period of 15 years to restrain the development and marketing of auto exhaust control systems. Unfortunately, because of the lack of an antitrust constituency for the public, that case began with the grand jury, was deescalated to a civil complaint, and now I understand this afternoon finally to a consent decree—the go-and-sin-no-more sanction.

That case could have had great potential in alerting the public to the internal connections between corporations who want to restrain the development of or the rate of technological change because of investment commitments and other reasons. It could have facilitated the basis for private treble-damage actions. It could have affected the law of trade associations, which are really very serious obstacles to reform in this area.

Secondly, I think a purpose of the law is to generate independent and public research and make it public, fast and comprehensively and authoritatively. We have two pollutants coming out of the motor vehicle operation, lead and rubber, that have been virtually ignored. René Dubos has said on a number of occasions that rubber particulates from tires may well turn out to be the worst of the pollutants. I have inquired of the tire companies and auto companies. None of them has conducted any research about it. We have also been, of course, very remiss in governmental research in this area. The reasons why heart and cancer research is so much greater than environmental research are reasons that would not make a very respectable analysis in scholarly journals. The reasons basically are that the former had the advocacy of a number of extremely dedicated and savvy people over a period of years. The latter has not had that blessing until very recently.

This raises the question: Can we tolerate a reliance on industry merely to define the problem much less to suggest a solution? I think past years have indicated that we cannot. The very definition of the problem of photo-chemical smog came from a professor at Cal Tech in the early fifties, not from the auto industry, which was not interested in trying to find out.

A third purpose would involve disclosure—disclosure all the way to articulating a broader and deeper set of values and concerns among the population, as well as opening the channels of communication that are blocked, as we know, because of the controversial nature of the subject matter.

A fourth purpose would be innovation. We should have learned about this long ago from Napoleon's successes with developing primitively canned foods as a result of a prize he offered in order to facilitate long treks of his army. Innovation was stimulated.

We have not yet developed a fundamental governmental role here, using all kinds of incentives—not just research grants—to develop prototype operational hardware (a non-polluting vehicle) useful for production. This is another area of severe neglect.

Fifth—and this I think is one of the most important—law without sanctions is really nothing more than public exhortation, and we are at an extremely primitive level in developing and applying sanctions. We usually end up with no sanctions or, much less frequently, sanctions that are so severe that they are not going to be deployed.

But this gets us to the corporate structure as a body of private government, to its constituency, its charter and the matrix of law surrounding it as well as to the personalities of the gentlemen who run corporations. If I have to choose one focus here, I would choose an emphasis on developing the law of sanction in a very, very selective manner, and applying it to corporate behavior, to the corporate institution and to the officials right up to the top. I would begin with the constitution of the corporation that is at least a century out of date and is monopolized by the State of Delaware, which has turned corporation law into a rather significant state industry, *e.g.* 13 per cent of the state's income. The State of Delaware, to a great extent, determines the basic constitutional charter of the American corporation, whether small or megacorporations the size of General Motors.

I would move from the charter to such intriguing problems as the due process of the corporate government. One of the great problems facing individuals who are trying to connect empirical and theoretical knowledge with legal policy-making is the widespread prevalence of invisible chains around specialists in corporate structures as well as scientists and engineers and other specialists elsewhere. There are in the land inhibitions to keep people from speaking out.

A case study: Colorado—nerve gas storage. It didn't start this year. Also, the drilling 12,000 feet deep, a few miles from Denver, for the disposal of chemical wastes did not start last year. Scientists in the Denver area knew about it but only last year did they somehow feel free to speak out about it.

This kind of fear is, I think, a cardinal subject of concern on the part of the legal profession. The inability of a scientist to speak out within a corporate structure without being subject to ostracism, demotion, rejection, or other violations of this due process, is a critical matter. I think we must begin to develop something on the order of a bill of rights for people in large, non-public organizations that have the ability to invoke arbitrary power. Technical societies, for another example, are a similar reflection or mirror image of the corporate malaise in this area.

Finally, I might add that it is the primary responsibility of the law to develop advocates for the law, and in this sense the development of internal ombudsman structures or external public interest lawyers is a critical tool without which very little is going to be moved.

Any society that requires an act of courage for statements of truth or expressions of pending doom is one that reflects great rigidities and great obstacles. We must allocate some of its resources clearly and unabashedly toward development of public-interest advocacy.

MR. NASON: I am not a trial lawyer, so I am not that familiar with practice and procedure, but following Mr. Nader's suggestion that we examine microscopic techniques, it seems to me that on the face of it we might have an opportunity to use the mandamus action perhaps a little bit better.

Through the use of mandamus—requiring the responsible agencies to enforce laws that are on the books—we can perhaps avoid the necessity of raising the huge amounts of money that are necessary to carry a case forward. Otherwise, what happens is that a small group of people are charged with the financial burden of carrying forward a case in the interests of the broad general public, which I think is unfair.

I think also in some of the kinds of cases that have been discussed, we get involved in a non-glamorous issue. It is difficult to raise the kind of money necessary to carry such a case forward. For instance in the area of air and water pollution control, when we in various states and at the federal level passed some very good legislation that seeks to bring about pollution control, not a heck of a lot seems to be done. It seems to me that the proper use of mandamus to require public officials to exercise their responsibility might not be a bad idea. Therefore, I am asking about this remedy, when can you use it, how it should be used, and what are its disadvantages?

MR. SIVE: I can just tell you that there is a well-recognized rule that you can't use mandamus to have a court order a public officer to perform a non-ministerial act if the act involves judgment. Generally, mandamus is not available. Now, that is what we have to work with, and we have to reshape it a bit. So that is the problem.

MR. PLAGER: So that if the government official has discretion to act or not to act, mandamus is typically not a remedy.

MR. SIVE: That is the traditional rule. Maybe some of you professors who have taught equity know this better than I.

MR. ROISMAN: You don't obligate officials to do anything but ministerial duties except in two kinds of cases. You can try to prove abuse of discretion, which is a very difficult suit. It may be that in some circumstances involving ecological problems it is possible to show that it is clearly abusive because of the clear evidence on the other side.

Another way to get around the problem is to reframe it slightly. There is the doctrine that if an administrator has the obligation to make a decision and hasn't made it, you can force him to make the decision.

Now, you may come up with the wrong answer when you force him to make a decision. You have to hope to some extent that other forums —the newspapers, the legislature—may help you by focusing attention on what you are trying to do.

A good case would be the sort of things that the Corps of Engineers tends to do. It looks at a very narrow spectrum and decides on a very narrow set of circumstances. If you frame the question on the ultimate issue, that is, whether or not the Corps should have approved the particular project, then you would run into the problem that it was a discretionary act and you probably would have great difficulty winning the case.

But if you raise it on the ground that the Corps was obligated to make a decision about ecological questions, you may in effect avoid the problem with mandamus. You may force the Corps to make an ecological decision, and it may be put in such a position that it just can't say, "Okay, you want me to make a decision, my answer is no harm, period"; you have been able to focus on some facts that will put the Corps on the spot. It will have to have a hearing, and take in evidence. And if the evidence is strong, it will have a difficult time.

We do have a lot of problems, I think, where administrators are not even deciding ecological questions; in these situations, mandamus to force them to do so would be appropriate, even if the ecological standards weren't specifically written into that piece of legislation.

Congressman McCloskey suggested that you take it from the preamble of another act—and this is done in other areas. You read into all federal agencies' mandate some concept of public interest, and say that any decision they make must be made in light of the public interest. You show that the public interest includes, in this case, an environmental concern.

MR. NASON: Is a state attorney general guided by the same principle? Is he charged with the responsibility of protecting the interests of the general public?

MR. ROISMAN: Any government official would be treated under the same principle. You always run into the difficulty of a government litigator responding, "I have made a discretionary decision that, given my limited resources, I can only take a certain group of cases. I am not going to take any cases that have anything to do with environmental problems." But I think when you force him to make the answer, you sometimes get what you need to prove the abuse of discretion needed to win an ultimate mandamus case.

MR. JORLING: The Water Quality Act of 1965 provides that all federal agencies shall operate pollution-free. However, it adds an escape clause that provides that they need only do so if they have the necessary appropriations or that matters of "national interest" preclude compliance with water quality standards.

The legislation that the Senate Public Works Committee reported out, S.7, has withdrawn those two escapes and now makes it mandatory that all federal agencies comply with applicable water quality standards.[6]

Now, assuming it is enacted in the Senate form, it is obvious that neither the Attorney General nor the President is going to enforce this; therefore, practicing lawyers might give some thought to the kind of action available for such enforcement.

DR. JEANS: I am disappointed so far that we have had no real reaffirmation by some of the lawyer members of the panel of the genius of common law nor of its ability to adapt itself to changing conditions. We are faced with a unique situation here. The populace is finally recognizing the magnitude of the harm that might befall us because of pollution of the environment, and I believe that under prompting from this unique and new threat the common law will react. It will react best through a proliferation of litigation with imaginative lawyers seeking some relief from the court. I am sure that the necessary changes will take place if we can get litigation along the traditional lines. The tort theories and nuisance theories are going to work. If my recollection of legal history is correct, the idea of fault was a new concept about 300 years ago. Before then it was the actor causing the harm who was responsible. Perhaps we will have to go back to that. With some subtle shifts in legal procedure, and if enough imaginative lawyers continue to present cases as they come up, I believe that we are going to get these changes within the common law.

MR. GREEN: My difficulty with this approach is that I don't think we have enough time to acquire the experience necessary to make the common law do the job.

DR. JEANS: The damage suit in common law is the attack on the

[6]This provision of S.7 was incorporated in the Water Quality Improvement Act, Pub. L. 91-224 (April 3, 1970).

jugular, which in this case is the pocket book. You don't bring the corporate conscience to bear by threatening the corporation with some type of wrist-slapping through an administrative regulation or some agency action. The history of products liability has proven that to be true.

There are a lot of regulations about how drugs should be labeled, but it took a couple of $100,000 civil law actions before the industry was brought up short and some of these changes were effected. I believe at that time the trial bar was able to educate themselves to the sophistry of drugs as they have been able to educate themselves in some sophisticated and esoteric terms of products liability. I think they will rise to the same challenge in this instance if they are given the chance, with the cooperation of scientists, and the help of gentlemen such as you who are experts in this field.

MR. NADER: As a former enthusiast of the common law in this area, I must disagree with Dr. Jeans. I think one of the most interesting tort seminars that can be developed at law schools in the near future is one that addresses itself to the question: Is torts obsolete?

We are dealing, first, with an extremely different kind of violence that is the root of tort actions—the very silent type, often long-range, difficult to detect, and coming from multiple sources that converge before the tort reveals itself.

We are also dealing with immense evidential problems, such as the nagging question of incidence.

You can attend almost any meeting of trial lawyers in this country, watch them stand up and talk about the great victories in products liability law. The first question you ask is the frequency of such cases, and you are down to the lower regions of the arthmetic. You ask them what is the replicative effect, the penumbra, and it is very small.

I have yet to see, for example, a single instance where an auto liability case has had an impact on the design back at the plant. True, we have no studies showing a link one way or the other except for the final evidence of what rolls off the production line every year. Suffice it to say that in one of the relatively easier areas of tort action—that is, determining the trauma of an automobile on a human being and proving legal cause or strict liability, then moving for damages and attributing them to the design negligence of the manufacturer—to date there has not been a single appellate court upholding a favorable jury verdict in this area.

Here we have an artifact that rolls off the production line at the rate of 9,000,000,000 a year, is involved in 4,500,000 injuries annually, and lawyers who are more or less conversant with it all over the country.

I would not, however, minimize the effect even of failure in this kind of litigation. The failure of this kind of litigation may be countered by the success of its factual disclosures. As a disclosure tool, the common law is still an extremely potent and impressive instrument, particularly in the early stages when the entire political and economic structure is arrayed against the challenger.

MR. MOORMAN: I do want to point out that the traditional damage action isn't going to save Mineral King or any *de facto* wilderness area or any endangered wildlife. We have to recognize that when dealing with the public domain especially, and many resources that are very dear to our hearts, we often can't prove a nickel's worth of damages, nor would it make any difference if we could.

MR. BENNETT: Another thing about the common law that strikes me is that even though Dave Sive may win a victory in New York, it really does not set a national precedent. It doesn't stop the building of a nuclear plant in California. And unless you have a national standard somewhat rigidly applied you have a case-to-case situation.

As far as damages are concerned, that is just the cost of doing business, and you and I are simply paying a little more for those judgments when we buy our automobiles or drug products.

Now, as far as the law is concerned, and the system within which this law operates, I have had an antitrust case going on now for almost 12 years. Each time I think I have won it I end up losing it through various devices including Congressional legislation. So I go back to the U.S. Supreme Court and still don't know the result. Antitrust enforcement is not permitted by a capitalist system. In terms of our interest here today we should really be discussing whether or not capitalism permits conservation. I am beginning to have my doubts.

MR. NADER: Who calls this system capitalism? It is corporate socialism.

OPPORTUNITIES
AND MECHANISMS
TO MEET THE NEEDS

Counsel for the Concerned

Charles H. W. Foster

The material to follow is addressed to the prospective conservation attorney. For the grizzled veteran of conservation wars, there may be little he does not already know. For the already-involved attorney, the lack of factual depth may prove somewhat disappointing.

The principal sources are the author's several decades of personal experience in public and private affairs, but he has also received valuable advice and guidance from many helpful respondents. The material is admittedly subjective in character and, in places, provincial in outlook.

The new recruit may conclude that conservation is elusive, mercurial, intemperate and even irrational. As a newcomer to the cause, he must learn to make the best of such uncomfortable facts of life, for these are characteristics that make conservation alive, exciting and, to many of us, a profession of vital significance for the future.

Conservation and the law have been inextricably intertwined from earliest times. Ancient customs and taboos encouraged the conservation of scarce animals by insisting upon the use of those that were abundant and in season. Contained in the Mosaic law was an actual prohibition against the taking of the female bird in favor of its young or its eggs. As early as 700 B.C. the Assyrian King Sennacherib had developed a formal game preserve. In 1066 A.D. William the Conqueror took over all forest, game and wildlife in England as property of the king, and Kublai Khan, scourge of all Asia, introduced systems of food patches, cover control and winter feeding for wildlife as early as the 13th century A.D.

In the New World, the charter of the Province of Massachusetts Bay, granted by the reigning monarchs William and Mary in 1691, made express provision for the continuation of the New England fisheries and imposed a stiff penalty for the felling of trees "fit for masts." The Great and General Court of the Province enacted a statute for the regulation of the mackerel fishery before it saw fit to establish courts of justice.

Though motivated by essentially pragmatic circumstances, these early manifestations of the law did enunciate man's determination to express his policy convictions and govern his social actions in conservation in some orderly and systematic fashion. The evolution to institutional and organizational devices was, in a sense, inevitable, for these were to be the most persuasive devices, and the most practical means, to insure compliance with an expressed, collective objective.

CONSERVATION ORGANIZATIONS IN GENERAL

Conservation organizations are, of course, formed for a variety of reasons, perhaps the most common being the desire to achieve some sort of secure status for an area of interest or course of action. A Society for the Preservation of Purple Martins, for example, exhibits much the same basic motivation as the primitive tribe or pioneer village banded together for protection against outside hostile elements.

The reverse of security, aggressive action, can also become a prime motivating force in conservation. A National Coal Association, protecting a vested interest, or a group of ardent wilderness advocates such as the Sierra Club, can become intensely partisan in its representations. The fine line between security and aggression lies principally in the eyes of the beholder.

A third common objective in the movement is that of economic efficiency, allowing individuals to accomplish a desired goal more effectively by sharing talents and applying their energies on a collective basis. Thus, an association of landowners, such as the Committee for Safety and Conservation in Milton, Massachusetts, banded together to oppose the projected route of Interstate 95 through the Fowl Meadow Reservation, can command more resources and exercise more influence than would each landowner operating individually.

Finally, as social animals, men have founded conservation groups to foster group relationships and a form of fellowship they both enjoy and need. A Boone & Crockett Club, a Michigan United Conservation Clubs, or a Maryland Garden Club Federation can become militant forces in conservation, but one should clearly recognize that this is not their basic reason for being.

In general, those conservation organizations most likely to succeed have a convincing cause, a sizable constituency, sufficient means for program operations, and responsible leadership. Although each of these elements is to a considerable extent mutually supportive, few organizations have, in fact, been able to maximize all variables at once. Whereas all of the essential elements must be present for a conservation organization to succeed and endure, only one is required for its initial creation.

In the maturing process that the conservation organization inevitably undergoes, it tends to grow conservative and even complacent, particularly if its initial actions attracted a measure of public acclaim. At this point, it can become over-institutionalized, difficult to identify with, and unresponsive to current need. It may then decline and disappear, although this is not often the case, or linger on, sustained only by its previous record of success. More likely it is eventually captured by new leadership and invigorated as the opportunities presented by new public concerns and interests raise provident and compelling voices. On the other hand, sheer economic necessity, underscored by declining membership and an inability to compete for public recognition and support, may itself provide the needed lubricant for reform and revitalization.

A direct result of organizational maturity seems to be a broader view of conservation as a whole. Typically, the institution begins with a specific and compelling mission which gathers to it a hard core of enthusiastic and dedicated individuals. The adversary nature of its actions makes its objectives crystal-clear and readily supportable, but as time goes by it is increasingly difficult to define its organizational objectives. One of the most difficult questions facing conservation today is how to sustain the organization that is broadly concerned with environmental values and dedicated to a balanced use of natural resources by economic as well as other interests.

THE NATIONAL CONSERVATION MOVEMENT

Statistics on activity by organized conservation groups are fragmentary at best for the nation as a whole. Periodic listings have been attempted over the years by such organizations as the U.S. Fish & Wildlife Service, the American Forestry Association, and the Natural Resources Council of America. Seven editions of a national conservation yearbook were published during the period 1952-1962 under the editorship of Erle Kaufman. The yearbooks included a wealth of statistical information in various resource areas and also a listing of what appeared to be the principal conservation organizations and agencies in each of the states.

Since 1954, however, the principal onus for compiling a national conservation directory has rested with the National Wildlife Federation in Washington. In order to keep the project within reasonable bounds, entries are accepted on a word-of-mouth basis with little effort made to evaluate the actual extent of activity claimed. Questionnaires are distributed annually to the organizations previously listed in order to obtain an up-to-date record of the names and addresses of the principal officers. The 1969 edition, for example, contained information on more than 500 private organizations and public agencies. With all its admitted draw-backs, the Federation directory remains the single most useful device of its kind today.

The directory entries permit classification of conservation organiza-tions in a number of different ways. One relates to the level at which the organization operates, *e.g.* international, national, multi-state or re-gional, state, or local. This classification offers some complications, how-ever, for several operating levels may be embraced by a single organization. The National Wildlife Federation itself, for example, is a national organization that consists of state affiliates which are, in turn, composed of local clubs. Its structure is further complicated by a large, national, associate membership unrelated to its individual state affiliates.

A second classification relates to the essential character of the organi-zation. Institutions may be wholly private, quasi-public, academic, or governmental. Public agencies are particularly complex since they may embrace a single jurisdiction—federal, state, or local—or may be inter-state in character, or be federal-interstate agencies, such as river basin commissions, where the federal government is actually party to the com-pact. Finally they may be international in scope, such as the many special commissions for fisheries and wildlife created by convention or treaty among nations. Similar complexities are encountered at the regional or local levels, particularly where metropolitan problems are involved.

A third way of examining conservation organizations involves their particular spheres of interest. Specific resource areas commonly repre-sented by such institutions include soil conservation, water resources, forestry, fish and wildlife, marine resources, parks and recreation. Func-tional categories include land preservation, nature study and conserva-tion education, science and research.

Organizations may also be viewed in the light of their individual partic-ipants. The professional societies, such as the American Fisheries Society or the American Institute of Biological Sciences, represent the interests of a particular technical skill. Occupational associations, such as the American Forestry Institute, are spokesmen for a given business or trade. Special interest clientele in conservation run the gamut from sportsmen's and women's groups to industry and labor organizations.

Finally, multi-organizational institutions, such as natural resources or conservation councils, conservation congresses, or environmental cen-ters and institutes, are a relatively recent phenomenon in the non-gov-ernmental field. In a recent study of such organizations, The Conservation Foundation identified some 35 state and regional conserva-tion councils. It observed that, in general, organized conservation inter-ests have been far better staffed and focused to face national issues than they have been to deal with state and local ones.

This brief review of the structure of the conservation movement shows that the conservation organization is as varied as the resources themselves, changing with the interests and convictions of its leaders and constituents. The movement suffers the handicaps of overlap and duplication of effort, yet also enjoys the vitality of an institutional pattern readily adaptable to change.

The essential fact is that conservation thrives on personal participation. For seemingly every conviction, there will either be an appropriate institutional expression or one will shortly be found. The newcomer, however, must recognize that even those organizations professing like objectives will differ widely and, at times, radically in their interests, methods, skills, dedication, and financial capabilities. Such clarity of vision will prevent the new recruit from wasting valuable time and effort and should make the energies he devotes to organizational work many times more productive.

ORGANIZATIONAL ACTIVITY IN CONSERVATION LAW

To define the interests of these organizations for the conservation-minded attorney, some 49 organizations were selected from the 1969 Conservation Directory of the National Wildlife Federation, and individual officials were contacted by letter to ascertain their present use and future needs for services of a legal nature. A degree of geographic spread and a reasonable mix of organizational types and subject interests were attempted.

In the international arena, organizations are currently engaged in the compilation of conservation statutes and the preparation of model laws for game, parks and nature reserves. International conventions for the protection of fisheries and wildlife are also of concern, as are the problems of ocean and river pollution, and the legalities of the ownership and control of the resources of the high seas and the continental shelf. Weather modification and rainfall stimulation efforts are posing new and potentially explosive questions of liability and other legal complications in arid regions.

Within the continental United States, land use conflicts and control have tended to dominate the attention of the urbanized northeast region. New and largely untested state regulatory actions are being employed to preserve wetlands, to prevent encroachment of active flood plains, and to insure sufficient open space in newly developed areas.

Farther south, water resources problems are high on many organizational priority lists. Particularly pressing are such matters as interbasin transfers of water, and the ownership of river beds and other submerged lands.

In the Midwest, typically controversial issues include questions of environmental contamination. Pertinent examples are the use of pesticides by public agencies and the sensitive question of whether existing surface water quality should be allowed to be degraded by new uses. Encroachment of parks and natural areas by highways, flood control, and other public projects has also given rise to litigation and court action of some significance in recent months.

In the Gulf and Pacific Southwest regions, the potentially adverse impact of oil and gas development on other resources has occupied the attention of many conservation organizations. Dredging of estuaries for commercial deposits of shell has also raised apparently serious threats to the continued productivity of the coastal waters.

The future of the public domain and, in particular, the deliberations of the Public Land Law Review Commission have occupied the primary resources spotlight in the Rocky Mountain and Great Plains regions. Conflicting interests of hard-rock miners, ranchers, and recreationists have posed distressing substantive, procedural and moral problems for all parties.

In the Pacific region, issues have ranged from the advocacy of extensive, untrammeled wilderness in the northwest to the hazards of air and oil pollution along the southern California coast. Alaskans are currently grappling with problems of state lands selection, native land claims, timber and mineral development, and the basic issue of state versus federal jurisdiction.

Among the specific organizational activities reported, the following will exemplify the range of current legal or potentially legal concerns of conservation organizations.

The Society for the Protection of New Hampshire Forests has been instrumental in the creation of a New Hampshire Land Use Foundation designed to promote proper planning and zoning practices at the local level and also provide a vehicle for the actual development of land under sound conservation and environmental principles.

The Water Resources Association of the Delaware River Basin, in conjunction with the Wissahickon Valley Watershed Association, has engaged legal counsel to insure court recognition of the validity of flood plain regulation ordinances.

The Wildlife Management Institute has expressed support for a major scientific symposium which would focus attention on problems of deep water channeling, rights of access, and conversion of water bottoms throughout the entire southeastern United States.

The "Ding" Darling Foundation, Inc., utilizing a special contractual arrangement with cooperating landowners, has sponsored a pilot program for the replanting of trees along the famous Lewis and Clark Trail Route in western Iowa.

The park and recreation committee of the National Institute of Municipal Law Officers reported that the Minneapolis Board of Park Commissioners won the first round of an important test case involving the taking of a portion of the city park system by the State Roads Commission.

The Executive Secretary of the Indiana Division, Izaak Walton League of America, has urged strict enforcement of the public information section of the Administrative Procedures Act as a deterrent to the misuse of authority by federal agencies.

Enterprising law students in the Washington, D.C., area, acting through a Greater-Washington Alliance to Stop Pollution (shortened appropriately to G.A.S.P.), have announced plans to take legal action against air pollution from local buses.

The Conservation Division of the General Federation of Women's Clubs is actively seeking the establishment of special trail systems for the blind and handicapped in the states of Montana and New Mexico.

Advance land options and contractual arrangements have been advocated by the Thorne Ecological Foundation to insure preservation of the fragile Florissant fossil beds near Colorado Springs. Similar approaches have been proposed by the Appalachian Trail Conference to safeguard the wilderness character of the 2,000-mile Appalachian Trail.

The legal committee of the Atlantic States Marine Fisheries Commission, upon examining a preliminary compilation of individual state statutes, regulations and court decisions, concluded that a state-by-state overhaul of present practices was urgently needed to properly protect salt marsh and estuarine values along the entire east coast.

The state of New Mexico, abetted by other sympathetic intervenors, disputed the Department of the Interior in Federal District Court on the question of Interior's jurisdiction over resident species of wildlife on federal lands.

The Rocky Mountain Center on Environment, with the help of 25 experts drawn from the eight-state region, has uncovered some 27 regional environmental problems requiring legal and other remedies.

The Federation of Western Outdoor Clubs has expended at least 500 hours of legal time over the past two years in opposing the efforts by private power companies to obtain an irrevocable license to flood out the scenic gorges of the Snake River.

Conservation Associates in California, over a period of almost 10 years' time, has assumed the major burden of title clearances, payment schedules, taxes, closing documents, gift transfer deeds, and estate sales transactions in order to help the state of California acquire key portions of a new state park.

Recent discussions of the Washington Environmental Council have attempted to identify possible prime issues for litigation. High on the list of possibilities is the application of equitable remedies to the correction of instances of environmental contamination, such as air and water pollution, use of pesticides, and destruction of the environment by highways.

A move to reserve a portion of the forest wilderness in southeastern Alaska has brought the Alaska Conservation Society and others into direct confrontation with the U.S. Forest Service, which has executed a 50-year contract for the sale of timber on Admiralty Island.

Among several important projects, the Commission on Legislation of the International Union for the Conservation of Nature and Natural Resources at Morges, Switzerland, is seeking solutions to the plight of the Atlantic salmon, now subject to intensive exploitation by commercial fishermen from Denmark and other nations.

Limited though the above sampling has been, it is evidence of the wide variation in the legal assistance now being sought and utilized by conservation organizations. The scope and substance of the services required can take an organization into virtually every nook and cranny of the law.

Generally, public agencies were found to have more ready access to competent legal talent than private organizations, either through established legal agencies of their jurisdiction, their own staff attorneys, or their ability to obtain outside assistance on a fee basis. In contrast, private organizations either "borrowed" legal services from a sympathetic agency or were forced to rely on volunteer attorneys. Furthermore, although the latter were often highly competent, the pursuit of a rewarding professional career tended to place the burdens of conservation service on the younger attorney, committed morally to the cause but still relatively inexperienced in his chosen profession. Overall, from the opinions received, it seems abundantly clear that the public interest is rarely represented as ably as are the commercial interests when conservation issues are at stake.

ELEMENTS OF A CONSERVATION LAW PRACTICE

For the potential conservation practitioner, the nature of the services needed tend to fall within a number of broad categories.

The first and largest category of services come within the descriptive term *organizational housekeeping.* Included here are the tedious and unromantic chores of bylaw preparation, drafting of charters, constitutions, and articles of incorporation, and the procedural requirements of filing and reporting under various state and federal charitable statutes. Organizational housekeeping also includes the preparation of a proper employee retirement program; the conduct of labor and personnel relations negotiations; registration, patenting and copyrighting of emblems and publications; problems associated with building locations, office leases, or the purchasing of materials and equipment; and such transactions as bank loans, investments, or capital improvement financing.

A special problem for park and recreation organizations is liability for user injuries. Similarly the area of conflict of interest appears to be of growing concern to all public officials, along with general questions of administrative procedure and legality of actions.

In the aftermath of the Sierra Club's widely-publicized confrontation with the Internal Revenue Service, many private organizations were understandably concerned with their status as charitable organizations. The extent of legislative activity permitted, the handling of contributions and, in particular, the degree to which outside income could be considered non-taxable, have become serious issues for many private organizations.

Legislative activity is the second major area requiring legal services. Most organizations devote considerable time to the review and drafting of legislation and in making representations as requested, before appropriate legislative bodies. As the governmental burden becomes more complex, and legislative bodies tend to hold lengthier sessions, the need for competent legal research and lobbying assistance on conservation issues has grown correspondingly large. The trend among private organizations seems to be to institutionalize and professionalize these services, often on a multi-organizational basis, using the trained attorney rather than the traditional dedicated volunteer.

Related closely to legislative activity is the emerging field of *governmental regulation.* Just as the task of drafting such regulations generally falls to a professional attorney, a corresponding need is felt by the conservation interests affected by such regulations. They often seek legal help in charting a proper course through a seemingly inconsistent and confusing body of governmental red tape.

A fourth area of active service involves *land preservation.* In recent years public and private agencies alike have devoted substantial time to acquiring key tracts of land and water for recreational and other purposes. Although availability of funds has been a key factor, there has also been something rather straightforward and simplistic about land preservation that has made it a popular priority activity within the conservation movement. Land transactions inevitably require appraisals, title examinations, and the drafting of suitable instruments and deeds. Negotiation of the transaction has also been a common practice. This, in turn, has led to professionally-intriguing techniques of land preservation through easements, options, mutual covenants, or other types of contractual agreements. Acquisition projects often bring up other useful applications of the law, such as aspects of estate management or tax planning.

Litigation, of course, represents a fifth area in which attorneys have already played an important, even pivotal role in conservation. Actions have been both civil and criminal, undertaken in prosecution and defense. Some have been strictly client-oriented, such as a resources trade association opposing a potential business competitor, or cause-oriented, such as the suits of the Environmental Defense Fund to ban the use of DDT. Litigants have used injunctive processes with some success, along with the *amicus curiae* approach. The legal actions of the Sierra Club's various chapters have helped build up a particularly valuable series of precedents in the matter of citizen standing in court.

ROLE OF THE ATTORNEY IN CONSERVATION

The question remaining seems simply this—can the legal profession make a meaningful contribution to the conservation and environmental field? The answer is strongly in the affirmative. It can and has performed significant services, but its full potential is far from realized.

Our quick look at the field would indicate that conservation organizations have rarely been healthier. If variety is any measure of vitality, the movement thrives. Environmental quality is firmly in the public mind, and our continuing affluence and leisure opportunities should sustain the public interest in the years ahead. The consequences of man's technological advances, as they become known, will provide additional fuel to the movement.

The opportunities to participate in conservation are already extensive, promising to become even more so in the future. Nevertheless, plurality and proliferation of organizations, though indicating vitality, are obstacles at times to real progress and accomplishment. The process of institutional sorting and regrouping, and the search for mutual approaches now under way, should vastly strengthen the movement's capacity for meaningful action.

Inevitably, however, there remains important missionary work to be done among the conservation organizations and the members of the legal profession. Although the interchange between them has been fragmentary at best in years past, the advent of new institutions such as the Conservation Law Society of America, the Conservation Law Foundation, the Environmental Defense Fund, and the developing legal interests of older organizations, offers promising new opportunities for bridging previous communication gaps.

Influential voices are now being raised within the legal profession itself. Senator Henry M. Jackson, for example, Chairman of the Senate Committee on Interior and Insular Affairs, has publicly advocated the active involvement of the legal profession in the development of a body of law encompassing man's environmental rights.

"Man's environment is under constant pressure from new technology and increasingly competitive demands for resources," the Senator told the Seattle King County Bar Association. "Lawyers have an opportunity to play a key role in preserving and protecting these resources for the future good of mankind."

It remains to be seen, however, whether conservation law *per se*, can, by virtue of its breadth and complexity, offer a viable profession to the lawyer. The time may certainly be approaching when no major law firm will find it advisable to omit an environmental specialist from among its senior associates. But it would appear that the day of a lucrative private practice in environmental areas is, in most places, still some distance away. There are some, in fact, who argue that conservation's basic credibility lies in the volunteer nature of its participants and that lawyers— like physicians, scientists, or businessmen—should be willing to donate time to the cause.

If conservation law practice cannot yet sustain itself, there is an unfilled need for public defender and legal aid organizations or, at the minimum, informed environmental law clearing-houses where legal materials and references to cases, and available practitioners can be provided. These services could be institutionalized under the general oversight of a bar association, or established as an independent public possibly within an academic setting. In the latter instance, the opportunities of building active conservation law training into the law school curriculum seem particularly attractive.

A final area of great promise to the legal profession and the conservation movement should be mentioned involving the hitherto-unexplored field of environmental conciliation. Most conservation issues would appear to lend themselves readily to negotiation provided a suitable third party is at hand to guide the way towards consensus. The resolution of frequent disputes involving competing segments of the public interest, as in the case of the encroachment of a public park by a public highway, should offer a fascinating challenge to the trained attorney and an opportunity to exercise the analytical and negotiating skills characteristic of his profession.

An Interdisciplinary Program
for Law Students
in the Environmental Field

James N. Corbridge, Jr.

The University of Colorado Law School Environmental Intern Program was developed as a response to a number of perceived shortcomings in natural resources legal education, particularly as it relates to the effect of the law on the quality of the environment. Few law schools have presented, even recently, substantial course offerings in the natural resources field, and interest has been concentrated in those areas of the country where water law, oil and gas, or mining problems are likely to confront the practicing attorney in the ordinary course of events.

Natural resources course content has stressed the private law aspects of the subject matter, approached, with some notable exceptions, through the traditional study of appellate cases to the virtual exclusion of other materials. Little attention has been paid to the "public law" of resources, or to the administrative and political processes which play a dominant role in the allocation and management of the country's natural resources, particularly in the West.

In addition to these shortcomings specifically related to resources law, law schools have generally been confronted, often through student initiative, with the question of how to move away from the case law approach during the final few semesters in order to sustain student interest and involvement, introduce the student to other significant aspects of the legal process, and create meaningful research programs in a particular subject area. A number of devices have been suggested to enable more students to participate in the type of research and writing experience which has traditionally been available only to members of the law review staff. Nevertheless, there remains a feeling among law students and teachers that additional new programs and approaches should be developed which would be effective vehicles for teaching and research, while providing students with an opportunity to observe at first hand the workings of the legal system in a particular area of law. Field research can make a substantial contribution toward the attainment of this last goal, in our case by putting the student in a position to get an insider's view of the practical aspects of resources administration.

With these considerations and needs in mind, the University of Colorado School of Law, under a grant from the Ford Foundation, has developed an intern program involving two semesters and an intervening summer, and designed to allow students to become familiar with basic principles of environmental law and its administration. The program is open to selected law students who are entering their fourth full semester of school. During that semester they participate in a seminar on the fundamentals of environmental quality control. Interdisciplinary faculty participation is involved, so that students are exposed to economic and scientific aspects of the subject matter as well as to the statutory, administrative, and judicial phases of environmental legal problems. During the following summer, the students are sent as interns to various federal, state and local agencies which have a direct or collateral concern with the quality of the environment. The primary occupation of each student is to accomplish field research on a preselected topic, the details of which have been arranged in advance with the participating agency. As a secondary goal, we expect that the students will become closely familiar with the practical and political considerations which have an impact on the complex decision making process of the agency. Each student devotes a period of 10 weeks to the summer research, for which time he receives a fellowship from the law school.

During the summer the other co-director of the program, Professor Donald Carmichael, and I closely supervise the scope and direction that each project is taking, to assure, among other things, that the research does not get untracked and that close working relations with each agency are maintained.

After returning in the fall, the students participate in a weekly two-hour seminar elaborating on their summer experiences. The student will also pursue further research and complete a major paper of publishable quality in a form determined by the nature of each student's project.

This year's papers all involve case studies which will then serve as a basis for evaluations of agency effectiveness and, in most cases, proposals for statutory revisions, model legislation, or changes in agency operating procedures.

We now have 12 students involved in the first year of the program. Although there has been no experience with the fall semester phase of the operation, we have accumulated experience which has answered a number of questions that arose at the outset, and which has enabled us to evaluate some of our original criteria regarding selection of students, agency participation, project content, and similar problems. While I have made arbitrary classifications for purposes of discussion, in fact many of these areas are closely interrelated.

SELECTION OF STUDENTS

In addition to the basic requirement of having completed three semesters of law school, a number of other criteria were employed to select 12 interns out of a large number of applicants. Grade point averages were employed, for better or worse, but without determinative emphasis. Far more important in our minds was a demonstrated interest in natural resources and, where possible, work or study experience in the field. A surprising number of candidates were qualified in this respect, and subsequent experience in supervising and observing summer research has demonstrated the validity of this criterion. Maturity, judgment, motivation, and our estimate of the candidate's ability to work harmoniously in a group situation were also considered, in order to select students who could do independent work without continuous supervision.

Although several courses in natural resources law are offered at Colorado, completion of these was not made a prerequisite for participation in the program. Many of the interns took one or more of these courses concurrently with the spring seminar.

SELECTION OF AGENCIES

It became obvious from the beginning of the project that the selection of appropriate agencies and the establishment of a close working relationship with them would be critical to success. Because the program was conceived as covering environmental problems in the broadest sense, we felt it desirable to select agencies involved in a wide spectrum of environmental activities, rather than limiting the choice to the more traditional concerns of air and water pollution. At the same time, consideration was given to the desirability of having experience with federal, state, and local agencies. Student backgrounds and interest preferences were also taken into consideration. Although the intent of the program is to encompass the Rocky Mountain region (and beyond, where appropriate), the location of many federal agencies in Denver made it possible to place about half of the students within commuting distance of their residences in Boulder. The agencies eventually chosen for the first year were: Army Corps of Engineers (Albuquerque); Denver Building Department (air pollution authority); Boulder County Planning Department; Bureau of

Land Management (Denver); United States Geological Survey (Denver); National Park Service (Yellowstone National Park); Oregon State Water Resources Board (Salem); Colorado Game, Fish and Parks Department; Federal Water Pollution Control Administration (Denver); Bureau of Outdoor Recreation (Denver); and Lake Tahoe Regional Planning Agency, which accepted two students.

One of our initial concerns was that agencies might be unenthusiastic about having an "outside" researcher on the premises for the summer, perhaps fearing an exposé or "investigation" of their operations. We found it helpful to assure agency personnel that their views regarding the drafts of final papers would be solicited. Ultimately, no difficulties were encountered in obtaining enthusiastic agency participation. Indeed, projects within a number of agencies initially contacted had to be deferred to another year because of the limited number of student interns. Cooperation between the agencies and the interns has consistently been excellent, and agency personnel have cooperated willingly in making information available to researchers. Several, in fact, have commented to law faculty members on the value of having their agency's operations examined by an "informed" outsider. It is worth noting in this respect that in addition to the assigned reading for the spring seminar, each student was required to do further background reading, suggested by the faculty supervisors, in his area of project specialization and in the legislative and administrative background of the agency with which he would be working. The interns therefore arrived for the summer with a substantial degree of familiarity with their agency and the kinds of problems it faced. Students were also briefed in advance on interviewing techniques and matters of protocol to observe while in the agencies.

SELECTION OF PROJECTS

Assigning the students to research projects which are meaningful and appropriate was considered equal in importance to the selection of the proper agencies, and much the same criteria were employed. Again the projects were selected to cover as broad a range of environmental problems as possible, so that the discussions in the fall seminar could embrace the entire spectrum of environmental concerns. Moreover, each project was structured so that its subject matter would generate conclusions of sufficient breadth to enable them to be applied to questions of resource management beyond the scope of the individual project. Student backgrounds and interests were obviously of importance in project selection. In some cases alternative possibilities were suggested to the student, with the final choice his.

We considered it essential to consult closely with each agency regarding the scope of the project the particular intern would be undertaking, for several reasons. Obviously agency personnel would be more enthusiastic about a project which they themselves had helped to outline. Furthermore, agency cooperation would be fostered by the assignment of projects having some practical value to the agency when completed, while at the same time providing the optimum educational value to the researcher. We found, in fact, that several agencies already had in mind potential research projects of broad scope, which they had been unable to undertake for themselves because of the press of business or insufficient funding.

On the basis of the foregoing criteria, the following specific projects were selected for research during the past summer.

Army Corps of Engineers: An examination of the administrative practices by which the Corps solicits public opinion regarding proposed projects and how that opinion is reflected in project decisions, with particular attention to the proposed Arkansas River Channelization Project.

Denver Building Department: An analysis of the interrelationship between various Colorado and federal agencies as it relates to the control of air pollution in the Denver Air Basin.

Boulder County Planning Department: A study of the effectiveness of state and Boulder County ordinances and planning procedures in regulating subdivision development in the Rocky Mountain foothills.

Bureau of Land Management: An analysis of the substance, legality, and enforcement of various types of stipulations which the Bureau includes in the lease forms for Leasing Act Minerals.

United States Geological Survey: A study of the development of ground water resources in the high plains region of eastern Colorado, and its relationship to water quality control for agricultural purposes.

National Park Service: An analysis of the Park Service's administrative and planning responses to increased user pressures on the parks, and the impact these responses will have on the ecology of Yellowstone National Park.

Oregon Water Resources Board: A case study of the interdisciplinary inputs and administrative procedures used by the Board in withdrawing quantities of streamflow from appropriation for purposes of conservation and amenity preservation.

Colorado Game, Fish, and Parks Department: An analysis of the present state of the art and the inputs necessary in assuring that concern for environment and ecology are reflected in the planning processes undertaken by various selected Colorado and federal construction and acquisition agencies.

Federal Water Pollution Control Administration: An examination of the water laws of the western states, as they affect the control of water pollution and the goals of the FWPCA, with particular attention to excessive salinity in the Colorado River Basin.

Bureau of Outdoor Recreation: An analysis by case studies of the effects which enabling statutes and administrative procedures used in selected Rocky Mountain States have on the prices paid for the acquisition of recreational land and a consideration of alternative acquisition procedures and devices, including less than fee acquisition.

Lake Tahoe Regional Planning Agency: A case study of the development of the California and Nevada Lake Tahoe Agencies, the interstate compact, and the functions and powers of bi-state agencies as they relate to the preservation of the environment in the Lake Tahoe Region.

Finished papers reflect the results of these summer research projects.

SPRING AND FALL SEMINARS

Finally, it may be useful to go into greater detail regarding the content of the spring and fall seminars in which the interns participate.

The purpose of the spring seminar is two-fold. First, to acquaint the students with the general spectrum of problems which face decision makers in the environment quality field. This includes a presentation of the scientific, economic, technical, administrative, and legal aspects of specific problem areas. Secondly, the seminar is designed to allow each student to become quite familiar with the particular agency (and problem area) with which his research will be concerned. Because of the scope of the problems to be covered and the limited amount of class time available, the basic materials and class discussion are somewhat general, while the additional outside reading assigned to prepare the individual students for their projects is quite specifically oriented.

No one collection of published materials which suited our purposes in the spring seminar was available, so Professor Carmichael and I put together our own materials in mimeographed form for general class discussion. The materials were primarily a collection of cases, statutes, administrative rules and regulations, and articles dealing with control of environmental quality and related topics. Included were sections on administrative law, agency organization, air pollution, water pollution, weather modification, land use, and environmental planning. For some of the more technical presentations, we relied on the good graces of several of our colleagues at the University of Colorado, including an ecologist, a research chemist, and a resources economist. We are by no means completely satisfied with the organization of the seminar, nor with the basic materials, which are being subjected to continued revision for future years. The basic approach of the seminar seems sound, however. One modification which we would make in future years would be the inclusion of more field work in the spring in such important areas as air and water pollution.

The fall seminar was planned to have each intern make a one-hour presentation of his project, focusing on the effectiveness of the agency in coming to grips with the environmental problems in its area of responsibility. Included in the presentation will be an examination and discussion of the strengths and weaknesses of the administrative and decision making processes which the student has been observing during the summer. Wherever possible, personnel from each agency will be invited to participate in these discussions, so that issues raised may be more fully explored and agency policy articulated. For the final sessions of the seminar, selected problem situations tie together the summer projects and stimulate general consideration of the problems of managing the environment.

SUMMARY

The first year of the program, at this writing, has progressed to the point where the student research papers are being completed. Some tentative conclusions can be drawn from these papers and from the discussions of the fall seminar.

One advantage which we see in the research aspect of the program is that it provides for informational feedback which can be used to suggest changes in agency administrative practices or to pose topics for more extended investigation in the future. The work of this first year suggests that there are some common problems running through the practices of agencies operating in the environmental field, and that these problem areas are reducing the ability of governmental units to function in a manner conducive to protecting the public interest in the maintenance of a viable environment.

First among these is that scientific information, where it is available, is not being fed into administrative decisions in a systematic or efficient manner. Agency scientists all too frequently fall at one end or the other of the policy spectrum—taking a client-oriented view on the one hand, or adopting a "pure" devotion to their own scientific disciplines on the other. It is not necessary to make a value judgment between these somewhat polarized positions; in either case they make little objective contribution to the practical decision making process, and not infrequently it is the scientist's unfortunate lot to be disregarded by the administrator.

A further problem is poor communication between an agency and the public it is designed to serve, and this communications failure runs both ways. Many agencies have faulty or undeveloped mechanisms by which the views of the affected public may be solicited prior to the making of policy or administrative decisions. Where public hearings are held, the stress tends to be on local rather than national viewpoints, even where decisions are being formulated which will affect the public interest at the national level. On the other hand, public agencies are all too frequently guilty of a highhanded attitude in attempting to "explain" their policies to the public, with resort to autocratically condescending pronouncements or stress on "public relations" rather than presenting facts and alternatives for objective public evaluation.

Internal structure of agencies is an area which deserves further examination, from both the legal and public administration viewpoints. One of the foremost problems is the short shrift given to alternative solutions to particular problems. The research of our summer interns indicated two sources of this phenomenon: first, the large numbers of personnel in particular agencies who are drawn from a single profession with a single point of view and, second, the low level at which many decisions affecting the environment are "locked" into a project to the point where fundamental changes become costly and, therefore, unattractive to agency decision makers.

These and other problems are being brought into sharper focus by the student reports. Agencies have been enthusiastic and cooperative, providing excellent opportunities for student effort and initiative. One of the most important goals of the environmental intern program is to generate law student concern about the quality of the environment, and in this respect it appears to be succeeding.

Current Trends in the Development of an Environmental Curriculum

A. Dan Tarlock

DEBATE OVER THE FUTURE OF LEGAL EDUCATION

This is a survey of current law school curricula, literature and teaching materials related to legal analysis of environmental management, and a review of current discussion over the future direction of legal education. After sketching the principal issues in this debate, I shall focus on the following questions: (1) What is meant by the term "environmental management as a field of study? (2) Should it be considered a new field and thus the subject for new course offerings or should the study of the problems of environmental management be incorporated into existing courses? (3) What present courses include subject matter directly related to problems of environmental management? (4) Where are such courses being offered and in what combinations? (5) If new courses are created, what should be their content? (6) To what extent are published or unpublished teaching materials concerned with problems of environmental management? (7) What is the optimum method for teaching lawyers to deal creatively with environmental management problems? More specifically, is meaningful analysis of the underlying ecological, economic and institutional problems possible within the highly structured 50-minute academic hour, undertaken two or three times per week, which moves at a stately pace through a carefully selected set of materials? (8) What specialized legal literature now exists in this area? (9) What future research is needed?

First, I acknowledge a post-legal realist orientation.[1] I recognize that

[1] For a discussion of this development in the context of secularization in intellectual thought see C. Woodward, "The Limits of Legal Realism: A Historical Perspective," 54 *Va. L. Rev.* 689 (1968).

we can no longer be content with the simple balancing of interests as a method of solving resource allocation conflicts or with a narrow focus on the litigation process. Attention must be focused on all sources of authority—both public and private—which effect the environment, and the study of the legal aspects of environmental management should be viewed as a search for insight into a complex and open-ended process of decision-making.

Second, we must be primarily concerned with study and defining the role the legal system plays in society.[2] As Abraham Goldstein observed, "Legal realism was a short-lived enthusiasm that, in fact, has left a legacy of expectation rather than accomplishment. The lessons of the '20s and '30s have been hardly absorbed at all. The empirical research, the close study of legal institutions, the exploration of behavioral suppositions have not come into being."[3] Surely, in order to determine what law can and should do we must be prepared to engage in the empirical research necessary for sophisticated model building and testing that shows how law functions in society.

As we move toward a "planned society" the use of long-range plans prepared by experts as a basis for decision-making will increase. Crucial decisions may be taken long before their impact is perceived by the regulated or the general public. We will need new legal doctrines to accommodate the participatory values of our political system to newer and more sophisticated forms of planning and regulation. We need to know at what stage in the decision-making process interested parties should intervene if they wish to have an effective voice in the decision.[4] The recent judicial involvement in urban renewal planning and current proposals for various types of ombudsman institutions perhaps point the way.

Third, we are moving into a field of study which cuts across disciplinary boundaries from the social to the physical and natural sciences. As lawyers, our primary function will be to mediate between the "claims of technology and the claims of democracy."[5] In so doing we will be forced

---

[2] See S. Macaulay, "Law Schools and the World Outside Their Doors: Notes on the Margins of 'Professional Training in the Public Interest,' " 54 *Va. L. Rev.* 617 (1968). The standard history of the involvement of legal education in the broader problems of law and society is B. Currie, "The Materials of Law Study," 3 *J. L. Ed.* 331 (1951) and 8 *J. L. Ed.* 1 (1955).
[3] A. Goldstein, *The Unfulfilled Promise of Legal Education, Law in a Changing America,* 157, 158 (1968).
[4] See J. Dukeminier, Jr., "The Coming Search for Quality," 12 *U.C.L.A. L. Rev.* (1965) for some interesting speculations on the future structure of environmental management decision-making institutions.
[5] F. Michelman, "The Legal Profession and Social Change," "The Challenge to the Law Schools," "The Path of the Law from 1967," *Proceedings and Papers of the Harvard Law*

to raise a number of basic questions about the role of political institutions and science and technology in shaping the environment in which we live. Even to pose the proper issues for analysis, an increased scientific and technological sophistication on the part of law professors, lawyers and law students will be necessary as well as a heightened appreciation of the role of social sciences.

While we will still find it necessary to train lawyers to represent private and public clients in an adversary context, we must recognize that the role of law and the adversary proceeding in shaping major technologically oriented decisions is diminishing.[6] If the law is to continue as a viable structure, capable of shaping a humane economic and scientific policy, lawyers must be trained in new techniques of decision-making, such as systems analysis.

Professor Joseph Sneed observed, "The lawyer best fulfills himself when he is transforming the data of technicians into material upon which those to whom final authority is given can act wisely."[7] I believe that the lawyer will need increasingly more sophisticated information to perform this function in the future. It is unrealistic to continue to glorify the lawyer's traditional generalist role, especially if the impact of the adversary process on policy formation continues to decline.[8] We law teachers must consequently acquire knowledge of other disciplines through formal or informal self-education.[9] This may be imperative if we are to communicate with today's student. We should not try to meet all the problems through our own curricula,[10] but should devise methods to incorporate specialists from other disciplines into the teaching process, and encourage students to take relevant courses elsewhere in the university.

Fourth, it is time to reject the Langdellian case method as the principal

School Convocation Held on the One-Hundredth Fiftieth Anniversary of Its Founding, 135 (1969).

[6] See A. Yarmolinsky, "Responsible Law Making in a Technically Specialized Society," Law in a Changing America, 97 (1968).

[7] J. Sneed, "Some Anxieties of Legal Education," 21 Sw. L. J. 617, 623 (1967).

[8] See A. Goldstein, supra n.3 at 161-63.

[9] If specialized instruction is to be possible, greater leave for inter-disciplinary work or self-study must be provided faculty members early in their teaching careers. See F. Allen, "One Aspect of the Problem of Relevance in Legal Education," 54 U. Va. L. Rev. 595 (1968). We have, however, made considerable progress in integrating law schools into the university community since Thomas Reed Powell charged his fellow law professors, "We ally ourselves with high schools rather than our fellow graduate departments of the university." T. Powell, "The Recruiting of Law Teachers," 1926 Handbook of the Association of American Law Schools and Proceedings of the Twenty-Fourth Annual Meeting 57.

[10] See R. Speidel, "A Matter of Mission," 54 U. Va. L. Rev. 606 (1968) for a discussion of general problems of specialization and curricular reform.

form of instruction in this area.[11] The following observations of Professor David Cavers succinctly describe the difficulties inherent in an analysis of urban problems based on the case method. They are equally applicable to the broader perspective of environmental management.

"Urban problems would not often yield questions that could be . . . neatly packaged. Knowledge would have to be imparted of an unfamiliar environment and its people, their difficulties and discontents. Relevant legal structures and processes would have to be analyzed as systems, and not simply described by inference or assumption. Orientation to the single case, explored by the give and take of traditional law school classroom dialogue, would yield in large measure to the flow of problem cases, explored by exchange and evaluation of information, often in substantial volume."[12]

Concepts of legal teaching reform should be based on the fact that the practice of law is becoming increasingly specialized. In the future the term "lawyer" may well become irrelevant for a substantial percentage of the bar just as today the term "doctor," without reference to his specialty, has little meaning. Inevitably, the lawyer will emerge from law school as a naissant specialist and seek work consistent with his interests.

The proposed methods of training this future lawyer can be roughly divided into two schools. The first would seek to adapt the model of the graduate schools to legal education while the second would turn the student into the real world for some form of clinical or intern experience.[13] Both schools seem to place emphasis on the student as his own teacher. My own preference is for Professor Lefcoe's view that the law schools must remain primarily concerned with model building in an attempt to explore the interrelationship of societal forces. Otherwise, "Without a comprehensive body of theory that has been proven by repeated testing, the chances are excellent that practice-oriented classes convey misinformation because those who conduct the classes overgeneralize from their own base of experience or are inartful in formulating a rich theoretical framework for perceiving whatever they perceive when they are in the field and then relaying it as the basis for classroom inquiry

---

[11]For a discussion of the origins of the case method see E. Patterson, "The Case Method in American Legal Education: Its Origins and Objectives," 4 *J. L. Ed.* 1 (1951).

[12]D. Cavers, "Legal Education in a Forward Looking Perspective," *Law in a Changing America*, 139, 147 (1968).

[13]For one version of this debate see the 1968 AALS Curriculum Committee Report drafted by Professor Charles J. Meyers and Professor George Lefcoe's response to it. *Proceedings, Part One: Reports of Committees and Projects, Section II, Association of American Law Schools* 7-38 (1968). A useful discussion of the problems inherent in the use of clinical programs in legal education is H. Sacks, ed., *Proceedings: The Ashville Conference of Law School Deans on Education for Professional Responsibility* (1965).

and instruction."[14] Student involvement should be for the purpose of gaining data by which models can be built and tested rather than for the purpose of skill training. Operationally, future instructional forms would thus include more faculty directed student research and small group instruction that would last longer than the present semester or quarter including, perhaps, carefully selected internships.

There has historically only been one law school model—that of the Harvard Law School developed by Dean Langdell.[15] But if specialization is to be made possible, either law schools must assume differentiated skills and subject matter development among themselves or the curriculum at each school must become divided into a series of tracks.[16] For example, Professor Quintin Johnstone of Yale University has proposed four models for the future law school.[17] The three basic approaches would be directed individually toward policy, legal doctrine and skills. There would also be a combined purposes school. While it is unlikely that schools are seeking voluntarily to differentiate themselves from each other, the development of internal tracks is now taking place at many law schools and is likely to accelerate. The chief objective would be to allow the student to begin training in the area of his specialty by the middle of his first year or the beginning of the second. The third year would be devoted to an in-depth study of a major problem area.[18]

A final word on the problem of relevance. There is and will continue to be great pressure for those of us who work in this field to be "relevant." My precious comments have been an endorsement of an intensive and expanded analysis of the role of law in contemporary society, but the

[14]Proceedings, *supra* n. 13 at 28.

[15]*See* A. Harno, *Legal Education in the United States* 53-64 (1953) and A. Sutherland, *The Law at Harvard* (1967).

[16]Law schools must face squarely the elitist implications of tracking. It may well be that the majority of our students are kept in law school too long and not sufficiently trained in the craft-skills of practice. Perhaps law schools should begin to practice the oft asserted theory that all the basic analytical skills are conveyed by the first two years at maximum and grant a degree after two years to most students. Advanced study would be reserved for those who wish to be trained for more specialized policy formulation rules. A system of financing could be devised to permit students to return for further study after an early graduation. As a corollary the legal profession should increase its reliance on continuing education as a means of conveying needed information to the practicing lawyer. *Cf.* Paul Goodman's most perceptive article, "The New Revolution," *The New York Times Magazine* 32, September 14, 1969.

[17]Q. Johnstone, "Models for Curricular Reform," 21 *U. of Miami L. Rev.* 544 (1967). *See also* A. Goldstein, "Educational Planning at Yale," 21 *U. of Miami L. Rev.* 520 (1967) for a discussion of a "Graduate-oriented" curriculum at Yale.

[18]For a lucid discussion of some of the costs and benefits of differentiation and specialization among law schools, see D. Riesman, "Some Observations on Legal Education," 1968 *Wis. L. Rev.* 63, 77-82.

values of teaching environmental management with a historical perspective should not be forgotten. The rise of planned resource management is one of the most fascinating chapters in America's reaction to its complex economic society. The law has developed in response to a series of adjustments to the demands of major economic and social problems.[19] If taught within this context, the law can furnish a useful perspective to view the kinds of adjustments which are being demanded today.

Through the work of Willard Hurst[20] and his students, such as Earl F. Murphy,[21] a start has been made on tracing the development of the law of natural resources. The history of the public domain is well documented. We are developing a good historical literature on the conservation movement and the planning euphoria evident during the early New Deal and which continues to furnish the ideological base for many current and proposed management policies. If the curriculum in this area develops along the lines of small group instruction and self-study, it should be possible to integrate a considerable amount of historical material into the student's training without unduly detracting from needed analysis of contemporary problems.

DEVELOPMENT OF AN ENVIRONMENTAL MANAGEMENT CURRICULUM

It is not easy to define the subject matter of environmental management with which lawyers should be concerned in terms other than traditional law school course categories. To borrow from Kenneth Boulding's *The Economics of the Coming Spaceship Earth*, the broad problem areas are the problems of capital resource exploitation, consumption, and maintenance,[22] which in our case might be defined as the tolerable disruption of existing ecosystems[23] From an exploitive and consumptive perspective, we are primarily concerned with the process of decision-making by private and public groups and its effect on the spatial distribution of our physical resources.[24] Emphasis on the spatial allocation of resources would appear to be a useful matrix from which to study the

---

[19] W. Hurst, *Law and Economic Growth: The Legal History of the Lumber Industry in Wisconsin 1836-1915* (1964).

[20] *See* R. Brooks, "The Jurisprudence of Willard Hurst," 13 *J. L. Ed.* 257 (1966). *See generally* L. Friedman, "History and the Future Law School Curriculum," 44 *Denver L. J.* 43 (1961).

[21] E. Murphy, *Water Purity* (1961).

[22] K. Boulding, *The Economics of the Coming Spaceship Earth, Beyond Economics* 275 (1968).

[23] *See generally* E. Kormondy, *Concepts of Ecology* (1969).

[24] I am indebted to the geographers for this concept. *See* Mayer, "The Pull of Land and Space," in G. Gottmann and R. Harper, *Metropolis on the Move*, 23, 24-26 (1967).

exploitation of our land, water and air. The economic and social consequences of optimal and non-optimal spatial distributions suggest a set of criteria for evaluating the performance of the legal system. From another perspective we can focus on the consequences of human intervention in existing ecosystems, permitting us to formulate a different set of criteria to evaluate the legal system.[25] In this paper I have concentrated on courses concerned with these broad problem areas, and I have not, therefore, dealt extensively with curricular developments organized around the concept of human poverty.

If environmental management is to win a firm place in the law school curriculum, its objectives must not be narrowly viewed. The function of law schools is not to train a specialized group of lawyers to represent conservation groups trying to modify or halt development projects. Rather, it must be directed toward training a generation of lawyers who will be influential in improving the quality of resource management in this country and throughout the world. As I will describe, the law schools have been making considerable progress toward training in resource management. The task ahead is to sensitize all levels of resource management curricula, from first year property to specialized seminars, to the problems of environmental quality.

INTRODUCING LAW STUDENTS TO CONCEPTS OF ENVIRONMENTAL MANAGEMENT IN THE FIRST YEAR

Most discussions of specialization in legal education have concentrated on the second and third years. But if a meaningful level of sophistication is to be reached by the student during this period, he must be introduced to the broad underpinnings of his specialty in the first year. Thus, the Langdellian cluster of basic courses must be reevaluated in light of its impact on specialized tracts existing in the second and third years. Not only must we be concerned with the skills taught in the first year, we must be equally concerned with their substantive context. Sources of authority and behavioral influence are proliferating. If the first-year courses are confined to the traditional run of cases in most casebooks, the student risks emerging with neither substantive background nor skills needed to function usefully in contemporary, let alone future, society.

---

[25] *Cf.* Professor Milton Kaplan's definition of the content of the environmental curriculum: "The primary concern of 'environmental law' is with the legal implications of man's conflict with his natural environment, and the manipulation of resources affecting the quality of his environment. The problems are 'external' and 'physical'. . . ." M. Kaplan, Memorandum to the Faculty of Law and Jurisprudence, State University of New York at Buffalo on Environmental and Urban Law Problems, ii (April, 1968) (unpublished).

Law schools have historically maintained that they are teaching basic skills rather than conveying substantive information. However, unless law schools focus on current substantive problems the student is given a distorted view of the evolution of the legal system. He will consequently be unable to work effectively within it.

Two approaches to the problem of introducing the student to the legal problems of environmental management are being developed. One is a restructuring of the first year course in real property and the other is a required first year course which incorporates environmental considerations, resource management and environmental control. In this section I will review the current teaching materials in real property.

The first year real property course underwent a revitalization in the years following World War II when Professors Casner and Leach of Harvard joined issue with Professors McDougal and Haber of Yale. In 1947-48 Casner and Leach published their *Cases and Text on Property* and McDougal and Haber published their catalytic *Property, Wealth, Land: Allocation, Planning and Development.* The latter attempted to implement the concept of legal education that McDougal and Laswell expressed in their 1943 article, "Legal Education and Public Policy: Professional Training in the Public Interest."[26] These two books have dominated thinking about the property curriculum.

Casner and Leach proceeded from the assumption that the basic property course should be concerned with the creation and exercise of private rights, with a heavier emphasis on commercial real estate transactions than had previously been the case. They explicitly rejected the McDougal and Haber approach on the grounds that the best training for future policy makers was the mastery of a closed doctrinal system.[27] Others such as Allison Dunham rejected McDougal and Haber not because of its basic objectives but because of the assumptions which underlay its conception of the role of the legal system in planned resource management. Dunham correctly criticized the book's abstract characterization of planning objectives because it gave the false impression that a consensus as to ends existed, and that the only question before the legal system was the provision of an efficient means for decision. He called for a more

---

[26]Laswell & McDougal, "Legal Education and Public Policy: Professional Training in the Public Interest," 52 *Yale L. J.* 203 (1943).

[27]Leach, "Property Law Taught in Two Packages," 1 *J. L. Ed.* 28, 49 (1948). He had this afterthought about the importance of public controls. "For better or for worse, the lawyer dealing in real estate has to concern himself with these matters very little . . . zoning ordinances and a few rules forbidding certain types of restraints and conditions are all the conveyencer has to contend with. They should be treated . . . but, in our view the first year property course is basically and primarily a private law course dealing with the representation of private clients."

critical examination of the division of function between various components of the legal and planning systems.[28]

While McDougal and Haber's casebook stirred a great deal of controversy, it was not widely adopted, apparently on the theory that it was
"unteachable." The more elegant and focused Casner and Leach work
became the leading casebook during the 1950's.[29] Thus, debate over the
scope of the property curriculum proceeded from the basic assumptions
laid down by Casner and Leach, although McDougal's ideas gained
acceptance as the Casner and Leach casebook came under increasing
criticism for failing to include material on the public control of land
development. The subsequent *Cases and Materials on Property*, by Cribbet, Fritz, and Johnson,[30] in turn became popular because it was considered to have "consolidated the reform initiated by Casner and Leach and
pushed it a step further"[31] by paring down the materials on classification
of estates and including a chapter on land use controls. Subsequent
casebooks such as Browder, Cunningham, and Julin's *Basic Property
Law*[32] have focused even more sharply on land transfer and development
but have not varied in their basic approach.[33]

While these casebooks became widely used, there was a growing recognition that the model of land development implicit in the first-year
materials was too static and simplistic.[34] The first major effort to construct a course based on a dynamic perception of the real estate market
was Dunham's *Modern Real Estate Transactions*.[35] This landmark casebook made the most significant contribution since McDougal and Haber
joined issue with Casner and Leach. Its utility was somewhat limited
because it dealt only with the development of residential housing. Today
it may be partially supplanted by Professor Krasnowiecki's recently published *Housing and Urban Development*,[36] which provides a more contemporary treatment of commercial land-development problems.

There is now widespread acceptance of the notion that advanced work
should be offered in land development and related public-regulation is-

---

[28]Dunham, "Book Review," 62 *Harv. L. Rev.* 1414 (1949).

[29]Tarlock, "Book Review," 21 *Stan. L. Rev.* 1266 (1969).

[30]J. Cribbet, W. Fritz & C. Johnson, *Cases and Materials on Property* (1960).

[31]Meyers, "Book Review," 46 *Cornell L. Q.* 377, 378 (1961).

[32]O. Browder, R. Cunningham & J. Julin, *Basic Property Law* (1966).

[33]Spies, "Book Review," 20 *J. Legal Ed.* 234 (1967). For a contemporary justification of the
introductory survey course *see* Cribbet, "Property in the First Year," 18 *J. Legal Ed.* 55
(1965); this position is criticized in Jacob, "Book Review," 20 *J. Legal Ed.* 373 (1968).

[34]Berger, "The Research Frontiers of Real Property Law: Commercial Land Transfers," 15
J. Legal Ed. 282 (1963).

[35]A. Dunham, *Modern Real Estate Transactions* (1952).

[36]J. Krasnowiecki, *Housing and Urban Development* (1969).

sues; there is no agreement on how this ought to be done or in what year of the curriculum it should be placed. Casner and Leach and their progeny are sorely out-dated, not because they are insensitive to the relationship between social and economic change and the legal system, but because their model of change no longer raises the critical issues in land development. They focus on the interaction between the vestiges of the feudal system and private decisions to transfer wealth or land; their thesis is basically that a more efficient system of land and wealth transfer will result from the elimination of artificial conceptual barriers stemming from the feudal system.[37] While this is to some extent still true, the danger is that the student may leave the property course with a very static and unrealistic model of land development. He simply may not see how modern land development is structured by the complex interrelationships between private money markets and the institutions of public control. It is true that much of the "law" found in any property casebook is applicable to modern transactions, but unless the student is given a model other than the feudal system to evaluate the doctrines he studies, a course in real property falls far short of its potential. But when the feudal system is removed as an organizing focus without an adequate substitute, what remains is a mechanistic approach that carries with it the high risk of leaving the student without new criteria to evaluate the process he is studying. Thus, one standard by which a new casebook can be judged is the extent to which it combines analytic training with a new model of land development.

Two new approaches to property-law teaching are represented by the casebooks of Professor Berger and Professor George Lefcoe. Both authors are graduates of Yale and former students of Myres S. McDougal. It is probable that future debates about the real property curriculum will no longer revolve around the Harvard-Yale debate of the 1940's and 1950's, but on the most effective methods of implementing the models developed by McDougal and Haber in their catalytic casebook. Professor Berger and Professor Lefcoe both have tried to incorporate the insights McDougal shed on the function of property in contemporary society into a set of materials suitable for first-year students. Professor Lefcoe did so by applying the general McDougal model to one industry, the large-scale housing developer, while Professor Berger's response was less of a break with traditional first-year casebooks.[38]

Lefcoe's *Land Development Law* denies the utility of the traditional concept-oriented property course and instead would introduce the first-year student to a sophisticated model of the land-development process,

---

[37] *See* W. Leach, *Property Law Indicted* (1967).
[38] G. Lefcoe, *Land Development Law: Cases and Materials* (1966).

although the more complex financing materials are also deferred until advanced courses. Professor Ina M. Heyman has concisely described the thrust of *Land Development Law* and its implications for the property curriculum:

[Lefcoe's] major focus is on the development of raw land, primarily for housing in American suburbs. Lefcoe's book is enormous—1681 pages. Yet it omits many of the topics included in the usual real property course offered in American law schools. There is little of relevance to the transmission of wealth —no estates in land, no trust and life estates, no statute of uses and rule against perpetuities; little on joint ownership (except partition as a potential means for avoiding subdivision regulation); nothing on matrimonial property. Nor does the book seek to develop an inclusive political, doctrinal, or philosophical theory of property by examining, for instance, the control, exploitation and transfer of "non-real" forms of wealth such as copyrights, governmental franchises, or land-related substances such as water and oil.

The book fastens, rather, on the legal structure facing the private housing developer; it investigates with skill and zest his activities and problems (and those as well of his lawyer and of the community in which he operates). The housing developer's complex activities, of course, relate to many of the doctrinal problems of "property" often taught to first-year students. Professor Lefcoe's approach, therefore, requires a reorganization of at least the property curriculum. The course offered by his book is not an advanced subject to be added to today's introductory treatment. It is a substitute, at least in part, therefor.[39]

Berger's thesis, on the other hand, is that a study of commercial land transfers should be deferred until the second or third year because

[r]eal estate transactions—as they are practiced today—are pregnant with considerations of income taxation, financing and contract. Except possibly for contract, a beginning law student lacks the necessary background in these areas, and if we ignore them, we waste everyone's time.[40]

His casebook, *Land Ownership and Use,* has thus reduced the content of the first year to what the author considers its minimum core and added to it a large chunk of the traditional separate course in land use planning. All materials on land transfer are omitted so that they may be covered in an advanced course, for which Professor Berger is now preparing another casebook. A preliminary edition of Axelrod, Berger and Johnstone, *Land Transfer and Finance,* is available in mimeographed form. It contains an expanded treatment of the gist of the traditional conveyancing course with the addition of material on real estate taxation and the more sophisticated forms of real estate "deals" such as the syndicate

[39]Heyman, "Book Review," 77 *Yale L. J.* 1260 (1968).
[40]Berger, *Land Ownership and Use* ix (1968).

and investment trust. It also contains a section on low income housing and shopping center development. Professor Lefcoe has recently published his advanced materials. *Land Finance Law* generally complements *Land Development Law,* which constructs a partial model of the real estate market. Thus, he does not duplicate much of the technical material on conveyancing (omitted entirely in Professor Berger's *Land Ownership and Use*). Instead he devotes considerably more attention to the problems of financing low income housing and to the operation of the mortgage market. Chapter Three, "The Banking Institutions as Mortgage Lenders," breaks new ground for property materials.

Land Ownership and Use is still concept oriented. It is organized into three chapters. Chapter I, "The Institution of Property," is an introduction to the nature of the concept of property *à la* McDougal and Haber. Chapter II, "Formation of Interests in Land," covers the basic materials on estates in land with emphasis on the landlord-tenant relationship. Chapter III, "Allocation and Development of Land Resources," covers the private, judicial, and administrative methods of controlling land use and constitutes almost half the book. The book thus covers a much narrower range of subjects than is conventionally found in the first-year course and is best suited for a four-unit introductory course followed by a three- or four-unit advanced course in modern real estate transactions.

A survey of law school catalogues and conversations with many of my property colleagues indicate that many courses are still organized around traditional doctrinal areas. Nevertheless, I believe that the dominant trend in the preparation of first year real property materials is toward the inclusion of subject matter areas formerly reserved for advanced courses. While casebooks prior to Berger and Lefcoe considered the public regulation of land use a proper subject to tack on to the first year course, these latter two books consider it to be a major focus for the course. The first year course has thus expanded from an examination of a series of narrow conceptual constructs to an evaluation of the legal system in terms of its impact on human activity and the physical environment. There is now an increased awareness that the manner in which institutions are structured influences their decisions and, ultimately, the way in which resources are distributed. Consequently the law student needs to be trained in the design and appraisal of institutional structures, as opposed to the study of an appellate decision viewed as an isolated conflict. He should be made to understand the public and private institutions that produced the decisions leading to conflict and to appraise the consequences of the result in terms of the kinds of choices a legal principle is likely to constrain or induce.

The implications of this shift in the content of the first year property course for advanced work in environmental management are encouraging. The student will receive an introduction to the process of resource allocation by private markets and public institutions while he is mastering the basic skills of case synthesis and doctrinal analysis. He should become accustomed to evaluating the legal system in terms of increasingly sophisticated economic and social criteria and will be better prepared for advanced work.

DEVELOPMENT OF THE LAND USE PLANNING CURRICULUM

The contemporary course in land use planning has its antecedents in the real property and municipal corporations curriculum. Prior to the publication of McDougal and Haber's *Property, Land and Wealth*, the property course's coverage of public regulations was confined to the common law of nuisance and restrictive convenant schemes. Whatever consideration was given to the public regulation of land was found in the municipal corporations course, but as Dan Mandelker had observed, "the early casebooks were preoccupied with the private law of municipal corporations."[41] While McDougal and Haber brought property into the twentieth century with coverage of the legal aspects of public regulation of land and water resources, Dean Jefferson Fordham did the same for municipal corporations with his casebook.[42] He rejected total reliance on the private corporation model and began to explore the impact of federal and state programs on the local level. He also began to focus on the problems of environmental management through the inclusion of materials on land use controls and public housing. But the book was still largely concerned with the internal operation of the city, and this division continued to dominate courses in local government. In 1949, at the annual meeting of the Association of American Law Schools,[43] Dean Fordham, McDougal, and Professor Richard Powell of Columbia debated whether land use regulation should be taught in a property course in municipal corporations or in an advanced property course. Although law schools approach land use regulation from both perspectives, the development of published teaching material generally proceeded from a property perspective.

The first casebook in land use planning was published in 1955. Professors Frank E. Horack, Jr., and Val Nolan's *Land Use Controls* had been preceded by the McDougal and Haber materials in 1948 and Dunham's *Modern Real Estate Transactions* in 1952, but theirs was the first book

---

[41] D. Mandelker, *Managing Our Urban Environment* vii (1966).
[42] J. Fordham, *Local Government Law* (1949).
[43] D. Mandelker, *supra* n. 36 at viii.

concerned solely with land use planning. It reflected two organizing principles: land use planning was a logical outgrowth of the basic real property course and was concerned principally with the administration of city and county zoning ordinances. *Land Use Controls* was offered as a supplement to the traditional first year course or in the alternative as an advanced seminar. The bulk of the book consisted of a good selection of important, recent zoning cases with a liberal use of text. Aside from an introductory chapter on the nature of property, only 33 pages were devoted to subdivision control and urban renewal. The book was justly criticized by Professor Jesse J. Dukeminier because it did "not include a great deal of information about what actually goes on in the planning process, without which discussion is blind and problems obscure."[44] He called for a collection of empirical case studies to supplement the reported cases.

In 1959 Horack and Nolan was supplanted by casebooks published by Professors Jacob H. Beuscher of the University of Wisconsin[45] and Charles Haar of Harvard.[46] Both casebooks were similar in content. They merged examination of the areas of the basic course in real property, which had been concerned with land use regulation, nuisance, restrictive covenants and equitable servitudes, with the techniques of public regulation. Each area could, as a result, be appraised from the perspective of its impact on the economic and social development of the community. Both authors expanded their coverage of subdivision regulation, official mapping and urban renewal compared with Horack and Nolan.

The most important difference between the Beuscher and Haar casebooks is their approach to the function of the planning process. Professor Beuscher viewed planning and regulation as a means of attacking certain well-defined physical problems.[47] Professor Haar took a more philosophical and skeptical view toward the function of planning. The result is a more sophisticated teaching tool. It raises the hard problems resulting from tension between traditional notions of freedom and the restriction of individual choice that land use planning entails. He clearly demonstrates that no consensus exists about the function of land use regulations and their ultimate goals, thus sparing the student the naive approach developed during the New Deal; i.e. planning is good and non-planning bad.

---

[44]Dukeminier, "Book Review," 8 *J. L. Ed.* 545 (1956).

[45]J. Beuscher, *Land Use Controls—Cases and Materials* (The College Typing Co., Madison, Wisconsin 1959). It should be noted that considerable attention is given to rural land use problems while Haar is confined to urban land.

[46]C. Haar, *Land Use Planning* (1959).

[47]*See Land Use Controls*, Ch. III "Modern Land Problems and Legal Tools."

In 1966 Professor Daniel R. Mandelker of Washington University synthesized the property and local government approach to land-use planning in his casebook *Managing Our Urban Environment.* He eliminated the artificial distinction between "the substance of controls over land use and reuse" and "the government structure within which these controls are exercised."[48] The first part of the book did not deal systematically with the range of functions of local government. It did cover the traditional sources of limitations of their power to innovate. Extensive coverage was given to the methods by which a city acquires jurisdiction over its territory as well as the modern substitutes for such governmental forms as the special district.[49] The traditional land use controls materials were presented from a functional rather than doctrinal perspective. The remainder of the book was organized around three generally accepted spatial divisions of the city. After two introductory chapters on the planning process and the constitutional basis of land use planning and regulation, the subsequent three chapters dealt with typically inner-city, suburban and rural-urban fringe problems. This enabled the author to suggest some performance criteria to judge the adequacy of the legal system. The strength of *Managing Our Urban Environment* is that it clearly focuses the student on the fact that land use planning and regulation is carried on by a maze of jurisdictional units and participants often with inarticulate or contradictory objectives. It also does a superb job of indicating the legal system's failure to develop modern doctrines responsive to the dynamism of urban development.

Professor Mandelker was a student of the late Professor Beuscher and the book reflects both the strengths and weaknesses of Beuscher's practical approach to urban development or inner-city decay. This process is perceived as a series of specific problems requiring definite public response. Thus, while Mandelker makes use of considerable writing and studies by planners, he does not venture far into some of the more philosophical and economic questions which increasingly come to the surface as the law is called upon to respond to the demand for "environmental quality."[50] Problems of securing adequate recreational and other open space facilities, preservations of eco-systems within or adjacent to urban areas, and methods of insuring innovative design and an "interesting" urban environment are not emphasized although they are raised. This neglect is not the result of insensitivity, but a function of the hard choices necessary in preparing a set of primary materials. Despite the soaring rhetoric now stemming from planners, the problems of policy

---

[48] D. Mendelker, *supra* n. 36.
[49] *See* Y. Wilburn, *The Withering Away of the City* (1964).
[50] *See* Tarlock, "Book Review," 20 *J. L. Ed.* 117 (1967).

coordination, minimal efficiency in the provision of urban services, and the prevention of the shifting of the more obvious external costs are still pressing and in need of new legal approaches. I would suggest that for the immediate present it would be sound pedagogical policy to integrate materials with a more explicit emphasis on environmental policy into courses such as the one contemplated by *Managing Our Urban Environment* and to leave more intensive consideration of them until advanced courses.

Land Use Planning has only become a relatively standard curricular offering within the past few years. Yet, the specialized advanced course may soon become obsolete due to the innovations in the first year real property curriculum. Much of the conventional course in land use controls and portions of the local government course dealing with jurisdiction over territory may be merged into the basic first year property course. The constitutional basis of land use regulation, the basic structures and powers of local governments and the administration of zoning, subdivision, and mapping regulatory schemes will be covered in considerable detail. This will free the curriculum for more advanced courses in specific areas and more intensive student research efforts.

In the past few years a number of innovative seminars and workshops have developed which hopefully give an indication of the future direction of this field. A seminar in urban renewal has been offered at Columbia and the University of Michigan, and Professor Daniel Mandelker has offered a seminar in urban housing problems at Washington University and directs empirical research projects.[51] Professor Norman Williams of Rutgers offers a seminar in the master plan. Professor Robert Covington of Vanderbilt University offers a seminar in regional economic development which is primarily concerned with TVA and Appalachian development. Emory University, the University of New Mexico, St. Mary's, Wisconsin, and Harvard have offered courses in eminent domain.[52] St. Mary's offers a course in the regulation of construction under the police power. Professor Robert I. Reis of the State University of New York at Buffalo offers a course in the preservation of open space. This school has also offered advanced work in the special problems of development planning on the Niagara Frontier. Under the direction of Professor Charles Meyers, Stanford has developed a Community Development Labora-

---

[51]For a discussion of Professor Mandelker's urban law program see D. Mandelker, "The Urban Legal Studies Project at Washington University School of Law," *Proceedings, The Ashville Conference of Law School Deans on Education for Professional Responsibility* (Howard Sacks, ed.) 63 (1965).

[52]This was taught by Professor Frank Michaelman but was dropped after one year because the problems were not "meaty" enough for student research and writing.

tory. Advanced law students work with architecture, business, and engineering students "to devise a general plan for the development (or redevelopment) of some nearby California community."[53] A similar program has also been developed at the State University of New York at Buffalo. The University of Washington offers a land use planning workshop in addition to a regular course.

Municipal Corporations (or Local Government) has long been a standard curriculum offering; my survey found that it is currently offered at some 74 schools. In the past few years Land Use Planning has also become a standard offering and is now given at some 60 schools. In some schools, such as Georgetown and Indiana University, Bloomington, land use problems are covered in local government law. But, as some 36 schools now offer both courses, the trend seems to be the separate coverage of the land use materials from the internal management of the city.

DEVELOPMENT OF THE WATER RESOURCES CURRICULUM

Historically the natural resources curriculum has been property oriented. The allocation of water was categorized as a right incident to the possession of land.[54] Courses focused on the allocation of resources between competing private claimants and, to a lesser extent, on conflicts between public authority and a private claimant. This approach reflected the prevailing economic assumptions of the 19th century. Resource exploitation was a desirable objective in an underdeveloped country, and the law accommodated itself to this thrust, as Willard Hurst has demonstrated so ably. Not until the last three decades of the 19th century did many become concerned that the rapid exploitation of our natural resources would result in their depletion.[55] From this fear the conservation movement was born and it gained widespread public acceptance during the presidency of Theodore Roosevelt. The Governor's Conference of 1908 and the Inland Waterways Commission drew attention to the need for public resource planning and management. Public intervention in the

---

[53] Stanford School of Law, *1968-69 Bulletin* 26.

[54] *See* H. Bigelow and J. Madden, *Cases on Rights Incident to the Preservation of Land* Ch. IV-VI (2nd ed. 1934).

[55] *See* R. Dana, *Pioneers and Principles, Perspectives on Conservation*, H. Jarrett, ed. 24, 25-26 (1958). In 1873 the American Association for the Advancement of Science appointed a committee to petition Congress on the importance of promoting the cultivation of timber and preserving the forests.

planning and management of our natural resources has increased steadily since that time, but the law schools have been slow in responding to this change.

The natural resources curriculum developed from two interrelated sources which have served to give it its present focus and structure. These are the basic courses in real property and specialized courses such as water rights, oil and gas rights, and mining rights offered at the far western schools. The amount of coverage given to natural resources was not extensive. In 1934 the AALS curriculum committee reported that there were 10 water and six oil and gas law courses.[56] In 1949 Professor Clyde Martz observed, "Many schools treat natural resource subjects only incidentally in their courses in property."[57]

The natural resources curriculum in the West crystallized into a series of discrete property-oriented courses geared to a regional demand for practicing lawyers trained in the legal technicalities of the acquisition and protection of exploitive rights.[58] In a 1965 survey Professor Robert Emmet Clark of the University of Arizona found that from 1948-49 to 1964-65 schools in both the West and East initiated or added one or more of the above offerings. He noted that during this period "the substance and the coverage of individual courses" did not change significantly.[59] Until the past two or three years, the only exposure most law students outside of the West have had to natural resources problems, aside from oil and gas, has been through the first year property course or perhaps an advanced course in land use controls. Judging from the scant published literature and teaching materials, there was little effort to relate these courses to the developments at Yale during the 1930's and 40's to expand the horizons of the traditional first year property course.

The first course that I have been able to discover that developed around the new concepts of regional resource planning and public management was entitled "Legal Problems in the Development of River

[56] "Report of Committee on Curriculum," 7 *Am. Law School Review*, 1032 (1934).
[57] Martz, "The Study of Natural Resources Law," 1 *J. L. Ed.* 588 (1949). Some people refused to accord any classification to the area. In a 1950 report at the AALS Curriculum Committee, the survey of property courses specifically excluded "Special courses in Oil and Gas, Water Rights, Mining, etc. . . ." Agnor, "A Survey of Present Law School Curriculum," 2 *J. L. Ed.* 510, 511 (1950).
[58] Professor Corwin Johnson of the University of Texas reports that the first set of water rights materials at Texas were prepared around 1945 by Professor W. O. Huie for use in a course in Texas Land Titles. A seminar in water rights did not emerge until 1948 and a separate course until 1950. Letter from Professor Corwin W. Johnson to author, June 3, 1969.
[59] R. Clark, "Teaching Natural Resources Law," 18 *J. L. Ed.* 165, 166 (1965). The Martz concept of a unified course was not followed in other schools nor at his own school in Colorado. *Id.* at 168 n. 18.

Valley Regions." It was offered by Professors George D. Braden and David Haber at Yale University.

Professor Myres McDougal has described the intellectual antecedents of the course in the following letter to the author.

From a historical perspective you might wish to go back to some of the early publications of the National Resources Planning Board on river valleys. Morris Llewellyn Cooke did more than anyone I know to develop the concept of interdependences as the appropriate characterization for a region. You will find this concept fully developed in a book by Maurice Rotival and myself entitled *Regional Planning with Special Reference to New England* published by the Yale University Press in 1947. Long before this Charles Runyon, who was my research assistant for a time, and I had been working on water law problems with ideas that we derived in the beginning from Underhill Moore. Moore had the notion that it was the type of use that determined the decision in water law. After some months of study, Runyon and I of course discovered that there were multiple uses in every dispute of any importance and that the only appropriate approach was through the unified region. If you will note carefully the sequence of cases and footnotes in chapter 10 of McDougal and Haber *Property, Wealth, Land,* you will see a sort of history in which our own ideas grew with the ultimate culmination in something like the TVA. We decided that our own intellectual progression was perhaps the best way to teach the materials, and during the years when I taught the book I found this to be reasonably effective.[60]

There is no evidence that the course was imitated. Water law continued to evolve as a specialized property course during the 1950's and early 1960's, especially in the states west of the 100th meridian.

More recently the legal study of water resource allocation and distribution is increasingly offered as part of the standard curricula since the subject has become a matter of national concern. To chart this evolution I will examine the following leading casebooks: Martz, *Cases on Natural Resources;* Sato, *Water Resources Allocation;* Sax, *Water Law;* Trelease, *Water Law;* Beuscher, *Water Law;* and Sax, *Water Law, Planning and Policy.*

The first post-war publication by a national casebook company was Professor Clyde Martz's *Cases on Natural Resource Law.* Prior to this time, schools generally used mimeographed materials usually tailored to one jurisdiction.[61] It should be noted, however, that the first water law casebook was by Professor Gavin W. Craig of the University of Southern

---

[60]Letter from Professor Myres S. McDougal to author, June 19, 1969.

[61]Professor Edward Clyde prepared a set of mimeographed water law materials for use at the University of Utah in 1947. They consisted, in the copy I have been able to locate in the Indiana University Library, of brief one paragraph précises of the case holding organized around conventional conceptual categories.

California in 1910,[62] primarily a collection of California cases with no text or notes. Several years later Professor Joseph Walter Bingham of Stanford University brought out the first casebook designed for a national audience.[63] It was an advanced collection, for its time, with emphasis on topics such as pollution and federal-state relations.

The function and scope of the Martz course was clearly defined in the first sentence of the introduction. "Natural Resource Law is concerned with the techniques by which private interests in water, minerals and land of the public domain or in *publici juris* are acquired; the nature of these interests; and the common law and statutory responsibilities that individuals who exploit the resources of the country owe to others who hold like interests and to the public."[64] The casebook contained a brief introductory chapter on federal public domain policy but the remainder was confined to a presentation of the doctrinal complexities of three subject matter areas: water, hard rock minerals, and oil and gas.[65] The final portion of the book, "Conservation Techniques," did deal with some public policy problems. However, apart from a fairly detailed analysis of the administration of oil and gas conservation the section was primarily composed of excerpts from federal and state statutes. The book made no attempt to present a set of criteria by which the public interest might be defined and the law evaluated.[66]

In 1962 Professor Sho Sato of the University of California published a three-volume set of mimeographed materials entitled *Water Resources Allocation*. The publication of a separate set of materials devoted to water reflected a rejection of the Colorado plan of combining water, hard rock minerals, and oil and gas in a separate course. The book contained a more contemporary selection of cases and materials, especially in the area of federal-state relations, reflecting the crystallization of the expanded federal authority since 1951.

Sato's approach differed from Martz in two significant ways. He broadened Martz's relatively narrow emphasis on the relationship of claimants *inter sese* to a crude consideration of the short- and long-term public interest in water allocation. He stated in his introduction, "Unlike some

---

[62]G. Craig, *Selected Cases on Water Rights and Irrigation Law in California and the Western States* (1910).

[63]J. Bingham, *Cases on the Law of Water Rights* (1918). Professor Bingham's introduction is still useful reading for its discussion of the possible scope of the course.

[64]Martz, *Cases on Natural Resources Law* 1 (1949).

[65]The casebook was developed from a five-hour course at the University of Colorado which combined the three subject matter areas. The primary reason seems to have been a desire to offer the student an introduction to the area without requiring a heavy commitment to specialized study. *See* Martz, "The Study of Natural Resource Law," 1 *J. L. Ed.* 588 (1949).

[66]*See* C. Johnson, "Book Review," 4 *J. L. Ed.* 503, 504 (1952).

areas of the law where consideration need be given only to temporal relationship of man to another, the law with respect to control and allocation of natural resources must necessarily include other dimensions —our relationship with nature and the effect on future generations."[67] While the book was still primarily a collection of cases and textual notes, the second volume did contain excerpts from two economists. Sato also differed from Martz by his increased emphasis on water distribution organizations.

In 1965 the Martz volume was superseded by a casebook authored by Dean Frank Trelease and Professors Bloomenthal and Geraud of the University of Wyoming. It was still primarily oriented toward western problems[68] and faithful to Martz's conception of a single course in resource development. Nevertheless the three subject matter areas were taught as separate courses at the University of Wyoming. Then in 1967 Dean Trelease published his portion of the 1965 volume, with some updating and revision, as a separate casebook entitled *Water Law: Cases and Materials*. The book differed in several aspects from Martz's earlier volume. It was less conceptually oriented than its predecessor; the first two chapters, which contained the bulk of the book, were organized around the topics of acquisition and exercise of water rights. The text notes made more extensive use of inter-disciplinary materials, primarily economic, than had previous casebooks, but there was no attempt to organize the material around a series of regional or national problems. The book also reflected the growing national concern with environmental quality, long a concern of Dean Trelease's, by including a substantial amount of legal and economic materials on the problems of the recreational use of water.

The western monopoly on water materials was broken in 1967 with the publication of Professor Jacob Beuscher's *Water Rights*. It is impossible to overstate the contributions of Professor Beuscher to this area. Concerned with problems of environmental quality when few others were, he also pioneered in devising courses and curricula to present them. His book had a two-fold focus which differentiated it from its western counterparts. It was concerned primarily with water problems more typical to the humid East than the arid West. The law of prior appropriation was covered but not systematically, for the topic was basically designed to

---

[67] S. Sato, *Water Resources Allocation* 101 (1962).
[68] C. Johnson, "Book Review," 7 *Natural Resources J.* 142, 143 (1967). The book was not solely western oriented, however, as it contained in addition to materials on riparian rights an expanded coverage of pollution and conservation problems of nation-wide significance. For a very brief discussion of the book's utility in the east see Brown, "Book Review," 2 *Land and Water Law Review*, 462, 462-64 (1968).

provide the necessary perspective for the student to evaluate and understand recent and proposed statutory modifications in the common law of riparian rights. The second focus reflected Professor Beuscher's long-standing concern for the criteria and methods available to create and maintain a quality environment. Extensive coverage, compared with previous casebooks, was given to pollution control and public limitations on the acquisition and exercise of private rights. Here the book emphasized problems of preservation of natural ecosystems and recreation and expansion of public rights.

Water Rights was still primarily a property book. While the author made excellent use of the Four State study he directed for the Department of Agriculture, tracing the evolution of administrative allocation of water, he made little use of inter-disciplinary materials.[69] Professor Beuscher was, however, far from insensitive to the relationship between law and economic development. He simply chose to present this relationship from a historical perspective as has his distinguished colleague, Willard Hurst. The casebook strongly emphasized the historical development of the economic assumptions which underlie judicial reasoning through the use of seminal 19th century cases.

Most of the teaching materials have been primarily concerned with the allocation of water between competing claimants rather than its subsequent distribution. It seems reasonable to assume that distributional problems were not emphasized in the classroom because its urban aspects have historically been studied either in the public utilities or the municipal corporations course.

The public utilities course, or Public Service Companies as it was first called, was one of the first law school responses to "the growing complexities of modern business and economic life."[70] It was a rallying point for those advocating greater emphasis on public law[71] and it firmly established itself in the legal school curriculum in the 1920's and early 1930's.[72] As it developed, it was increasingly combined with trade regulation, as

[69] *See* A Tarlock, "Book Review," 3 *Land and Water Law Review* 471 (1968).

[70] Stone, "The Future of Legal Education," 6 *Am. Law School Review* 331 (1924).

[71] *See e.g.* Judge Cuthbart W. Pound's 1922 Association of American Law Schools Address, "The Law School Curriculum as Seen by the Bench and Bar," 5 *Am. Law School Review,* 66, 70 (1922) and Wesley Hobfeld's extremely far-sighted paper, "A Vital School of Jurisprudence and Law: Have American Universities Awakened to the Enlarged Opportunities and Responsibilities of the Present Day," *Proceedings of Fourteenth Annual Meeting of American Association of Law Schools* 76 (1914).

[72] In 1933, 55 out of the 66 member AALS schools offered Public Utilities making it the most popular new public law offering and second only to constitutional and criminal law. Report of 1934 AALS Curriculum Committee, *supra* note 56 at 1083. However, its popularity appeared to decline by 1938. See Curriculum Committee Report, 9 *American Law School News* 212, 213 (1938).

was contemplated at Yale in 1928, and taught as Government Control of Industry.[73] From this merger came the first sophisticated efforts at integrating the study of law and economics.[74]

Treatment of the regulation of basic urban services was generally assumed by the municipal corporations course. In the past few years there has been a renewed interest in the relationship between urban development, environmental stability and the institutions providing urban services. For example, Professor George Lefcoe has included a section on utility service in his first year property materials and Professor Daniel R. Mandelker has included similar material in *Managing Our Urban Environment*. These developments indicate that future teaching materials concerned with environmental quality will be increasingly concerned with problems of public utility performance.

The water law casebooks surveyed thus far are primarily property oriented and concerned largely with the problems of agricultural use. While they stress to varying degrees the shift from judicial to administrative allocation of water, their focus has remained the acquisition and exercise of private rights. Although they have not neglected the urbanization trends, they have not squarely confronted the fact that most future problems will center around water allocation and distribution to urban populations. Witness the Bureau of Reclamation's emergence as a major urban supplier in the west.

The first published set of materials to break out of this pattern is University of Michigan Professor Joseph Sax's *Water Law, Planning and Policy*, published in 1968. It is a testimony both to the author and to the growing importance of the field that this book produced the greatest amount of scholarly criticism. A detailed review of the objectives and content of Professor Sax's book provides an excellent opportunity to chart the future development of the water resources curriculum.

Water Law, Planning and Policy is a bold effort to place water law problems within the context of economic policy and the politics of regional planning and decision-making. The first chapter, "Public Planning for Water Use," contains a selection of readings on the strengths and limitations of benefit-cost analysis and the politics of legislative and administrative project evaluation and selection. Part two of the chapter focuses on the legal problems of inter-state water transfer using the proposed northwest-southwest diversion as a model. The second chapter, "Managing Water Use," contains the meat of the traditional water law

[73]Hutchens, "Modern Movements in Legal Education," 6 *American Law School Review* 402, 403-04 (1928).

[74]For a description of the early Chicago program see Katz, "What Changes Are Practical in Formalized Legal Education," 10 *American Law School News* 1184 (1941).

course, although the format continues to be innovative. It discusses three water management institutions: the Bureau of Reclamation, the Delaware River Basin Compact Commission's involvement with New York City's water supply and the private water appropriation system. Even in studying the appropriation system the emphasis is on the rapid urbanization of the West; the section deals primarily with the private and public mechanisms for transferring an appropriative right in order to shift water from agricultural to urban uses. The selection of the Bureau of Reclamation reflects the fact that the important legal problems of water use are likely to continue to center around its distribution rather than its initial allocation. A case study of the city of New York's water problems explores the optimum institutional decision-making framework for allocation and how it is shaped by legislation and administrative agencies. The third chapter, "Recreation, Conservation, and Aesthetics," contains a brief introduction to the concept of navigability as a source of public regulation and an examination of the special problems of applying riparian principles to the solution of recreational conflicts. The bulk of the chapter is devoted to an analysis of the Scenic Hudson Preservation Conference using the briefs on rehearings. In Professor David Currie's words, "His choice is a brilliant one, for the briefs illustrate most tellingly the painstaking factual and technical analysis that must go into any informed decision on resource use."[75] Materials on pollution, ground water and liability for damage caused by surface drainage conclude the casebook.

Professor Sax has paid a high price in teaching efficiency for his efforts to modernize water law by shifting its emphasis to the broader problems of environmental management. To provide the necessary inter-disciplinary perspective, he has had to pare to the bone both the legal and non-legal materials. The result is not always satisfactory. The student is given an incomplete picture of both the legal and non-legal complexities of the problem. For example, the legal aspects of the allocation of federal-state power and the relationship between common law pollution remedies and the administrative process deserve much more attention than Professor Sax has given them.[76] The materials include only 18 cases, making it difficult to use the book in a medium-sized or large class since large amounts of outside reading cannot be expected from the students. It is both a strength and weakness that the book is almost self-teaching because of the author's frequent use of his incisive commentary. In many instances the student can reach a decent level of comprehension by just reading the book carefully; but often the student is not given a sufficient

[75]Currie, "Book Review," 56 *Calif. L. Rev.* 1811, 1814 (1969).
[76]See Corker, "Book Review," 4 *Land and Water Law Review* 219, 220-23 (1969).

analytic construct to start him thinking about a problem. The book is still a useful starting point for a discussion of the broader aspects of the legal doctrine. Perhaps, it will be most successful for a seminar because, to answer the more sophisticated problems posed by the author, the student must have read the cases and secondary sources cited by the author along with some other materials.

The need for the student to have a fairly comprehensive understanding of the subject prior to any discussion is not peculiar to environmental management, but it is one which must be faced if we are to achieve any sophistication in our presentation of the problems. I shall discuss this at greater length in connection with my survey of seminar developments. Perhaps, it should be recognized that materials should no longer be expected to provide comprehensive coverage of a given subject, but should function only as a jumping-off point for more extensive reading. The criteria for evaluating a casebook might be reformulated not in terms of what it includes but rather what it does not omit. It might thus be adopted if it is cheaper to have the student purchase the casebook, along with reproduced supplementary materials, rather than to reproduce a complete new set of materials.

Despite these criticisms Professor Sax has made a valuable contribution to teaching water resources. He has taken the first significant step since McDougal and Haber to place the problems in the context of regional management policies and the constant shift from rural to urban uses.

A course in water resources law is rapidly becoming a standard curricular offering throughout the United States. My survey of law school catalogues for the period 1968-70 reveals that there are at least 46 courses exclusively or substantially concerned with the subject. They are offered at almost all western law schools, most major state universities and, increasingly, at smaller schools throughout the East and Midwest. For example, courses in water resources law have recently been added at Drake University in Iowa and Washington and Lee University in Virginia. To date the major private schools have only offered such courses on an irregular basis. There are no members of the Columbia, Harvard, Pennsylvania or Yale faculties with a primary interest in the subject. However at Stanford Professor Charles Meyers offers the water law course on a regular basis and directs a substantial amount of related independent research, while at the University of Chicago Professor David Currie has recently entered the field.

I have not attempted to survey systematically the content of the various courses. Many follow the organization of the casebooks previously discussed. There are two significant differences between the traditional western course and those being developed in the East. Eastern courses are often offered as Natural Resources and cover related topics in resource management such as land conservation. They emphasize pollution control and the reservation of non-consumptive uses for recreation and the maintenance of natural ecosystems to a greater degree than is often the case in the West. It is certain that, since these problems are now national, these differences will diminish in the near future.

OIL AND GAS AND OTHER MINERALS

Oil and gas and, at some schools, hard rock minerals, have generally been considered one of the major specialized courses within the natural resources curriculum. They should not, however, be considered an essential part of a curriculum organized around the concept of environmental management. These subjects are still best taught as specialized courses in commercial transactions or taxation. Despite the fact that the basic doctrines that allocate competing claims to oil and gas and water have their origins in the common law of property, the oil and gas course is basically concerned with the interpretation of highly technical written documents and regulatory legislation. The casebooks now in use in the area are based on these assumptions and in my judgment are excellent teaching tools.[77] "Natural Resources" courses that combine oil and gas with water problems are organized around a construct with no pedagogical utility. Those aspects of oil and gas and hard rock mineral production with important environmental consequences—such as off-shore drilling, drilling in urban areas, and strip mining—should be considered in environmental management courses.

My survey found that some 30 schools offer courses in oil and gas. The courses are generally confined to the oil and gas states with the exception of some major national law schools, such as Columbia and the schools in Washington, D.C. Some courses listed under water resources also include segments on oil and gas, so the number of schools offering some instruction in the area is larger than the list suggests. The greatest concentration of courses in this area is, most appropriately, at Southern Methodist University in Texas.

THE EMERGING ENVIRONMENTAL LAW CURRICULUM

Tradition versus contemporary need. The teaching profession has long been dissatisfied with the efficiency of our mode of classroom teaching. Under the chairmanship of Karl Llewellyn, the 1944 AALS curriculum

---

[77] H. Williams, R. Maxwell, C. Meyers, *Oil and Gas* (2nd. ed. 1964) and W. Huie, A. Walker and M. Woodward, *Oil and Gas* (1960).

committee made an incisive critique. They focused on the second and third years of law school and found the case method failing under the weight of "a constant accession of new and more complex materials and new and more complex demands which are made upon all case-courses at once and indiscriminately." They concluded that the continued analysis of appellate cases is not useful to train lawyers in the skills of statutory construction, appellate advocacy and simple drafting and counseling. The report was mainly concerned with the "private law" curriculum, defined as areas "where the main lines of policy are relatively settled." Its final section, however, noted that the case method was also inadequate in training lawyers to operate in the public law area where policy formulation was so fluid. The committee's conclusions have influenced legal teaching in this field ever since.

> The three conclusions which seem to us persuasive in regard to "public law" material are therefore: (1) that it can and should be selected and above all taught with primary reference to giving effective training in craft-skills of general application; (2) that it should be selected and above all taught in terms of a steady attempt at widening perspective; (3) that both can be more effectively accomplished by deep and sustained work centered on particular areas and problems of particular administrative bodies than they can by any effort at wider or more inclusive class coverage of informational subject-matter. Again we believe the information and skills developed by returning instructors to point the road. Such men return, we repeat, equipped with specialized knowledge and experience which has a uniquely useful twist. As law teachers, they have sized up their experience with an eye to articulate communication; again as law teachers, they will on their return to reworking and rethinking with an eye to lines of instruction which can make study of the particular yield light on the general. If their fresh knowledge and initiative are put to work before either stales, our profession at large will have promise of developing within a relatively brief period techniques for effective teaching on the still puzzling "public law" side which can hope to rival the effectiveness of classic case-instruction. And it pays to recall again in this connection that the heart of case-instruction for class purposes is not use of judicial opinions as such but instead of the concrete situation (of which the judicial "case" is but one type), presenting a concrete problem or series of problems, with the class really grasping the background and the problems, being trained in solution by actually trying to solve until solving becomes a thing each member of the class knows how to do, and moreover does by trained habit.[78]

Subsequent curriculum committee reports voiced the same objections.[79] The more recent reports manifest a greater sense of urgency as

---

[78]1944 Committee on Curriculum of Association of American Law Schools, "The Place of Skills in Legal Education," 45 *Colum. L. Rev.* 345, 388 (1945).
[79]*See e.g.* Association of American Law Schools, "Report of the Curriculum Committee," *1960 Proceedings*, 166.

the boredom of second- and third-year law students seems to increase. The 1968 curriculum committee report, authored by Professor Charles J. Meyers, was sharply critical of the last two years of law school labeling them "too rigid, uniform, narrow and repetitious"[80] It suggested more intensive individual work and clinical-intern experiences. Nevertheless, most schools continue to rely on the appellate case-oriented survey course to carry the bulk of instruction during the entire three years.[81] It is difficult to judge if this inertia is the result of the financial constraints under which American legal education operates or a lack of initiative on the part of American law teachers.[82]

In my opinion effective legal teaching in the field of environmental management requires drastic reduction in our reliance on appellate cases, periodic one-hour classes covering a small portion of predigested materials and our use of the survey course. At the time Langdell devised the case method, it was useful in teaching the process of decision in many areas. However, it is not an accurate method of understanding the process of public and private decision in environmental management for four principal reasons.

First, the information necessary for an intelligent discussion of the problems cannot be conveyed Socratically. It must either be treated by lecturing or the student must do a large amount of outside reading. This is especially true of interdisciplinary materials. The lawyer's function is to evaluate their relevance to the solution of specific controversies, but before he can do so he must understand how other disciplines conceptualize problems.

Second, appellate decisions often give only a small portion of the facts relevant to the decision. Reasoning from real factual situations was the core of the case method, but the legal realists such as Jerome Frank in *Law and the Modern Mind*, showed the gap that exists between facts relevant to a decision and those reported by appellate courts. This gap is especially evident in environmental management cases. The complex process of decision may originate in some remote policy stage of planning and be the product of a variety of participants. It is a process that is seldom well analyzed in an appellate decision, even in such a well-reasoned opinion as that of Judge Hays in *Scenic Hudson*. The subtle play of formal legal rules and "softer" policy decisions by those in author-

[80] *See* Meyers, *supra* n. 13.
[81] Langdell devised the casebook because it was impossible to give all students ready access to the original reports in the library. E. Patterson, "The Case Method," 4 *J. L. Ed.* 1, 11 (1951).
[82] *See generally* Special Committee on Law School Administration and University Relations, Association of American Law Schools, *Anatomy of Modern Legal Education* (1961).

ity can only be understood by detailed case studies of specific decisions using agency and trial transcripts and public documents such as planning studies.

Third, most appellate decisions do not have great precedential value. Richard Babcock in his book *The Zoning Game* has described the limited influence appellate cases have on similar controversies. The same is true for most problems in environmental management. There is no systematic body of principles that can be synthesized and digested as Langdell and Beale assumed. Instead, we are studying an ongoing process of constantly changing variables.

Finally, appellate cases seldom furnish criteria to test the efficiency and utility of the legal system. The value premises that should underlie the "good" management decision are not fixed and cannot be stated in such cozy generalities as "security of title" or "full utilization of resources." I believe the law in this area can only be evaluated by its performance in allocating resources to the satisfaction of the community. Its impact on human activity must be charted and ethical judgments made on the basis of this data.

These criticisms of the case method and the call for wider perspectives in the study of the role of the legal system should not obscure the fact that legal education is primarily skill training. Courses in "contemporary" problems such as environmental management often run the risk of providing little more content than can be gained by a sustained reading of *The New York Times*. A dash of economics and political science combined with a pinch of biology served up with some interesting cases does not make a course in the legal problems of environmental management. Besides the traditional skills of formulation and application of doctrine and legal drafting, students need to be trained in such skills as: the extraction of authoritative principles, from a mass of official and semiofficial public documents, that will help decide specific controversies; the use of inter-disciplinary materials to shape legal principles and to test their validity (as well as understanding the limits of inter-disciplinary materials and empirical data);[83] the evaluation of decision-making institutions in terms of the kinds of decisions they are likely to produce; understanding how new legal institutions and structures might be created and organized; and understanding the use of scientific and economic data in the decisional process.

The thrust of my position is that law schools ought to merge their traditional skill training with that developed by those branches of politi-

[83] *See* H. Kalven, "The Quest for the Middle Range: Empirical Inquiry and Legal Policy," *Law in a Changing America*, 56 (1968).

cal science[84] and economics[85] that deal with policy formulation and public administration. In the 1930's law schools separated the study of administrative law from public administration and focused on "the law which establishes the procedures and methods of the executive branch in its contacts with private interests and provides for judicial checks on its authority,"[86] rather than on the substantive law that administrative agencies develop. Seen in historical perspective this was a logical and necessary development in order to win public acceptance of widespread delegations to administrative agencies. But, it is a totally inadequate response to contemporary problems. The emphasis on procedure has deflected attention from the role that law plays in the resolution of the policy questions inherent in this country's attempts to adjust to years of uncritical acceptance of technological innovation.

CURRENT SPECIALIZED OFFERINGS

Course offerings in environmental management are the forefront of the search for new methods of training law students. Professor David Cavers of Harvard offered a course in the legal problems of environmental quality for several years prior to his retirement[87] and, along with Professor Sax at Michigan, pioneered curricular developments in this area. This section reviews the organization and content of several seminars in the legal problems of environmental management and several first year courses designed to provide the student with a good foundation for advanced work. The distinguishing feature of these courses compared with those previously surveyed is that the old curricular categories which separated water and mineral problems from land use regulation are being discarded. The environment is viewed as a series of interrelated subsystems and courses are being organized around this construct. These courses are less concerned with the resolution of conflicts between a limited number of parties than with the role of the legal system in protecting some notion of the public interest in environmental quality. The focus is thus on the process of planning and decision-making for resource management and on the stages and methods of effective public intervention.

---

[84] For insight in future tasks faced by lawyers, *see* L. Caldwell, "Administrative Possibilities for Environmental Control," F. Darling and J. Milton, editors, *Future Environments for North America* (1966).

[85] *See generally* G. Wunderlich, "Training in Economics for Natural Resource Lawyers," 21 *J. L. Ed.* 538 (1969).

[86] R. Fuchs, "An Approach to Administrative Law," 18 *N.C. L. Rev.* 183, 196 (1940).

[87] Professor Cavers' course examined the deterioration of environmental quality resulting from the increased use of technology. Air and water pollution and the regulation of nuclear reactors were the principal topics.

Courses on environmental quality include traditional survey as well as research courses. The emphasis on in-depth research is illustrated by two seminars offered at the University of Minnesota and at Indiana University, Bloomington.

Professor Thomas Bryden offers a yearlong seminar in natural resources at Minnesota. It covers a shifting range of topics of current interest. Scheduled for 1970 are control of water pollution, pesticides, preservation of parklands from highways and wetlands from drainage. The course will meet once every three weeks. Three or four sessions will be devoted to each topic and a short written assignment is required from each student for each session. The object of the class is a "group effort to produce and edit an article suitable for presentation to a law review, or memorandum for a government agency."[88]

In 1969-70 I shall introduce a colloquium on environmental quality at Indiana University, Bloomington. Its objective is to provide a small group of students, five, with in-depth research and tutorial experience. The students will be assigned topics in the first week and will have a month to prepare a comprehensive bibliography. A 100-page paper will be required, preceeded by an outline and rough draft. The topics chosen for next year are the regulation of powerline placement, thermal pollution, highway route selection procedures in selected urban areas, noise abatement and the role of law in encouraging or constraining innovative building design. The group will meet together during the first half of the course to discuss certain common problems such as constitutional limitations on the public's power to implement planning proposals, the role of the judiciary in reviewing decisions delegated to non-judicial bodies, the allocation of power between expert and citizen, and the impact of technology on the law. Throughout the course a number of speakers from within the university, such as Professors L. K. Caldwell and Jerome Milliman, will meet with the students to present different perspectives on the problem of environmental quality. The bulk of the instruction will be by individual tutorial sessions of about one half hour each week. When rough drafts of the papers have been completed they will be shared with the other students and the writer will defend it before the colloquium.

Seminars in environmental quality are also offered at Denver University, the University of Michigan, Rutgers, Newark, Stanford University and the University of Washington. Professor Sax has concentrated on the problems of securing adequate land for recreational use and conservation. The seminar at the University of Denver is taught by a variety of faculty members and outside guest lecturers. The topics

---

[88]Letter from David P. Bryden to author, May 14, 1969.

vary and "usually cover areas of current interest."[89]

The Stanford course, Conservation Issues, is offered by Professor Girard and is an in-depth examination of environmental management problems currently being faced in the Bay Area and the state. Preservation of open space and forest management have been selected as this year's topics. Professor Girard is the draftsman for a state legislative committee concerned with open space preservation, and the objective of the course is to devise practical methods of preserving open space. A course with a similarly pronounced activist orientation is offered at the University of Washington. Students are encouraged to do case studies of recent or pending policy decisions such as the location of a freeway.[90]

The following table lists some of the specialized offerings in environmental management.

ENVIRONMENTAL QUALITY

1968-69	Harvard	Legal Problems of Environmental Quality
1969-70	Michigan	Legal Problems of Environmental Quality
1969-70	Indiana University (Bloomington)	Colloquium in Selected Problems in Environmental Quality
1968-69	State University of New York at Buffalo	Comparative Environmental Law
1968-69	State University of New York at Buffalo	Problems of Open Space Preservation
1969-70	Stanford University	Conservation Issues
1969-70	University of Denver	Natural Resources Seminar
1969-70	Rutgers	Environmental Quality
1969-70	University of Washington	Protection of Environmental Quality

THE EMERGENCE OF A REQUIRED FIRST-YEAR COURSE IN ENVIRONMENTAL MANAGEMENT

At least three schools require a course in resource planning or environmental management in the first year. To date Denver University, the State University of Iowa and the State University of New York at Buffalo require these courses. Basically, they are designed to give first year students an overview of the problems of environmental management.

---

[89]Letter from Thomas P. Brightwell to author, June 3, 1969.
[90]William Rogers Memorandum, Seminar on Environmental Protection, August 22, 1969 (unpublished).

Their curricular function is generally to illustrate the operation of portions of the legal system that are not stressed in typical first year classes such as the role of law and legal institutions in the formulation and implementation of broad societal objectives and the interplay between legislatures, administrative agencies and the courts. Most of them require substantial outside reading from a variety of disciplines, and thus another objective is a high degree of information transfer.

In 1967 Professor N. William Hines organized a course in resource planning at the State University of Iowa that was focused on the "quality of our living environment." Professor Hines has described the pedagogical methods and substantive content of the course as follows:

If required to characterize the course in one phrase, I would call it a public law of property course. It concerns matters traditionally classed as property topics, but its orientation is one of public and not private law. The subject matter coverage of the course is revealed by the attached table of contents of this year's materials. Consistent with the purposes the course was originally designed to fulfill, the emphasis is placed on structure and process. In teaching it, substantive law coverage is relegated to a secondary position in relation to examination of the private and public institutions involved in resource allocation and management and study of the processes by which these institutions function.

Perhaps the best way to describe the content of the course over and above the factual transmission of existing legal rules and principles affecting the problem areas studied would be to suggest some of the major "themes" that permeate the class discussions. Many of these themes can be stated in terms of conflicts. A repeating theme is the conflict between the tradition of free enterprise in resource development and the desire to recognize and protect the interests of future generations. The problems in the development and implementation of a conservation ethic are closely related to this theme and also to a second major theme: power and the preservation of the quality of physical life. Among other things, consideration of this issue requires wrestling with the difficulties of trying to devise measures more meaningful than the standard economic indicators for use in broad scale social cost accounting.

Another pair of themes relate to the constraints that operate to reduce the range of alternatives available to resource planners. One theme is the conflict between the community's powers to act in the public interest and the individual's rights to determine the use of his private property. A related theme is the conflict between the interests of the existing community and the needs of the potential community. Putting content into such terms as "taking" and "public interest" are exercises that illustrate the former theme; elitist land development requirements such as large lot zoning, minimum floor size, and architectural review boards are examples of the latter.

Another major theme that pervades the entire range of problems studied is the conflict between the need to improve the efficiency of resource planning and management and realization of the democratic ideal of broad citizen participation in government decision making. Illustrative questions falling under this rubric are such matters as the openness of administrative hearing procedures, the appropriate composition of various local boards of review and appeal (expert v. layman), designing of agencies that meaningfully represent and protect the public interest, the many puzzling problems associated with trying to assure that the sentiments of the affected citizenry are considered at a timely point in the planning process, and the scope of review to which administrative decisions should be subjected.[91]

The University of Denver course is entitled "Environmental Control and Natural Resources." A substantial amount of background reading in economics and political sciences is required. The first half of the course consists of an overview of land-use planning and zoning with emphasis on the new forms of controls, the economic and social discrimination zoning fosters and its use of aesthetic objectives. The second part of the course is an overview of air and water pollution and the allocation of water resources. Some public land mining problems and oil and gas are tacked on at the end.

The first year course at the State University of New York at Buffalo is entitled "Environmental Management." The objective is similar to the other two courses, but its method of implementation is different. A small number of judicial decisions have been selected for intensive study. The course has a heavier emphasis on the constraints imposed by existing government structures in environmental management and is primarily concerned with the regulation and development of urban land. Air and water pollution problems are, however, also covered.[92]

The recently revived school of law at Northeastern University is also contemplating requiring an upper division course in environmental management. The school is built on two principles that distinguish it—in theory—from the majority of American law schools. Serious attention is given to training the student to practice law through a cooperative plan where the student alternates between a law office and school; at graduation the student will have nine quarters of school and five of office work. The second principle is the belief that law school curricula have failed to reflect a genuine concern for the urgent problems of American society.[93] Thus, the curriculum has been shaped "around significant issues in contemporary life, especially those which arise with increasing urgency in our populous metropolitan areas."[94] Courses designed to

---

[91]W. Hines, "Resource Planning," background paper prepared for this conference (unpublished).
[92]Syllabus, Environmental Management, Spring, 1969.
[93]Conversation with Dean O'Toole, Boston, Massachusetts, April 11, 1969.
[94]*Bulletin*, Northeastern University 10-11 (1968-69).

correct this deficiency on the drawing board are law and population, workshop in urban land problems and the proposed course in environmental management.[95] This course has not yet been designed but Dean O'Toole has informed me that it will concentrate on the problems of the Northeast such as land conservation and pollution.

ONE EXAMPLE OF A COMPREHENSIVE PROGRAM IN ENVIRONMENTAL AND URBAN LAW

Most law schools are fortunate if one member of the faculty has a major research and teaching interest in environmental management. But, at the State University of New York at Buffalo an ambitious, coordinated teaching and research program is in the formative stages. Under the leadership of Professor Milton Kaplan, a group of some five law professors has been assembled. Earlier Professor Kaplan had surveyed the extent of law school involvement in this area for the Ford Foundation and he drew on this experience in presenting his recommendations for a program in Environmental and Urban Law to the Buffalo faculty. The geographical focus for the program was the Niagara Frontier, which represents an excellent laboratory for exploring the dynamics of urban development and environmental change. The program was by no means parochial because courses and graduate study in comparative environmental law are contemplated if financing can be obtained. Professor Kaplan offered the following general guidelines for his program:

> The program would cut across all the major functions of faculty-professional training [J.D. and advanced degree candidates]; teaching students of other disciplines; research by faculty members and students; interdisciplinary studies; clinical programs; student internships; faculty curriculum development; community service and contributions to law reform. . . . Each element must serve and reinforce the others.[96]

Professor Kaplan believes that the substantive problems should be studied from a functional perspective but wisely noted, "One man's function may be another man's category."[97] He offered four guidelines for the structuring of the curriculum:

> Problem settings and problem interrelationships should be given serious consideration in the designing of courses. . . .
> The curriculum should demonstrate the uses of law as a positive force in the solution of the problems exposed.

---

[95] *Id.* at 8.

[96] Memorandum to the Faculty of Law and Jurisprudence, State University of New York at Buffalo, *supra* note 22 at 51.

[97] *Id.* 53.

The subjects of teaching should be organized around real-life situations wherever possible.

To achieve the foregoing ends, we should take advantage of opportunities accorded by ties with other faculties of the University and by the geographical setting of the University.[98]

All forms of instruction discussed in this paper are being used or are contemplated—the required survey course with a heavy informational content in interdisciplinary perspectives, specialized seminars and courses, field research and participation in legal aid and internship programs. The sweep of the program can be grasped by the course titles from the school's 1968-69 bulletin:

1. LAND TRANSACTIONS

2. LEGAL PROBLEMS OF THE METROPOLITAN COMMUNITY

3. STATE AND LOCAL TAXATION

4. PUBLIC FINANCE AT THE STATE AND LOCAL LEVEL

5. SELECTED PROBLEMS IN DEVELOPMENT PLANNING

6. SELECTED PROBLEMS OF WATER RESOURCE LAW

7. INSTITUTIONAL ASPECTS OF PUBLIC AND PRIVATE DECISION MAKING IN THE ALLOCATION OF LAND AND RESOURCES AFFECTING THE DEVELOPMENT OF LAND

8. COMPARATIVE ENVIRONMENTAL LAW

9. SEMINAR ON THE LEGAL CONTROL OF AIR AND WATER POLLUTION

10. PROBLEMS IN HOME RULE

11. URBAN PROBLEMS

12. PROBLEMS OF OPEN SPACE PRESERVATION AND REJUVENATION IN METROPOLITAN COMMUNITIES

13. INTERSTATE COOPERATION, REGIONAL PLANNING, AND FEDERAL INTERVENTION IN WATER RESOURCE ALLOCATION THE PROBLEMS OF MUNICIPAL SUPPLY AND WATER POLLUTION

14. PROFESSIONAL COURSES FOR OTHER FACULTIES

15. SELECTED PROBLEMS OF WATER RESOURCE LAW

16. INSTITUTIONAL ASPECTS OF PUBLIC AND PRIVATE DECISION MAKING IN THE ALLOCATION OF LAND AND RESOURCES AFFECTING THE DEVELOPMENT OF LAND

SPECIALIZED LEGAL PERIODICALS AND SYMPOSIA

There are three specialized legal periodicals and one annual publication concerned with aspects of environmental management. The first to

---

[98] *Id.* at 54-55.

be published was the *Natural Resources Journal* started in 1961 by the University of New Mexico School of Law. It serves both as a national inter-disciplinary journal and a state law review. The natural resources section has consistently presented a broad spectrum of resource management literature from legal scholars as well as the natural and social sciences. In 1966 the University of Wyoming School of Law converted its law review to the *Land and Water Law Review* with the same bifurcation of specialized and state functions as the *Natural Resources Journal.* However, to date the *Land and Water Law Review* has been less interdisciplinary than its New Mexico counterpart. In 1966 the University of Detroit converted its law journal to the *Journal of Urban Law.* The coverage of the *Journal* ranges far beyond environmental management, for it is concerned with the implications of all areas of the law for the urban dweller.[99]

A most significant annual publication was inaugurated in 1967 by Professor Daniel R. Mandelker of Washington University. *The Urban Law Annual* "has two major purposes—to publish the results of empirical research into legal problems in urban areas and to publish articles on new and innovative ideas for legal controls, especially as they take statutory form."[100] The content of the first two issues indicates that articles will not be confined to those dealing with the central city and its suburbs, but will be concerned with regional environmental management problems.[101]

In the past several years there have been a substantial number of law review symposia dealing with problems of environmental management. As with all legal writing they vary widely in quality. Some are merely random collections of articles built around a general common theme.[102] Others are organized around more specific topics and often provide valuable in-depth insight into the dimensions of a problem. The 1965 symposia in the *Washington University Law Quarterly* on "New Towns," the 1965 *Pennsylvania Law Review* on "Planned Unit Development," and the 1964 *Temple Law Review* of "Pleasure Boating and the Law," are examples of the best type of this symposium. *The Journal of Law and Contemporary Problems* has continued its tradition of providing high quality interdisciplinary examinations of important problems in-

[99]See J. McAuliffe, "The Urban Law Program of the University of Detroit." 20 *J. L. Ed.* 53, 91-92 (1967).

[100]Mandelker, Preface, 1 *Urban Law Annual* (1968).

[101]Protection, 1 *Urban Law Annual* 128 (1968) and W. Kochelman, "Wisconsin's Water Resources Act of 1952," 2 *Urban Law Annual* 141 (1969).

[102]*See, e.g.,* "Water Use—A Symposium," 9 B.C. *Ind. and Comm. L. Rev.* 531 (1968); "Land Use Symposium," 50 *Iowa L. Rev.* 243 (1965) and "Recreational Planning: A Symposium," 55 *Ky. L. J.* 745 (1967).

cluding environmental management.[103] The recent symposia on "Housing, Urban Problems and Prospects" and "Air Pollution" are valuable contributions to the literature of this area.

Perhaps the most encouraging development has been the student designed and written symposia. One of the first was a 1964 collection of student notes in the *Northwestern Law Review* entitled "Apartments in Suburbia: Local Responsibility and Judicial Restraint."[104] The notes were primarily confined to commentary on appellate cases and secondary scholarly writings, but it was an encouraging effort at the coordination and concentration of student research toward an examination of important societal problems.

Law reviews combined with intensive research seminars can play a creative role in furthering our knowledge of the problems of environmental management. Law schools have historically been handicapped by the lack of faculty research assistance and thus our knowledge of the actual operation of the legal system in society remains meager. The sources of student research energy we do have, the law reviews and a small additional reserve of competent second- and third-year students have often been diffused on small and uncoordinated projects. This has resulted in a substantial loss to legal scholarship that can no longer be tolerated. In fact, it seems clear that the coming generation of students, trained in the behavioral sciences, will demand that we move from the narrow analytic framework in which most law is taught to greater involvement in empirical research. One means of meeting the student demand for a more meaningful analysis of the legal system is to design research projects in which the student can participate for a substantial period of his legal education. As more and more law reviews recruit their members on the basis of open competition, it should be easier to coordinate student research projects with classroom work for the promise of publication will function as a useful incentive.

Coordinated large-scale student projects can improve the quality and utility of the vast majority of our law reviews. Most law reviews are slavish imitations of our large national law schools. The resulting duplication of research and trivial end product has often been deplored. One remedy would be for most law reviews to focus in depth on the special problems of their state or region leaving to Harvard the task of counseling the Supreme Court. By state or regional problems I do not mean trite

---

[103]Professor Cavers, founder of the journal, was an early advocate of specialized legal periodicals with an inter-disciplinary component. D. Cavers, "New Fields for the Legal Periodical," 23 *U. Va. L. Rev.* 1 (1936).

[104]Symposium, "Apartments in Suburbia: Local Responsibility and Judicial Restraint," 59 *Nw. L. Rev.* 344 (1964).

comments on the latest folly or "mal-reasoned" effort of the state supreme court.[105] Rather I envision projects that study actual resource
management problems. These projects would often be done by teams of
students under faculty supervision in connection with a continuing seminar. They would serve legal scholarship in two ways beyond the functions
currently being performed by the vast majority of student law review
writing. They would focus on important but less publicized sources of law
such as the decisions and regulations of state administrative programs.
They would involve empirical research into the role of law in environment management. I realize that these kinds of projects have been undertaken in the past and that many are under way at present. Professor
George Lefcoe's study of the provision of low-income housing in the
New Haven area is an excellent example of the kind of study I envision.
The point I wish to emphasize is only that coordinated student research
projects should be considered an integral part of an environmental management curriculum.

The potential for creative student work is best illustrated by a symposium prepared by students at the Berkeley campus of the University
of California in 1967.[106] The symposium analyzed several regional resource allocation and development problems in the Bay Area such as air
and water pollution, regulation of bay fill, rapid transit and urban
renewal. Case and statutory analysis was combined with field research
and thus in some instances the authors were able to suggest some crude
form of quantitative evaluation of the effectiveness of a given regulatory
program. Their use of unpublished technical material and other hard-to-
obtain sources of information was also useful for other scholars not
familiar with the work of government agencies in the area.

Conclusion

Since this conference was held, environmental quality has emerged in
the public mind as our most urgent domestic priority. Legal education
has responded predictably. As was poverty and the urban crisis in the
mid 1960's, the environment has been "discovered." New courses are
rapidly being created and law review symposia produced. However, I
view this response somewhat skeptically. The basic role of the universi-

---

[105]See J. Werner, "The Need for State Law Reviews," 23 *U. Va. L. Rev.* 49 (1936) for a
discussion of the conventional role of single-jurisdiction oriented law reviews.
[106]"Symposium: The San Francisco Bay Area—Regional Problems and Solutions," 55 *Calif.
L. Rev.* 695 (1967). Three years earlier two students had produced an excellent study of the
Lake Tahoe Region. Pagtar and Wolfe, "Lake Tahoe: The Future of a National Asset—
Land Use, Water and Pollution," 52 *Calif. L. Rev.* 563 (1964).

ties must be to train a new type specialist. Persons trained in one discipline with the ability to synthesize and apply the insights of related fields are needed for future decision making. However, a recent report of the Office of Science and Technology, *The Universities and the Environment: Committment to a Focused Education*, questions the ability of the university to restructure itself to train this new type of specialist. Hopefully this paper will play some small role aiding law schools and universities in the necessary cross-disciplinary restructuring, which is necessary to allow them to play a more meaningful role in environmental management.

DISCUSSION

George Lefcoe, CHAIRMAN   David P. Currie
James N. Corbridge, Jr.   N. William Hines
Charles H. W. Foster   Michael E. Levine
A. Dan Tarlock

MR. LEFCOE: The first focus of our discussion is going to be on the law schools and the prospects and problems for training people who have interests in the environment.

Hank Foster surveyed the opportunities and needs for legal services among various conservation groups. A good place to start might be to ask that he summarize what he found. What opportunities are there? What work needs to be done?

MR. FOSTER: Thank you, George. I feel somewhat out of place up here in this nest of law professors, and maybe a little bit like the California sea lion in the Santa Barbara oil slick. (Laughter)

MR. LEFCOE: We are the sea lions. (Laughter)

MR. FOSTER: I think there are a few non-lawyers in the group, and I will try to uphold our end of the bargain here. It was my interesting assignment to try to reproduce for the prospective environmental attorney at least a facsimile of the kind of conservation clients he might be confronted with. Of course, no human being can do this properly, but the material pulled together will give you a rough idea of what you might be letting yourselves in for.

MR. LEFCOE: You have described a need for legal services but no capacity to support them financially. You have described an abundance of work that any competent lawyer, conventionally trained, could do such as drawing up corporate bylaws or trying cases. To the extent any of that is learned in law school, it is in courses that are found in the standard, existing curriculum—nothing novel. Perhaps this should not be surprising; lawyers doing the most distinguished trial work today in environmental law had no special environmental training in law schools.

In comparing the kinds of courses that people are developing we might consider two rather diverse models. At one end of the spectrum is the activist approach. Under this approach the students are supposed to throw themselves into the fight, and earn credit for obstructing the orderly processes of degradation. (Laughter) They join a lawyer in fighting a case or present an administrative argument. As an activist class this model resembles the clinical and legal aid programs in poverty law in which students are sometimes given academic credit for practicing law under supervision.

The theory of this model might well be that there is nothing unique at all about environmental law. It is a way of applying other aspects of law to a particular set of facts or events. The best way to get some idea about that is to do it.

On other end of the spectrum are the conventional programs that law schools have had, the traditional classes in natural resource law. A more contemporary example, with no bias whatsoever in favor or opposed to conservation interests, might be a class in resource economics. It simply purports to teach the existing law of economic analysis, just as you might teach the existing water law, however inadequate that body of law might be for some purposes. I would call these rather passive models, without intending a pejorative.

The questions I want to put to the panel are: What are your courses about? Are you training people for the work Hank Foster describes? Are your classes activist? Are they morally neutral? Would they help a lawyer for an oil company to better serve his client's interest, narrowly conceived, just as they might help a conservation man do his job better? What is the content, direction and purpose of the programs that you have each designed?

MR. CURRIE: One way to approach the question is to ask whether we are doing anything that responds to Mr. Foster's statement of needs in this area. I can say rather flatly that I am not doing anything that would contribute to turning out people who are going to be good at, for example, drawing up bylaws for conservation organizations. That kind of work is rather thoroughly taken care of in traditional courses on corporations. Some of the tax implications are taken care of in tax courses and there is no reason why those should be treated by people who are particularly concerned with the environment.

Some of us start out with a bias in favor of preserving the environment and try to do something that will promote a better preservation. This affects our courses, and one way to accomplish it would be to take an activist position and send our students out to do good. But some of them may not want to do good in our way and that is something of a problem.

MR. YANNACONE: Flunk 'em.

MR. CURRIE: I think I would prefer to set them up on projects where they can go out and do whatever appeals to them that would be of educational value in this field.

One thing that I think students can really contribute in this area is in finding out what is going on. We have, as some people suggested yesterday, quite a lack of information in many areas. I found in dealing with my seminar last year that the best thing the students did was to gather simple facts on what was happening. I then tried to have them propose solutions to difficult resource problems that they had discovered in the community. We had more trouble because we discovered we really do not have the kind of confidence in approaching an essentially legislative policy problem that we have in something like statutory construction. One thing I would like to do in this kind of course is to heighten the students' appreciation of the problems that exist in the environmental field and of the inquiries they have to make to find out what is going on, the need to utilize the services of people in other disciplines, and the different kind of decision-making process they will have to go through in attempting solutions.

We will get somewhere in these courses if we introduce the lawyers to environmental problems. Then we can turn out some people who are more alert to the threat to the environment. We can make a contribution by conveying information, a function that is sometimes looked down upon in law school. But in this field there is quite a lot of information that needs to be conveyed—just main substantive information. What is the law? What are the facts? What is some of the technology?

We can make a contribution by trying to work toward solutions of these problems with our students, illustrating the difficulty and the thought processes that are necessary. Maybe one thing we can do is try to turn out people who will help make better decisions about how to use resources.

Beyond these environmental goals I think some of us have more abstract educational goals in attempting to teach a course on resource use. The resource course, as I see it, is somewhat different from the usual law school curriculum in three ways. First, it is interdisciplinary. Law schools have had too much of a tendency to assume that lawyers work independently of everyone else.

Second, the subject matter cannot be dealt with adequately through a study simply of appellate judicial opinions. That is how we teach most law school subjects and it is unfortunate, because there is an awful lot of law in this field (and in some others) that is not found in appellate opinions. Somewhere along the line students ought to deal with the non-appellate law.

And thirdly, to use the common term, this is a relevant subject. It gives the students something of an outlet for their desire to do something positive, and it helps show the students that law has a function in modern society that is not just a consideration of problems no longer of any significance.

So, we are trying to do two things. We are trying to use the resource course as a vehicle for training lawyers generally, sharpening some skills that they might not use as well in other courses, and we are trying to impart some learning about conservation problems and how they ought to be approached.

Now, whether this meets the needs of the conservation associations I don't know. I would be interested in hearing the views of some of the people here—trial lawyers and conservationists—about what they would expect and what they hope the law schools would do to help those in the field.

MR. JORLING: Have you determined that your courses respond to student demand or have you designed the courses to stimulate students into this area?

MR. CORBRIDGE: Our own summer program was not developed in response to student demand. I think there has been an increased student demand for more work in the natural resources area along traditional lines and this is indicated by the size of classes, if nothing else, and desire for greater offerings in this particular field. But I do not think that there has been any measurable widespread student demand for courses that are specifically oriented to preserving the quality of the environment.

MR. JORLING: In other words, you have sensed no student shift, say, from what has been popular in the law schools recently, a shift from the poverty or the legal-aid fields into the environmental area among the students. I am interested in whether law students are reflecting what we sense in the rest of society.

MR. CORBRIDGE: There is an increased concern about a noticeable lag between what students read in the newspapers and what they suggest to the curriculum committee. But the option to suggest courses isn't always available to them.

MR. CURRIE: Our students are still much more interested in poverty than they are in conservation, but we are hoping to divert some of their energies.

MR. LEFCOE: I was going to ask Jim Corbridge while he is speaking here just to summarize how his course works. It is rather an unusual model for law school classes.

MR. CORBRIDGE: Ours is basically a summer intern program that takes advantage of some slack time in the students' schedule. We are more concerned with an in-depth exposure to particular problems than we are with covering a wide area of subject matter.

It is really two semesters and an intervening summer. The first semester is devoted to study of administrative law, ecology, economics, some chemistry and engineering, but basically research in ecologically oriented material in a setting of administrative practices. Then the students go out in the summer and work for 10 weeks on a pre-selected project with one particular agency at the state, federal or local level that has either a primary or collateral concern with environmental quality control. They come back in the fall, give presentations, discuss material and bring in agency personnel, finishing up with a major paper that is pretty much determinated by the project. It might be model legislation, traditional legal research or a critique of agency operations. Our present program is for 12 students a year.

MR. TARLOCK: I would say that the picture is a lot more mixed. I was just out at my alma mater, Stanford, where there is a course entitled Conservation Issues that focuses on the Bay area. Because of Stanford's emphasis on writing, it is a restricted course. The instructor indicated that he has been under tremendous pressure from the students to expand the enrollment. There, I think, conservation and student radicalism seem to be fusing.

At my own school, Indiana, when I first announced a course more or less slanted along these lines there was a great deal of student interest. I take kind of a dim view of this, however.

When it appears to some students that they are not going to be able to just emote about the problems, but may actually have to work, there is some slackening of interest. (Laughter) This is a problem that you face in areas that are contemporary and relevant.

MR. HINES: Most of the courses and programs that have been described and probably will be described are very small programs in the total law school picture. There has been a notion abroad in the law school community for a long time that subject matter really doesn't count for very much in law school, that actually what we are teaching is process, so you can do it in one context about as effectively as you can in another. Capitalizing on this theory, we have adopted the tack in our freshman program at Iowa of using environmental quality, we call it resource planning, as a unifying subject matter to introduce the student to administrative procedure and to the planning function of law in a number of problem areas. In the process, we are subjecting our entire first-year class to a treatment of environmental quality problems, not particularly for the sake of environmental quality as a subject matter but because it meets the test of relevance that Dave Currie was talking about a moment ago, and it raises some of the nicest current problems that we can try to work out through the legal process as it is now evolving. We are almost incidentally exposing the law school to the environmental quality problem.

Now, responding to the question of whether this is stimulated by student demand, our students are mostly Midwesterners, usually no more than one generation removed from the farm, and they are strongly moved by conservation issues once they learn about them. But our local issues perhaps are not as dramatic as they are in the wilder country or on the coasts. Once the freshmen are exposed to this they become very interested in the whole problem. As yet, we have not really experienced the phenomenon taking place on the West Coast where militant students are actually taking up the conservation issue as a cause.

While I am speaking let me respond to one other question asked very early about whether we are doing the job of preparing lawyers for employment in conservation.

Two years ago, almost to this day, I attended a conference in Denver sponsored in part by the Mineral Law Foundation, put together by the resource industry in conjunction with the law schools. The problem was to determine how law schools could turn out more and better people to perform lawyerlike functions for the industry. Joe Sax was there, as I recall, and we had somewhat the same discussion about whether law schools actually could do something to help.

After a day and a half of discussion we reached the conclusion that what the industry actually wanted was good lawyers who were interested in working for the industry. The subtle pitch, at least to the western law schools, was to try and interest more good law students in this kind of a career possibility.

I take it that we have somewhat the same situation here today from the other side. What we really need are able, competent lawyers willing to contribute or participate on the conservation side in some of these battles. Whether that happens will depend to a large extent on whether the law school stimulates this interest. In terms of the number of lawyers needed, I suppose the small-group approach is adequate. There is reason to believe that law schools are beginning to turn out a group of people who are really interested, well informed, and likely to become involved.

MR. LEFCOE: So, Bill, people would take your resource-oriented class, learn some economics and related matters. Many will become interested in resource problems who otherwise might not have. On graduation, those who remain interested and have become more competent and knowledgeable than law students ever were in this subject area, will have two choices. They may practice corporate law and occasionally, *pro bona publica,* represent conservation interests. Or they may take one of the many attractive opportunities in industry, practicing resource law for, say, the petroleum people. Some students will make one choice, some the other, and both groups will be equally improved in their competence and fattened in their numbers by your class.

MR. HAIK: Just a comment on that. Your last statement ignores the reality of private practice in the resource area. What this gentleman is producing in Iowa is the kind of awareness about social problems that we need among lawyers. Some 75% of the practice in our 13-man firm comes from public law work and not from the private sector. We need lawyers who are aware of the problems and who are concerned and willing to work in the public area. Soon you are going to have to make the choice between going to work with industry or going to work for conservationists at night.

MR. BENNETT: When you get out of law school there will be somebody from Tennessee Gas Transmission or Humble Oil or some other producing industry and if you are married and going to have some children you must elect between $20,000, $25,000, $30,000 or more a year assured income, or doing conservation work part-time.

Now, that is no choice. The system is against helping conservation causes because the corporations have all the money. Unless you change that, this is just part-time legal aid to save society. That is all it is.

MR. CORBRIDGE: You have to make a choice, but that doesn't detract in any way from the value of Bill's program or any one of those programs.

MR. BENNETT: I quite agree.

MR. CORBRIDGE: It is dangerous when you start talking in terms of turning out a better conservation lawyer. We should drop the phrase. We ought to just turn out better resource management lawyers, good people who are aware of these problems.

All we are doing is expanding the scope of the materials that are covered to make students aware that these other problems exist and it is possible to do it within the framework of the traditional courses.

MR. BENNETT: Resource management lawyers today are working for the real resource managers of America, basically the oil and gas industry, the mineral extractors and all the rest. That is where they are working. They are managing your resources and you had better face up to that.

MR. LEVINE: Isn't it all the more important, then, to train them to be sensitive to the kind of problems involved? Resource management is both the representation of future interests in present activities and considering an activity's compatibility with other activities in the environment.

MR. BENNETT: Of course, but give that boy a real choice, not to be just a poverty lawyer all his life but a well-paid conservation or poverty lawyer. The way it is today, economically there is no real choice unless you want to be an ascetic like Ralph Nader and possibly never get married.

MR. LEVINE: Gee, I don't see too much success out here, either.

MR. HAIK: You just insulted me. I work in the resource field and I don't work for a corporation. I work in the public sector through special-purpose governmental units, institutional forms that are new, that are growing and should be growing in the country to deal with resource management problems. If all that law school in Iowa does is acquaint the future lawyer with how we make the resource decisions in this country, I am satisfied that that young student, if he is idealistic about social problems in the urban centers, will be astute enough to come to the same conclusion that I did many years ago: that is, I don't like the way we make the decisions.

Now, we have two choices coming out of this whole conference today. We have Mr. Yannacone and the others saying that the answer lies in the great litigation route. Some of us have gone that route and are still going that route. But the answer really lies in the public awareness—the law does change, as Professor Green noted when he quoted Holmes. The common law does reflect the attitudes of society and the "felt necessities of the time." We need students coming out of law school who are aware of the environmental problems, who are aware of how a resource decision is made, and who have insights into how you can change the subtle legislative process affecting the use of the resource.

You can make these legislative changes and you can also do it by using litigation to highlight the problem. The choice is not simply: "Do I work for the oil and gas industry or do I work as a poverty lawyer?" You may not make as much money, but we have lawyers coming into our office out of law school who want to work in a small group. The only thing is, we don't have that much work to give them. But they will come and we have had some come for $2,000 or $2,500 a year less than they were offered by major firms. They want to work in this area because they were made aware back at Iowa Law School.

MR. HANSEN: Let's look at this matter from another angle. There are a few of us here who are lawyers and also directors of conservation organizations, all of whom are notoriously poverty-stricken, and if we had available just one student, we would double our legal staff overnight. Hopefully we in the Rocky Mountain region will be the beneficiaries of this summer intern program that Jim Corbridge described. The University of Denver Law School is also starting an intern program that may help us.

Now, you can call the impact of these programs small, but if Mike

McCloskey in San Francisco and Ben Nason in Massachusetts and Brock Evans in Seattle and others like them could have available at their neighborhood law school a ready made intern, this alone would double their capacity to perform the legal services that Hank Foster outlined. It might seem like a lot of minor detail such as bylaws and so forth, but this is the guts of the stuff that we have to do on the firing line. This is where the real world is.

MR. LEVINE: You are asking us to fight again in the law schools the battle that some of us have fought and thought we resolved with respect to poverty issues. We would not like to regard our students as a form of relatively cheap labor for causes, however worthy, unless they are going to learn a great deal from the experience. We are being paid outrageous sums of money that still don't pay the even more outrageous costs of educating them. They deserve to get the most educational value for that money.

We have set up extensive clinical programs in the poverty area and have found that we have to be very careful in designing these programs or else the students become law clerks in a very worthy cause, getting the kind of education that 70 or 75 years ago we abandoned as an inadequate form of legal education.

You will get your hands on these students after they graduate, we would hope, and they will be able to really do a job for you. They won't be just a group of people who have six months more experience than they otherwise would have had when they start out.

MR. HANSEN: But it will be years before I can afford to hire some of the products of this experience.

MR. PLAGER: Maybe we were wrong 75 years ago, Mike.

MR. LEVINE: That is conceivable. In rejecting completely the experience of the law office, we were wrong, but we need not return to it in the form that we abandoned it, that is, simply placing law students in a relatively unstructured clinical situation and saying "Learn by experience." It seems to me that what we have learned (and if we have come full circle we have come full circle at a slightly higher level) is that you can place law school students in a rather controlled clinical environment, ask them to question what is happening and to analyze what they are doing. Unfortunately, the more you do this the less useful they are to the organization with whom they have been placed. In fact, at U.S.C. we are tending more and more to use artificial clinical situations because they are more manageable from an educational point of view, although not necessarily useful at that moment to the community at large.

MR. CORBRIDGE: Let me add in response to Roger Hansen that although I think sending a man to ROMCOE for the summer would be an excellent educational experience, ROMCOE and other conservation-oriented groups are rather atypical agencies for our program. A more typical agency is the Corps of Engineers, and that is a long way from throwing warm bodies into the trenches. It's throwing them into the trenches, but not to fight. (Laughter)

MR. HANSEN: It's digging the trenches.

CONGRESSMAN MCCLOSKEY: I would like to ask the panel a question having to do with legal ethics. The issue came in very strongly yesterday morning. I think most environmental lawyers would concede that this is a field of law perhaps more demanding in the matter of legal ethics than any other. As soon as that law student of yours graduates and practices law in practically any community in this country, particularly the smaller towns, eight or ten citizens are going to come in and ask him, "Will you help us block this dam that the local power company wants to build on our favorite trout stream?" or "Will you help us block this cement plant?" They are going to go to him because he is a new young lawyer and is not known to charge large fees.

What are the law schools doing to apprise these young men who are now aware and going out to throw their bodies into the trenches that there are really severe problems of legal ethics focused on yesterday by Mr. Yannacone when he said, "Let's invent a cause of action, no matter how outrageous; let's test the issue and make the public aware of it."

The first time that young lawyer calls a press conference to expand and publicize his cause he is probably violating the canons of ethics. Yet, as I recall, most courses in legal ethics are taught by somebody who never practiced law and is not aware of these practical problems.

MR. HINES: Let me respond. Law schools are moving away from the course in professional responsibility and moving toward a more functional approach. Questions such as ethics are taken up within the subject matters where they naturally arise.

I have been a teacher of such a course for two years and the first problem you raise is not one that I had thought of. Not having an adequate practice background, it is not one that was readily apparent to me. I appreciate your raising it. I assure you it is one that will be discussed in the future.

This perhaps highlights the need for a good interchange between the teaching lawyer and the practicing lawyer about the real problems that these cases generate.

MR. CORBRIDGE: Along those same lines, as a negative response to your question, I suppose that running the kind of program where a student gets his credits by going out and stirring up trouble is hardly an ideal way to point out the ethical problems.

MR. LEVINE: At the same time, you know, there are two dimensions to that question. A great deal of what we call legal ethics is really a kind of guild hall mentality that is intended to keep as many people as possible out of the trade or at least keep those in the trade from stepping on each other's toes. In another context we would call those antitrust violations. U.S.C. did have, until last year, a course in professional responsibility and will probably have one this fall. We have changed our emphasis in that course, though, from the traditional droning through the canons of ethics to a general questioning about the structure of the legal profession. This accomplishes a lot of what has been discussed here this morning—it asks which of the canons of ethics are intended to protect clients and which are intended to protect lawyers. Some canons are protection against the immoral conduct of a fellow lawyer but more often they are directed against his "unsportsmanlike" conduct in competing with his fellow lawyers. Because we have such a shortage of legal services (since we can't afford the kind of legal services that we say we need, especially in the public area) the time has come to question the extent to which these restrictive practices have artificially raised the cost of legal services to the whole society. There is pressure for paralegal services in the poverty area, and I have no doubt that in the environmental area some of the same skills could be taken up.

I have no doubt that Professor Sanders could in a year of part-time study probably learn enough law to serve some of his purposes and that he could competently, and perhaps more competently than most lawyers, do some legal work to advance his purposes in the cause of conservation.

MR. DURNING: I note the session is entitled "Opportunities and Mechanisms to Meet the Needs." All through yesterday and today the word money has been repeated again and again. That seems to be more need than opportunity, but in other fields things that we haven't even discussed yet have been happening rather rapidly. We are getting to them gradually.

This panel started off, gentlemen, as if you were the academicians on the hill at the university of a thousand years ago, as if this were a nice pleasant exercise in professional education, and that there really isn't any urgency involved. Yet, Professor Roberts and others have asked how much time we have in a livable environment. If we are in an environmental crisis, the scale of response is not yet in step. If we believe that, then we need more rapid and larger-scale responses than have yet been approached through small-group seminars and internships from law schools.

The fact is that the poverty program did produce some revolutionary things in legal ethics and methods of practice.

I believe the solution to the money problem lies in group practice. I would like to hear some comment about the possibilities of consumers' unions or labor unions negotiating into their contracts prepaid legal care with benefits for environmental causes in planning, zoning and air pollution, just as they build in the benefits for workman's compensation claims and the like. If large numbers of people were covered by insurance plans negotiated with employers that included benefits for environmental causes, then we might have clients that we could support.

Maybe it is a wild idea, but Brock Evans told me another. The first stage of the conservation movement was when we rushed to the legislatures. The second stage was when realized we couldn't get there fast enough, so we are rushing to the courts. The third stage is the Green Panthers. (Laughter) Can the legal response work soon enough or will we go into the third stage?

MR. CORBRIDGE: Everybody would agree we are short of time. I don't think there is any dispute about that. And the only thing I would say is, if we want to talk about crash programs, let's get out of the educational area. Universities, believe it or not, are still in the business of educating people, not solving the world's problems by bringing lawsuits and forming battalions of students to race out and activate their own preconceived notions.

MR. LEVINE: Would it be relevant for universities of law to provide model statutes to change legal ethics, to provide group practice programs that include environmental law?

MR. CORBRIDGE: Absolutely, if you can answer yes to one question: Does it have some educational value?

MR. LEVINE: Does it?

MR. CORBRIDGE: If you have a proposed program, put it to the educational test.

MR. LEVINE: The students at the University of Washington are saying if it doesn't have some relevance it doesn't make sense as an educational experience. I would say if it is relevant, maybe it is educational.

MR. BENNETT: It is quite plain that the law schools are uncommitted to this particular cause. There is just no question about it.

MR. LEVINE: Is it the role of the law school to be committed to particular causes?

MR. BENNETT: Maybe the system says it's supposed to be that way, but you are collectively uncommitted and that, for the most part, is why you are getting these neutral graduates.

MR. LEVINE: Well, George mentioned that you could characterize courses as active and passive and, contrary to my performance yesterday and today, I am afraid I teach a passive course in that sense.

MR. BENNETT: In California you would not be permitted to teach a course in the techniques of blocking the construction of nuclear plants on the California coastline, would you?

MR. LEVINE: My dean would permit me to each anything I care to, I suppose.

MR. HOFF: A great deal of what you say is true, but by the same token, my own experience has been that of all the institutions that need reform, education perhaps needs it the most. And sometimes I think all of you might take a look at your so-called educational tests.

What is educational in the context of today's problems? There has been a great failure on the part of our colleges and universities as a whole, without singling out any particular department, to review what constitutes education in today's terms—including the techniques, I might add.

MR. CORBRIDGE: Phil, I would make a distinction between trying to teach students to recognize these problems and cranking up a bunch of robots. If you just acquaint students with the facts of the environment they will see the need. If you want to propagandize, we don't need universities. We can get ad agencies to do that.

MR. MOORMAN: I don't want them to propagandize but I want the law schools to act. There has been a big movement toward clinical legal education recently, with sincere students working with full-time lawyers in the poverty area, handling cases. If every law school had a clinical legal professor who would similarly bring environmental actions, we would be on a par with corporate counsel. This professor would supervise and educate the students while filling a desperate need.

MR. SIVE: That still doesn't answer the ethical problem that I mentioned yesterday and that was cavalierly treated. The canons of ethics still say in the judiciary law of New York that the lawyer shall not encourage and promote litigation. He shall not speak to the press, and you still have a problem of champerty. Somebody with a little bit more time than we have to study ethics should guide us and tell us how to meet the problems.

Now, there is one thought that has occurred to me on several occasions, being a conservation organization officer and a lawyer litigating its problems. I know this matter has been raised in the courts with reference to civil rights groups, particularly the NAACP Legal Defense Fund. Perhaps they have evolved an answer, but somebody has to study the canons of ethics as now written because the one who will face the proceeding of the bar association can't simply say that some professor said the system is wrong.

MR. LEVINE: I am sorry to have sounded cavalier, if that was your interpretation. I think all I was suggesting in my own overdogmatic way was the same sort of thing that has been suggested here. The university basically exists to examine what is, and to make students aware of the implications of what exists. What we do when we study the canons of ethics is to make law students aware of the fact that they are inadequate to meet today's conditions.

Now, I suppose that does not teach them what to say when they are hauled in front of the local bar committee. I suppose we don't have really good answers for that problem. The NAACP Legal Defense Fund and others have apparently worked out problems in the way that practicing lawyers do, just by litigating them. There are several relatively sympathetic courts and the Supreme Court decided *NAACP v. Button* and all those other good things.

CONGRESSMAN MCCLOSKEY: May I respond to that? If the goal of the law schools is to turn out lawyers who are aware of environmental problems then I think you have an obligation greater than you have in other fields to acquaint students with the perils they are going to face immediately on graduation. In California we have found that many of the kids who were suspended or disbarred were not aware of the ethics problem.

MR. LEFCOE: If I can report consensus, I think that we are all impressed with the importance of that suggestion. If we don't seem to respond to it, it may be that it catches us short, largely because there are so few occasions when academic people and practicing lawyers have these exchanges.

There might also be a consensus that one of the most important things law schools can do is not only inform the students about the existing state of legal ethics but help students join a community of those who would amend or remove the most indefensible canons.

MR. TARLOCK: To amplify that, last year I thought of devoting considerable time and resources to the problem of class actions to control air and water pollution. Then it suddenly occurred to me that, aside from the technicalities of class actions under the federal rules, I didn't know a thing about what would happen if one started litigating. It looked like a terrible ethical problem. Next year I will try to correct that within my limitations.

In the last few years many of us in teaching have been more concerned with the development of environmental quality standards by administrative agencies than with their enforcement through the courts. I think in the future there will be an increased emphasis on litigation since we now have quality standards in many areas. This will necessitate an infusion of professional responsibility materials into the courses.

MR. TIPPY: I would like to suggest another topic for the agenda in the matter of operational skills. I think Dan Tarlock's paper made a very good point—the lawyer in this area can't operate as the elegant generalist that his classical three-year legal education is designed to create and that the few courses in resources helped significantly to depart from. It is my observation that in New England more than nodding familiarity with engineering terms is just about essential, and I wonder if you think the law schools have the capacity to provide this.

Now the issue of interdisciplinary approaches, I would assume, is resolved. Mail certainly is strong on this. Yale turns out people who speak fluent economics and fluent planning, but the sort of lawyer that speaks fluent engineering is very rare.

Whether we speak of civil engineering or public health or pesticides or any of the technological areas, how can we get the lawyer with a commitment? Many of them from now on will be matriculating the first year with interest in the environment, but how can the law schools put in this technological fluency?

MR. KRIER: I have heard a lot of dissatisfaction voiced with legal education specifically and education in general. I suspect that the conservation movement—and it probably is a movement now—is where it is today almost wholly because of what formal education has contributed to the public knowledge and awareness of what is going on around us. So today, when we are talking about the environment, we don't just talk about how nice green grass is. We can talk in sophisticated ecological terms.

As far as the law school's job is concerned, everyone here seems to talk about his experiences as though that were the only relevant horizon, so I will do that, too, for a minute.

Based on my experiences I don't think that there is a legal-service supply problem. There is a demand problem affecting interested young lawyers. I know literally tens—and that is a large enough number, literally tens—all right I know literally thousands (Laughter) of young lawyers who want to go out and work for "causes" including the conservation cause. The law schools have already done far more than their share to create a demand for the supply they are producing. It gets kind of silly because we get in a circle. We perceive a need, so then we create a supply of lawyers to go out and answer that need, and then there is no demand. By demand, too, I mean you have to give these people something to live on, because lawyers do make their living practicing law. They do a lot of it at night for which they don't get paid. We are supposed to create a demand for the supply created and at the same time are criticized because we haven't created a different kind of supply.

I think you, too, have a responsibility to create a demand for the kind of people that exist today that want the kinds of jobs that you want them to take.

I had a fellow in my office the other day who had what I would call modest credentials. He was Phi Beta Kappa, Berkeley, and cum laude from Harvard Law School. That may or may not be good, I don't know. He had just taken the California Bar exam and he wanted to work, believe it or not, no, not for air pollution. (Laughter) This fellow wanted to work against air pollution. He was something of a zealot, and he didn't really care how much he got paid as long as he could feed his wife, who was a small woman. (Laughter) So I called the County Counsel's office in Los Angeles first. I talked to some lady there, I don't remember her name, which is for her own good, I think.

I said, "I have a fellow here who is a lawyer and he wants to work helping you in your air pollution problems. Do you think he could come down and talk to someone about a job?" And she said, "He is a lawyer?" I said, "Yes." "Does he have a background in chemical engineering or something like that?" I said, "Lady, you know, a lawyer drafted the air pollution law. This guy can do something for you." She said, "Well, we don't hire people just to work on air pollution. They have to do other things, too."

So, then, I called the Los Angeles Air Pollution Control District and I had a long distance call in to HEW to see if they would just give him some money under the 1967 Act just to think about air pollution for a year when I remembered that UCLA might have some money of its own to hire this guy.

What I am trying to suggest again, because I guess my experience is a relevant horizon, is that there is a real demand problem, not a supply problem, and if anybody can create a demand for people who want to work for conservation causes, I for one can tell you where you can get supplies of people who incidentally did not graduate last in their class at Taiwan Law School but really are very well qualified people. (Laughter)

MR. NASON: May I suggest that there really isn't a demand problem but a capacity to finance the demands that we have. There is a lot of demand. It is just that we don't have the resources to be able to hire the people who are available.

MR. KRIER: I guess it is how you define demand. I have always thought demand is more than saying, for example, "You can be the mother of my child but I don't want to marry you." (Laughter) Demand means I want to hire you. I want you to work for me for pay, for something in fair exchange. Now, there are certain limitations. I can't pay you $25,000 a year. Okay. But a lot of students today don't want to go work on Wall

Street. They don't want to go work for big Washington firms and for conglomerates. They really want to *take on* a lot of those interests and they can do it very, very well. In fact, I think pretty soon the legal talent out of Wall Street is going to do better than the legal talent in Wall Street.

MR. STEVENS: I think that perhaps the problem comes when the brilliant student, introduced or not introduced, comes to the door and says, "I want to be an environmental lawyer or I want to be an air-pollution lawyer."

This is fine. We can certainly use environmental lawyers and air-pollution lawyers, but the fact remains that in any office of any size or scope it is necessary to conduct other types of practice, too.

The preferable approach would be to say that I am interested in public service. I am interested in environmental problems. I am also interested in practicing law because I think basic to a successful practice in environmental law is the ability to practice law generally, the ability to produce evidence, the ability to analyze points, the ability to understand procedure and to carry on a successful law practice. I think it would be unfortunate to encourage students to reduce themselves to a narrow specialty, because the conversations of the past panels have convinced me that as a specialty *per se*, there are relatively few places left for the full-time environmental lawyer. There are a great many places available and mine is one office that I think would welcome with open arms the good lawyer who is capable of conducting a good practice and who is also interested in and perhaps has special abilities in this field.

MR. KRIER: I don't want to disagree with your choice of words but I think environmental law is a big enough field so that one is generalizing enough if he specializes in environmental law. Frankly, I think specialization is a good development in the law. I know, for instance, that the best United States attorney's office in the world, in the technical competence sense, is in the Southern District of New York. I think anyone who has ever had the unpleasant experience of defending a case up there knows that those people are good. They know all the relevant bodies of law they have to deal with and it is an awfully large area.

MR. PLAGER: I am glad Jim Krier made his statement because it certainly gives us a warm feeling as to what some of the law schools are doing, but I think we also have to look at another facet of the problem.

In yesterday's discussion there was, I thought, a pretty general understanding and consensus about the limitations of certain institutions, such as Congress and various agencies, to deal with different kinds of problems. I think there are also limitations on universities generally and, relevant to this topic, law schools are not fully appreciated. These are limitations that are inherent in the institutional role *vis-à-vis* other institutions in society, and they are limitations that arise from our own perceptions.

By and large, anybody who looks to the universities and to the law schools to make a major contribution toward solving environmental problems is looking into an empty hole. The kids have been marching into the universities in the last few years telling us *we* have got to solve society's problems. *We* have got to end the war in Vietnam. I think most of the academics here have found themselves being called by various presidents and chancellors and ordered to go meet and try to solve these problems. I don't know why they turn to the law faculties, but typically they do. The law schools have been very much aware of the fact that the institutions are not only unable to solve the war in Vietnam, but equally unable to solve the problem of how to get competent secretarial help to type the reports so that they can tell people they can't.

Legal education has been generally accepted over the years. We have been able to fake it very well because of what lawyers have been doing over these years. In the past they have gone out in little country towns to hang up their shingles, or they have gone to Wall Street where they make a lot of money.

We thought we taught them how to recite the litany and the myths that are a part of the trade. Now, as Jim suggests, many of our students today don't want to go out and play the practitioner bit. They want to do a lot of other things and they think we are going to train them to do it. The truth is, of course, that we don't know what makes a good lawyer.

What we do know—or think we know—is that there are certain kinds of things that most people who work in this field find useful. A lot of us think that what is useful no longer means doctrine and rules, but something else. We aren't quite sure what that something else is, so we are busily setting up new programs. The clinical bit is the latest attempt to kid the students into thinking that they are really getting something they can use, the idea being that we are going to give them a taste of the real world. But I think we have come around the Toynbean circle when somebody suggests that we now are setting up simulated clinical situations.

MR. Krier: The next step is a simulated law teacher. (Laughter)

MR. PLAGER: All I am trying to say is that we do have a role but I think we all have to recognize that our role as academic institutions is really a very limited one in terms of what we can actually do. It seems to me that if our problem is how to develop a certain type of professional competence in a specific field, maybe we need to give some thought to alternative institutions.

MRS. STRONG: The joint program we have just started at Penn speaks to this. This is the first year we have offered a four-year joint program in city planning and law. We have eight law students in the program this year and there were more who applied. Since we also have joint programs with operations research, civil engineering, and regional science, we had to limit the number. We have Ph.D. students in economics, planning, sociology, and public administration who are taking many of the same courses, which should provide a useful interchange. I think that law students particularly need resource economics, a basic course in ecology, and a systems course.

With such courses we will turn out people who are better trained. More city planners than law students come to the program with bleeding hearts. They are the ones who, long before the law students, have had a desire to go out and spend much of their time working for a volunteer organization. We have felt the need to push them towards some of the rigors of law school.

But on the other hand, many of the students at the law school have felt that there is insufficient opportunity to learn more about the substantive areas that interested them first, such as poverty. Now the interest in the environment is increasing.

I am very interested in the University of Colorado's summer program. We have had this only for the poverty people so far, for both law students and for planning students, but we haven't had it in the environment.

MR. CORBRIDGE: There are time limitations on using the interdisciplinary approach. Students may get only a cocktail party familiarity with the subject. A far more efficient way of doing it is simply to attract to law schools people who already have this information. We have done very little of this, possibly because of an old folk tale that the only route to a law school is through the Department of Political Science. Utter nonsense.

MR. LEVINE: We have been telling people for some time that the important thing in terms of pre-law preparation is simply learning any discipline well. In fact, I have a pet theory that if I could ever attract a music composition student to law school he would probably make a superb lawyer because he has learned to manipulate a symbolic system in a very complicated way. This would probably train him very well to master the ins and outs of procedure and trial tactics.

But let me make a plea in general for the thousand-year university that has been so roughly treated here this morning. Everyone here is talking about "training" and "warm bodies for the firing lines," and next we will hear about bodies to stack up to make dikes. I suppose that those are all useful things to teach people to do in a metaphoric way. But I would like to make a plea for understanding the consequences of various ways that we have organized society and trying to figure out what went wrong, what it means to go wrong, and what it means to be doing it right. We should try to educate people about what our objectives really are in organizing society and how we can tell whether what we are doing is right. The interesting thing is that the economists have gone over to econometrics and the political scientists have gone over to some of the more arcane corners of political theory. In fact, nobody seems interested any more in the problems of organizing society. I would make a plea for teaching this in the law school and would submit that this is not entirely irrelevant over the long run to getting the kind of environment we want.

MR. MOORMAN: You are too modest. I am a little bit disturbed that so many high-powered law professors here take such a retiring role in this environmental business. Frankly, the environment is far more important than classical legal education, which is simply a tool.

The biggest array of talent we have in this country outside the corporate structure is you professors and your students. Maybe you ought to hire a lawyer or two and start sponsoring a few lawsuits. You can do it. You have the libraries, you have the talent, and you can consult with your colleagues. Frankly, someone must do this. The corporate legal establishment is pretty big, and I am not sure the lone practitioners can take it on unless they get strong institutional support. You are the people to do it and don't say you can't. You can.

MR. PLAGER: How long do you think the state universities will survive if they start sponsoring legal actions to shut down all the corporate interests that control the legislature?

But I think all that Jim Moorman is suggesting is that we have a reserve of legal talent now inefficiently employed in terms of solving environmental problems.

MR. MACDONALD: We have another area of demand, which I am sure all of us have been aware of but that hasn't been considered in the discussion. That is the demand for legislators. I have seldom been aware of the fact that I was teaching a student who was about to be a legislator, and yet all of us are aware that a large percentage of Congress, the state legislatures, and people in a policy-making position in the administrative agencies throughout the country are lawyers. If we can give them some insight into problem solving in the environmental area and make them aware of what the present law is and is not able to accomplish, maybe they can in the long run do as much through awareness as we do through litigation or through attempting to influence legislation. Of course the students themselves are seldom aware that they will become legislators. Yet the impact here can be tremendous.

The other thing I want to mention is in this interdisciplinary area. There should be increasing emphasis on interdisciplinary classes or seminars where students go out and find problems, learn the facts, talk about solutions, and, when possible, are put in teams—one lawyer and one graduate student who is a biologist or a limnologist or a structural engineer—to train each other. They would at least become acquainted with each other's approach and each other's language.

MR. BALDWIN: I want to get my licks in just once without being too critical of my own law school represented here by Mr. Currie. Unfortunately, he wasn't teaching environmental law four years ago.

It seems to me that environmental law courses should be compulsory in the first year for all the reasons that Mr. Currie discussed earlier.

The kind of courses that are now compulsory or are necessary to pass the bar exam—contracts, torts, property, tax or modern real estate—hardly excite the imagination of many law students. It has been possible for one to come out of law school with a jaundiced view of a lawyer's possibilities and absolutely no indication of how much he can do in behalf of the public in the environmental field.

MR. LEVINE: Mal, I think the problem is that you are before your time.

MR. ROBINSON: I am the only student in this room and I can't get a course at Columbia University Law School on environmental subjects.

VOICE: Transfer.

MR. ROBINSON: Beyond courses in environmental law, I think there is a need to impress on the legal teaching profession not represented here that there is a role for some environmental law in all courses; so if you want to teach legal methods through an environmental course, fine.

Further, recognizing the legal service needs of those who "have no rights," or are poor and gasping, helps define the function of the law school and the legal profession. If the law schools provide uniform codes or ideas for uniform codes, might they not also inquire into the structure of the legal ethics with a little more vigor? Perhaps too, Jim Krier is right in saying that the firms and the people who are in the profession have bigger responsibilities here than the law schools. Certainly many more practicing attorneys have got to go into a place like Columbia or other law schools and do a little prodding on their own and then offer jobs, as they do in the civil rights field. It should be possible to work for a firm in Wall Street and take time off, without a loss in income, to work in environmental affairs.

MR. MOORMAN: Do you realize the potential conflict of interest the Wall Street firm has in this field? I know one firm has considered setting up a public service law branch and it isn't easy to do.

MRS. STRONG: I have explored it in Philadelphia. A major firm agreed at first to release people for two situations: one was airport location and they said they had clients involved, and the other was stream pollution and they had industrial clients involved in that. They said, "You find something that won't be controversial and we can help."

MR. MONTGOMERY: It can be done. I have the year off with pay from Arnold and Porter to develop cases in the environmental field as well as in the poverty field.

MRS. STRONG: Can you sue any of Arnold and Porter's clients?

MR. Montgomery: No, but we don't represent everybody in the world, contrary to what *The New Times* reports. (Laughter)

MR. LEVINE: The theory being that Covington & Burling will sue your clients and you will sue Covington's clients?

MR. DURNING: We shouldn't criticize because it is not perfect. It is a big step forward. I have never heard of it before. My mind boggles at the idea that any major firm would give a man of that talent a year off. I think we should have a committee that calls on other firms to do the same thing. I know it is not perfect but I think it is great if you take on Covington's clients and vice versa.

MR. LEFCOE: Is there anyone who thinks that Arnold and Porter ought not to do this, just forget it? Let this man go back and practice the way he practiced last year?

MR. YANNACONE: I will not mention the name of the firm, but two years ago I was asked to report to the National Audubon Society on the possibility of a major lawsuit against the Army Corps of Engineers involving the Florida Everglades and their drought. I suggested a Ninth Amendment suit and a direct attack on the sugar trusts and the developers and a few other people involved.

Two senior partners of a major Wall Street law firm were called into that meeting to review my proposal. After four hours of cross-examination, the two lawyers left and wrote a report to the foundation that was going to fund the case that said in words of one syllable that if I was successful on these theories, the attack would be so broad and the precedents so great that the American private enterprise system, which they represented, would be in jeopardy. They would not condone National Audubon Society's lending its name to any legal attack that was so radical.

Later on that summer, that same partner called me and said they had hired a group of *Harvard Law Review* students to come and prepare a memorandum for a client. They had taken good notes on my theory but they had missed a few points and they wanted to know if I would go into New York and meet with these students and give them the information. I said, "Write me a letter and I will send you an opinion, and by the way,

is this a public service operation?" "Oh, yes, it is a public service operation." "Will you tell me the name of the clients?" "No." "Who is it for?"
"It is going directly to the client." "Well, you are sure it is a public
service?" "Yes." "Are you going to pay me a fee?" "No." "Are you
receiving a fee?" "We can't tell you. It is a public service job."

After this went on for about 15 minutes and they kept telling me it was
my public duty to inform their undisclosed clients of everything I knew
and thought on the strategy of this lawsuit I finally told them, "Gentlemen, the last public service your firm performed was to bury the
founder," and I haven't been bothered since. (Laughter) I have great
respect for the Wall Street law firms. They represent all the might of the
legal profession and, as Ralph Nader said, they represent the head of the
profession. The legal profession, like a dead fish, rots from the head
down.

When the Pennsylvania State Bar Association called me to talk about
environmental law in Pennsylvania, I opened by telling them the legal
mind has been likened to a steel trap and for the past 100 years it has
behaved like a steel trap, rusted shut. But let's cease the anecdotes and
get back to business.

We are trying to talk to professors about what to do in law schools, and
at least one thing has been missed. Professor MacDonald, who was
hosting me while we were in Madison, Wisconsin, trying DDT and a few
other people, tackled the problem of writing an ecologically sophisticated, politically feasible pesticide law. Now Representative McCloskey and everybody else who is familiar with Congress knows that
Gaylord Nelson has been trying to ban DDT for the past five or six years
and so have a number of other legislators. But what nobody seems to
realize is if you ban DDT, it is probably going to be replaced with dieldrin
which is a hundred times more biologically active and probably a hundred times worse.

Professor MacDonald and I tackled the problem of writing the law
from the point of view of enforceability and this is what the law schools
must do. Ninety percent of the legislators in the state of New York are
attorneys. In the whole course of their legal education the only exposure
to legislation they ever had was seeing an appellate decision that rendered the legislation constitutional or unconstitutional. The only effective legislation is the legislation that is enforceable. Therefore, you ask
if it can be enforced by an agency? Can it be enforced by the general
public? If it is enforceable by an agency, will the limited vision of the
agency cloud the effect of enforcement? We discovered with the pesticide
laws that exist, or were being proposed, that if the pesticide control board
was going to be controlled by conservationists it was a good law. If it was

going to be controlled by the Department of Agriculture it was a bad law. We have litigated most of the bad laws and the good laws aren't enforceable, so we decided we would write a law that is immune to the makeup of the board. How? By providing for procedural due process, providing for adversary procedures and having the board sit as judge, rather than judge, jury and executioner.

The law schools should teach their students that a good law is an enforceable law, and that the law must be enforceable by any special interest group who might have a case—citizen, legislator, administrator, public interest organization, industry—even the worst exploiter in the world should be entitled to procedural due process. And if you look at the hundreds of environmental bills including the Air Pollution Control Act and Federal Water Pollution Control Act you will find out that very few of them are enforceable in the trial sense. This gets us to the final part of what I want to say. There has been no talk about educating the trial lawyer. Presentation of evidence is the part of environmental law that counts. A great deal can be done in the way of public education and by lobbying—that dirty word—if you want to risk your tax exemption. But where the defendants, or in the DDT case, where the National Agricultural Chemical Assocation, can spend $1.5 million to buy advertising space in the media, how are you going to meet that public relations attack? The only place you are going to be able to raise the questions that have to be raised is in a forum where the issues are tried—something akin to an administrative proceeding of an adversary nature or a lawsuit. Yet, all around the country many of the lawyers who would like to help have no tools.

This gets to the prerequisites of how to become a lawyer. Very few lawyers will come to law school with any scientific background. One big failure is our inability to provide a way of continuing legal education, in the nature of environmental or ecological survey courses, right there at the law school. The other failure is that in the entire law school education process, there is very little room for encouraging the student to go into the courtroom when he gets out of school, or even sometimes during school, and utilize the tools, tactics and techniques allowed by the rules of evidence and good pleading practice. There the lawyer can frame environmental issues, so that you can then go back and meditate in the hallowed halls of the law school and figure out what ought to be done legislatively.

It is nonsense to spend three years reading nothing but appellate opinions and forgetting that the underlying basis of those opinions was facts developed in that courtroom—probably butchered because somebody didn't do it right.

This is the big failing I found in the law schools and in my own law school education.

MR. CAVERS: Probably the law teachers of America are the only group in the whole field of higher education that could spend as many hours as we have spent this morning and never allude to a research function. This is a peculiarity of our tribe because we have been able to perform research in the interstices of our teaching duties and this research up until rather recently has been thought of as wholly adequate.

Environment is a field where we have to know something. We have to know not only some of the scientific impacts of technological developments on the environment but also a great deal more about what is actually being done by way of law enforcement, by way of response to law enforcement by those to whom the enforcement efforts arc supposed to be directed.

It seems to me we can consider our educational responsibilities not only in terms of disseminating learning to students and providing a training function, but also in terms of whether lawyers can't add to knowledge.

In this area it is going to be very difficult for them to work wholly in isolation from other disciplines. There is perhaps a more vivid need for interdisciplinary work and research here in teaching than in most fields. But I believe we ought to recognize that this is one of the responsibilities of the legal educational system.

It is going to be difficult to discharge because the law schools have been set up on a "B" budget basis. They have been able to have a faculty that is relatively small in relation to student body and they don't have the large array of students that have provided other disciplines with shock troops in research.

I think the kind of joint program we have just heard about at Penn is going to be emerging in a good many schools. I know it is at Harvard. I am not sure whether we have gotten to the city planning school as yet, but it is, I think, one of the trends that is coming to the fore, and this will help to correct the imbalance on the research side.

MR. TARLOCK: I just want to make three comments which I think will amplify what Professor Cavers has been saying. First, it is probable that most of us here, while a little paranoiac, are regarded by our own faculties as somewhat unsound or at least curious because we read things other than West's advance sheets and the *Harvard Law Review*.

The second is that actually we are quite close to what Vic was saying. It seems to be if we do concentrate on what we perhaps too cryptically call the process, we are providing students with exactly the skills needed to draft legislation and appreciate why it is or is not going to work.

The third comment amplifies what Professor Cavers was saying. The disillusionment with clinical programs in large part stems from the fact that the information flow-back to the universities is very minimal. I was hoping a program like Jim Corbridge's and others will get a greater informational inflow into the university and thus into teaching and research projects.

MR. HANSEN: Let me say something about the interdisciplinary dialogue that has been raised about eight times this morning.

Yesterday I suggested that we have to seat in one great orchestra economists, sociologists, ecologists, paleobotanists, sociologists and architects, and conduct them in one grand environmental symphony. But the discussion is going this morning as though we can make a one-man band out of every lawyer.

MRS. STRONG: I certainly didn't mean to suggest that we at Penn were going to turn out a lawyer-ecologist or an engineer-civic designer. We share the fear of trying to turn out a generalist who knows nothing in depth. We have gotten into the joint degree program because it is terribly important that we prepare someone with a general background in the field of environment but also with a specialty.

MR. LEVINE: The function of interdisciplinary studies in the law school—interdisciplinary studies is probably the wrong name for it—is not simply to have a dialogue with some other profession.

I am teaching the problem of organizing the society in those areas in which we want to marshal resources for productive use. I don't see how I can teach my students to make intelligent noises about such problems if they do not master certain concepts. I do not make economists out of them. I am not an economist myself. I am a lawyer who has had a little bit of training in economics.

The purpose of what I am doing is, once again, to make them good lawyers. One of the functions is to train people to deal with these things intelligently at the legislative level and that means also training them to understand the subject area about which society is legislating. And it seems to me that the best thing we can do there is to teach them those aspects of the other disciplines that enable them to do their job better—not to turn them out to be qualified lawyer-economists, or qualified economists who have had a touch of law. It is all a question of what problems you are trying to solve and what skills you need to solve them, and it is only within that framework that I think interdisciplinary material, if that is what you want to call it, means anything.

MR. CURRIE: A word on the other side of the same question. I don't think we need to worry that we are watering down unduly the legal content of the law school curriculum. There is a great deal of slack in that curriculum right now. We don't need three years to cover the basic legal concepts we are teaching them. There is plenty of room to teach them a little more in addition.

MR. CORBRIDGE: Inflexibility is the problem. Has there ever been a professor who didn't think that removing his course from the curriculum would be the end of civilization as we know it? Curriculum reform is much overdue and I say that so somebody who is not a law professor won't have to.

MR. LEFCOE: One of the functions of this discussion it seems to me is for law teachers to hear the kinds of things that people in the field are concerned about—and we have heard a number of things. People here have talked about not so untraditional skills that don't have anything particularly to do with environment. How do you appraise legislation? How do you draft it and how do you design studies to appraise whatever legal structures you have set up?

But, you see, none of these are uniquely environmental. These are skills that one could use in absolutely any subject matter you can conceive of. The question that occurs to me is whether there is such a thing as resource management. Is this field totally anecdotal? Is each experience really unique? Are they linked only on the one hand by traditional skills, trial strategy, legislative drafting, legislative appraisal, and on the other by a certain amount of scientific information which, from the discussion of standards yesterday, I gather is itself largely anecdotal in the sense that there isn't a lot you can say in the way of promulgating general standards without knowing specific scientific contacts. If we are creating programs in environmental law, is there a management science? Are there strategies, institutional or litigatory, that have special connections from one resource area, one resource dispute, to another that we can study? If not, the choice of environment as the focus of inquiry may simply have the effect of increasing interest, increasing legislative interest on behalf of students who will be legislators or students who may go into trial work, but it does not itself constitute a law subject in any special sense.

I would not necessarily complain about that incidentally. I don't think such a conclusion speaks against having these classes. There is a lot more reason for conducting classes in environmental contexts than for classes in a lot of other contexts we have.

MR. GREEN: I get into this field of environment through the back door. I get into it because the main field of my interest is the relationship between law and science and technology.

I am the director of a program at George Washington Law School, now in existence for five years, that involves a cluster of five seminar courses, each looking at the interface between law and science-technology in a somewhat different manner. The fact of the matter is that probably the most important consideration in all of these five courses is what science and technology are doing to the environment. This area of science and technology *vis-à-vis* the law, *vis-à-vis* the environment, may not cover the entire area of environmental concern but I think it does cover a very substantial portion of it. I believe that here we have a unique subject that I would define as follows:

First, how do scientific and technological developments affect the substantive law?

Second, how does the response of the law to scientific and technologic development in turn affect science and technology?

And third what is the process by which private and governmental bodies—private and governmental actors in the evolution of science and technology and the law—make their decisions? Who makes the decisions on the basis of what inputs of information? And how should it be done in the public interest?

MR. LEFCOE: I want to ask you something about this. Can you make statements that are meaningful, that are neither obvious nor fairly trivial, and which hold from one environmental or scientific setting to another? Or is it all anecdotal in the sense that you can only make statements that apply comfortably to a particular instance? Can you make a meaningful statement about the relationship between law and technology that has predictive force?

MR. GREEN: You can.

The general conclusion that I have reached, and I am not sure it is completely valid as applied to all instances of environmental abuse stemming from science and technology, is that we must draw a distinction between that type of environment use that is a product primarily of profit-seeking investment in our society and that kind of environmental abuse that is the consequence of government's interference in one way or another with the market structure: that is, government-sponsored, as opposed to privately sponsored, abuse.

Now, whether this distinction has complete validity across the board I do not know, but I do think this is one way of defining the problem. Indeed, one of the problems I have is that those people who are trying to create a structure for technology assessment have not made this distinction, which I think is crucial.

MR. LEFCOE: What kind of statements can you make about this distinction that are significant to those people who want to see it better?

MR. GREEN: Well, I would say that when government steps in to accelerate the development of any particular technology, the effect of government intervention is largely to preempt the operation of the market system and the operation of the legal system as determinants of the rate of technological advance.

MR. CURRIE: George, when you start with a field nobody knows much about, things are somewhat anecdotal, but it is not long before you can start utilizing the traditional lawyer's process of induction in the hope of developing some general principles. And I think as we continue to work in this field and to treat it as unified because of some of the common physical and technological problems overlapping the various areas, we will discover increasing numbers of common elements.

I hope, for example, that we can work toward the development of general conservation strategies, to what extent it is useful to use legislation, to what extent it is useful to go to the courts. I think we can work toward the development of methods of problem solving and resource management, the proper role to be played by something like benefit-cost analysis, the proper role to be played by a conservation ethic. We can work toward a common body of law that might have application to a number of different resource problems. We can work toward a common understanding of the proper role that science plays in the solution of certain kinds of legal controversies. One way that we can approach this entire problem is to make very intensive studies, interdisciplinary studies wherever possible, of very narrow particular problems.

This is one place where law students can come in by participating in research projects and where the law schools can do something other than teaching. They can participate in the development of a body of knowledge.

MR. YANNACONE: You certainly asked the key question. Is there any overview body of knowledge technique that can put some of this in general perspective?

There are two. One is systems analysis and the other is operations research. They are two sides of what basically amounts to the same mathematical coin and they have one key element that has been totally lacking in this whole discussion for two days, and that is the feedback mechanism.

In January 1969 I made a proposal to the Ford Foundation that furnished an answer to the questions of what we do about the lack of feedback both to the scientific community and to the legal community, and how we account for and capitalize on the awesome addition to the body of knowledge on pesticides, since the first lawsuit, as a result of the need to overcome evidentiary problems during the trial.

The proposal was very simple. Let us take the academic science community that is interested in the environment as represented by a number of environmentally oriented scientific organizations, and gather them in a consortium much like the Associated Universities that have handled atomic energy research. Let us take the big law schools that are interested as represented here and gather them in consortium. Let us take those who would go forth and litigate with the special skills, whatever they might be, involved in litigation and gather them in consortium. And let us feed back and exchange the demands and the needs of one group with the other.

For example, let's say the scientists say they can prove that the reduction of species diversity because of DDT is bad for the environment. I go to court and bring a lawsuit. In the middle of the lawsuit we suddenly discover that there are three missing pieces of data. We pick up the phone and call the scientist who called in the first place and say, where is the data? He says it is going to take five years to get it. You tell him that the hearing is next Thursday and he must have it by then. The following Thursday, with luck and good fortune (as happened in Wisconsin), he comes up with the data.

The same thing applies when we are about to be dismissed because we have raised a Ninth Amendment argument and nobody has heard of the Ninth Amendment and nobody can find a copy of the Constitution to look it up. We pick up the phone and we make some frantic calls around and, lo and behold, a week later we have a brief on the Ninth Amendment.

What is involved? The process of interdisciplinary feedback without the attempt to squeeze a particiular group into a new mold. Leave everybody in their molds, in their own particular place. Open the lines of communication not just in one direction, but make sure the feedback is fed back where it can be meaningfully acted upon. Unless the major law schools and the minor law schools that can afford it and the major scientific organizations and the trial bar agree that each has something to tell the others, and, more important, that each has some questions to ask the others, we will get nowhere. We will be trying to make monsters —people who are experts in everything and knowledgeable about nothing.

I don't ask the law schools to turn out a bunch of law professors or a bunch of trial lawyers. The best regional planner that a regional planning school or regional planning group turns out is only as good as the local zoning law. To sit in a vacuum in a vast room and talk about zoning and planning without recognizing the fact that there are regional planners around the corner who have something to say is to waste the time of the law students and the law professor as well as to frustrate the regional planner.

Gentlemen, let's put the people in their proper perspective, open the lines of communication and listen for the feedback.

MR. FOSTER: I must say that I have a growing conviction that a prime need is some mechanism that can link the academic world with the world of reality. I don't mean only law professors, but other university scientists, and specialists as well. And I speak with some feeling on this, having been a state administrator and having been astonished at how little the academic world often really knows about the priority needs of a particular state.

If we can establish the kinds of relationships we have discussed between the people on the firing line and the people in the institutions, I think we can not only make an input into the educational process, but also provide help to private organizations and public agencies. Most important, we can keep the academic community really up to date on some of the issues now being debated.

MR. HOWE: It seems to me that all of you and perhaps the average attorney across the country has a great deal of competence that is needed by the civic constituency of environmental quality, especially at the community and state level.

The town conservation commission that wants to develop a new ordinance, the League of Women Voters group that is trying to analyze a piece of state law or a proposed law, the Nature Conservancy chapter that needs help acquiring a piece of land—all of these groups will require a lawyer's help. I hope that in the next session we can develop some recommendations on how to apply your legal competence to these places of need.

Conclusion

Mr. Philip H. Hoff
Rep. Paul N. McCloskey, Jr.

MR. HOFF: As you may know, I have been on a seven-year sabbatical from the law, including that year when I did nothing but campaign. In all honesty, as I sat here listening I think I had forgotten how knowledgeable attorneys are, and I hadn't quite realized they were the source of all solutions to our environmental problems.

Perhaps I am a little less optimistic than some of you with respect to instituting the theories under either the trust fund or the Ninth Amendment, but I am more optimistic about what will happen in a legislative sense. We are going to be deluged with environmental legislation from all quarters in the period of the next few years. Therefore, one of the greatest needs emphasized time and time again here is the need for enforceable draftsmanship.

For example, we have outlawed all off-premise billboards in Vermont and have severely limited on-premise billboards. From a draftsman's point of view it is one of the worst pieces of legislation that I have ever encountered. We accepted this as a price of getting it through with the thought that ultimately we would clean it up.

This is just one of many cases where model legislation would have been useful—prepared and submitted to interested people in various states.

I am optimistic that major environmental solutions will come through legislation if for no other reason than when industry sees the writing on the wall, it is most likely to accept reforms that would apply equally to all rather than to put a few at a competitive disadvantage.

The legal actions to date have served a very useful purpose primarily, I think, in focusing public attention on the issues and scaring the hell out of industry. Industry now lives in mortal fear of lawsuits, particularly in terms of the delays involved. And we are also getting some new responses from regulatory agencies that have been notably absent before. For example, the Atomic Energy Commission appeared with 36 people in a public hearing at Burlington, Vermont, last night.

This was the first time that the AEC had ever appeared at such a forum in this particular manner. And so there are encouraging signs.

Which brings me to the matter of priorities. The more serious things —those that threaten our very existence—we hopefully will respond to immediately. Those dealing with aesthetic values, which are terribly important to most of the people in this room, will be harder to come by.

The middle and lower middle classes are still much beset with the business of earning a living. They aren't going to give much of a damn about aesthetic qualities if somehow these qualities interfere with the ability to earn a living. This is a hard fact of life. We must do a better job of making the ordinary citizen understand that aesthetic destruction has an impact on him as well. We should understand some of the psychological costs of closing people off to access to clean water and clean air and a place to sit on a rock and just let the stream go by. Perhaps, as this psychological evidence continues to mount, we can convince more people of the importance of aesthetic values.

CONGRESSMAN MCCLOSKEY: It is fortunate perhaps that since the Constitutional Convention, when I think 33 out of 55 of the framers were lawyers, that two-thirds of the Congress generally are lawyers. They do not seem for the most part to be lawyers from large cities. They run heavily to small town types, and for that reason I think there is great hope that conservation is going to have a very, very sharp focus in Congress in the next few years. The man who comes from a small town, who sees a city encroaching on it, who sees the streams that he has fished become polluted and populated with summer cottages, is inclined to feel a strong motivation to conserve and to protect.

Now, Congress and the executive branch are in a position to move with increasing speed to honor conservation principles, but their education is somewhat lacking. And I would like to speak to that point for just a minute.

First of all, I want to suggest that there is a vehicle that hasn't been discussed today: the investigative committee of your state legislature or Congress. The time of these individuals is taken up with so many problems that it would be of immense assistance to them (and to me, in particular) if someone with expertise on a given problem in his local community, seeing the need for developing facts on a subject such as a nuclear power plant or a power line or stream pollution, were to write to his congressman on one of the relevant committees suggesting that hearings be held on this subject. I would go so far as to suggest that in that letter you indicate the witnesses you feel should be called that would cast light on the given subject, that perhaps you list specific questions to be addressed to those witnesses, and that you attach a bibliography of documents so that the congressman can know as much as those witnesses do. Then, as any cross-examining lawyer must do in the preparation of his case, he can extract the facts by virtue of his own knowledge of the subject.

This would have been of immense help to the congressional committees that recently investigated the Santa Barbara oil spill, where congressmen were largely unacquainted with the technical details. If we had known what was requested by Professor Sanders I think we could have extracted that information. Unfortunately, sometimes we may abuse our power as congressional investigating committees. We are not bound by all of the rules of the Fifth Amendment and some of the rules of relevance, some of the rules of hearsay. Unfortunately, some of our members aren't bound by propriety in the types of questions that they ask. But I think we are geared to extract facts and put them into the public realm, and we can be of assistance in that respect. Every lawyer in this room could be of assistance to legislative bodies if he would write that kind of letter to his legislator.

Perhaps the true enemy of preservation of our environment is our own system of government. By that I mean local governments and county governments, entirely dependent upon the property tax and the increase of their payroll structure, are the true enemy of conservation today. It may be that we must revise the entire tax structure of the United States. It may be that conservation can never take place so long as a local government, which has charge of the primary things to be conserved, must for financial survival get new tax bases, new development, new payrolls into its boundaries.

I think that law schools might very well be the ones to coalesce the necessary fields of expertise—the economists, the planners, the geologists, the various scientists.

Also, I think population growth is a major problem that law schools might address. We may need a national abortion law and a national land-use policy. We may need to ask, when developing new towns to absorb population in the next 50 years, what kind of corporation we should charter. Should we do as the English did with the old trading-colonizing companies, the Virginia Company and the Massachusetts Bay Company?

What do we do to take care of a population that will double in the next 60 years? Where do we put these people? By what form of legal mechanism do we create the garden cities that we have been talking about for 70 years? How do we do this if each locality has the right to zone, if we don't have statewide zoning as Phil Hoff has suggested?

In Hawaii, where they have statewide zoning, and in Denmark, where they have established conservation, agricultural and urban areas, men have shown that they know what to do when they condemn somebody's land: they take a scenic easement. The man has to be paid for his land. But what do we do when by zoning or governmental action we improve the value of his land? We do not have the legal mechanism by which to take that increment of value of the man's land and say, "Your land will be urban, a new town, and thereby increase in value 50 times." We have no way to apply that increment in value to the cost we are going to expend when we say to the next man, "Your land is so lovely we insist you retain it for farming."

This is work for lawyers. Law schools have an obligation to focus on these problems, to draw all of these conflicting sciences and disciplines together.

Finally, I offer a precise recommendation to conservationists. Our great problem has been lack of information. When you tackle a utility company or you tackle the Atomic Energy Commission it is very difficult to find experts outside those areas, particularly in industry, who are not bound to testify on behalf of their particular clients.

I recall trying to find an expert to testify against the Pacific Gas and Electric Company on underground transmission in the Woodside case some years ago. No private power company engineer would testify because of an agreement among private power companies that precluded them from being disloyal in their war with public power companies. They really didn't want to testify against one another. And even in the public power field it was hard to find an engineer who would dare to suggest the possibility that transmission lines should go underground and create a precedent that would be followed throughout the country.

Now, I think that the way to lick this problem of information is for our conservation groups to latch onto experts from among those who have been considered the enemies of conservation or among those against whom a conservation battle is being fought. Let me list one example.

Last month a very wonderful individual retired. He had been the Corps of Engineers District Engineer in San Francisco. Rather than allow him to go back into some industry-related organization, the Sierra Club might possibly hire this kind of man to tell them how to do battle with the Corps in the next 10 years on the filling of waterways, the damming of river systems and this sort of affair.

If we can get the ablest men who have been connected with the development process, we can begin to know how to attack and slow development down, to turn it around. I suggest that we form some sort of central clearing house from which it will be made known who can testify on what matter, who is an expert on the internal problems of the utility companies, the Corps of Engineers, the chemical companies.

Perhaps the answer to conservation lies in the very industries that have been polluting the atmosphere. By gaining expertise from those individuals associated with those industries, we can add to our ability to conserve and preserve. I do not know one company that despoils the atmosphere of the landscape that does not have some employees who resent bitterly what that company is doing, and would be the first to offer information in some way if they would not lose their jobs or the chance to advance in them.

RECOMMENDATIONS

Following the remarks of Mr. Hoff and Congressman McCloskey, participants and observers were asked to suggest specific recommendations for action after the conference. The major suggestions, in addition to those made in previous sessions, are summarized below.

Environmental Law Reporter. A legal information service was cited by most participants as the greatest immediate need. The conference generally endorsed plans of The Conservation Foundation and the Public Law Education Institute to set up the *Environmental Law Reporter.*

Plans for the *Reporter,* as described by Mr. Baldwin and Mr. Alder, were undertaken in response to widely voiced requests for legal research and basic information useful to lawyers confronting environmental issues as advocates, counsellors, government officials, and teachers. The *Reporter* would be a comprehensive information service issued monthly in loose-leaf form, cumulating to 1,000 to 1,500 pages. Separate sections of the *Reporter* would be: Newsletter, Court Decisions, Administrative Proceedings, Statutes and Administrative Regulations, Analytic Comments, Digest Bibliography, and Index. Part of the information service would be to make available pleadings, briefs and other legal documents to interested lawyers.

A spokesman for the American Trial Lawyers Association (Mr. Jeans) noted that ATLA had established an Environmental Law Committee and that the *Reporter* could be tied in with the Committee's planned seminars for ATLA's 23,000 members, each of whom represented a prime source of information to the *Reporter.*

Mr. Brenneman suggested that there was additional need for an early warning system about major environmental modifications and proposals, permitting public comment and criticism before the event.

National Environmental Law Organization. An organization similar to the American Civil Liberties Union is needed in the environmental field, pointed out Miss Kessler. The organization would be primarily volunteer—offering help to citizens seeking environmental protection—with local and national professional staff brought in later.

Law School Research for Environmental Lawyers. Mr. Sive suggested the need for law school mechanisms to channel research to practicing lawyers lacking the time and resources to do it themselves. Mr. Carmichael noted that this kind of assistance was best left to environmental law student clubs, and cited the opportunity for a national network of such groups. Law students might take the lead in university-wide interdisciplinary efforts in the environmental field, said Mr. Roisman. Observing that student interest in the environment was on the rise, Congressman McCloskey pointed out that it needed translation into specific opportunities for work that might be handled by a national clearinghouse. Mr. Jorling noted that law student help could greatly aid congressional committees and their staffs.

Speaking for young law professors, Mr. Tarlock suggested that they not be required to wait so long before taking sabbaticals. Instead, they should be encouraged to engage in environmental research, establishing expertise early in their careers. Research might entail working for and "psyching out" an administrative agency or experimenting with interdisciplinary studies in the university.

Alliance with Political Leaders. It was suggested by Mr. Tufo that those seeking changes in environmental laws ally themselves with sympathetic political figures running for local and state executive offices. And Congressman McCloskey noted that political candidates over the next decade might find conservation the strongest single interest of the electorate and a potential source of political strength.

National Land-Use Policy. Mrs. Strong emphasized the need for reallocation of land-use powers, economic planning and population distribution plans at the national level. The Congressman observed that various congressional committees were making some progress but were still moving slowly. Discussing the importance of the Public Land Law Review Commission work, Mssrs. MacDonald, Moorman and Hansen stressed the need for independent evaluation of the Commission's reports and legislative recommendations. Mr. Hoff, citing his own experience in Vermont, endorsed the concepts of state land-use plans and state-wide zoning.

Environmental Use Taxes. Mr. Levine recommended that federal, state, and local units of government set up a system of "environmental use taxes" based on the external impact of private use of natural resources. Where for political reasons taxes are not feasible, subsidies in the amount of the proposed taxes ought to be paid.

Future Generations Fund. Mr. Levine further recommended that such a fund be set up by the federal government to buy at fair market value the rights to develop resources in ways that will not deny them to future generations. For each purchase made, the administrators of the fund should consider the value of present use and the probable value of future use, giving appropriate weight to possible technological developments now or in the future that would affect the economic value of the resources in question. Scenic and recreational values should be appropriate justification for purchases by the fund.

Administrative Reform. The administrative system needs to be overhauled to better respond to ecological data, said Mr. Corbridge. New federal legislation on environmental quality, now being considered by Congress, might correct some of these administrative flaws, responded Congressman McCloskey, but the problem of Congressional committee conflict and overlap remains. Mr. Haik emphasized the need for hard analysis of resource-agency mandates and procedures, administrative economic assumptions, the extent of congressional supervision and the environmental effects of their decisions. Because resource allocation would be the primary problem in the future, he suggested that new legislative and administrative recommendations resulting from such studies arc vital.

Ad Hoc Committee. Conference participants generally agreed that an *ad hoc* committee should be appointed to consider the suggestions made and begin to help implement some of them. It was decided that Mr. Howe should appoint such a group. Among the matters suggested for the committee's immediate consideration were ways to finance the litigation of the environmental bar (Mr. Moorman), the finding and creating of positions for those wanting to work in environmental law (Mr. Howe), and helping to educate the public generally to the role that lawyers can play in environmental matters (Mr. Hansen).

The conference adjourned with the sentiment that another should be called within 2 years to assess future needs and past progress.

Environmental Law Bibliography

Contents

I. Bibliography of Reference Works and
Government Documents

II. Bibliography of Legal Articles

III. Index

I. BIBLIOGRAPHY OF REFERENCE WORKS AND GOVERNMENT DOCUMENTS

Prepared for the Conservation Foundation by Cheryl Prihoda

The following bibliography is a guide to reference tools and government documents, related to environmental policy issues, since 1965. Within each of the categories, entries are arranged alphabetically by title. Citations follow the rules outlined in the Harvard Law Review Association, *Uniform System of Citation*, (11th ed. 1967), with some modifications:

(1) The *total* number of pages appears after the titles.

(2) Publishers whose works are not entered under their name are indicated in parentheses before the date of publication. All other materials are Government Printing Office publications; however, they are not necessarily for sale by the Superintendent of Documents (e.g., Committee Prints are generally not available to the public).

Bibliographies

1. Citizens Committee for the Outdoor Recreation Resources Review Commission Report, *Action for Outdoor Recreation for America* 37 (rev. ed. 1964)
   Publications from government and private sources, with annotations and a list of agencies and organizations concerned with recreation.
2. Science and Technology Division, U.S. Library of Congress, *Air Pollution Publications* 522 (Public Health Service Publication No. 979, 1969)
   Includes mostly technical articles and monographs, but also some legal and administrative materials, from 1966 through 1968.
3. G. Bennett & J. Hostman, *Bibliography of Books on the Environment—Air*,

Water, and Solid Wastes 52 (Dept. of Chemical Engineering, University of Toledo, 1969)

An international bibliography of books, journals, and proceedings of conferences.

4. Library, U.S. Dep't of Housing and Urban Development, A/MP-108, *Bibliography on Housing, Building, and Planning* 43 (1969)

". . . [A] selection of approximately 400 recent books and periodicals available in the United States on housing, building, and planning."

5. Library, Bureau of Public Roads, U.S. Dept. of Commerce, *Bibliography on Right-of-way Acquisition* 27 (Supp. 1966)

Contents: Administration; Personnel and Training; Appraisal, Damage, and Compensation; Eminent Domain; Public Utilities; Relocation Aspects; Land Acquisition Methods and Procedures; Billboards.

6. Charles L. Smith, *Bibliography on the Anti-Monopoly 160-Acre Water Law* 7 (1969)

Materials dealing with the workings of the National Reclamation Act of 1902 and related aspects of conservation up to 1969.

7. Council on Planning Librarians, *Exchange Bibliography Series.*

The Council issues many short bibliographies on a variety of specific subjects. Among them, the following contain a substantial amount of law-oriented materials:

M. Knobbe, *Air Pollution*, No. 83 (1969)

L. Betebenner, *City Planning and Zoning in American Legal Periodicals*, No. 28 (1965)

G. Menges, *Historic Preservation*, No. 79 (1969)

C. Stoots, *Metropolitan Organization for Planning*, No. 50 (1968)

G. Hagevik, *Planning for Environmental Quality*, No. 97 (1969)

W. Goodman, *Planning Legislation and Administration*, No. 57 (1968)

M. Vance, *State Outdoor Recreation Plans*, No. 34 (1967)

8. Law Library, California State Library, *Legal Aspects of Air Pollution* 12 (1967)

An alphabetical listing of journal articles, monographs, and documents of various states, which reflects the holdings of the California State Library.

9. Urban Land Institute, *Open Space Land Planning and Taxation* 54 (1967)

A guide to references on the role of taxation in urban open space planning, including land economics, legal aspects of open space action, taxation-land-use relationships, and public finance.

10. J. Pinkerton & M. Pinkerton, *Outdoor Recreation and Leisure* 336 (School of Business and Public Administration, University of Missouri, 1969)

Part I, ". . . a survey of major recreation reference sources published from 1953 through 1967." Part II, ". . . a selected bibliography of references on outdoor recreation . . . from 1959 through 1968." Includes monographs, periodicals, series, yearbooks, and articles, with annotations.

11. Library, Bureau of Land Management, U.S. Dep't of the Interior, *Public Lands Bibliography* 106 (Supp. 1965, 1968)

Citations to holdings in the Library of Congress, Dep't of the Interior Library, and National Archives.

12. L. Caldwell, *Science, Technology, and Public Policy: A Selected and Annotated Bibliography* 2 vols. (Program of Advanced Studies in Science, Technology and Society, Indiana University, 1968-69)

> v.1: Books, Monographs, Government Documents, and Whole Issues of Journals
>
> v.2: Articles in Journals
>
> A subject-arranged list of materials published in English from 1945 through 1967. Some topics included in the concept of science policy: energy, resources and environment, public institutions for policy-making, legal aspects of technological application, and international programs for scientific cooperation. Volume 2 covers more environmental materials than does volume 1.

13. U.S. Dep't of Housing and Urban Development, *Selected Abstracts of Planning Reports* 98 (1969)

> Contains summaries of planning studies supported by HUD throughout the country during 1967 and 1968. Reflects the beginnings of planning that deals with law enforcement, codes and ordinances, government management and coordination, and physical development policies.

14. R. Netherton, *Selected Materials on Highway Law and Administration* 57 (Highway Research Board Bibliography No. 49, 1969)

> ". . . [A] compilation of references to current literature dealing with the problems of development and administration of highway transportation systems. . . ." Includes control of access, air space rights, contract administration, eminent domain, easements, land acquisition and land use control.

15. J. Jacobstein & R. Mersky, *Water Law Bibliography, 1847-1965; Source Book on U. S. Water and Irrigation Studies: Legal, Economic, and Political* 249 (Jefferson Law Book Co., 1966)

> A selection of judicial decisions, statutes, administrative policy statements, non-legal treatises, and unpublished doctoral theses grouped by broad categories and by states. A "Legislative Histories" section summarizes all federal laws on water and their amendments, and cites all documents published concerning them. A separate bibliography on water pollution law is planned for the near future.

Digests, Compilations of Laws

16. House Comm. on Banking and Currency, 91st Cong., 1st Sess., *Basic Laws and Authorities on Housing and Urban Development* 952 (Comm. Print 1969)

> "The laws, Executive orders, and other authorities contained in the print are those which authorize the functions and activities of the Department of Housing and Urban Development, or which are closely related to them."

17. Senate Comm. on Public Works, 89th Cong., 1st Sess., *Compilation of Documents on Public Works and Economic Development* 48 (Comm. Print 1965)

> Analysis of the Public Works and Economic Development Act, Area Redevelopment Act, Public Works Acceleration Act, and Appalachian Regional Development Act.

18. Senate Comm. on Commerce, 89th Cong., 1st Sess., *Compilation of Federal Laws Relating to the Conservation and Development of Our Nation's Fish and Wildlife Resources* 472 (Comm. Print 1965)

"The Federal laws contained in this compilation are in their amended form with certain minor editorial changes and sectional subheadings. . . . Appropriate citations to the U.S. Statutes at Large and the U.S. Code are found at the beginning of each amended statute."

19. *Abatement and Control Development Programs, A Compilation of Selected Air Pollution Emission Control Regulations and Ordinances* 146 (Public Health Service Publication No. 999-AP-43, rev. ed. 1968)

Major cities discussed in terms of their implementation of state and local pollution control laws. "The regulations and ordinances compiled were selected to represent the different methods of controlling emissions by law and to represent varying degrees of control."

20. Senate Comm. on Labor and Public Welfare & House Comm. on Interstate and Foreign Commerce, 91st Cong., 1st Sess., *Compilation of Selected Public Health Laws* 489 (J. Comm. Print 1969)

Includes the Public Health Service Act, Clean Air Act, Solid Waste Disposal Act, and National Housing Act, with statutory provisions in effect as of Jan. 1969.

21. Agricultural Stabilization and Conservation Service, U.S. Dep't of Agriculture, Handbook No. 361, *Compilation of Statutes Relating to Soil Conservation, Acreage Diversion, Marketing Quotas and Allotments, Wheat Certificates, Commodity Credit Corporation, Price Support, Export and Surplus Removal, Public Law 480, Crop Insurance, Sugar Payments and Quotas, Nutrition, Food Stamp, and Related Statutes as of Jan. 1, 1969* 384 (1969)

22. U.S. National Park Service, *Compilation of the Administrative Policies for the National Recreation Areas, National Seashores, National Lakeshores, National Parkways, National Scenic Riverways (Recreational Area Category of the National Park System* 64 (1968)

A compilation of administrative policies that ". . . implement the mandates of Congress and . . . prescribe guidelines for the management of recreation areas." Three main categories are covered: resource management, resource use, and physical development policy.

23. Economic Research Service, U.S. Dep't of Agriculture, ERS-355, *Digest of Federal Natural Resource Legislation, 1950-1966,* 62 (1967)

". . . [S]ummarizes natural resource legislation applicable to agriculture, forestry, and related programs, enacted by the 81st through 89th Congress." A quick reference tool for locating legislation and corresponding statutes.

24. Shepard's Citations, Inc., *Digest of Public Land Laws; Prepared for the Public Land Law Review Commission* 1091 (1968)

"The digest was designed to assemble in one work a brief summary of each of the statutes currently in effect relating to the administration, management, or disposition of public lands. . . ."

25. National Center for Air Pollution Control, U.S. Public Health Service, Pub. No. 711, *A Digest of State Air Pollution Laws* 556 (1967)

Summaries of the essential elements of state air pollution control laws, both existing and proposed.

26. T. Witmer, *Documents on the Use and Control of the Waters of Interstate and International Streams: Compacts, Treaties, and Adjudications*, H. R. Doc. No. 319, 90th Cong., 2d Sess. 815 (1968)

". . . [A]ll of the interstate compacts in force Sept. 30, 1968 among States . . . have [have to do with] the consumptive use of the waters of interstate streams, . . . pollution of such waters, or . . . floods and problems associated therewith."

27. M. Naftalin & J. Earner for the House Comm. on Merchant Marine and Fisheries, 90th Cong., 2d Sess., *Federal Authority for Marine Science Activities* 149 (Comm. Print 1969)

"A study of the legal authorities under which the U.S. Government is conducting and supporting marine science activities." Note especially Appendix A: "A Compendium of Statutory Materials."

28. Document Room, House of Representatives, *Federal Power Commission Laws and Hydroelectric Power Development Laws* 261 (1959)

A bit out of date, but useful in a historical perspective. Laws arranged chronologically, from the 66th through 86th Congress.

29. Bureau of Reclamation, U.S. Dep't of the Interior, *Federal Reclamation Laws, Without Annotations* 204 (1966)

"A chronological reprint of public statutes of the United States affecting the Bureau of Reclamation, June 23, 1959-November 8, 1965."

30. Secretary of the Army, *Laws of the United States Relating to the Improvement of Rivers and Harbors*, H.R. Doc. No. 182, 90th Cong., 1st Sess. 4189 (1968)

"A compilation of laws relating to the improvement of rivers and harbors, passed between January 2, 1939 and October 22, 1966, pursuant to the provisions of section 106 of the River and Harbor Act of 1948."

31. Document Room, House of Representatives, *Laws Relating to Federal Aid in Construction of Roads* 380 (1966)

Chronological reprint of laws from 1912 through 1966.

32. Document Room, House of Representatives, *Laws Relating to Forestry, Game Conservation, Flood Control, and Related Subjects* 607 (1966)

Some specific subjects: game refuges, beach erosion, rural electrification, forest land management, tree planting along highways, watersheds. Laws from 1911 through 1966.

33. United Nations, *Natural Resources, Restrictions, Regulations, Agreements: Oil, Land, Minerals* 98 (International Review Service, v. 10, no. 80, 1964)

Discusses legislation of various countries, and international agreements, several of which include the U.S. An appendix gives resolutions of the General Assembly and the Economic and Social Council.

34. *State Laws Enacted in 1968 of Interest to the Department of Housing and Urban Development, as Reported by the Commerce Clearing House and Other Unofficial Sources* 122 (1969)

Brief summaries arranged by subjects under each state. Some of the subject headings: codes and zoning, land sales regulation, eminent domain, pollution, open space, mass transportation.

35. Foreign Affairs Division, U.S. Library of Congress for the Senate Comm. on Commerce, 89th Cong., 1st Sess., *Treaties and Other International Agreements Containing Provisions on Commercial Fisheries, Marine Resources, Sport Fisheries, and Wildlife to Which the United States Is a Party* 410 (Comm. Print 1965)

A compilation of U.S. multilateral and bilateral treaties both in force and in process as of 1964

Summaries of Legislation

For every Congress, each committee usually publishes a review of its activities in a Committee Print. Some of these prints for the 90th Congress follow, along with other histories of environmental legislation.

36. Science Policy Research Division, U.S. Library of Congress for the Subcomm. on Oceanography of the House Comm. on Merchant Marine and Fisheries, 89th Cong., 2d Sess., *Abridged Chronology of Events Related to Federal Legislation for Oceanography, 1956-66* 39 (Comm. Print rev. 1967)

"A Summary of Federal Funding in Oceanography" and a bibliography follow the Chronology.

37. House Comm. on Interior and Insular Affairs, 90th Cong., 2d Sess., *Accomplishments of the Committee on Interior and Insular Affairs . . . During the 90th Congress* 38 (Comm. Print No. 13 1968)

Summaries of the legislation considered by each subcommittee.

38. House Comm. on Government Operations, 90th Cong., 2d Sess., *Activities of the House Committee on Government Operations, 90th Congress . . .* 187 (Comm. Print 1968)

Reviews investigations, legislation, miscellaneous activities, and committee prints published, for each of the subcommittees.

39. Senate Comm. on Commerce, 91st Cong., 1st Sess., *Activity Report of the Committee on Commerce, 90th Congress* 9 (Comm. Print 1969)

Brief account of the committee's concern with communications, electric power, aviation, consumer protection, transportation, fisheries, oceanography, and wildlife.

40. Senate Comm. on Interior and Insular Affairs, 90th Cong., 2d Sess., *A Brief Presentation of the Committee's History and Jurisdiction, and a Summary of Its Accomplishments During the 90th Congress* 61 (Comm. Print 1968)

Reviews full committee activities and those of each subcommittee.

41. Legislative Reference Service, U.S. Library of Congress, for the Senate Comm. on Interior and Insular Affairs, 90th Cong., 2d Sess., *History of the Implementation of the Recommendations of the Senate Select Committee on National Water Resources* 215 (Comm. Print 1969)

A history of legislation on water resources planning and water research.

42. G. Doumani for the Subcomm. on Oceanography of the House Comm. on Merchant Marine and Fisheries, 91st Cong., 1st Sess., *Oceanography in the 90th Congress* 84 (Comm. Print 1969)

Summary of ". . . major events of concern to both bodies of Congress, which took place in 1967 and 1968, . . . [giving] background information, legislative measures and results of hearings and Congressional action."

43. Subcomm. on Science, Research, and Development of the House Comm. on Science and Astronautics, 90th Cong., 2d Sess., *Policy Issues in Science and Technology: Review and Forecast* 54 (Comm. Print 1968)

Summarizes the activities of the subcommittee, delineates areas of science needing further investigation, and suggests new methods of meeting some critical problems.

44. Science Policy Research Division, U.S. Library of Congress for the Subcomm. on Science, Research, and Development of the House Comm. on Science and Astronautics, 91st Cong., 1st Sess., *Science, Technology, and Public Policy During the 90th Congress* 343 (Comm. Print 1969)

". . . [I]lluminates the two principal aspects of governing science and technology: fostering science and technology, their resources and applications; and controlling these applications to prevent or mitigate unwanted, unanticipated side effects."

45. Senate Comm. on Public Works, 90th Cong., 2d Sess., *Summary of Legislative Activities and Accomplishments* 110 (Comm. Print 1969)

Summary of the committee's activities, such as authorization of river and harbor flood control projects, legislation on curtailing air and water pollution, and authorization for regional development projects. An appendix lists all hearings held pursuant to each bill.

Indexes to Congressional Hearings, Reports, and Documents

46. House of Representatives, *Calendars of the United States House of Representatives and History of Legislation* (final eds.)

A complete index to all bills and reports of both the House and Senate for each Congress. Bills are listed numerically with a complete history of all actions taken, including the committees from which they were reported, the report number, dates of passage, and resultant law number. A subject index lists bills with their assigned Senate and House numbers.

47. Senate Library, *Cumulative Index of Congressional Committee Hearings*, 74th through 85th Congress (1959, Supp. 1963, Supp. 1967)

House and Senate hearings arranged by subject (giving dates, Congress, and bill number); by committee; and chronologically by bill number. First Quadrennial Supplement: 86th through 87th Congress. Second Quadrennial Supplement: 88th through 89th Congress (with an additional section listing committee prints).

48. Science Policy Research Division, U.S. Library of Congress for the Subcomm. on Government Research of the Senate Comm. on Government Oper-

ations, 89th Cong., 2d Sess.-91st Cong., 1st Sess., *An Inventory of Congressional Concern with Research and Development* 4 pts. (Comm. Print 1966-1969)

". . . [A] systematically documented reference work listing all congressional hearings, reports, documents, and public laws on science policy." Committee prints are not included. Some topics: energy, environmental quality, natural resources, oceanography, transportation, and urban affairs.

Part I: 88th and 89th Congresses
Part II: 89th Cong., 2d Sess.
Part III: 90th Cong., 1st Sess.
Part IV: 90th Cong., 2d Sess.

49. *Numerical Lists and Schedules of Volumes of the Reports and Documents of the . . . Congress* (1933-   )

Issued annually. Titles of Senate and House reports and documents listed chronologically, with their corresponding Serial Set number.

Hearings, 90th-91st Congress

The following list is a model of the types of legislation on the environment considered in Congress during a three-year period. All hearings, including those previous and subsequent to these, appear in the Cumulative Indexes of the Congressional Committee Hearings (see entry no. 47).

90th Congress, 1st Session

50. Hearings on *Air Pollution* Before the Subcomm. on Air and Water Pollution of the Senate Comm. on Public Works, 90th Cong., 1st Sess. 4 pts. (1967)

Considers ". . . problems and progress associated with control of automobile exhaust, the Air Quality Act, and related matters pertaining to the prevention and control of air pollution."

51. Hearings on *Electric Vehicles and Other Alternatives to the Internal Combustion Engine* Before the Senate Comm. on Commerce and the Special Subcomm. on Air and Water Pollution of the Senate Comm. on Public Works, 90th Cong., 1st Sess. 550 (1967)

"Bills . . . to authorize an investigation and study to determine means of propelling vehicles so as not to contribute to air pollution . . . and . . . to authorize a program of research, development, and demonstration projects for electrically powered vehicles."

52. Hearings on *Estuarine Areas* Before the Subcomm. on Fisheries and Wildlife Conservation of the House Comm. on Merchant Marine and Fisheries, 90th Cong., 1st Sess. 486 (1967)

"Bills to authorize Federal-state action to protect, develop, and make accessible estuarine areas of the nation which are valuable for sport and commercial fishing, wildlife conservation, recreation, and scenic beauty, and for other purposes."

53. Hearings on *Federal Role in Urban Affairs* Before the Subcomm. on Executive Reorganization of the Senate Comm. on Government Operations, 89th

Cong., 2d Sess.-90th Cong., 1st Sess. 21 pts., 4437 (1966-1967)

54. Hearings on *Governing the Use of Ocean Space* Before the Senate Comm. on Foreign Relations, 90th Cong., 1st Sess. 44 (1967)

55. Hearings on *Highway Beautification and Highway Safety Programs* Before the Subcomm. on Roads of the Senate Comm. on Public Works, 90th Cong., 1st Sess. 46 (1967)

56. Hearings on *Natural Gas Pipeline Safety Regulations* Before the Senate Comm. on Commerce, 90th Cong., 1st Sess. 426 (1967)

57. Hearings on *Policies, Programs, and Activities of the Dept. of the Interior* Before the House Comm. on Interior and Insular Affairs, 90th Cong., 1st Sess. 6 pts. (1967)

58. Hearings on *Review on Highway Beautification* Before the Subcomm. on Roads of the House Comm. on Public Works, 90th Cong., 1st Sess. 1097 (1967)

59. Hearings on *Water Pollution* Before the House Comm. on Public Works, 90th Cong., 1st Sess. 247 (1967)

60. Hearings on *Water Pollution* Before the Subcomm. on Air and Water Pollution of the Senate Comm. on Public Works, 90th Cong., 1st Sess. 721 (1967)
Includes several water pollution bills and a review of the Federal Water Pollution Control Administration.

90th Congress, 2d Session

61. Hearings on *Air Pollution* Before the Subcomm. on Air and Water Pollution of the Senate Comm. on Public Works, 90th Cong., 2d Sess. 3 pts., 1132 (1968)
Includes air pollution compacts and air quality criteria.

62. Hearings on *Environmental Quality* Before the Subcomm. on Science, Research and Development of the House Comm. on Science and Astronautics, 90th Cong., 2d Sess. 588 (1968)

63. Hearings on *Estuaries and Their Natural Resources* Before the Senate Comm. on Commerce, 90th Cong., 2d Sess. 158 (1968)
Bills to study the nation's estuaries, make them accessible for sport and recreation purposes, and protect their natural resources.

64. Hearings on *Highway Safety, Design and Operations: Freeway Signing and Related Geometrics* Before the Special Subcomm. on the Federal-Aid Highway Program of the House Comm. on Public Works, 90th Cong., 2d Sess. 661 (1968)

65. Hearings on *Highway Safety, Design and Operations: Roadside Hazards* Before the Special Subcomm. on the Federal-Aid Highway Program of the House Comm. on Public Works, 90th Cong., 2d Sess. 1243 (1968)

66. Hearings on *Housing and Urban Development Legislation of 1968* Before the Subcomm. on Housing and Urban Development of the Senate Comm. on Banking and Currency, 90th Cong., 2d Sess. 1433 (1968)

67. Hearings on *Intergovernmental Cooperation Act of 1967 and Related Legislation* Before the Subcomm. on Intergovernmental Relations of the Senate Comm. on Government Operations, 90th Cong., 2d Sess. 536 (1968)
Includes also the Joint Funding Simplification Act and the Grant-in-Aid Review Act—bills to coordinate long-range physical planning on the state-local levels.

68. Hearings on *Intergovernmental Cooperation* Before a Subcomm. of the House Comm. on Government Operations, 90th Cong., 2d Sess. 233 (1968)
   Witnesses for the Intergovernmental Cooperation Act of 1968 and other bills on grants-in-aid, land acquisition policies, and uniform relocation.

69. Hearings on *Joint House-Senate Colloquium to Discuss a National Policy for the Environment* Before the House Comm. on Science and Astronautics and the Senate Comm. on Interior and Insular Affairs, 90th Cong., 2d Sess. 233 (1968)

70. Hearings on *Marine Resources Conservation and Development Act* Before the Special Subcomm. on Submerged Lands of the House Comm. on the Judiciary, 90th Cong., 2d Sess. 108 (1968)

71. Hearings on *Natural Gas Pipeline Safety* Before the Subcomm. on Communications and Power of the House Comm. on Interstate and Foreign Commerce, 90th Cong., 1st and 2d Sess. 351 (1967, 1968)

72. Hearings on *Oceanography Legislation* Before the Subcomm. on Oceanography of the House Comm. on Merchant Marine and Fisheries, 90th Cong., 1st & 2d Sess. 229 (1967, 1968)

73. Hearings on *Surface Mining Reclamation* Before the Senate Comm. on Interior and Insular Affairs, 90th Cong., 2d Sess. 375 (1968)

74. Hearings on *Thermal Pollution* Before the Subcomm. on Air and Water Pollution of the Senate Comm. on Public Works, 90th Cong., 2d Sess. 1394 (1968)
   Discussions on ". . . the extent to which environmental factors are considered in selecting powerplant sites, with particular emphasis on the ecological effects of the discharge of waste heat into rivers, lakes, estuaries, and coastal waters."

75. Hearings on *Timber Management Policies* Before the Subcomm. on Retailing, Distribution, and Marketing Practices of the Senate Select Comm. on Small Business, 90th Cong., 2d Sess. 577 (1968) ;
   "The subject: What are the wood needs of the future, and how will they be met?"

76. Hearings on *Uniform Relocation Assistance and Land Acquisition Policy* Before the House Comm. on Public Works, 90th Cong., 2d Sess. 615 (1968)

77. Hearings on *Waste Management Research and Environmental Quality Management* Before the Subcomm. on Air and Water Pollution of the Senate Comm. on Public Works, 90th Cong., 2d Sess. 451 (1968)
   Discussions on the need to establish a national environmental quality policy and federal research activities and strategies in pollution control.

78. Hearings on *Water Pollution* Before the Subcomm. on Air and Water Pollution of the Senate Comm. on Public Works, 90th Cong., 2d Sess. 2 pts., 822 (1968)
   Includes a review of the activities of the Federal Water Pollution Control Administration and consideration of S. 2525 and S. 3206.

91st Congress, 1st Session

79. Hearing on *Control, Regulation, and Management of Fish and Wildlife*

Before the Senate Comm. on Commerce, 91st Cong., 1st Sess., 52 (1969)

Considers bills to grant to the states authority and responsibility for the management, regulation, and control of fish and wildlife on federal lands within their own territorial boundaries, ". . . and to provide procedure under which federal agencies may otherwise regulate the taking of fish and game on such lands."

80. Hearings on *Effects of Population Growth on Natural Resources and the Environment* Before a Subcomm. of the House Comm. on Government Operations, 91st Cong., 1st Sess. 256 (1969)

81. Hearings on *Federal Involvement in Hazardous Geologic Areas* Before a Subcomm. of the House Comm. on Government Operations, 91st Cong., 1st Sess. 184 (1969)

Study to determine ". . . the extent to which Federal agencies, FHA and VA . . . responsibly exercised their authority in these problem areas and . . . whether they have acted . . . to protect the public. . . ."

82. Hearings on *International Implications of Dumping Poisonous Gas and Waste into Oceans* Before the Subcomm. on International Organizations and Movements of the House Comm. on Foreign Affairs, 91st Cong., 1st Sess. 151 (1969)

83. Hearings on *National Environmental Policy* Before the Senate Comm. on Interior and Insular Affairs, 91st Cong., 1st Sess. 234 (1969)

"Bills to authorize the Secretary of the Interior to conduct investigations, studies, surveys, and research relating to the nation's ecological systems, natural resources, and environmental quality, and to establish a Council on Environmental Quality."

84. Hearings on *National Mining and Minerals Policy* Before the Subcomm. on Minerals, Materials, and Fuels of the Senate Comm. on Interior and Insular Affairs, 91st Cong., 1st Sess. 155 (1969)

85. Hearings on *Oil Pollution* Before the House Comm. on Merchant Marine, 91st Cong., 1st Sess. 493 (1969)

"Bills to amend the Oil Pollution Act, 1924, for the purpose of controlling oil pollution from vessels, and for other purposes."

86. Hearing on *Pipeline Safety* Before the Subcomm. on Communications and Power of the House Comm. on Interstate and Foreign Commerce, 91st Cong., 1st Sess. 109 (1969)

87. Hearings on *Policies, Programs, and Activities of the Dep't of the Interior* Before the House Comm. on Interior and Insular Affairs, 91st Cong., 1st Sess. 6 pts. (1969)

Briefings with the several bureaus within the Department.

88. Hearings on *Population Trends* Before the Ad Hoc Subcomm. on Urban Growth of the House Comm. on Banking and Currency, 91st Cong., 1st Sess., pt. 1, 803 (1969)

89. Hearings on *Radiation Standards for Uranium Mining* Before the Subcomm. on Research, Development, and Radiation of the Joint Committee on Atomic Energy, 91st Cong., 1st Sess. 414 (1969)

90. Hearings on *Resource Recovery Act of 1969* Before the Subcomm. on Air and

Water Pollution of the Senate Comm. on Public Works, 91st Cong., 1st Sess. 495 (1969)

"A bill to amend the Solid Waste Disposal Act in order to provide financial assistance for the construction of solid waste disposal facilities, to improve research programs pursuant to such Act, and for other purposes."

91. Hearings on *Uniform Relocation Assistance and Land Acquisition Policies Act of 1969* Before the Subcomm. on Intergovernmental Relations of the Senate Comm. on Government Operations, 91st Cong., 1st Sess. 306 (1969)

Consideration of a bill "to provide for uniform and equitable treatment of persons displaced from their homes, businesses, or farms by federal and federally assisted programs and to establish uniform and equitable land acquisition policies for federal and federally assisted programs."

92. Hearings on *Water Pollution* Before the Subcomm. on Air and Water Pollution of the Senate Comm. on Public Works, 91st Cong., 1st Sess. 4 pts., 1584 (1969)

"Bills to amend the Federal Water Pollution Control Act, as amended, and related matters pertaining to the prevention and control of water pollution."

Other Documents

Congressional

93. U.S. Dep't of Transportation for the House Comm. on Public Works, 90th Cong., 1st Sess., *Advance Acquisition of Highway Rights-of-Way Study* 107 (Comm. Print 1967)

A report to Congress, as required by the Federal-Aid Highway Act of 1966, discussing federal and state legal authority for land acquisition, management of property, agency coordination efforts, and planning procedures.

94. Legislative Reference Service, U.S. Library of Congress for the Senate Comm. on Interior and Insular Affairs and the House Comm. on Science and Astronautics, 90th Cong., 2d Sess., *Congressional White Paper on a National Policy for the Environment, Submitted to the U. S. Congress* 19 (Comm. Print 1968)

Part 1, "Aspects of Environmental Management"

Part 2, "Alternatives for Congressional Action"

Part 3, "Elements of Policy"

95. House Comm. on Government Operations, *Federal Involvement in Construction in Hazardous Geologic Areas*, H.R. Rep. No. 429, 91st Cong., 1st Sess. 27 (1969)

"The purpose of the study is to determine whether the Federal Housing Administration and Veterans' Administration . . . have responsibly exercised their authority in areas of potential geological instability, so as to afford maximum protection in housing against hazards. . . ."

96. Subcomm. on Economic Progress of the Joint Economic Comm., 90th Cong., 2d Sess., *Federal Programs for the Development of Human Resources* 2 vols. (J. Comm. Print 1968)

Note especially Part V of Volume 2, "Housing and the Quality of Man's Environment," which includes papers on national housing goals, providing facilities for outdoor recreation, and combating environmental pollution.

97. Special Subcomm. on the Federal-Aid Highway Program of the House Comm. on Public Works, *Federal-State Highway Management Practices and Procedures*, H.R. Rep. No. 1506, 90th Cong., 2d Sess. 110 (1968)

Investigation into states' compliance with title 23 of the Federal-Aid Highway Act of 1956, especially with regard to planning procedures and administrative implementation.

98. U.S. Dep't of Transportation for the House Comm. on Public Works, 90th Cong., 1st Sess., *Highway Relocation Assistance Study* 235 (Comm. Print 1967)

Evaluates existing relocation programs and legislation, and explains a "Joint Development Concept" as set forth in the Federal-Aid Highway Act of 1966.

99. Subcomm. on International Organizations and Movements of the House Comm. on Foreign Affairs, *Interim Report on the United Nations and the Issue of Deep Ocean Resources*, H.R. Rep. No. 999, 90th Cong., 1st Sess. 289 (1967)

Reports the results of the Committee's investigation into legal definitions of "sea," "resources," and "jurisdiction," and presents some recommendations for U.S.–U.N. activities in international cooperation on marine exploitation.

100. John E. Stephen & L. Tondell, for the Subcomm. on Transportation and Aeronautics of the House Comm. on Interstate and Foreign Commerce, 90th Cong., 1st Sess., *Legal and Related Aspects of Aircraft Noise Regulation* 206 (Comm. Print 1967)

Papers presented at the International Conference on the Reduction of Noise and Disturbance Caused by Civil Aircraft, London, Eng., Nov. 22-30, 1966. Titles of the papers: "Regulation by Law of Aircraft Noise Levels, from the Viewpoint of U.S. Airlines," and "Legal, and Related Aspects of Airport Land Use Planning."

101. Subcomm. on Science, Research, and Development of the House Comm. on Science and Astronautics, 90th Cong., 2d Sess., *Managing the Environment* 59 (Comm. Print 1968)

". . . A summary of current information from hearings, subcommittee consultants, and staff studies . . . [concerning] . . . the means by which science and technology can serve the national goals of environmental quality and economic progress."

102. U.S. Commission on Marine Science, Engineering and Resources, *Marine Resources and Legal-Political Arrangements for Their Development*, H.R. Doc. No. 42, 91st Cong., 1st Sess., pt. 4, 204 (1969)

Reports by:

(1) Panel on Marine Resources, discussing the present physical, economic, and legal conditions under which resources are exploited, the deterrents to their development, and future recommended programs.

(2) International Panel, discussing increased U.S. participation in worldwide oceanic development through various suggested legal-political frameworks.

103. L. Caldwell for the Senate Comm. on Interior and Insular Affairs, 90th

Cong., 2d Sess., *A National Policy for the Environment* 35 (Comm. Print 1968)

"A report on the need for a national policy for the environment; an explanation of its purpose and content; an explanation of means to make it effective; and a listing of questions implicit in its establishment." Note two appendixes: B) "Environmental Legislation Introduced in the 90th Congress" and C) "Federal Administration of Environmental Programs."

104. Subcomm. on International Organizations and Movements of the House Comm. on Foreign Affairs. *The Oceans: a Challenging New Frontier*, H.R. Rep. No. 1957, 90th Cong., 2d Sess. 128 (1968)

A report, together with hearings and supplemental summaries by the legal and the economic and technical working groups on meeting the challenges of the ocean.

105. Senate Comm. on Public Works, 90th Cong., 2d Sess., *Recommendations of the Committee on Public Works to the Committee on the Judiciary Regarding the Conditional Consent of the Congress to Various Interstate Air Pollution Control Compacts* 9 (Comm. Print 1968)

Reports on the Illinois-Indiana Air Pollution Control Compact, the Mid-Atlantic States Air Pollution Control Compact, and the West Virginia-Ohio Air Pollution Control Compact.

106. Panel on Science and Technology of the House Comm. on Science and Astronautics, 91st Cong., 1st Sess., *Science and Technology and the Cities* 126 (Comm. Print 1969)

Topics covered at the meetings: urban crisis, urban and interurban transportation, the socio-economic syndrome, the application of science and technology to urban problems.

107. Joint Comm. on Atomic Energy, 91st Cong., 1st Sess., *Selected Materials Concerning Future Ownership of the AEC's Gaseous Diffusion Plants* 495 (J. Comm. Print 1969)

A compilation of several studies and reports, including ones from the AEC, the General Accounting Office, and the Atomic Industrial Forum, Inc.

108. Joint Comm. on Atomic Energy, 91st Cong., 1st Sess., *Selected Materials on Environmental Effects of Producing Electric Power* 553 (J. Comm. Print 1969)

A consolidation of several background documents dealing with the problem of meeting greater power demands while still protecting the environment. Includes excerpts from hearings on the AEC and the environmental effects of nuclear power; a report on the AEC's authorization legislation; and reports by the Energy Policy Staff of OTS and the Federal Power Commission.

109. Select Subcomm. on Real Property Acquisition of the House Comm. on Public Works, 88th Cong., 2d Sess., *Study of Compensation and Assistance for Persons Affected by Real Property Acquisition in Federal and Federally Assisted Programs* 522 (Comm. Print 1965)

Considers all federal land acquisitions—highway programs, public works, urban renewal, military programs—in the context of ". . . the just compensation provision of the 5th amendment and the due process clauses of the 5th and 14th amendments."

110. Science Policy Research Division, U.S. Library of Congress for the Subcomm. on Science, Research, and Development of the House Comm. on

Science and Astronautics, 91st Cong., 1st Sess., *Technical Information for Congress* 521 (Comm. Print 1969)

"A series of case studies of selected past decisions by Congress involving the interface between science and politics." Note the following chapters:

XI, The Office of Coal Research: the Use of Applied Research to Restore a "Sick" Industry

XIII, The Water Pollution Control Act of 1948: the Dilemma of Economic Compulsion Versus Social Restraint

XV, The Insecticide, Fungicide, and Rodenticide Act of 1947

XVI, Congressional Decisions on Water Projects

111. Comm. on Science and Public Policy, National Academy of Sciences for the House Comm. on Science and Astronautics, 91st Cong., 1st Sess., *Technology: Processes of Assessment and Choice* 163 (Comm. Print 1969)

Studies various types of constraints which inhibit the advancement of technology (e.g., economic and jurisdictional) and sets forth guidelines for improving technology assessment.

112. House Comm. on Government Operations, *Views of the Governors on Tax Incentives and Effluent Charges (Water Pollution Control and Abatement),* H.R. Rep. No. 1330, 89th Cong., 2d Sess. 75 (1966)

Based on a study made by the Committee's Natural Resources and Power Subcommittee to consider the reaction of state governors to the proposal that ". . . pollution control would be accelerated if incentives were provided for industry, such as tax writeoffs of expenditures, subsidies, research grants, etc." Non-Congressional

113. U.S. Citizens' Advisory Comm. on Environmental Quality, *Annual Report to the President and to the President's Council on Environmental Quality* (1968-)

Specific and concrete recommendations on national environmental problems, each year focusing on one or two different issues.

114. U.S. Citizens' Advisory Comm. on Recreation and Natural Beauty, *Report to the President and to the President's Council on Recreation and Natural Beauty* (1967-)

Recommendations for citizen action in conservation and protection of the environment.

115. U.S. Bureau of Mines, Special Pub., *Automobile Disposal: A National Problem* 569 (1967)

"[Area] case studies of factors that influence the accumulation of automobile scrap," with a general discussion on the auto wrecking industry, economic aspects of scrap disposal, and legal considerations.

116. U.S. White House Conference on Natural Beauty, *Beauty for America* 782 (1965)

Reports of fifteen panels dealing with such topics as federal-state-local partnership in environmental planning, highway landscape control, open spaces, underground installation of utilities, and citizen action programs.

117. U.S. Office of Economic Opportunity, *Catalog of Federal Programs for Individual and Community Improvement* 414 (1965)

"A description of governmental programs to help individuals and communities meet their own [economic, social, and environmental] goals." Gives the major eligibility requirements for each program.

118. Energy Policy Staff, U.S. Office of Science and Technology, *Considerations Affecting Steam Power Plant Site Selection* 133 (1968)

". . . [A] factual presentation of public interest considerations affecting generating site selection based on existing information. . . . [I]dentifies such issues as the prospects and problems of metropolitan siting, underground transmission lines, the need to protect scenic areas and the quality of our air and water, and yet meet the Nation's need for reliable, low-cost power supply."

119. V. Burgin, *Decisions and Opinions of the U.S. Department of the Interior* 2 pts. (1969)

A decennial index-digest of opinions voiced by the Department in hearings, court cases, contracts, etc., from Jan. 1, 1955 through Dec. 31, 1965.

120. U.S. Bureau of Outdoor Recreation, *Federal Outdoor Recreation Programs* 224 (1968)

Information on federal programs that deal with meeting America's recreation needs. Part A: directory of federal agencies. Part B: description of various programs, with the legislative authority under which each operates.

121. U.S. President's Council on Recreation and Natural Beauty, *From Sea to Shining Sea: A Report on the American Environment—Our Natural Heritage* 304 (1968)

Proposals and recommendations representing ". . . a statement of long-term comprehensive goals for the Nation . . . which will stimulate Federal, State, local, and private action . . ."

122. National Air Pollution Control Administration, U.S. Dep't of Health, Education, and Welfare, *Guidelines for the Development of Air Quality Standards and Implementation Plans* 53 (1969)

Furnishes guidance to state governments in carrying out functions assigned to them under the Air Quality Act of 1967.

123. U.S. Advisory Commission on Intergovernmental Relations, *A Handbook for Interlocal Agreements and Contracts* 197 (1967)

Describes the major features of interlocal agreements and includes some model contracts. An aid to local legislative bodies in preparing legislation and negotiating contracts, sharing facilities, exchanging information, and engaging in joint regional development projects.

124. P. Gates, *History of Public Land Law Development* 828 (Public Land Law Review Commission 1968)

A history of U.S. laws since Colonial times.

125. *International Conference on Water for Peace; Papers* 8 vol. (1967)

Contents:

      I Speeches and Country Situation Reports

      II-IV Water Supply Technology

      V Organizing for Water Programs

      VI-VIII Planning and Developing Water Programs

Note volume V, a discussion of various governmental agencies on water resource development and in analysis of modern water law and legislation.

126. Norman Williams, *Land Acquisition for Outdoor Recreation—Analysis of Selected Legal Programs* 67 (ORRRC Study Report No. 16, 1962)

Analysis of the legal implications of acquiring land for recreational purposes and open space, with a focus on federal acquisition. Includes a discussion on easements, their legal basis, and problems of acquisition.

127. U.N. Conference on the Law of the Sea, *Law of the Sea: Convention on Fishing and Conservation of the Living Resources of the High Seas Between the United States of America and Other Governments, Done at Geneva April 29, 1958* 49 (Treaties and Other International Acts Series, No. 5969, 1966)

Complete text of the Convention, in English, Chinese, French, Russian, and Spanish.

128. G. Derrickson, Business and Defense Services Administration, U.S. Dep't of Commerce, *Motor Vehicle Abandonment in U.S. Urban Areas* 51 (1967)

A report based on a questionnaire survey of local governments, with suggestions for more effective legal ways of handling the problem.

129. U.S. General Accounting Office, *Need for Improving Procedures to Ensure Compliance with Law Regarding Deposition of Industrial Waste Solids into Navigable Waters, Corps of Engineers (Civil Functions) Dep't of the Army* 25 (1966)

A report directed to Congress, ". . . because the review concerns compliance with Federal law and because . . . the corrective measures . . . could significantly reduce Government costs for maintenance dredging."

130. U.S. General Accounting Office, *Need to Improve Procedures for Compensating Municipalities for Relocation of Facilities Necessitated by Construction of Federal Water Resources Projects, Corps of Engineers (Civil Functions) Dep't of the Army* 35 (1968)

Recommendation that ". . . no facilities be provided beyond those necessary to serve eligible residents who have indicated their intent to move to the relocation area."

131. Ann L. Strong, Urban Renewal Administration, U.S. Dep't of Housing and Urban Development, *Open Space for Urban America* 154 (1965)

An analysis of federal, state, local, and private open space action programs, which ". . . explores planning and land acquisition techniques, sources of finance, [and] methods of operation . . ."

132. Law Division, U.S. Dep't of Justice, *A Procedural Guide for the Acquisition of Real Property by Governmental Agencies* 64 (1965)

Outlines briefly the basic elements of land acquisition by direct purchase or by condemnation.

133. Economic Research Service, U.S. Dep't of Agriculture, Misc. Pub. No. 1122, *Public Access to Public Domain Lands: Two Case Studies of Landowner-Sportsman Conflict* 64 (1968)

Examines the Piceance Creek Area and the Caliente Mountain Area cases, focusing on the issue of access to public lands for recreation purposes.

134. Environmental Pollution Panel, U.S. President's Science Advisory Comm., *Restoring the Quality of Our Environment* 317 (1965)

A series of reports on soil contamination, health effects of environmental pollution, solid wastes, combined sewers, agricultural wastes, and other similar topics.

135. Task Force on Environmental Health and Related Problems, U.S. Dep't of Health, Education, and Welfare, *A Strategy for a Livable Environment* 90 (1967)

Policy-making recommendations for action against the present pollution conditions and for protective measures against further contamination.

136. U.S. Dep't of the Interior, *Surface Mining and Our Environment: A Special Report to the Nation* 124 (1967)

Identifies 2 million acres of surface-mined area which should have reclamation treatment. Acid mine drainage and other water quality factors are considered.

II. BIBLIOGRAPHY OF LEGAL ARTICLES
Prepared for the Conservation Foundation *by William Sitig*

The following annotated bibliography of articles, comments and notes on environmental law represents a selection of entries appearing in the *Index to Legal Periodicals, 1965-1969.* An annotation was made either to summarize the article or present one of the author's major conclusions or recommendations. This list is not intended to be comprehensive, but rather to represent a wide variety of environmental issues and laws of several governmental units.

The form used is consistent with Harvard Law Review Association, *A Uniform System of Citations* (11th ed. 1967), except that at the end of each citation the total number of pages are included.

137. Adinolfi. "First steps toward European cooperation in reducing air pollution —activities of the Council of Europe," 33 Law & Contemp. Prob. 421 (1968). 6 p.

An exposition of the resolutions adopted concerning air pollution.

138. "Administration of public lands: symposium," Natural Resources J. 149 (1967). 117 p.

The Public Land Law Review Commission and mining laws are highlighted.

139. Agee. "Aesthetic zoning: a current evaluation of the law," 18 U. Fla. L. Rev. 430 (1965). 10 p.

The author suggests that Florida "abandon the present link between aesthetics and tourism."

140. "Agricultural pesticides: the need for improved control legislation," 52 Minn. L. Rev. 1242 (1968). 19 p.

A review of federal and state legislation and suggestions for improvement.

141. "Air pollution—automobile smog: a proposed remedy," 14 De Paul L. Rev. 436 (1965). 9 p.

This comment suggests ". . . federal standards coupled with local control and enforcement."

142. "Air pollution symposium," 10 Ariz. L. Rev. 1 (1968). 96 p.

Articles include "Air pollution and government structure," "Industry—the views of the regulated," and "The Misdemeanor approach to pollution control."

143. "Air pollution symposium," 1968 Wash. U.L.Q. 205 (1968) 120 p.

This student symposium examines the nature of air pollution and local, state, interstate and federal regulation.

144. "Air quality act of 1967," 54 Ia. L. Rev. 115 (1968). 26 p.

Increased state control activities are seen as the major effect of this act.

145. "Airplane noise, property rights, and the Constitution," 65 Colum. L. Rev. 1428 (1965). 20 p.

The author suggests that "airport authorities, perhaps with financial aid from the federal government" should take "affirmative action to compensate injured landowners."

146. Alekshun. "Aircraft noise law: a technical perspective," 55 ABAJ 740 (1969). 6 p.

"Law is lagging behind technology when it refuses to recognize" that noise is a distinct invasion of property rights.

147. "American bar association national institute on marine resources," 1 Natural Resources Law. 1 (1968). 264 p.

The papers presented at this institute range from U.S. policy regarding marine resources to the technological aspects of exploitation.

148. Arkin, Burdick, Joyner. "Sonic boom—a legal nightmare," 19 Okla. L. Rev. 292 (1966). 13 p.

A discussion of available remedies.

149. Ayres. "Air pollution in cities," 9 Natural Resources J. 1 (1969). 22 p.

This paper discusses "major sources of pollution . . . , physical effects, economic costs, and alternative pollution control policies and technologies."

150. Baxter. "SST: from Watts to Harlem in two hours," 21 Stan. L. Rev. 1 (1968). 57 p.

A scientific analysis of the sonic boom and recommended legal adjustments for damage.

151. Beazley. "Conservation decision-making: a rationalization," 7 Natural Resources J. 345 (1967). 16 p.

The author urges wider participation in a stable framework for conservation decision-making.

152. Behan. "Succotash syndrome, or multiple use: a heartfelt approach to forest land management," 7 Natural Resources J. 473 (1967). 12 p.

The author calls for a more flexible, critical appraisal of multiple use, not its rigid application.

153. Bennett. "Public land policy: reconciliation of public use and private development," 11 Rocky Mt. M.L. Inst. 311 (1966) 34 p.

An argument from the viewpoint of a mining interest lawyer.

154. Berger. "Air pollution as a private nuisance," 24 Wash. & Lee L. Rev. 314 (1967). 6 p.

This comment advocates the adoption of the Absolute Nuisance Rule.

155. Berger. "Standing to sue in public actions: is it a constitutional requirement?" 78 Yale L. J. 816 (1969). 25 p.

After a historical survey, the author concludes ". . . the notion that the constitution demands injury to a personal interest as a prerequisite to attacks on allegedly unconstitutional action is historically unfounded."

156. Bermingham. "Federal government and air and water pollution," 23 Bus. Law. 467 (1968). 26 p.

An article designed ". . . to help your client in a compliance program or in meeting government attacks for alleged failures to comply."

157. Bernfeld. "Developing the resources of the sea—security of investment," 1 Natural Resources Law. 82 (Jan. 1968). 9 p.

The author suggests dividing up the entire sea-bed among the nations in order to solve existing legal complications.

158. Boerner. "Standing to appeal zoning determinations: the 'aggrieved person' requirement," 64 Mich. L. Rev. 1070 (1966). 16 p.

The author urges that ". . . statutory grants of aggrieved party status to third parties should be liberally construed."

159. Bosselman. "Control of surface mining: an exercise in creative federalism," 9 Natural Resources J. 138 (1969). 28 p.

The article discusses, among other things, the effects of the industry on the environment and the division of regulatory power.

160. Boston. "A cause for injunction," 20 J.A.G.J. 47 (1965). 6 p.

The author "deals with cases where the government, as plaintiff, sues for an injunction to prevent encroachment upon naval activities and conflicting uses of adjoining property when administrative remedies fail to rectify a hazard to government interests." .

161. Bower. "Some important research problems in the water resources field," 5 Natural Resources J. 286 (1965). 12 p.

Water quality improvement benefits and water resources planning in metropolitan areas are among the problems discussed.

162. Bowers. "Police power and the design of buildings," 5 Natural Resources J. 122 (1965). 27 p.

The author criticizes Albuquerque's "use of the police power in furthering the interests of a self-regulated monopoly" and recommends that building permits be "issued on all plans certified either by registered engineers or by registered architects."

163. Broesche. "Land-use regulation for the protection of public parks and recreational areas," 45 Tex. L. Rev. 96 (1966). 36 p.

The author suggests that in Texas "the soundest approach to implementations would be through statewide regulation promulgated by a state agency."

164. Brooks. "Legal problems of the geothermal industry," 6 Natural Resources 511 (1966). 31 p.

The author concludes that S. 1674 89th Cong., 1st Sess. (1965) "as amended, appears to provide a practical framework within which geothermal exploration and development on federally owned lands can proceed."

165. Brooks. "Strip mine reclamation and economic analysis," 6 Natural Resources J. 13 (1966). 32 p.

The author argues that "the private profit signals to which coal stripping firms must and should respond to maximize their profits are not adequate guides for maximizing social welfare."

166. Browning. "United Nations and marine resources," 10 W. & M. L. Rev. 690 (1969). 15 p.

The author sees great hope in the International Decade of Ocean Exploration.

167. Bryan. "Water supply and pollution control aspects of urbanization," 30 Law & Contemp. Prob. 176 (1965). 17 p.

Two of the author's suggestions are increased reuse of water and reorganization of political boundaries for more effective pollution control.

168. Burke. "Contemporary legal problem in ocean development," 3 Int. Law. 536 (1969). 24 p.

"The regulatory difficulties of marine fisheries" are discussed.

169. "Can law reclaim man's environment?" 5 Trial 10 (1969). 19 p.

A symposium with short articles by Sen. Muskie, Gov. Guy of N.D., Prof. Sax, and others.

170. Carmichael. "Forty years of water pollution control in Wisconsin: a case study," 1967 Wis. L. Rev. 350 (1967). 70 p.

A comprehensive survey highlighting drainage basin regulation and the control efforts of municipalities and large industries.

171. Carver. "Administrative law and public land management," 18 Ad. Law. Rev. 7 (1965). 12 p.

The author discusses the legal aspects of the Public Land Law Review Commission.

172. Carver. "Pollution control and the federal power commission," 1 Natural Resources Law. 32 (Jan. 1968). 6 p.

A general discussion of the FPC's role in the area of pollution.

173. Carver. "Role of the federal government in land management," 11 Rocky Mt. M.L. Inst. 345 (1966). 24 p.

A discussion of the activities of the Public Land Law Review Commission by the Under Secretary of the Interior.

174. Cassell. "The health effects of air pollution and their implications for control," 33 Law & Contemp. Prob. 197 (1968). 20 p.

"Because of the multifactorial nature of air pollution and its effects, control based primarily on standards for individual pollutants may be inadequate to the problem."

175. Clary. "Air and water interstate compacts," 1 Natural Resources Law. 60 (Oct. 1968). 8 p.

A review of the existing compacts and a discussion of the compact as an organizational form.

176. Clement. "Pesticide problem," 8 Natural Resources J. 11 (1968)). 12 p.

A review of J. Headly & J. Lewis, *The Pesticide Problem: An Econoomic Approach to Public Policy* (1967).

177. Clyde. "Legal problems imposed by requirements of restoration and beautification of mining properties," 13 Rocky Mt. M.L. Inst. 187 (1967). 45 p.

The author urges the mining industry to formulate programs before the work of others is imposed on them.

178. "Conservation of natural resources: a panel," 60 L. Lib. J. 362 (1967). 17 p.

Includes selected bibliography on conservation of soil and water resources.

179. "Constitutional law—governmental regulation of surface mining activities," 46 N.C. L. Rev. 103 (1967). 26 p.

Pros and cons of state-level regulation.

180. Cooley. "State land policy in Alaska: progress and prospects," 4 Natural Resources J. 455 (1965). 13 p.

The author argues for a balanced cautious approach between economic development and conservation.

181. Corbridge & Moses. "Weather modification: law and administration," 8 Natural Resources J. 207 (1968). 29 p.

In order to ensure against errors, the author suggests an international system of licensing, inspection and reporting.

182. Crocker. "Some economics of air pollution control," 8 Natural Resources J. 236 (1968). 23 p.

The author states that ". . . economic theory and quite incomplete empirical evidence give some indication that increased real per capita incomes and improved environmental quality are directly related."

183. Cunningham. "Scenic easements in the highway beautification program," 45 Denver L.J. 168 (1968). 99 p.

This comprehensive article discusses federal and state experience with scenic easements and the constitutional and technical legal problems involved.

184. Davis. "Standing: taxpayers and others," 35 U. Chi. L. Rev. 601 (1968). 36 p.

The author believes that the holding in *Flast v. Cohen*, 392 U.S. 83 (1968) should be extended "to all constitutional and statutory limitations on the authority of officers."

185. Delogu. "Effluent charges: a method of enforcing stream standards," 19 Maine L. Rev. 29 (1967). 19 p.

Suggestions for effective water pollution control in Maine by "combining the tools of the economist, planner, water resources engineer, and the state government."

186. Delogu. "Legal aspects of air pollution control and proposed state legislation

for such control," 1969 Wis. L. Rev. 884 (1969). 24 p.

The author offers a model air pollution control statute.

187. Delogu. "Taxing power as a land use control device," 45 Denver L.J. 279 (1968). 17 p.

The author outlines a range of tax programs which could induce desirable land use.

188. Dempsey. "World ocean; a plan for international action," 18 Catholic U.L. Rev. 491 (1969). 33 p.

A critical examination of the report of the President's Commission on Marine Sciences, Engineering, and Resources.

189. DiCello. "Aesthetics and the police power," 18 Cleveland-Mar. L. Rev. 384 (1969). 8 p.

". . . Aesthetics as a controlling factor behind municipal housing ordinances poses a very real threat to the individual's right to use property in a reasonable manner in harmony with the rights of others."

190. Dunkelberger. "Federal-state relationships in the adoption of water quality standards under the federal pollution control act," 2 Natural Resources Law. 47 (1969). 15 p.

"This article focuses upon the authority of the Secretary of the Interior to require a State to include specific provisions in its water quality standards as a condition of his approval of those standards. . . ."

191. Edelman. "Federal air and water control: the application of the commerce power to abate interstate and intrastate pollution," 33 Geo. Wash. L. Rev. 1067 (1965). 21 p.

An examination of the constitutional basis for federal pollution controls.

192. Edwards. "Legal control of thermal pollution," 2 Natural Resources Law. 1 (1969). 6 p.

Includes discussion of proposals for pre-construction review of atomic plants by federal agencies.

193. Edwards. "Legislative approach to air and water quality," 1 Natural Resources Law. 58 (Jan. 1968). 12 p.

A summary of federal law and legislative history relating to pollution control.

194. Ely. "American policy options in the development of undersea mineral resources," 1 Natural Resources Law. 91 (Jan. 1968). 5 p.

The author discusses suggestions to revise the Geneva Convention and other proposed conventions.

195. "Environmental policy: new directions in federal action," 28 Pub. Admin. Rev. 301 (1968). 47 p.

Emphasis in this symposium is on coordinative aspects of environmental policy and programs concerned with complex segments of the environment.

196. Erichsen-Brown. "Legal implications of boundary water pollution," 17 Buffalo L. Rev. 65 (1967). 5 p.

The work of the Canadian-American International Joint Commission in the field of pollution is discussed.

197. Eveleth. "New techniques to preserve areas of scenic attraction in established rural-residential communities—the Lake George approach," 18 Syracuse L. Rev. 37 (1966). 12 p.

The author discusses the Lake George Park Commission, "which is empowered to encourage property owners . . . to execute restrictive covenants and easements. . . ."

198. "Federal regulation of air transportation and the environmental impact problem," 35 U. Chi. L. Rev. 317 (1968). 25 p.

"This comment is concerned with the extent of the authority of the CAB and the FAA to consider noise in their respective certification proceedings."

199. Fleming. "Aircraft noise: a taking of private property without just compensation," 18 S.C. L. Rev. 593 (1966). 16 p.

The author urges the South Carolina Supreme Court to permit recovery, shunning a strict view of trespass.

200. Forer. "Preservation of America's park lands: the inadequacy of present law," 41 N.Y.U. L. Rev. 1093 (1966). 31 p.

The author analyzes impediments of existing law and suggests legal machinery to 1) restrict the taking of parks, 2) provide citizens' methods for court tests, and 3) prescribe appropriate remedies.

201. Freeman. "Advocacy and resources allocation decisions in the public sector," 9 Natural Resources J. 166 (1969). 10 p.

The author suggests "some form of subsidy might be granted to organizations advocating more widely distributed potential benefits" to offset the influence of wealthy large single-interest groups.

202. Fromson. "History of federal air pollution control," 30 Ohio S. L. J. 516 (1969). 21 p.

Legislative history of the Air Quality Act of 1967.

203. Gerhardt. "Incentives to air pollution control," 33 Law & Contemp. Prob. 358 (1968). 11 p.

A short analysis of "basic policy alternatives available to those who would control air pollution."

204. Gibbons. "Public lands—whence? whither? a midstream view of the Public Land Law Review Commission," 2 Natural Resources Law. 179 (1969). 13 p.

A comment on four years' work of the commission.

205. Gormley. "Urban redevelopment to further aesthetic considerations: the changing constitutional concepts of police power and eminent domain," 41 N.D. L. Rev. 316 (1965). 17 p.

Focuses on analyzing *Berman* v. *Parker*, 348 U.S. 26 (1954).

206. Green. "State control of interstate air pollution," 33 Law & Contemp. Prob. 315 (1968). 26 p.

The author suggests that interstate compacts, in partnership with the federal government, might offer the best solution.

207. Grunawalt. "Acquisition of the resources of the bottom of the sea—a new frontier of international law," 34 Mil. L. Rev. 101 (Oct. 1966). 33 p.

The author recommends "placing the resources of the deep ocean floor under the exclusive control and jurisdiction of the U.N."

208. Hagevik. "Legislating for air quality management: reducing theory to prac-

tice," 33 Law & Contemp. Prob. 369 (1968). 30 p.

"This paper first attempts to set down some basic social science theory about the economics of air pollution and about decision making in general."

209. Haight. "Developments in the United Nations relating to sea-bed and ocean floor," 2 Natural Resources Law. 119 (1969). 12 p.

A review of U.N. work in this area during the 23rd General Assembly (1968).

210. Haight. "Seabed and the ocean floor," 3 Int. Law. 642 (1969). 32 p.

A discussion of the 1968 activities of the U.N.'s Ad Hoc Committee on the Sea-bed and Ocean Floor.

211. Haight. "United Nations affairs: Ad hoc committee on seabed and ocean floor," Int. Law. 22 (1968). 9 p.

A short discussion of the committee.

212. Halloran. "Water pollution control in New York," 31 Albany L. Rev. 50 (1967). 12 p.

The author shows how the statutory remedies in N.Y. evolved from the common law doctrine of riparian rights.

213. Hamill. "Process of making good decisions about the use of the environment of man," 8 Natural Resources J. 279 (1968). 23 p.

The author presents "an operational theory of wise (planned) resource use."

214. Hammond. "Wilderness act and mining: some proposals for conservation," 47 Ore. L. Rev. 447 (1968). 23 p.

Discussion of the decision of Kennecott Copper Co. to start open pit mining in the Glacier Peak Wilderness Area in Washington State.

215. Hauver. "Water for recreation: a plea for recognition," 44 Denver L.J. 288 (1967). 12 p.

The author suggests regulation of surface waters by a permit system.

216. Hennigan. "Essence of standing: the basis of a constitutional right to be heard," 10 Ariz. L. Rev. 438 (1968). 18 p.

Emphasis on recent decisions, especially *Flast* v. *Cohen,* 392 U.S. 83 (1968).

217. Hines. "Nor any drop to drink: public regulation of water quality," 52 Ia. L. Rev. 186, 432, 799 (Oct. 1966-Apr. 1967). 120 p.

A comprehensive discussion of state, interstate, and federal efforts toward water pollution control.

218. Huard. "Roar, the whine, the boom and the law: some legal concerns about the SST," 9 Santa Clara Law. 189 (1969). 38 p.

Although recognizing the problems of its use, the author argues for public acceptance of the SST.

219. James. "Economic analysis of recreational reservoirs," 55 Ky. L.J. 822 (1967). 22 p.

A justification for large expenditures for recreational reservoirs.

220. "Jet noise in airport areas: a national solution required," 51 Minn. L. Rev. 1087 (1967). 31 p.

An examination of the scope of the problem, present status of legal relief, and the financial burdens involved.

221. Johnson & Austin. "Recreational rights and titles to beds on Western lakes and streams," 7 Natural Resources J. 1 (1967). 52 p.

A review of federal and state cases in the trans-Mississippi West.

222. Jost. "Cold facts on hot water: legal aspects of thermal pollution," 1969 Wis. L. Rev. 253 (1969). 17 p.

"The greatest difficulty will be encountered in isolating thermal pollution as a separate entity and getting the public and legislature to recognize the hazard so that effective controls may be administered."

223. Juergensmeyer. "Control of air pollution through the assertion of private rights," 1967 Duke L. J. 1126 (1967). 30 p.

The author contends that ". . . although traditional legal concepts may provide the framework for obtaining adequate relief in individual cases, the overall pollution control consequences of private actions are at best piecemeal and not a substitute for effective government regulation."

224. Kahan. "Federal taxpayers and standing, *Flast* v. *Cohen*, 392 U.S. 83 (1968)," 16 U.C.L.A. L. Rev. 444 (1969). 12 p.

The author believes that the federal standing doctrine was beclouded by the *Flast* decision.

225. Kaito. "Federal water pollution control act as applied to the city and county of Honolulu," 1 Natural Resoures Law. 70 (Jan. 1968). 7 p.

The author advocates more local decision-making and control of pollution problems.

226. Karabus. "*Flast* decision on standing of federal taxpayers to challenge governmental action: mirage or breach in the dike?" 45 N. D. L. Rev. 353 (1969). 10 p.

An examination of the decisions in *Frothingham* v. *Mellon*, 262 U.S. 447 (1923) and *Flast* v. *Cohen*, 392 U.S. 83 (1968).

227. Kennedy & Weeks. "Control of automobile emissions—California experience and the federal legislation," 33 Law & Contemp. Prob. 297 (1968). 18 p.

Legislative histories of the Calif. and federal laws.

228. Kieser. "Animals ferae naturae—Commonwealth not permitted to recover damages in trespass for negligent killing of fish by pollution," 72 Dick L. Rev. 200 (1967). 8 p.

The author pleads for state legislative action to protect fish life from pollution.

229. Kissel. "Permissible uses of New York's forest preserve under 'forever wild,'" 19 Syracuse L. Rev. 969 (1968). 28 p.

This comment describes how the constitutional provision of "forever wild" has been widely interpreted.

230. Kleinhaus. "Architectural control: urban environment and the law," 1 Colum. J.L. & Soc. Prob. 26 (1965). 13 p.

The author concludes that "the proper exercise of aesthetic review can be expected to describe broad parameters within which healthy variety—even experiment—can flourish."

231. Knodell. "Liability for pollution of surface and underground water," 12 Rocky Mt. M.L. Inst. 33 (1967). 67 p.

An argument for a more gradual evolution of water pollution control law.

232. Kohn. "Achieving air quality goals at minimum cost," 1968 Wash. U.L.Q. 325 (1968). 36 p.

The author presents economic criteria for the reduction of sulfur dioxide pollution in the St. Louis area.

233. Kovel. "Case for civil penalties: air pollution control," 46 J. Urban L. 153 (1968). 19 p.

The author believes that "the use of the criminal law" for social welfare regulation "is inappropriate, cumbersome, and rarely helpful."

234. Kreuger. "Mineral development on the continental shelf and beyond," 42 Calif. S. B. J. 515 (1967). 19 p.

A short review of "internal-municipal and international law regarding the sea" since 1945.

235. Land. "Unraveling the urban fringe: a proposal for the implementation of proposition three," 19 Hastings L.J. 421 (1968). 25 p.

The author examines "the role of the property tax as a factor contributing to the depletion of California's natural resources and examines existing and proposed relevant legislation."

236. Landstrom. "Citizen participation in public land decisions," 9 St. Louis U.L.J. 372 (1965). 18 p.

Includes discussion of administrative procedures and expressions by organized groups.

237. "Law of administrative standing and public right of intervention," 1967 Wash. U. L. Q. 416 (1967). 20 p.

An examination of the case law, including *Office of Communication of United Church of Christ* v. *FCC*, 359 F.2d 994 (D.C. Cir. 1966) and *Scenic Hudson Preservation Conference* v. *FPC*, 354 F.2d 608 (2nd Cir. 1965).

238. "Legal control of water pollution," 1 U.C.D. L. Rev. 1 (1969). 273 p.

This whole issue is devoted to a comprehensive analysis of many aspects of water pollution (ground water, oil, pesticides, etc.) and its control.

239. "Legislation to preserve and control open space land," 6 Harv. J. Legis. 57 (1968). 38 p.

Presentation of a Model Open Space Statute.

240. Lewis. "Phantom of federal liability for pollution abatement in condemnation actions," 17 Mercer L. Rev. 364 (1966). 17 p.

The author concludes, "Irrespective of the government project, it is the obligation of the industry or municipality to abate the pollution by treatment."

241. Ludwig. "Air pollution control technology: research and development of new and improved systems," 33 Law & Contemp. Prob. 217 (1968). 22 p.

The author examines the control of pollution from stationary sources and vehicles, air pollution instrumentation, and meteorology.

242. Lynch, Gindler, Stanton. "Coordinated resource development: legal controls of water quality and oil pollution in a marine environment," 44 L.A.B. Bull. 154 (1969). 9 p.

A short survey of applicable legislation, with a suggestion for more emphasis on preventive as well as punitive measures.

243. McCloskey. "Can recreational conservationists provide for a mining industry?" 13 Rocky Mt. M.L. Inst. 65 (1967). 21 p.

The Conservation Director of the Sierra Club discusses points of conflict between mining interests and conservationists.

244. McCloskey. "Landscape policy for public lands," 45 Denver L. J. 149 (1968). 18 p.

The author "charges the federal agencies who administer federal lands with the failure to develop coordinated policies for classification and protection of scenic resources despite existing statutory authority."

245. McCloskey. "Wilderness act of 1964: its background and meaning," 45 Ore. L. Rev. 288 (1966). 34 p.

A comprehensive review of the Act.

246. McKee & Venable. "Converting a city street into a pedestrian mall: shade trees, fountains and lawsuits," 28 U. Pitt. L. Rev. 293 (1966). 26 p.

The authors suggest that comprehensive mall legislation is the best method to overcome legal obstacles.

247. Malley. "Supersonic transport's sonic boom costs: a common law approach," 37 Geo. Wash. L. Rev. 683 (1969). 24 p.

Before any damage occurs and investment is made, the courts should provide the "private users with an economic indication of the costs involved."

248. Maloney, Plager, Baldwin. "Water pollution—attempts to decontaminate Florida law," 20 U. Fla. L. Rev. 131 (1967). 17 p.

The authors examine Florida's pollution control laws, which they believe to not satisfactorily meet the growing problem.

249. Mann. "Political implications of migration to the arid lands of the United States," 9 Natural Resources J. 212 (1969) 16 p.

The author urges careful planning for the increased urban population of the arid Southwest, with its concomitant strain on resources.

250. Martin. "Conflict resolution through the multi-use concept in Forest Service decision-making," 9 Natural Resources J. 228 (1969). 9 p.

The author concludes that the multiple-use formula has a desirable effect on decision-making.

251. Martin & Symington. "A guide to the Air Quality Act of 1967," 33 Law & Contemp. Prob. 239 (1968). 26 p.

"This article attempts to delineate the scope and ultimate effects in controlling air pollution attributable to stationary sources of contaminants."

252. Masotti & Selfon. "Aesthetic zoning and the police power," 46 J. Urban L. 773 (1969). 15 p.

"The courts seem to recognize aesthetics as a valid concept, but in practice they rely on auxiliary support."

253. Miller. "Aesthetic zoning: an answer to billboard blight," 19 Syracuse L. Rev. 87 (1967). 8 p.

This note traces the development of the law to the point where in N.Y. aesthetics per se is all that is needed to sustain a zoning ordinance.

254. Miller. "Electric transmission lines—to bury, not to praise," 12 Vill. L. Rev. 497 (1967). 10 p.

The author wonders if the people advocating undergrounding for aesthetic reasons will be willing to pay the additional costs.

255. Mock. "Human obstacles to utilization of the public domain," 12 Rocky Mt. M.L. Inst. 187 (1967). 38 p.

The author argues against bureaucrats managing public lands programs.

256. "Model interstate compact for the control of air pollution," 4 Harv. J. Legis. 369 (1967). 30 p.

This proposed compact "gives power not merely to recommend, but also to take immediate action to initiate regulatory action, and to require compliance with its rules, regulations, and orders."

257. Moody. "Air quality improvement—a look ahead," 2 Natural Resources Law. 7 (1969). 8 p.

The President of the National Coal Policy Conference urges industry, government, and public cooperation in air pollution control.

258. Moore. "Acquisition and preservation of open lands," 23 Wash. & Lee. L. Rev. 274 (1966). 21 p.

The most promising legal devices for preserving open lands seem to be "compulsory dedication, cluster zoning, and the purchase of conservation easements."

259. Morgan. "Standing to sue and conservation values," 38 U. Colo. L. Rev. 391 (1966). 16 p.

The author urges federal courts "to recognize the standing of conservation groups or private individuals who challenge public recreation policy."

260. Morse & Juergensmeyer. "Air pollution control in Indiana in 1968: a comment," 2 Val. U.L. Rev. 296 (1968). 19 p.

The authors address themselves to the problems of private and public control in Indiana in light of the federal Air Quality Act of 1967.

261. Moses. "What happened to multiple-purpose resource development?—a plea for reasonableness," 3 Land & Water L. Rev. 435 (1968). 7 p.

The author "examines recent decisions and suggests reasons for refusing to humbly defer to the preservationist."

262. Mulchay. "Camara (*Camara* v. *Municipal Court of the City and County of San Francisco*, 87 Sup. Ct. 1727) and See (*See* v. *Seattle*, 87 Sup. Ct. 1737): a constitutional problem with effect on air pollution control," 10 Ariz. L. Rev. 120 (1968). 18 p.

The warrant requirement of "*Camara* and *See* represent progress in the protection of the rights of individuals to their privacy."

263. Munro. "Aircraft noise as a taking of property," 13 N.Y.L.F. 476 (1967). 22 p.

Includes discussion of the implications of the decision in *United States* v. *Causby*, 328 U.S. 256 (1946).

264. Munroe. "Current governmental trends in public land management, environmental controls and taxation as they affect mining economics," 14 Rocky Mt. M.L. Inst. 1 (1968). 32 p.

The author argues from a viewpoint favoring the development of domestic mining and against government regulation and taxes.

265. Murphy. "Air pollution," 62 L. Lib. J. 84, 225 (1968). 17 p.

A bibliography of Congressional material.

266. Murphy. "Mobilization for the national program in marine sciences: organizational considerations," 29 Pub. Admin. Rev. 263 (1969). 13 p.

"A review of the efforts of the Executive and Legislative Branches to coordinate the national marine science program."

267. Nanda. " 'Torrey Canyon' disaster: some legal aspects," 44 Denver L.J. 400 (1967). 26 p.

The author urges international agreements "to develop minimum standards and effective safeguards" to combat oil pollution.

268. Nebolsine. "Today's problems of industrial waste water pollution abatement," 1 Natural Resources Law. 39 (Jan. 1968). 19 p.

The author concentrates on "the technical, operational and economic factors governing industrial waste water treatment."

269. Netherton. "Implementation of land use policy: police power vs. eminent domain," 3 Land & Water L. Rev. 33 (1968). 25 p.

An analysis "of these powers and the principles that control their use suggesting that a new rationale be used to determine the appropriate criteria to guide future policy."

270. "North Dakota weather modification act and the need for a comprehensive weather modification program," 45 N.D. L. Rev. 407 (1969). 17 p.

The author suggests creative federal and state legislation in this area.

271. Norton. "Police power, planning and aesthetics," 7 Santa Clara Law. 171 (1967). 17 p.

"This paper demonstrates that there is nothing in the concept of the police power . . . that requires the courts to discriminate against aesthetic regulation. . . ."

272. Norvell & Bell. "Air pollution control in Texas," 47 Tex. L. Rev. 1086 (1969). 38 p.

A history of Texas pollution control and an analysis of the present law.

273. O'Fallon. "Deficiencies in the Air Quality Act of 1967," 33 Law & Contemp. Prob. 275 (1968). 22 p.

". . . The lack of emphasis on immediate utilization of existing technology . . . severely weakens the Act."

274. "Oil pollution of the sea," 10 Harv. Int. L.J. 316 (1969). 44 p.

A comment on "the problems caused by oil pollutions of the sea and . . . the response given by the American and international community."

275. Olpin. "Recent developments affecting public lands of the states—1968," 2 Natural Resources Law. 229 (1969). 9 p.

Cases on ownership of navigable waterbeds, accretion, development of marine mineral resources, and ocean beaches are discussed.

276. Olson. "Progress and problems in Wisconsin's scenic and conservation easement program," 1965 Wis. L. Rev. 352 (1965). 32 p.

The author concentrates on the effect of Wisconsin's ORAP easements on property taxes and income tax treatment of easement payments.

277. O'Neill. "Zoning: aesthetics: the chameleon of zoning," 4 Tulsa L. J. 48 (1967). 21 p.

The author notes that Oklahoma recognizes aesthetics, but only with "the crutch of the police power."

278. "Open space legislation: suggestions for a model act," 2 Ga. L. Rev. 294 (1968). 17 p.

"Of utmost importance is the realization that the traditional concepts of real property taxation are in conflict with the preservation of open space land."

279. Oppenheimer. "Adminstering the Air Quality Act of 1967," 2 Natural Resources Law. 15 (1969). 5 p.

A review by the Assistant to the Commissioner, National Air Pollution Control Administration.

280. Ortner. "Sonic boom: containment or confrontation," 34 J. Air. L. 208 (1968). 15 p.

One of the author's conclusions is that "[i]f supersonic flight is here to stay, legislation is needed to identify government as the responsible control agency responsible for damages and empowered to settle claims."

281. "Park planning and the acquisition of open spaces: a case study," 36 U. Chi. L. Rev. 642 (1969). 23 p.

The techniques of purchase, transfer, condemnation, donation, and subdivision dedication are examined using Montgomery and Prince George's Counties, Md., as examples.

282. Pierce. "Legal aspects of weather modification snowpack augmentation in Wyoming," 2 Land & Water L. Rev. 273 (1967). 47 p.

A comprehensive survey, including a discussion of the problems of the weather modifier's liability.

283. Pleat & Lennemann. "Considerations for long term waste storage and disposal at USAEC sites," 8 Atomic Energy L.J. 1 (1966). 20 p.

A technical discussion concerning "high-level (radioactivity) wastes from irradiated nuclear fuel processing."

284. Plimpton. "Constitutional law—power of state to designate game preserves," 6 Natural Resources J. 361 (1966). 7 p.

The author calls "untenable" the broad language of *Allen* v. *McClellan*, 75 N.M. 400, 405 P.2d 405 (1965), in which the New Mexico Supreme Court "held that the State Game Commission could not enforce its inclusion of the plaintiff's privately owned twelve-acre plot in a game management area."

285. Poland. "Development of recreational and related resources at hydroelectric projects licensed by the Federal Power Commission," 4 Land & Water L. Rev. 375 (1969). 24 p.

An exploration of "the scope and exercise of the FPC's authority . . . to foster conservation measures."

286. Pollack. "Legal boundaries of air pollution control—state and local legislative purposes and techniques," 33 Law & Contemp. Prob. 331 (1968). 27 p.

"The need for future land-use planning . . . should not be allowed to dominate the purposes and directions of state and local legislative efforts to prevent and control air pollution at its source."

287. Porter. "Role of private nuisance law in the control of air pollution," 10 Ariz. L. Rev. 107 (1968). 13 p.

Private air pollution tort law can be quite effective in some jurisdictions, the author concludes.

288. Powe. "Water pollution control in Washington," 43 Wash. L. Rev. 425 (1967). 29 p.

Although the permit system has worked well with small polluters, the author feels that the Washington Pollution Control Commission has failed with large industries and municipalities.

289. Powell. "Analysis of demands for open spaces in Maryland subdivision regulations," 25 Md. L. Rev. 148 (1965). 17 p.

The author concludes that ". . . planning commissions have been influenced far more by the concepts of city planners than by judicial thinking."

290. "Preservation of Indiana's scenic areas: a method," 40 Ind. L.J. 402 (1965). 18 p.

The author advocates "preservation based on private initiative."

291. Pyle. "Water and watercourses: water pollution laws and their enforcement in Oklahoma," 22 Okla. L. Rev. 317 (1969). 29 p.

Oklahoma water pollution control laws and authority presented.

292. Quesseth. "Water pollution control laws of Oregon—problems of enforcement," 3 Willamette L.J. 284 (1966). 11 p.

A review of Oregon's past and present laws.

293. Rathwell. "Air pollution, pre-emption, local problems and the Constitution —some pigeonholes and hatracks," 10 Ariz. L. Rev. 97 (1968). 10 p.

"If the local governments may not set emission standards binding new motor vehicle sales in a particular area, does the locality or a person living therein have any recourse when otherwise effective federally set standards prove to be too low and fail to protect an acutely polluted area?"

294. "Reconciling competing public claims on land," 68 Colum. L. Rev. 155 (1968). 11 p.

The author feels that the decision in *Texas Eastern Transmission Corp.* v. *Wildlife Preserves, Inc.,* 48 N.J. 261, 225 A.2d 130 (1966) is a creative effort toward reconciling claims.

295. Reich. "Law of the planned society," 75 Yale L.J. 1227 (1966). 44 p.

A general discussion of administrative law, in which the author argues for more democratic representation in government planning.

296. Rein. "Obtaining boiler fuel gas to reduce air pollution: the policy of the Federal Power Commission," 33 Law & Contemp. Prob. 399 (1968). 22 p.

The author feels that the FPC can be persuaded to expend "limited quantities of natural gas as a partial interim solution."

297. Reis. "Policy and planning for recreational use of inland water," 40 Temp. L.Q. 155 (1967). 39 p.

The author tries to reconcile the competing values of private rights and public needs.

298. Reitze. "Pollution control: why has it failed?" 55 A.B.A. J. 923 (1969). 5 p.

The author believes that only large-scale public support will eventually be able to control pollution.

299. Reitze. "Wastes, water, and wishful thinking: the battle of Lake Erie," 20 Case W. Res. L. Rev. 5 (1968). 82 p.

A comprehensive survey of the sources of Lake Erie's pollutants, the legal response, and the author's recommendations for effective control.

300. Rempe. "International air pollution—United States and Canada—a joint approach," 10 Ariz. L. Rev. 138 (1968). 10 p.

The author traces the history of the International Joint Commission's dealings with air pollution problems, especially in the Detroit-Windsor area.

301. Renkey. "Local zoning of strip mining," 57 Ky. L.J. 738 (1968). 18 p.

A review of "recent developments [in Kentucky] in the continuing effort to balance the benefits to be obtained from the strip mining of coal against the environmental damage and pollution . . ."

302. "Resources of the sea; a symposium," 8 Natural Resources J. 373 (1968). 132 p.

Articles include: "Marine resources and the freedom of the seas" and "Legal aspects of offshore oil and gas operations."

303. Rheingold. "Civil cause of action for lung damage due to pollution of urban atmosphere," 33 Brooklyn L. Rev. 17 (1966). 17 p.

A thorough discussion, including newer causes of action and problems of proof.

304. Rice. "Estuarine land of North Carolina: legal aspect of ownership, use and control," 46 N.C. L. Rev. 779 (1968). 34 p.

Primarily an examination of "the legal history of estuarine ownership and use in N.C."

305. Rogers. "Administrative law—expansion of 'public interest' standing," 45 N.C. L. Rev. 998 (1967). 11 p.

"Perhaps the next step . . . will be judicial recognition of a constitutional right to be heard in the administrative process, founded on the first amendment."

306. Rogers. "Need for meaningful control in the management of federally owned timberlands," 4 Land & Water L. Rev. 121 (1969). 23 p.

The author urges an immediate "examination, and perhaps reappraisal, of the extent and right to judicial review of these . . . management decisions."

307. Rohrman. "Law of pesticides; present and future," 17 J. Pub. L. 351 (1968). 51 p.

A comprehensive discussion of "existing pesticide laws and common law principles applicable to the use of pesticides."

308. Rohrman. "Pesticide laws and legal implications of pesticide use," 23 Food Drug Cosm. L.J. 142 (1968). 20 p.

A description of existing federal and state laws.

309. Ross. "Airspace—aircraft noise—inverse condemnation absent overflight," 8 Natural Resources J. 561 (1968). 8 p.

Ferguson v. *City of Keene*, 89 N.H. 410, 238 A.2d 1 (1968) is primarily discussed.

310. Ryckman. "Eminent domain—conservation—evidence necessary to determine if a regulation restricting the use of property is invalid as a taking without compensation," 6 Natural Resources J. 8 (1966). 5 p.

A discussion of the finding in *Commissioner of Natural Resources* v. *S. Volpe & Co.*, 349 Mass. 404, 206 N.E.2d 666 (1965), in which the protection of marine fisheries was involved.

311. "The San Francisco Bay area—regional problems and solutions," 55 Calif. L. Rev. 695 (1967). 203 p.

This symposium includes discussions on control of air and water pollution and land use planning in the Bay Area.

312. Schiff. "Outdoor recreation values in the public decision process," 6 Natural Resources J. 542 (1966). 18 p.

"The confrontation of disparate value systems," the author contends, will lead to "a more interesting and dynamic environment."

313. Schmitz. "Pollution, law, science, and damage awards," 18 Clev. St. L. Rev. 456 (1969). 11 p.

The author strongly urges "promulgation of the concept that 'Polluters-Must-Pay.' "

314. Schoonover & Sheriff. "Public relations, law, environmental pollution," 18 Clev. St. L. Rev. 467 (1969). 6 p.

Having succeeded in passing a bond issue in Cleveland, the authors urge massive public relations activity to pass anti-pollution laws.

315. Seago. "Airport noise problem and airport zoning," 28 Md. L. Rev. 120 (1968). 16 p.

A review of the cases in this area with suggestions for airport zoning legislation.

316. Searles. "Aesthetics in the law," 22 Record 607 (1967). 8 p.

A short review of recent legal developments.

317. "Sierra Club political activity, and tax exempt charitable status," 55 Geo. L.J. 1128 (1967). 16 p.

The author suggests changes in the IRC "to permit some charitable organizations to participate in certain political activities."

318. Sigler. "Controlling the use of pesticides," 15 J. Pub. L. 311 (1966). 13 p.

This short presentation emphasizes the need for further research in this area in order to formulate public policy.

319. Sillin. "Environmental considerations facing the public utility industry," 2 Natural Resources Law. 20 (1969). 6 p.

An address by the President of Northeast Utilities.

320. Synder. "Toward land use stability through contracts," 6 Natural Resources J. 406 (1966). 18 p.

The author "presents a brief review of previous experience with land use control devices, a summary statement of the basic features of the California Land Conservation Act, and a discussion of some of the possible implications of his program for non-prime agricultural land and its effect on the local revenue and tax structure."

321. "Sonic booms—breaking the tort barrier?" 2 Ga. L. Rev. 83 (1967). 27 p.

"Although tort remedies of strict liability and nuisance appear the most promising of available judicial alternatives," court costs and the need for multiple actions are serious defects.

322. Spater. "Noise and the law," 63 Mich. L. Rev. 1373 (1965). 38 p.

The author presents "the cases dealing with the scope of the immunity of the government and government-authorized entities from legal action for objectionable noises or other nuisances."

323. Spengler. "Megalopolis: resource conservor or resource waster," 7, 8 Natural Resources J. 376, 505 (1967, 1968). 20 p.

The author suggests the imposition of taxes to prevent increased city size, which make for unproductive use of resources.

324. Stein. "Regulatory aspects of federal water pollution control," 45 Denver L.J. 267 (1968). 12 p.

". . . The success of regulatory measures depends upon the percentage of cases that can be effectively disposed of by federal-state negotiation and cooperative action—and not by court action."

325. Stoebuck. "Condemnation by nuisance: the airport cases in retrospect and prospect," 71 Dick L. Rev. 207 (1967). 33 p.

Discussion and analysis of this new "breakthrough in an important area of eminent domain law."

326. Stone. "The marine environment—recent legal developments," 2 Natural Resources Law. 26 (1969). 21 p.

A review of decisions clarifying the Submerged Lands Act and the 1958 Geneva Convention on the Continental Shelf.

327. Stone. "United States legislation relating to the continental shelf," 17 Int. & Comp. L.Q. 103 (1968). 15 p.

The discussion covers only oil and gas in the continental shelf.

328. Sweeney. "Oil pollution of the oceans," 37 Fordham L. Rev. 155 (1968). 54 p.

The author discusses "pollution caused by marine transport of persistent oils."

329. "Tale of two lakes—a new chapter in Washington water law," 43 Wash. L. Rev. 475 (1967). 9 p.

The author concludes that "[s]tate regulation of the lakes which it opens for public use is not only equitable, but also preserves established legal rights while furthering a sound social policy."

330. Tarlock. "Eminent domain—review of route selection made by public utility through private wildlife refuge," 8 Natural Resources J. 1 (1968). 10 p.

A review of *Texas Eastern Transmission Corp.* v. *Wildlife Preserves, Inc.*, 48 N.J. 261, 225 A.2d 130 (1966), in which the burden of proof was shifted to the condemnor to disprove the feasibility of proposed alternatives.

331. Tarlock. "Preservation of scenic rivers," 55 Ky. L.J. 745 (1967). 54 p.

"There has been little recognition that in some instances preservation of a river in its free-flowing condition should be its highest use . . ."

332. Taubenfeld. "Weather modification and control: some international legal implications," 55 Calif. L. Rev. 493 (1967). 14 p.

The author urges establishment of international weather programs and agreements before unfortunate conflicts occur.

333. Tenzer. "Jet aircraft noise: problems and their solutions," 13 N.Y.L.F. 465 (1967). 11 p.

Member of Congress reviews legal aspects of the problem and some of the proposals before Congress.

334. Tippy. "Preservation values in river basin planning," 8 Natural Resources J. 259 (1968). 20 p.

Specific decisions made by the Army Corps of Engineers, the FPC, and the Dept. of the Interior are discussed.

335. Tippy. "Roads and recreation," 55 Ky. L. J. 799 (1967) 23 p.

The author "suggests that highways should be constructed to provide easy access to and through our recreational parks without destroying their natural beauty."

336. Tondel. "Noise litigation at public airports," 32 J. Air L. 387 (1966). 21 p.

The author believes that the airport noise problem should be placed in the same legal perspective as other annoyance cases.

337. Trelease. "Policies for water law: property rights, economic forces, and public regulation," 5 Natural Resources J. 1 (1965). 48 p.

The author's policies for water use stress maximum benefit, whether it be "conservationist" or "utilitarian."

338. Twiss & Litton. "Resource use in the regional landscape," 6 Natural Resources J. 76 (1966). 6 p.

The authors propose four characteristics of the landscape—nature, beauty, meaning, and imageability—to be used as criteria for establishing public policy.

339. Tyler. "Methods for state level enforcement of air and water pollution laws," 31 Texas Bar J. 905 (1968). 13 p.

An examination of Texas' antipollution measures.

340. "Urban noise control," 4 Colum. J.L. & Soc. 105 (1968). 15 p.

"Ultimately, the only satisfactory method of noise control may result from market pressures on the manufacturers of noise-producing items or from particularized legal regulation of specific noise-producing sources."

341. Verleger & Crowley. "Air pollution, water pollution, industrial cooperation and the antitrust laws," 4 Land & Water L. Rev. 475 (1969). 12 p.

The authors conclude that "a joint response [to pressure for pollution control] by several companies comprising an industry is permissible."

342. Verleger & Crowley. "Pollution: regulation and the anti-trust laws," 2 Natural Resources Law. 131 (1969). 11 p.

The authors conclude, by examining recent court decisions, that "collaborative acts in the air pollution field . . . to obtain valid government action or inaction are protected."

343. Waite. "Public rights in Maine waters," 17 Maine L. Rev. 161 (1965). 44 p.

Focuses on rights to outdoor recreation.

344. Warne. "Water crisis is present," 9 Natural Resources J. 53 (1969). 10 p.

Problems of water supply and quality control in California are discussed.

345. "Water appropriation for recreation," 1 Land & Water L. Rev. 209 (1966). 14 p.

This comment suggests a nondogmatic rule for "allowing or forbidding the taking of water for . . . recreation."

346. "Water quality control in Georgia," 16 Mercer L. Rev. 469 (1965). 9 p.

Review of the Georgia Water Quality Control Act (1957) and the Georgia Resources Commission Act (1957).

347. "Water quality standards in private nuisance actions," 79 Yale L.J. 102 (1969). 9 p.

Although the Federal Water Quality Act has been "blunted by bureaucratic timidity and deference to industry," this note suggests that "a secondary effect of the Act may be to revivify private nuisance actions, and thus to help restore the quality of our water."

348. Weissberg. "International law meets the short-term national interest: the Maltese proposal on the sea-bed and ocean floor—its fate in two cities," 18 Int. & Comp. L.Q. 41 (1969), 62 p.

Discussion of UN action on the Maltese proposal, with special emphasis on U.S. reaction.

349. Wilkey. "Deep ocean: its potential mineral resources and problems," 3 Int. Law 31 (1968). 18 p.

The author's topics are "the comparative pace in law and technology" and "legal policy and problems relating to undersea mining."

350. Williams. "Legal techniques to protect and to promote aesthetics along transportation corridors," 17 Buffalo L. Rev. 701 (1968). 18 p.

The author focuses on scenery along highways.

351. Wilson. "Trees, earth, water, and ecological upheaval: logging practices and watershed protection in California," 54 Calif. L. Rev. 1117 (1966). 16 p.

This comment examines "the relation between watershed protection and land use in general" and criticizes "California's attempt by statute to regulate the relation between the logger and his land."

352. Wolf. "Legal aspects of air pollution," 5 Tr. Law. Q. 22 (1968). 10 p.

The author believes that legislation has not been effective because of powerful lobbyists, so that pollution problems can be best alleviated through the courts.

353. Wollan. "Controlling the potential hazards of government-sponsored technology," 36 Geo. Wash. L. Rev. 1105 (1968). 33 p.

The author urges creation of a Technological Hazards Board, "as a lobbyist for reduction and control of potential risks to the public and the environment."

354. Wolozin. "The economics of air pollution: central problems," 33 Law & Contemp. Prob. 227 (1968). 12 p.

The author suggests that air pollution must be studied in the total environmental context.

355. Wright. "Some aspects of the use of corrective taxes for controlling air pollution emissions," 9 Natural Resources J. 63 (1969). 21 p.

An economic analysis of air pollution control in relation to pollution abatement ordinances.

356. "Wyoming air quality act," 4 Land & Water L. Rev. 159 (1969). 26 p.

A discussion of the constitutionality and practical legal problems of the act.

357. Zielinski. " 'Public interest' standing for the federal taxpayer: a proposal," 17 Buffalo L. Rev. 887 (1968). 15 p.

"The apparent solution to granting taxpayer standing on the federal level lies in a controlled use of judicial discretion."

358. Zimmerman. "Political boundaries and air pollution control," 46 J. Urban L. 173 (1968). 25 p.

The author sees great promise in the "creative federalism" spirit of the Mid-Atlantic States Air Pollution Control Compact.

Index to Bibliographies

Index